Children's Literature, Briefly

SECOND EDITION

Children's Literature, Briefly

Michael O. Tunnell
Brigham Young University

James S. Jacobs
Brigham Young University

Merrill
an imprint of Prentice Hall
Upper Saddle River, New Jersey   *Columbus, Ohio*

Library of Congress Cataloging-in-Publication Data

Tunnell, Michael O.

    Children's literature, briefly / Michael O. Tunnell, James S. Jacobs.—2nd ed.

      p.   cm.

    Rev. ed. of: Children's literature, briefly / James S. Jacobs, 1996.

    Includes bibliographical references and index.

    ISBN 0-13-096214-7

    1. Children's literature—Study and teaching. 2. Children's literature—History and criticism.   I. Jacobs, James S.   II. Title.

    PN1008.8.J33   2000

    809′.89282—dc21   99-17130

                                                                    CIP

Cover Art: Illustration from *Musicians of the Sun,* ©1997 by Gerald McDermott, reproduced by permission of Simon & Schuster

Editor: Bradley J. Potthoff

Production Editor: Mary M. Irvin

Design Coordinator: Diane C. Lorenzo

Cover Design: Ceri Fitzgerald

Text Design: Pagination/Ed Horcharik

Production Manager: Pamela D. Bennett

Director of Marketing: Kevin Flanagan

Electronic Text Management: Marilyn Wilson Phelps, Karen L. Bretz, Melanie N. King

Marketing Manager: Meghan Shepherd

Marketing Coordinator: Krista Groshong

This book was set in Galliard by Prentice Hall and was printed and bound by R.R. Donnelley & Sons Company. The cover was printed by Phoenix Color Corp.

Printed in the United States of America

10 9 8 7 6 5 4 3 2 1

ISBN: 0-13-096214-7

Prentice-Hall International (UK) Limited, *London*

Prentice-Hall of Australia Pty. Limited, *Sydney*

Prentice-Hall of Canada, Inc., *Toronto*

Prentice-Hall Hispanoamericana, S. A., *Mexico*

Prentice-Hall of India Private Limited, *New Delhi*

Prentice-Hall of Japan, Inc., *Tokyo*

Prentice-Hall (Singapore) Pte. Ltd., *Singapore*

Editora Prentice-Hall do Brasil, Ltda., *Rio de Janeiro*

CREDITS

COLOR INSERTS

POEMS

PREFACE

WHY THIS BOOK?

The subtitle for this text should be "A children's literature textbook for people who don't like children's literature textbooks." In a combined 41 years of teaching children's literature at the university level, neither of us used a text, because the ones available were too expensive and too extensive for an introductory course. We own and regularly consult the available texts, but they seem more like reference books. Our biggest concern, though, was neither the cost nor the length but the hours stolen from students when they could be reading actual children's books. The focus of a children's literature course should be on those terrific children's titles. They are more important than any text, including this one, and we wrote this book on that assumption.

Children's Literature, Briefly is an overview written to shed light on children's literature and its use with young readers. Our job as teachers, whether university or elementary, is to introduce and illuminate children's books for our students. These books can offer insight and pleasure without having to be explained, analyzed, or used as objects of study. Yet some comment, if it is secondary to the books and does not become too self-important, can help teachers and children alike find their own ways to rewarding reading.

The goal of this text, then, is to provide a practical overview of children's books, offering a framework and background information while keeping the spotlight on the books themselves. That's why we kept the textbook itself and each chapter short.

And that's why we limited the book lists. The world of children's literature offers only one completely dependable book list—your own. Throughout the following chapters, we present ours, absolutely trustworthy in every way—to us. You are allowed to harbor serious doubts about our choices, but their value is that our titles may save you time wandering up and down library aisles. We organized our book lists at the end of the chapters under four different headings and offer a fifth on CD-ROM.

1. *Ten of our favorites*. The 10 books listed after each chapter in Part 2 (15 in the case of picture books) are terrific reading. These lists are very short, the result

of much negotiating, often emotional but largely friendly. The purpose of the 10 is to provide solid suggestions for those who wonder where to find a good book. Each title is annotated to give a brief idea of the content.

2. *Others we like*. These titles (generally around 20) are not annotated. Although they are the second level of recommendations, each is a book we like very much. Don't be surprised if you find some of them more appealing than the 10 of our favorites.

3. *Easier to read*. Next we have added 10 titles of shorter, generally popular books. These help the teacher find nonthreatening titles for children struggling to make reading a rewarding pastime.

4. *Picture books*. In most genre chapters, we have included 10 picture books we consider representative and outstanding. Not all of these titles are for use exclusively in the lower grades; many are appropriate for the upper grades as well.

5. *The CD-ROM*. The biggest list is on CD-ROM. (See the information inside the back cover on the last page of the book.) It is not comprehensive but certainly extensive with more than 10,000 titles. The database can be searched for key words or concepts to yield almost any specialized list you can imagine. Or you can search it by any of the 11 fields describing each title (author, title, illustrator, publisher, year of publication, grade level, genre, topics, description, awards, or comment). Once the database is installed on a hard drive, you may enter personal codes or comments that allow for completely individualized lists, plus you may add titles of your own.

ACKNOWLEDGMENTS

We would like to thank the reviewers of our manuscript for their insights and comments: Bonnie Armbruster, University of Illinois at Urbana-Champaign; Sam L. Sebesta, University of Washington; and J. Lea Smith, University of Louisville.

DISCOVER COMPANION WEBSITES: A VIRTUAL LEARNING ENVIRONMENT

Technology is a constantly growing and changing aspect of our field that is creating a need for content and resources. To address this emerging need, we have developed an online learning environment for students and professors alike—Companion Websites—to support our textbooks.

In creating a Companion Website, our goal is to build on and enhance what the textbook already offers. For this reason, the content for each user-friendly website is organized by topic and provides the professor and student with a variety of meaningful resources. Common features of a Companion Website include:

FOR THE PROFESSOR

Every Companion Website integrates **Syllabus Manager**™, an online syllabus creation and management utility.

- **Syllabus Manager**™ provides you, the instructor, with an easy, step-by-step process to create and revise syllabi, with direct links into Companion Website and other online content without having to learn HTML.
- Students may logon to your syllabus during any study session. All they need to know is the web address for the Companion Website and the password you've assigned to your syllabus.
- After you have created a syllabus using **Syllabus Manager**™, students may enter the syllabus for their course section from any point in the Companion Website.
- Class dates are highlighted in white and assignment due dates appear in blue. Clicking on a date, the student is shown the list of activities for the assignment. The activities for each assignment are linked directly to actual content, saving time for students.

- Adding assignments consists of clicking on the desired due date, then filling in the details of the assignment—name of the assignment, instructions, and whether or not it is a one-time or repeating assignment.
- In addition, links to other activities can be created easily. If the activity is online, a URL can be entered in the space provided, and it will be linked automatically in the final syllabus.
- Your completed syllabus is hosted on our servers, allowing convenient updates from any computer on the Internet. Changes you make to your syllabus are immediately available to your students at their next logon.

FOR THE STUDENT

- **Topic Overviews**—outline key concepts in topic areas
- **Electronic Blue Book**—send homework or essays directly to your instructor's email with this paperless form
- **Message Board**—serves as a virtual bulletin board to post—or respond to—questions or comments to/from a national audience
- **Web Destinations**—links to www sites that relate to each topic area
- **Professional Organizations**—links to organizations that relate to topic areas
- **Additional Resources**—access to topic-specific content that enhances material found in the text

To take advantage of these resources, please visit the *Children's Literature, Briefly* Companion Website at www.prenhall.com/tunnell

CONTENTS

CHAPTER TEN
Historical Fiction   105

CHAPTER ELEVEN
Biography   117

CHAPTER TWELVE
Informational Books   129

CHAPTER THIRTEEN
Picture Books   153

Children's Literature, Briefly

PART ONE

The Book

CHAPTER 1

Why Read?

Like most important questions, "Why read?" seems embarrassingly obvious. Reading simply *is* important. Period. We know that, and we assume everyone else knows that. Even in today's climate of constant controversy and limitless lawsuits, where no one appears to agree with anyone on anything, reading receives unanimous support. An antireading position has no voice, claims no champion, and gets no press. No magazine or newspaper prints an article about the evils of the reading act or how time spent with print is wasted. The push is always toward more reading. So why is reading universally acclaimed?

THE REWARDS OF READING

Like eating, reading is one of life's activities that simultaneously yields both pleasure and benefit. When we chomp down on a three-way chimichanga, the sensation of textures, temperatures, and taste rewards us right then. No one needs to confirm the results; from our own personal taste buds, we know immediately that the bite is satisfying. Any attempt to change our mind is a waste of words. In addition to the obvious pleasure, our digestive system now turns the agreeable mixture of beans, beef, lettuce, onions, and tortilla into nutrients that keep us going. Benefits automatically follow the pleasing meal—energy and good health—but the primary reason for lifting a fork is the immediate reward of tasting and chewing.

Similarly, immediate reward is the one dependable criterion for determining why people choose to read. Beyond that, it is impossible to predict how a particular reader will be affected by print, as illustrated by the following actual incidents:

- Conventional wisdom says that a reader must comprehend a certain percentage of written material for reading to be successful, yet three-year-old Bobby Morgan, whose parents read to him regularly, got up early to spend time with the *National Geographic,* which he preferred to picture books. His parents knew that he was comprehending only a fraction of the material, but he continued to spend hour after hour with the magazine.
- Common sense indicates that we seek comfortable surroundings when engaging in a long activity like extended reading, yet Sean, a college student, drove to the bookstore on a snowy day to buy a new book and decided to spend a few minutes looking it over in his car before heading home. Time passed, and the sun set. To continue reading, Sean had to hold the book to the window so the lights from the parking lot would shine onto the page. Four hours later, he started his chilled car for the drive to his apartment.
- Educational practice says to match individual reading abilities with the difficulty of a text, yet Bill, a junior high student with second-grade reading skills, chose a book far beyond his tested level. A part of his school day was spent in intensified reading instruction in a lab setting, the last half hour devoted to uninterrupted individual reading. Educator Dan Fader watched Bill during his 30 minutes of reading time until the bell sounded. "Still absorbed in his read-

ing, Bill closed the book, glanced at the cover, placed the book in his bag, and started for the door. Intrigued by this thirteen-year-old second-grade reader, I crossed his path at the door and walked with him as I asked, 'What are you reading?' '*Jaws.*' 'Is it good?' 'Yeah!' 'But isn't it hard?' 'Sure it's hard, but it's worth it!'" (Fader 1976, p. 236).

When we read words that have meaning for us, we know "it's worth it." No one needs to confirm the results. We, ourselves, have proven their value. Beyond the immediate satisfaction, a number of benefits come our way: expanded vocabulary, increased world knowledge, improved reading skills, better communication skills, strengthened knowledge of language, new insights, power to compete in an information-driven age, and perhaps a certain amount of additional confidence. Engaging in the act of reading leads us down the sure path to becoming educated, but the primary reason for turning pages is always the immediate reward. Some novels provide that appeal from the first paragraph, as with *The Ruby in the Smoke* by Philip Pullman.

> On a cold, fretful afternoon in early October, 1872, a hansom cab drew up outside the offices of Lockhart and Selby, Shipping Agents, in the financial heart of London, and a young girl got out and paid the driver.
> She was a person of sixteen or so—alone, and uncommonly pretty. She was slender and pale, and dressed in mourning, with a black bonnet under which she tucked back a straying twist of blond hair that the wind had teased loose. She had unusually dark brown eyes for one so fair. Her name was Sally Lockhart; and within fifteen minutes, she was going to kill a man. (Pullman 1985, p. 3)

Nonfiction can have the same appeal. In *The Human Body: And How It Works* by Steve Parker, a double-page spread focuses on the skin. The first paragraph reads:

> On the outside, you are dead. Your hair and the surface of your skin are made of dead cells. But less than a millimeter away under the surface of your skin are some of the busiest cells in your body. They are continually dividing to make new layers of skin cells which harden and die, to replace the top layer of skin as it is worn away. Every day millions of dead skin cells rub off as you wash, dry yourself with a towel, get dressed and move about. Much of the "dust" in a house is dead skin which has rubbed off the bodies of people. (Parker 1998, p. 10)

Real reading, then, offers us two rewards. The first is immediate. The text pulls us into images and ideas at the very moment we travel through the words: Suddenly we realize that dust particles in a shaft of sunlight are bits of our own skin! We find ourselves delighted with this new thought. The second reward of reading is long-term. The accumulated benefits—increased language and thinking skills plus additional knowledge, experience, and insight—add up to our becoming an educated person.

If we all agree that reading is so rewarding and beneficial, why don't more people spend more time at it? Why is our illiteracy rate so high? In 1992 the U.S. Office of Education commissioned an adult literacy survey with five levels of skills in the areas of prose, document, and quantitative proficiencies. Scores were not according to percentiles. All could have ended up in the highest level if all were highly skilled. Yet 40 million to 50 million adults (20 to 23 percent of the population) scored in the lowest level (Kirsch, Jungeblut, Jenkins, and Kolstad 1993, p. xiv).

The trend in the United States is not toward increased literacy. "The literacy proficiencies of young adults assessed in 1992 were somewhat lower, on average, than the proficiencies of young adults who participated in a 1985 literacy survey" (Kirsch et al. 1993, p. xvi). Scores on the verbal test of the Graduate Record Exam also show that college graduates' skills have dropped 9 percent from 1965 to 1992 (Snyder 1994, p. 310).

Why has reading declined among young adults during the last two decades (Zill and Winglee 1988)? Why is the United States dead last among 26 industrialized nations in the number of new titles published annually per capita (UNESCO 1990, Table 7.4)? Why does this powerful experience of being ravished by print seem to be limited to so few?

UNENGAGED AND ENGAGED READING

The reading we do tends to fall into two categories: unengaged and engaged. Unengaged reading is primarily the reading of necessity, the reading we do not choose but must do anyway. Usually work or school related, unengaged reading speaks to neither our heads nor our hearts. In the classroom, unengaged reading is frequently assigned reading. Instructional materials, particularly those with questions at the end, tend not to engage the reader. And even novels can be misused by well-intentioned teachers who unwittingly prevent their students from experiencing the power of a book in a variety of ways. Superseding the story with a specific task can provide a barrier to finding meaning and excitement in print. In an effort to improve vocabulary, for example, teachers assign students to find the nine examples of onomatopoeia in the first chapter of *Island of the Blue Dolphins* (O'Dell 1960). Before asking students to read a chapter, teachers introduce the difficult vocabulary and ask students to locate the words, define them, and use them in sentences. When students know that a traditional book report (plot, setting, theme, characterization, style, point of view) is expected, they read books from a different and less personal perspective.

No immediate benefits and few lasting by-products can come from unengaged reading. If the reader is not involved with the text—not engaged in the information or experience—the reading is empty and unproductive. It is even possible to read every word on a page and gain absolutely nothing from the activity. The deciding factor is always the heart and mind of the reader.

One reason so few Americans read a book after leaving school is that they never have gone beyond assigned reading. Despite having completed the required reading that marks the path to high school graduation, a surprising number of supposedly educated graduates never have known the sustaining thrill of reading a book that speaks directly and personally to them. The reading they did was for someone else, according to someone else's rules and expectations, with the result that life never was breathed into the books they completed for their classes. In short, the books never happened.

If the book and reader remain distant, literacy is at a dead end. Even the person with all the necessary skills to read well does not progress unless those skills are strengthened and polished by use. Without engaged reading, the person may be able to read but has become uninterested in doing so, or aliterate. The aliterate person has all the necessary know-how to unlock the meaning in print, but chooses not to pick up books. And, as the sign over a small school library reminds us, "The person who can read and doesn't is no better off than the one who can't read."

It is only in personal reading that meaning takes place, that we find the reason to turn to print. Those who engage in personal reading find their reward in two areas: locating information and gaining experience.

People who want certain information seek it out. We read for information when we check the sodium content in frozen dinners, plan the drive from Poughkeepsie to Pittsburgh, look in the dictionary for the meaning of *obfuscate*, scan the newspaper ads for a furniture sale, follow the so-called directions for assembling a barbecue grill, or scan the note from Harold's teacher. No one makes us do those things. We choose to do them because the messages locked in those passages of print are interesting to us. Yet in each of these cases, someone else could read and summarize the content, and we would be satisfied. In her transactional theory of literature and reading, Louise Rosenblatt (1978) calls this reading for information "efferent" reading. We are motivated by getting the facts. Yet someone else could do the reading for us, supply us with the desired information, and we would be equally as happy as if we had read the facts ourselves.

"Esthetic" reading is different from efferent because the goal is not the acquiring of information but participation in the experience. In esthetic reading, readers focus on what they are experiencing as their eyes pass over the words. This kind of reading cannot be summarized by another but must be done personally, because it is not centered on data. The facts are not the most important part; engagement with the experience is. Knowing the plot of *Tuck Everlasting* (Babbitt 1975) is not the same as experiencing with Winnie Foster her difficult choice between a natural life span and living forever as a young girl. Being told that Jeffrey in *Maniac Magee* (Spinelli 1990) topples the barriers between the black and white neighborhoods in Two Mills, Pennsylvania, comes nowhere close to being with him when he shakes up old prejudices. Reading for experience—esthetic reading—can no more be done by someone else and then reported to us than our eating can be done by another. We don't want information on food flavors; we want those flavors to flow over our own taste buds. When we read for experience, we aren't satisfied simply by knowing where the book ends up. We want to make that journey to the final page ourselves. When we participate in the experience of a good book, our lives are never quite the same again.

For reading to make a difference, it has to be personal. People do not turn to books because they want to study the author's use of vocabulary or have a desire to describe the major and minor characters any more than people attend movies to examine the cinematographer's use of the long shot or analyze the use of background music. We read fiction and go to the movies to get lost in the story, to see through eyes other than our own. Almost magically, participating in these vicarious experiences sheds light on our own lives. We compare, test, experience, and come away with new thoughts and visions, wondering how we ourselves would have responded in similar situations.

If someone forces us to shift our concentration from the experience to the externals—
the form, the theme, the use of language—these elements become the main reason for
reading or viewing. As a result, reading the book or attending the movie may become
no more than tedious labor. For instance, would our experience with a good movie be
enhanced by having the manager of the theater pass out mandatory study guides to be
completed while we watch the film? We would look over the questions, and our purpose for viewing the movie would shift from living the movie to ferreting out the correct responses. At the end, we haven't seen the movie at all. We have witnessed a collection of facts we needed to identify and isolate. To enjoy the movie, we would likely
choose to leave the theater and wait for the film to be released on videocassette.

Like viewing a movie, the act of reading can't serve two masters. We read either
for ourselves or for some other purpose. When anything comes between the reader
and the printed page, such as a teacher's expectation or an assignment, the reading
tends to be unengaged and remains artificial—even if eyes continue to march across
the rows of words. For example, how many of us have covered several pages of
assigned reading in a textbook, only to discover that we have not registered one
morsel of meaning? Yet we have also experienced being so consumed by a novel or
biography that we do not notice when the chapters begin or end.

A reader can respond differently even to the same book. Lloyd Alexander, an
author who attributes his success to childhood reading, discovered *Treasure Island* at
home as a child and loved it—pure engaged reading. He lived with Jim, he pondered
the story when he was away from the book, and he longed to return to the people and
events of the tale. Years later he was assigned the same novel in a high school English
class. This time the reading did not produce the same involvement. Class discussion
centered on elements he found uninteresting, assignments interfered with his experience, and he failed the final test "because I couldn't remember the construction of that
damned blockhouse" (Alexander 1993). The teacher held "discussions" with the class
but asked only factual questions, gave assignments that did not include Lloyd's focus,
and graded success based on a test of specific and unimportant details. Instead of
helping Lloyd get deeper into the story, the teacher's approach actually kept him from
the book, turning an earlier engaged reading experience into an unengaged one.

Does this mean that any book assigned in school automatically suffers the kiss of
death? Of course not. An assigned book may begin as unengaged, uninteresting
reading and yet become important, even invaluable, to the reader. For that to occur,
however, it must receive the reader's personal stamp of approval. Somewhere
between the covers, even with the full knowledge that the book is required reading
and a part of the final grade, the reader must become personally interested in the
book and engaged in the text. At that point, the book moves from assigned reading
to personal reading. If it never makes the switch, it never develops the power to
influence or affect that one reader. (See Figure 1–1.)

We need to be aware of our own interaction with the text. Some readers have
spent so much time reading for others that they have difficulty identifying their own
responses to a book. Even some good students respond automatically to "What did
you think about the book?" with thoughts like, "What should I have thought about
the book?" "What am I supposed to think about the book?"

FIGURE 1–1
Unengaged and engaged reading.

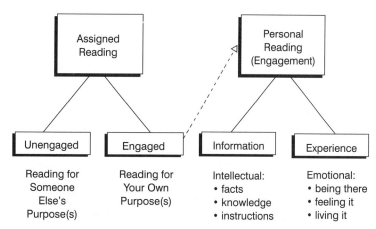

When we already have an interest in what we read, engaged reading comes naturally. No one wonders if the instructions to assemble a swing set for a much-loved but impatient three-year-old will make good reading. The purpose is determined, and the reading engages immediately. Before the first word is read, we know the instructions are worth it. At a bookstore sale table, a Civil War buff picks up a book on Stonewall Jackson and is likely to buy it. A child with an interest in dinosaurs is drawn to a book on the subject. Even when a book is not particularly well written, the person who is interested in the topic becomes an engaged reader without persuasion or effort.

Classic unengaged reading often comes during traditional reading instruction time at school. There the focus is not on the text as a purveyor of meaning but on the text as underbrush, where the secret skills of reading hide out. The sentences and paragraphs serve as camouflage for initial consonant blends, prediction questions, comprehension checks, vocabulary words, and the objects of a multitude of other skills lessons. This is not to say that the skills of reading are unimportant. The skills need to be learned, and students need the confidence that comes from understanding how language works and from an awareness that they are skilled and competent readers. The problem comes when students are given a good story to read with the primary goal of identifying skill components in it. This emphasis is a bit like sitting down to Thanksgiving dinner and seeing only vitamins and minerals on your plate or, worse yet, being served a pile of pills instead of the steaming turkey and trimmings because, after all, those nutritional elements are what is important for fueling our bodily furnaces.

How do we determine if a reader is engaged or unengaged? An engaged reader is not aware of the reading process. Engaged readers don't even see words after the first sentence or two at the beginning. In a story, they see scenes, people, action. In nonfiction, they test theories or think of applications or chew on the facts. But in neither instance do they focus on the skills of reading. They are unaware of how many pages they have read or how long they have been at the book. They pace themselves accordingly, gulping down great whacking passages quickly or dawdling over a line that gives them particular delight. They never say, "Look at me. I have chosen the correct sound of *y* at the end of *happy*—long *e*. I didn't confuse it with the long *i* like at the end of *fly*. I know the meaning of these words. I can use each of them in a sentence. I am comprehending the meaning of this paragraph and can pick out the topic sentence with 80 percent accuracy." During engaged reading there is no focus on skill, decoding, or vocabulary. When engaged readers come to a word they can't pronounce or define, they skip right over it without hesitation or guilt. A real reader engaged in a book is no more aware of reading skills than a running back threading his way through the defensive team is aware of his ability to run. He is not saying, "Right foot, then left foot, now pivot 45 degrees on the next step." His focus is on the game, and he simply uses his body to get where he wants to go. When something gets in the way, both the athlete and the reader improvise—self-correct—so the primary goal is still in sight and the pursuit continues.

So, why do we read? For personal and immediate reward. We read that which already interests us. And we learn new interests through reading a skillfully written account that takes us places we have never before been. And we can experience the genuine pleasure of having assigned reading work its way under our skin and become part of us. Author Gary Paulsen, whose early years in Minnesota were spent largely in the library, suggests we should "read like a wolf eats" (1987): in great hulking bites, with vigor, as often and much as possible. In the middle of this enthusiastic sampling of print, we will find those things that personally are worth it, while allowing other materials to slough off naturally. All the while, we increase our range of reading skills and strengthen our education without being aware of either. The very real benefits come predictably and automatically.

Occasionally, we even stumble onto a benefit beyond expectation. For instance, actor Walter Matthau may have discovered the ultimate bonus of engaged reading. In response to the question, "What book made the greatest difference in your life?" he wrote:

> The book that made the greatest difference in my life was *The Secret in the Daisy*, by Carol Grace, Random House, published 1955.
>
> The difference it made was enormous. It took me from a miserable, unhappy wretch to a joyful, glad-to-be-alive human. I fell so in love with the book that I searched out and married the girl who wrote it.
> Most sincerely,
> Walter Matthau (Sabine and Sabine 1983, p. 29)

REFERENCES

Alexander, Lloyd. 1993. Telephone conversation with James S. Jacobs, 2 March.

Babbitt, Natalie. 1975. *Tuck Everlasting*. New York: Farrar, Straus and Giroux.

Fader, Daniel. 1976. *Hooked on Books*. New York: Berkeley Books.

Kirsch, Irwin, Ann Jungeblut, Lynn Jenkins, and Andrew Kolstad. 1993. *Adult Literacy in America: A First Look at the Results of the National Adult Literacy Survey*. Washington, D.C.: U.S. Office of Education and Educational Testing Service.

O'Dell, Scott. 1960. *Island of the Blue Dolphins*. Boston: Houghton Mifflin.

Parker, Steve. 1998. *The Human Body: And How It Works*. Illustrated by Giovanni Caselli. New York: Dorling Kindersley.

Paulsen, Gary. 1987. "Books and Early Reading." Speech at Clarke County Library Association in Las Vegas, Nevada, 29 January.

Pullman, Philip. 1985. *The Ruby in the Smoke*. New York: Putnam.

Rosenblatt, Louise. 1978. *The Reader, the Text, the Poem*. Carbondale, Ill.: Southern Illinois University Press.

Sabine, Gordon, and Patricia Sabine. 1983. *Books That Made the Difference*. Hamden, Conn.: Shoe String Press.

Snyder, Thomas D., and Charlene M. Hoffman. 1994. *Digest of Education Statistics 1994*. Washington, D.C.: U.S. Department of Education.

Spinelli, Jerry. 1990. *Maniac Magee*. Boston: Little, Brown.

UNESCO. 1990. *UNESCO Statistical Yearbook*. Paris: UNESCO.

Zill, Nicholas, and Marianne Winglee. 1988. *Who Reads Literature?* Washington, D.C.: Child Trends.

CHAPTER 2

What Is a Good Book?

When adults select books for children, we want to pick out good ones. The trouble is, we're not always sure what "good book" means. Left to our own choosing, we thumb through titles trying to find something that seems beneficial and desirable for young readers. We forge ahead, sometimes unaware of the criteria we use to determine what is "good."

But criteria we have. All adults choose children's books according to some kind of standard, even though we may not be aware of exactly why we make our choices. Our first responsibility when selecting books, then, is to determine what our biases are. What *are* the criteria we respond to most? For instance:

1. The lessons they teach. We want children to learn the correct lessons about life. If a book teaches what we want taught, we call it a good book.
2. Large, colorful illustrations. Young eyes need stimulation, and color provides it better than black and white. Also, the pictures need to be large enough for children to see clearly.
3. Absence of harshness. Children will run into difficulty soon enough. Let them enjoy life now. Protect them from the tough side of living as long as possible.
4. Absence of scariness. We don't want to invite fears or nightmares.
5. Absence of swearing. We don't want books to model inappropriate behavior.
6. Short. Keep the reading easy.
7. Simple vocabulary. We don't want to frustrate or overpower children.
8. Familiar content. We think our child will respond to a book about zoos because we go to one often. If a book connects with a child's experience, it will be a better book.
9. Political correctness. We want the values and social views represented in the book to be what we consider appropriate.

A problem with the reasons just listed is that they are narrow and sometimes misguided; they focus on only a tree or two and miss the forest. If we want to help create lifelong readers by choosing books that appeal to the greatest range and number of children, we need to view the book as a whole instead of focusing on only a small element or two. And the most trustworthy standard for viewing the whole book is to look at the experience it offers. Titles of lasting value can almost be defined as experiences that re-create the very texture of life.

Problems can arise, however, in trying to convince others of the power of that experience. Generally, when we like a book—or don't like it—we assume the book deserves our response. When books please us, we think they are well written or have other measurable literary value. Works that leave us cold are somehow lacking in merit. It is largely human nature to think others will respond the way we do. The following two cases illustrate the extremes.

Case 1: "*The Wind in the Willows* [Kenneth Grahame] is a classic," he said. "It has received critical acclaim for almost 100 years, and I loved it. If you want a wonderful experience, take it now and read it." So she did. Her response was different, however: total boredom. How do we explain that one person is thrilled by a book of accepted literary merit, recommends it to another, and that person finds the supposedly wonderful book definitely ho-hum?

Case 2:   The librarian held up a book between thumb and forefinger like a five-day-old fish. "The Goosebumps books lack quality and merit. This series is predictable and weak." Alvin, fifth grade, reads the beginning of *Piano Lessons Can Be Murder* (Stine 1993) and can't put it down until he finishes. A trained educator judges a title to be substandard literature, and yet Alvin considers it a good book. How can this be?

People often don't see eye-to-eye when it comes to judging whether a book is worthwhile because *good book* is a common phrase with two different definitions, one based on quality and the other on taste.

QUALITY.   A good book is one created by a knowledgeable and skilled author where the elements of literature measure up under critical analysis. Quality is recognized by evaluating different elements of the book. Those elements may include the following: style and language, character, plot, setting, theme, tone, point of view, illustrations, mood, pacing, design and layout, and accuracy.

- *Style and language.* The words used to tell a story are at least as important as the story itself, and which words are chosen and how they are arranged is the style. The author's style can underscore or reflect an element of the story, as in Spinelli's (1990) *Maniac Magee,* where the short chapters and short sentences mirror the running and rapid movement of the main character. The arrangements of his words parallel the story itself, adding an additional element of unity. The skillful use of language not only draws readers into the writing but also is the foundation on which all the other elements of a book rest. (See Chapter 3.)
- *Character.* Good books must have characters that are unique and believable. Those who live between the covers of a book must be as real as those who live across the street. It is impossible to identify with or have feelings for a person unless we know the individual, and it is the author's job to show us the character's personality so we can become involved with that life.
- *Plot.* A good plot shows what happens to the people in the story in such a way that the reader cares about the outcome. Every plot must have a conflict, and how that conflict is resolved carries the book to its conclusion. Well-defined plots, according to author Pam Conrad, introduce a question early on that can be answered yes or no. She calls this the "major dramatic question" and cautions that it is not asked outright. It is, however, clear that something is going to happen either one way or another. Whether the answer is yes or no, and how the answer evolves, is the plot of the story. In *Hatchet* (Paulsen 1987), for instance, the question is, "Will Brian be rescued from the Canadian wilderness where he survived a plane crash?" In *Make Way for Ducklings* (McCloskey 1942), the question is, "Will the ducks make the trip safely from the Charles River to the Public Garden?"
- *Setting.* Where the book takes place is the setting, which can be as broad as a planet or as narrow as a room. When detailed and fleshed out, the physical surroundings add credibility and depth to the story.
- *Illustrations.* The art or photography in a book can strengthen and extend the content beyond the words. The marriage of illustration and text can yield an experience more powerful than either alone. (See Chapter 4.)

- *Theme*. The central idea of the story is the theme: friendship, coming-of-age, sibling rivalry, coping with the death of a pet, and adjusting to a new town, to name a few.
- *Tone*. The tone is the author's attitude toward the subject or audience in a particular book. Tone can reflect the range of human emotion: reverential, sarcastic, condescending, enthusiastic, and so on.
- *Point of view*. The point of view is the position taken by the narrator. Most stories are told in first person ("I") or third person ("he/she").
- *Mood*. The atmosphere evoked in the writing is the mood: spooky, hilarious, innocent, understated, exaggerated, caustic, and the like.
- *Pacing*. How quickly or slowly a story moves is pacing. While most books tell their stories at a relatively constant rate, pacing can vary in the same volume according to the author's desire to linger over the content or move the story along.
- *Design and layout*. Eye appeal of the cover, the colors, the margins, the spacing, the positions of page numbers—all visual elements of a book are a part of the design and layout. Although word order is not affected by the design and layout, word placement is—particularly in picture books. The visual appeal of a book can determine if a potential reader will pick it up or march right on by.
- *Tension*. Fiction without tension is bland. Tension makes the reader want to read on to see how the conflict is resolved and what happens to the people involved in the problem. Even in picture books, tension—a close relative of suspense—is what piques and sustains interest.
- *Accuracy*. Whenever books deal with real facts, whether centering on them in nonfiction or using them as background in fiction, they must be true. Writers need to do their homework in order to gain and keep readers' trust.
- *Believability*. The key to creating a good book is to make everything believable. We know that fiction is the product of an imagination. The people never lived. The story is made up. The setting is invented. So why do we care about these people who never were, doing things that never happened, in a place that may not exist? Because the emotional reality is absolutely true. Because their imagined lives reflect the realities of living, breathing people. Because we can get genuine experience through living side-by-side with fictional characters while they endure their own trials and enjoy their successes. We participate, we enjoy, and we learn—all simultaneously. Yet if anything in the book reminds us that what we read is invented, the story loses its power. All the elements in a story must be logical, sensible, and consistent. Much in the same way that the spell of a movie is broken when we notice a boom microphone hanging over the head of the police chief, authors are obligated to keep their facts and actions credible and their techniques out of sight when putting the book together.

Of the elements just listed, the first three—style and language, character, and plot—and the last—believability—provide the bulk of information when judging the quality of fiction. When a book reveals its story in powerful language, contains memorable characters, follows a compelling plot, and is believable, the fiction generally can be said to have "quality." To get a quick, thumbnail view of the potential power of the book, look at those four elements. But the presence of quality does not guarantee a positive reader response.

TASTE. The second definition of a good book is simply "a book the reader likes," quality or not. For instance, *Wind in the Willows* is judged to be quality literature for children. This prototype of modern animal fantasy skillfully delineates the four main characters, contains satisfying action sequences, and is told in a rich and varied language. But some children do not find themselves engrossed in the story when they try to read it, nor do they particularly like to have it read aloud to them. The book has definite literary merit—it is critically a good book—yet for those who are not taken by the story, it has no appeal. Conversely, the Goosebumps books win no literary awards. Yet they continue to be read by many who find pleasure in reading the tales of mystery and light horror. Thousands of children sail through the series and report that each Goosebumps story is a good book. Some adults may think that children who read such formulaic, shallow stories should at least feel shame for doing so, but so far no guilt has been detected in those who move quickly from one volume to the next.

So, when determining which books are good, an obvious problem surfaces: The positive feelings a reader has about a book are the same whether they come from a quality book or one of questionable merit. Readers call either book "good" as long as those feelings come during the time of turning pages. Were we able to correctly identify the sources of our positive responses, we would more accurately say, "I like this book because the author's skill took me places and showed me things I have not previously experienced." If the book is well crafted, believable, and supplies all the elements needed for a rewarding new experience, the author should take a bow. What the writer of the book brought to the work creates this response. On the other hand, if we respond to a book because it serves as a link to something already a part of us, we would say something like, "I liked this book because it connected with something I find appealing to me"—giving us a good scare, outwitting a bully, or reliving a personal memory. When our favorable response is triggered but not adequately developed by an author's writing, credit for the response goes to the reader. Yet we generally don't examine our responses this closely. When we read and like the experience, that is good enough for us. Figure 2–1 depicts the roles and results of book quality and reader response.

A book can be written well or badly, and a reader can respond well or badly to both strong and weak books. Quadrant 1 of Figure 2–1 shows that an author has written a book with literary merit, and the reader likes it. We have no problem with a reader who responds positively to quality writing. A well-crafted book deserves no less. Similarly, quadrant 4 presents no difficulty. The author shows little skill in producing a book of minimal merit, and the reader does not respond well to this flawed product. These two unshaded quadrants pose little problem for the teacher and student.

But problems may occur when a quality book is not well received. Quadrant 2 shows that an author has written a good book, but the reader doesn't care for it. Teachers who recognize quality may have a tendency to feel they are shirking their duty if they let a child believe that a book of high merit is of little value. Teachers who redouble their efforts to convince the unbeliever that something wonderful is being missed

FIGURE 2–1
Evaluating books: Four possible outcomes.

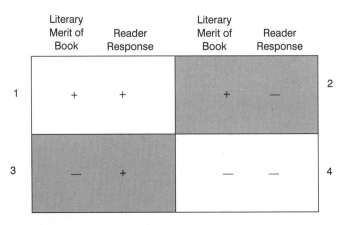

usually drive the unbelieving student further from the book. In quadrant 3, the reader accepts a weak book with open arms. This scenario is often played out as a teacher tries to show the young reader just how poor the book really is. These sincere attempts are generally as successful as trying to dam the Mississippi River using a teaspoon.

In both quadrants 2 and 3, the teacher needs to accept the honest feelings of the reader, misguided as they might be in the adult eye, and continue to provide and introduce the better books. Doing so carries no guarantee that young readers will like them, but it does increase the chances that this may happen. Direct attacks on positive responses to poor quality books, however, almost guarantee that a rift will develop between teacher and student and, in the case of quadrant 2, between a student and a genuinely good book.

Understanding that a positive response can be a result of either the author's skill or the reader's individual taste can help in solving some mysteries about how readers respond to books. A British reviewer of children's books was surprised when her daughter, Alison, chose as her favorite book one that was far inferior to the many quality titles in their home. The story told is of Peppermint, a pale kitten, who is last in a litter and alone after the others are matched with new families. Eventually, she is given to a girl who loves her, fusses over her, and prepares her so well for the cat show that Peppermint wins first prize. Alison's mother finally realized the appeal of Peppermint's story.

> Alison is an adopted child; her hair is pale straw, her eyes are blue; she was taken home, like Peppermint, to be loved and cared for and treasured. It was a matter of identification not just for the duration of the story but at a deep, warm, comforting and enduring level. . . . The artistically worthless book—hack-written and poorly illustrated—may, if the emotional content is sound, hold a message of supreme significance for a particular child. (Moss 1977, pp. 141–142)

When a class of 30 college students read a not-very-good biography about Maria Tallchief, a Cherokee ballerina who captured the attention of the dancing world in the early 20th century, all but an enthusiastic handful of female students pronounced the book mediocre. Those five who loved the book couldn't understand why the others were not impressed by this story that had meant so much to them. During the short discussion, it was determined that each of the five students had taken and loved ballet as children. When they read about Maria Tallchief, they were reading their own stories. For them, the book served as a link to an appealing personal experience. The others, without ballet backgrounds, did not find enough to interest them in the shallow way the author presented the story.

As adults working with children, we spend our time more productively in quadrants 1 and 2 in Figure 2–1 for two reasons. First, the more a book has to offer readers, the greater the chance the reader will respond. When Kevin Henkes (1990) identifies so precisely the reactions of an only child to the arrival of a new baby brother in *Julius, the Baby of the World*, the reader participates in the older daughter's jealousy and the turning point when a cousin's critical comments cause her to defend her new sibling. The author's range of emotion and humor is so broad that readers at a variety of levels are able to respond. The second reason we are more productive in quadrants 1 and 2 is that judging literary merit is easier than determining the idiosyncracies in readers that bring about positive responses to books. We have no way of knowing beforehand that Alison will find comfort in Peppermint or that five students will be linked to their ballet lessons by Maria Tallchief.

This whole evaluative process is somewhat like examining two new couches in Danish modern style. From a distance, they appear identical, but one reflects the true value of $1,800 while the other carries an honest price tag of $500. However, if allowed to inspect the couches at close range, even the nonprofessional should be able to determine which couch is of real quality and which is of lesser worth. We can determine the more expensive by examining the stitching, which should be close and even; the fabric, which should be tight and finely woven; the wood, which should be heavy, joined perfectly, well stained, and flawlessly finished; the padding, which should be thick and firm; the weight, which should be heavy; and the comfort, which should be evident on sitting. Once identified, however, the quality piece will not necessarily be welcomed into every living room. If Danish modern style does not appeal to me, it is of no importance that I now have the $1,800 couch. I can recognize its fine craftsmanship and can see that its shoddy counterpart is lacking in quality, but that does not make me want to own the fine couch if my taste runs counter to its appearance. Ultimately, the piece must please me before it gets my stamp of approval.

George Woods, the late and longtime children's book critic for the *New York Times*, addressed the topic of evaluating children's books in a speech to an auditorium of college students. "How do we know a good book?" he asked his audience. Pens came to the ready for the scholar's definition. "We know a good book . . . (pause) . . . because it hits us in the gut" (Woods 1977).

The worth of a book is proved on the individual reader's nerve endings. Yet we know that some books simply are better constructed than others, offering a clearer understanding of the human experience and a deeper sense of pleasure. These quality books are the ones we need to introduce to children because they generally have more power to stir up interest where none is apparent and, over time, will catch more readers than will mediocre books. Yet we can't force these quality titles on children—we can only offer. To become truly engaged readers, children must have the freedom to accept or reject a title. Just as we can't insist on a positive response to a book of quality, we can't erase a positive response to a poorly written book. Some young readers will respond with broad smiles and genuine affection to lower quality "good books." Attempting to change a convinced reader's mind that a book is not worthy of devotion is foolish and often counterproductive. All we can do, and should do, is continue to mention and offer different titles that may appeal to that reader. Allowing individual response is wisest in the long run. After all, if children read nothing, then our opportunity to broaden their taste and judgment about books is nonexistent.

In the end, the question of "good book" is one of respect: respect for the truly fine work of authors who pay their dues and create works of lasting value and also respect for the response of individual readers who cast the deciding vote on a book's appeal. There is, after all, only one list of good books that is completely dependable. Not the winners of a certain award. Not titles that have proven themselves over time. Not the books with the current highest sales figures. The only list we can trust without reservation is our own.

REFERENCES

Henkes, Kevin. 1990. *Julius, The Baby of the World*. New York: Greenwillow.

McCloskey, Robert. 1942. *Make Way for Ducklings*. New York: Viking.

Moss, Elaine. 1977. "What Is a Good Book?" In *The Cool Web*, edited by Margaret Meek, Aiden Warlow, and Griselda Barton. London: Bodley Head.

Paulsen, G. 1987. *Hatchet*. New York: Bradbury.

Spinelli, Jerry. 1990. *Maniac Magee*. Boston: Little, Brown.

Stine, R. L. 1993. *Piano Lessons Can Be Murder*. New York: Scholastic.

Woods, George. 1977. "Evaluating Children's Books." Speech at Brigham Young University, 17 September.

CHAPTER 3

What Is a Good Book? The Words

To evaluate the literary quality of a book is to make a judgment about how well the author uses words. "This book is well written" is a common badge of praise to be pinned on books of quality. What does *well written* mean? Often it means nothing more than the speaker's way of saying the book is pleasing. If it pleases me, it must be well written. When used as evidence that we responded well to a book, the phrase "well written" has become a generalized catchall.

If a book is truly well written, that means the words between those covers have been arranged in magical patterns that stir deep emotional responses in readers. The words do far more than relate the events of the story. The words make the book by defining character, moving the plot along, identifying the setting, isolating the theme, creating the tone, choosing the point of view, developing the mood, establishing the pace, making the story believable, and reporting information accurately. Isolating each element from the others, however, does not give us a clear picture of exactly what makes a book so memorable. Certainly plot must be well structured, but it cannot be separated from the major characters who are living the story. Conversely, well-defined characters lose their appeal if they are not involved in a compelling plot. The elements of writing are integrated, worked into an well-orchestrated whole, by a talented writer.

Talented writers create works that are clear, believable, and interesting. Whatever the subject or literary element (or intended age group, for that matter), the writing must first of all be understandable (clear), then it must seem real (believable), and finally it must have appeal (interesting). A story is not good because it is about a particular topic or peopled with certain characters; it is good because of the way it is presented. A work of nonfiction is not good because of the subject matter; it is good because of the way it views and reveals the subject. Consider the two perspectives from which the following event can be viewed:

Case 1.   The college football coach finished his twentieth successful season and was honored at a banquet where his praises were sung loud and long. As dishes were cleared and tables taken down after the festivities, the coach talked with his friend, the college president. At one point, the coach paused and then asked, "President, I appreciate this evening more than you'll ever know. Yet sometimes I find a nagging question in my mind: Would all of you still love me if I lost football games instead of won them?"

"Oh, Coach, we'd love you just as much," the president said as he reached out his arm, pulled him in close, and looked him right in the eye. "And we'd miss you."

Case 2.   A college student said to his classmate, "Did you hear that last night after the banquet honoring the football coach, the president said he'd be fired if he didn't keep up his winning record?"

In case 2, the reader gets all the pertinent information: the banquet in the coach's honor, the president and coach's conversation afterward, and the gist of their exchange. In the first example, the reader gets to participate in the event. A few details flesh out the scene, the coach shows some vulnerability, the president displays his administrative concern, and the reader has to figure out that the coach would be fired. The point is not revealed until the reader becomes a part of the story and draws that conclusion.

Human beings can't draw conclusions without information, and we gain information only through the five senses. If data can't enter through one of the holes in our heads (sight, sound, taste, or smell) or through contact with some part of the body (touch), they can't be processed. Good writers know readers need specific information—sensory detail—and take the trouble to provide it. Lesser writers generalize. The difference between providing sensory detail and generalizing is the difference between showing and telling. Where lesser writing *tells* by summarizing (as in case 2), quality writing *shows* the reader what is going on by providing enough sensory detail to allow the reader to make personal discoveries and come to personal conclusions (as in case 1). Consider, for instance, the opening paragraph of *The Illyrian Adventure:*

> Miss Vesper Holly has the digestive talents of a goat and the mind of a chess master. She is familiar with half a dozen languages and can swear fluently in all of them. She understands the use of a slide rule but prefers doing calculations in her head. She does not hesitate to risk life and limb—mine as well as her own. No doubt she has other qualities as yet undiscovered. I hope not. (Alexander 1986, p. 3)

The reader is solidly introduced to Vesper Holly. Alexander reveals Vesper's particular personality by *showing* her skills, accomplishments, abilities, and interests. Had Alexander begun by *telling* us about Vesper, he may have summarized her character by saying, "Miss Vesper Holly is courageous, intelligent, daring, a skilled linguist, delightfully irreverent, and headstrong." We would then know what to expect of her, but we wouldn't know her as well.

From details come real knowledge and understanding. If a friend who has been mostly a loner suddenly has a date and is excited, we share that excitement. We secure a promise to be telephoned immediately after the event. The phone rings very late. "Remember how excited I was to go out tonight?" "Yes." "Remember how I had my hopes built up, maybe even a little too high?" "Yes." "Well, the evening was ten times better than I had imagined. I'm tired now. Good night." Click.

As we sit holding the phone, we are unsatisfied. We want details, not because we are nosy but because we can't understand without them. We can participate vicariously in the evening only when we have enough facts: where they went, what they talked about, what our friend thought, whose hand brushed whose, and so on. The phone call *told* us about the evening; what we want is to be *shown*.

The detail we need from the printed page so we can participate in an experience comes to us in various forms: precise vocabulary, figurative language, dialogue, music in language, understatement, and surprise observations. These terms do not constitute a comprehensive list but are some examples of how words show detail in writing.

PRECISE VOCABULARY

By age four, children have acquired most of the elements of adult language (Morrow 1989). The only additional refinements take place in acquiring more complex structures and in semantics—learning new words and their meanings. Semantic development continues for the rest of their lives. With more than 800,000 words (300,000 being technical terms), English has the richest vocabulary of the 5,000-plus languages on the planet. One of the great pleasures of language is to find in this fertile and varied vocabulary precisely the right word to use in exactly the right place. Mark Twain described the difference between the right word and the almost right word as being like the difference between lightning and the lightning bug. And the only way to learn the fine differences between words and to develop a broad personal vocabulary is to be surrounded by precise words used accurately. When Newbery-winning author Elaine Konigsburg writes for children, she tries "to expand the perimeter of their language, to set a wider limit to it, to give them a vocabulary for alternatives" (1970, pp. 731–732).

William Steig is a master of precise vocabulary and wider limits. In *The Amazing Bone* (Steig 1976), Pearl the pig, dressed in her flowered dress and sun bonnet, took her time coming home from school: "On Cobble Road she stopped at Maltby's barn and stood gawking as the old gaffers pitched their ringing horseshoes and spat tobacco juice." (If this sentence were written by someone afraid it is not accessible to the younger reader, it would come out something like: "She stopped at the barn and watched the old men play horseshoes.") Naming the road and the barn gives the story depth and credibility—the place seems to exist. "Gawking" identifies exactly the kind of looking she did—wide-eyed, unabashed staring. "Ringing horseshoes" provides a dimension of sound to the game, adding an additional layer to the picture. And "spat tobacco juice" presents a side of the men and their activities that rounds them out. But the genius on this page is the selection of the word *gaffers*. English has a number of specific words for the phrase *old men*: patriarch, ancient, graybeard, Nestor, grandfather, gaffer, geezer, codger, dotard, Methuselah, antediluvian, preadamite, veteran, old-timer, old soldier, old stager, dean, doyen, senior, elder, oldest, first-born, seniority, primogeniture (Lewis 1961). The only ones general enough to be considered for this setting are codger, dotard, gaffer, geezer, and old-timer. The Oxford English Dictionary reports that each carries a specific view of old men:

> *Codger*: "A mean, stingy, or miserly (old) fellow; a testy or crusty (old) man" (*Compact Edition* 1971, p. 456)
> *Geezer*: "A term of derision applied to elderly persons" (*Compact Edition* 1971, p. 1125)
> *Gaffer*: "A term applied originally by country people to an elderly man or one whose position entitled him to respect" (*Compact Edition* 1971, p. 1103)
> *Dotard*: "One whose intellect is impaired by age; one whose dotage is in his second childhood" (*Compact Edition* 1971, p. 790)
> *Old-timer*: "[O]ne whose experience goes back to old times" (*Compact Edition* 1971, p. 1984)

Gaffer is the only term that is neither negative nor neutral. Its positive connotation complements the pleasant, unhurried scene while reflecting a strong image of the elderly.

The right words do not have to be fancy or obscure. Even ordinary words can be right. In *Temporary Times, Temporary Places* (Robinson 1972), teenaged Marilyn is stunned when she comes out of the church after an evening social to see her friend, Janet, walking away with the boy of their dreams, the one they have spent endless hours discussing. He has never spoken to either of them, and here he is leaving with Janet. Carrying her sweater in her hand, Marilyn can only stare: "She was standing on the steps of the church, mouth open, eyes wide, sweater dragging." With those six words—mouth open, eyes wide, sweater dragging—astonishment is *shown*. Robinson has thought about what astonishment in this situation looks like and presented it precisely. The reader sees what Janet sees. A lesser writer, who tells instead of shows, would have written something like, "She was standing on the steps of the church, a look of astonishment on her face." This sentence tells readers they should feel astonishment, but it does not create the image or the experience. In Robinson's hands, the scene is more specific, more complete, and more believable.

FIGURATIVE LANGUAGE

Simile, metaphor, personification, and imagery add layers of meaning and emotional power economically. *Maniac Magee* shows March, supposedly the month of spring, as a brute: "During the night, March doubled back and grabbed April by the scruff of the neck and flung it another week or two down the road" (Spinelli 1990, p. 149). Spinelli's personification of March reminds us vividly that this unpredictable month is given to sudden nastiness.

From *Tuck Everlasting* comes the lingering image of Mae Tuck, described as a "great potato of a woman" (Babbitt 1975, p. 7). In five words Babbitt creates a feeling for Mae's lumpy shape, her earthiness, her plainness, her lack of color, her solidness, her accessibility, and other earthy and dependable traits associated with a vegetable that is not spectacular, fragile, or rare but is a nutritional staple.

Figurative language can add power and insight to whole paragraphs. It is one thing to say that Winnie Foster was made to do housework continually, but in *Tuck Everlasting*, the author underscores the seriousness of cleaning in Winnie's household by loading the description with images of war.

> Winnie had grown up with order. She was used to it. Under the pitiless double assaults of her mother and grandmother, the cottage where she lived was always squeaking clean, mopped and swept and scoured into limp submission. There was no room for carelessness, no putting things off until later. The Foster women had made a fortress out of duty. Within it, they were indomitable. And Winnie was in training. (Babbitt 1975, p. 44)

When we read the paragraph, we get the solid impression that housecleaning in the Foster cottage is the focal point of life. Only when we go back and pick out the military terms Babbitt has chosen—double assaults, fortress, duty, in training—do we see the image of soldiers in battle that has helped persuade us of the Foster obsession with cleanliness.

DIALOGUE

Speech reveals character. When a person's mouth opens, truth emerges about personality, motives, desires, prejudices, and feelings. Bernard Waber has an ear for real speech that reveals the nuances, challenges, and bluffing responses of sibling conversation. In *Ira Sleeps Over*, Ira has been invited to spend the night at a friend's house—his first sleepover. When his older sister learns of his plans, she asks:

"Are you taking your teddy bear along?"

"Taking my teddy bear along!" I said. "To my friend's house? Are you kidding? That's the silliest thing I ever heard! Of course, I'm not taking my teddy bear."

And then she said: "But you never slept without your teddy bear before. How will you feel, sleeping without your teddy bear for the very first time? Hmmmmmmmm?" (Waber 1972, pp. 5–7)

In this brief exchange between brother and sister, Waber shows the older sister's need and ability to control her younger brother with what appears to be an innocent question: "Are you taking your teddy bear along?" What difference does it make to her if he takes it? None, but her job is to make his life miserable, and she performs it well. His reply, a little too quick and laced with false bravado, shows his insecurity. And her final statement is a knockout punch that leaves him no chance to get to his feet, reminding him that he has never slept alone, asking how that would feel, and ending with that taunting, "Hmmmmmmmm?"

If speech is not natural and not as individual as a particular personality, it shows the characters to be shallow and stiff, distracting from the story and consequently weakening it. Unnatural dialogue appears in *Fun at the Hospital* when Peter goes outside to see if he can get into the sandlot baseball game forming up near his house.

"Please let us play ball with you.
"We like to bat the ball and run,
"Playing baseball is so much fun."
It was Peter's turn to run around
When he slipped and fell down to the ground.

He ran into the house crying, "Mother!"
In back of him followed each brother.
"It hurts me, hurts me terribly, here!"
"Oh, let Mother look at it, dear." (Trepeck 1964, pp. 11–15)

Real boys and real mothers simply do not talk that way. This dialogue is written by someone who has forgotten what childhood is like, putting stilted words and formal sentences into the mouths of active boys. The author also seems out of touch with the way adults speak and react. This passage should show a screaming child and a frantic mother. Instead, we see cardboard people.

MUSIC IN LANGUAGE

The sounds of words add to the appeal and strength of the story as they blend together, create emphasis, repeat tones, establish patterns, provide a cadence, and add variety. The rhythm in "Hundreds of cats, Thousands of cats, Millions and billions and trillions of cats" (Gág 1928) rings in the ear and burrows into the mind. The rhyme in *Goodnight Moon* (Brown 1947) does the same: "Goodnight stars. Goodnight air. Goodnight noises everywhere."

Buford in *Buford the Little Bighorn* (Peet 1967) is a small mountain sheep whose horns have grown enormously, way out of proportion to his body. They cause him balancing problems, and he falls from craggy heights but is saved when his horns hook onto a small tree. From then on, his friends have to help him over the rough spots in their high, rocky world. To climb a steep ledge, two sheep from above grab his horns in their teeth and pull while one butts him skyward, giving "Buford a big boost from below" (Peet 1967, p. 3). Those explosive *b*'s echo the heavy sounds and sudden movements of butting and boosting as well as linking the phrase together by repeating the sound.

Because the eye does not reveal the fine points of language as accurately as the ear, it is common for authors to submit their writing to a final check by reading it aloud. In two versions of "Snow White," the queen questions the mirror in language that is subtly yet powerfully different. Submit the following two passages to the read-aloud test:

Mirror, mirror on the wall. Who is the fairest one of all? (Walt Disney Productions 1973, p. 2)

Mirror, mirror on the wall, Who is fairest of us all? (Grimm 1972, p. 2)

Uneven meter in the first one makes that passage more difficult to say aloud; the cadence is rougher and the sound choppier. The language in the second flows, falling smoothly and effortlessly from the mouth. The result is a more musical reading. The second also suggests an archaic form of speech that matches the "once upon a time" setting of the fairy tale.

Varied sentence length is another feature of language that appeals to the ear. In natural speech patterns, sentences are of differing length. These diverse sentences add variety to the language, creating balance, interest, and appeal. Read aloud the opening passages from the Disney and Grimm versions of "Snow White," paying attention to how they feel coming from the mouth and how they fall upon the ear.

Long ago there lived a princess named Snow White. She was a beautiful princess. And like all princesses she lived in a castle.

Her stepmother, the queen, also lived in the castle. The queen had a magic mirror. Every day she looked into the mirror and asked the same thing.

"Mirror, mirror on the wall. Who is the fairest one of all?"

The mirror always gave her the same answer. "Oh, queen, YOU are the fairest one of all." (Walt Disney Productions 1973, p. 2)

Once it was the middle of winter, and the snowflakes fell from the sky like feathers. At a window with a frame of ebony a queen sat and sewed. And as she sewed and looked out at the snow, she pricked her finger with the needle, and three drops of blood fell in the snow. And in the white snow the red looked so beautiful that she thought to herself: "If only I had a child as white as snow, as red as blood, and as black as the wood in the window frame!" (Grimm 1972, pp. 1–2)

For most readers, the many short sentences in the first example interrupt the flow of the story, creating a degree of choppiness. The varied sentence construction in the second helps produce a smooth and flowing narrative that reads with a musical quality. The first has ten sentences; the second four. The first has an average of 7.9 words per sentence; the second 23.5. More words per sentence are not necessarily an earmark of good writing, but in this case the longer sentences help weave stronger, more emotion-laden images.

UNDERSTATEMENT

When facts and feelings are presented clearly in writing, readers draw their own conclusions without being told precisely what to think. Readers then participate in the experience instead of being led through it. Part of this participatory process is understatement, which presents minimal but carefully chosen facts and details without any explanatory comment. Understatement is simply very brief "showing." The opposites of understatement are sensationalism and overexplanation.

The power of understatement is evident in *Tuck Everlasting* (Babbitt 1975). Angus Tuck tries to convince young Winnie Foster, whom he has grown to love like his own child, not to drink from the same magical spring that has transformed the Tucks into people who cannot age or die. When the Tuck family is forced to move away, Angus is uncertain of what Winnie will do—let her life follow its natural course, as he counseled, or submit to the enticements of living forever. In the epilogue, Angus and Mae Tuck return to Winnie's town 60 years later and visit the cemetery. When he discovers her tombstone, Angus's throat closes and he briefly salutes the monument, saying, "Good girl." No long discourses with his wife about Winnie's wise decision. No fits of crying or sentimental remembrances. Just "good girl."

In *A Summer to Die* (Lowry 1977), the family is going through a period of mourning as it becomes clear that teenage Molly is going to die. On the way home from a particularly good hospital visit, the family sings childhood songs, capturing the comforting feelings of what life used to be like before Molly became so ill. After that scene, the next words are, "Two weeks later, she was gone" (Lowry 1977, p. 108). No jarring telephone brings news of the inevitable. No heap of details describes her last moments. We have lived through the disease, joined in the family's efforts to understand and draw together, and now the inescapable has arrived. That's all we need to know. Understatement gives power to writing because of what is not said and shows that an author trusts readers to make important, personal connections with the story.

UNEXPECTED INSIGHTS

Like life, good stories contain occasional small surprises. We live with characters as they work their ways through problems but may be delighted suddenly by a small detour from the main story line or an eye-opening insight about the human experience. For instance, Maniac Magee wonders why the people in East End call themselves black. "He kept looking and looking, and the colors he found were gingersnap and light fudge and dark fudge and acorn and butter rum and cinnamon and burnt orange. But never licorice, which, to him, was real black" (Spinelli 1990, p. 51). "That's absolutely right," we find ourselves saying.

Lloyd Alexander is famous for such insights. In the five-book series, The Prydain Chronicles, Dwyvach Weaver-Woman presents a beautiful cloak to the girl Eilonwy. "Take this as a gift from a crone to a maiden," says Dwyvach, "and know there is not so much difference between the two. For even a tottering granddam keeps a portion of girlish heart, and the youngest maid a thread of old woman's wisdom" (Alexander 1968, p. 115). And in counsel to Taran, who is disappointed that he did not accomplish more while away on his quest, the enchanter Dallben points out, "There are times when the seeking counts more than the finding" (Alexander 1964, p. 215).

ELEMENTS OF WEAK WRITING

The easiest definition of weak writing is to say it is the opposite of good writing: not clear but fuzzy, not believable but implausible, not interesting but dull. Particularly in children's books, however, some weak elements stand out: didacticism, condescension, and controlled vocabulary.

Didacticism is writing that pretends to be a story but is actually a thinly disguised lesson. Good books can and do provide lessons, but in good books, the lessons are secondary. They are secrets to be discovered rather than sermons to be suffered. The learning and insight arrive as additional gifts, by-products from rewarding experiences.

Didacticism was more evident in books from earlier times when small children or animals who were, for instance, greedy or lazy learned the error of their ways and became model citizens. Although some of that still exists, today's didacticism tends to lean more toward political correctness. Lessons about ecology, acceptable social behavior, and the rights of special interest groups overshadow the story in contemporary didactic books.

Condescension may be slightly harder to pin down than didacticism. Evident mostly in books for very young readers, a condescending tone treats children as precious and overexplains with a certain wide-eyed amazement bordering on phoniness. Condescension dilutes the power of language in both nonfiction (labeling "esophagus" as "food tube") and fiction ("What fun! We like to share our toys with other boys and girls!").

Controlled vocabulary is based on the idea that children learn to read certain easy words first, then graduate slowly to more difficult ones to avoid frustration. However, so-called dumbed-down text, which overly controls vocabulary and arranges words in unnatural patterns ("I see the mat. The mat is tan. It is a tan mat."), often has proven to be more difficult for children to read and understand than text with interesting words and language patterns. The dumbed-down text does not correspond with what they have learned through the ear (Goodman 1988). Children can sometimes learn difficult words more easily than seemingly simple ones. If first graders are shown the words *surprise*, *was*, and *elephant,* the one they will learn to sight read first is *elephant*. Although it is longer and more difficult, it is also more specific. Try drawing a picture of a *surprise* or a *was*. The hardest of the three—the one that takes the most exposures to become included in children's sight vocabulary—is *was*.

In the '80s, basal companies recognized the power of natural text and began to include excerpts from authentic literature as a part of their reading programs. However, in the '90s, schools began buying and using sets of controlled-vocabulary paperback books instead of basal textbooks. Therefore, to meet demand, basal companies also began to include with their literature-based reading series sets of controlled-vocabulary readers. Today, teachers must choose wisely because, once again, reading materials available in the elementary schools may focus on a particular word pattern, largely ignoring the appeal of natural language and cohesive story.

The idea of controlled vocabulary goes too far when the author's primary purpose is providing word practice instead of telling a good story. When an author focuses intently on simple words and language patterns, the writing likely will be artificial and colorless. Can't an author write a book with rigidly controlled vocabulary and an interesting story at the same time? It is unlikely because a book can't serve two masters—the one more important to the author almost always takes over. Margaret Hillert's *Why We Have Thanksgiving* (1982) is a picture book designed as a controlled reader. The Thanksgiving story is filled with human pathos. It is a story of sacrifice and courage. But not so in Hillert's version, as this excerpt shows:

> Here we are on the boat. This is fun. Away we go. . . . What is this spot? Is it a good one? What will we do here? We have to work. We have to make a big house for boys and girls and mothers and fathers. (1982, pp. 14–15, 21–23)

> See this come up, and this, and this. It is good to eat. And here is something to eat, too. Something little and red. Something good. We can get some for Mother and Father. Now, sit down. Sit down. It is good to have friends. (pp. 28–31)

Never once does the word *Thanksgiving* appear or words like *corn* and *cranberry*. The text is so sparse, repetitive, and lacking in detail that a young reader can derive no sense of the human experience related to the first Thanksgiving. Not only does this book not show, but it doesn't even get as far as telling. It never answers the question implied in the title: Why do we have Thanksgiving?

Another title, Doreen Rappaport's *The Boston Coffee Party* (1988), is also written for fledgling readers and recounts in a historical fiction format an actual event in American history. Certainly, as evident in the brief excerpt that follows, the vocabulary is gently controlled, but there is a natural rhythm to the text and an honest sense of story. The characters seem like real people, and there are not the gaping holes in the plot that make the Thanksgiving story incomprehensible.

> Just then the door opened. It was Aunt Harriet. She looked angry.
> "Do you know what Merchant Thomas has done," she cried. "He locked up forty barrels of coffee in his warehouse."

"But why?" asked Mrs. Smith.

"He is waiting until no one in Boston has coffee," said Aunt Harriet. "Then he will sell his coffee for a lot of money."

"He is greedier than I thought," said Mrs. Homans.

"We must teach him a lesson," said Aunt Harriet.

"But what can we do?" asked Mrs. Smith.

The room was quiet.

"Let's have a party!" Sarah shouted suddenly.

"Silly girl, this is no time for a party," said Mrs. Homans.

"I mean a party like the men had when they threw English tea into the harbor," said Sarah. (Rappaport 1988, pp. 32–36)

In short, the standards for a well-written children's book are no different from the standards for any well-written book. The author treats the audience with respect and writes so that the text is honest and interesting. The literary devices employed to achieve that honesty and interest operate so smoothly they remain virtually invisible. The story (fiction) and the information (nonfiction) are so compelling that the reader sails along, engrossed in the precise language and unaware of the talent and time necessary for making the final product appear so effortless.

REFERENCES

Alexander, Lloyd. 1964. *The Book of Three*. New York: Holt.

Alexander, Lloyd. 1968. *The High King*. New York: Holt.

Alexander, Lloyd. 1986. *The Illyrian Adventure*. New York: Dutton.

Babbitt, Natalie. 1975. *Tuck Everlasting*. New York: Farrar, Straus and Giroux.

Brown, Margaret Wise. 1947. *Goodnight Moon*. Illustrated by Clement Hurd. New York: Harper & Row.

Compact Edition of the Oxford English Dictionary, The. 1971. New York: Oxford University Press.

Gág, Wanda. 1928. *Millions of Cats*. New York: Coward McCann.

Goodman, Kenneth. 1988. Look what they've done to Judy Blume!: The basalization of children's literature. *The New Advocate* 1, no. 1 (fall): 29–41.

Grimm Brothers. 1972. *Snow-White and the Seven Dwarfs*. Translated by Randall Jarrell. Illustrated by Nancy Eckholm Burkert. New York: Farrar, Straus and Giroux.

Hillert, Margaret. 1982. *Why We Have Thanksgiving*. Chicago: Follett.

Konigsburg, E. L. 1970. Double image. *Library Journal* 95 (15 February): 731–734.

Lewis, Norman. 1961. *The New Roget's Thesaurus in Dictionary Form*. New York: Putnam.

Lowry, Lois. 1977. *A Summer to Die*. Boston: Houghton Mifflin.

Morrow, Leslie M. 1989. *Literacy Development in the Early Years: Helping Children Read and Write*. Upper Saddle River, N.J.: Prentice Hall.

Peet, Bill. 1967. *Buford the Little Bighorn*. Boston: Houghton Mifflin.

Rappaport, Doreen. 1988. *The Boston Coffee Party*. Illustrated by Emily Arnold McCully. New York: Harper & Row.

Robinson, Barbara. 1972. *Temporary Times, Temporary Places*. New York: Harper & Row.

Spinelli, Jerry. 1990. *Maniac Magee*. Boston: Little, Brown.

Steig, William. 1976. *The Amazing Bone*. New York: Farrar, Straus and Giroux.

Trepeck, Conalee. 1964. *Fun at the Hospital*. Illustrated by David L. McKay. New York: Carlton Press.

Waber, Bernard. 1972. *Ira Sleeps Over*. Boston: Houghton Mifflin.

Walt Disney Productions. 1973. *Snow White and the Seven Dwarfs*. New York: Random House.

CHAPTER 4

What Is a Good Book? The Pictures

In this age of visual bombardment—daily overloads of images on computer screens, in magazines, on television, at the movies, and on the roadside—do children need even more images in picture books? The answer is a resounding "Yes!" The problem is not having too much to see but learning to be discriminating in what they see. We use the term *visual literacy* to describe this sort of discrimination. More than in any other generation, today's children need to develop discretion about what they view. Picture books are a perfect vehicle for opening a child's eyes to the beauty and power of art because they do not function like other books, in which words alone tell a story or convey information.

Illustrations in the better picture books share the function of storytelling or concept teaching. In fact, in wordless picture books the illustrations do the whole job. So the pictures beg for active participation in their viewing, unlike so many of the random images that are flashed daily in front of each of us. Text and illustration weave together to communicate. To get the full measure of meaning and fulfillment from a good picture book, the reader must attend carefully to both (Kiefer 1995).

Through the beautifully crafted picture books available today, young readers not only may become aware of the variety of artistic styles, media, and techniques that artists employ but also may develop a sense for judging quality.

DEVELOPING THE ABILITY TO "SEE"

Adults tend to sell children short when it comes to their abilities to perceive the world. Both of us have heard our university students, who are of course adults, say such things as, "This artwork is too sophisticated for children. Won't they OD on this?" One woman actually asked, "Why do they waste such great art on kids?" Truth be known, children are generally more visually aware and alert than most adults (McDermott 1974b). The older we get, the more our visual awareness is likely to be dulled by overload or by the real or imagined expectations our educational systems have imposed on us that alter the way we view images. Honest responses to art and other visual stimuli are programmed out of most children. They begin to ignore their own personal reactions and the fascinating detail in the art in order to second-guess their teachers' agendas, thus becoming basically less aware. This process is not much different from analyzing poetry with children until the beauty is beaten out of it.

As we have read to children over the years, they have shown us detail in picture book illustrations that our supposedly sophisticated adult eyes overlooked. For example, we had read *On Market Street* (Lobel 1981) many times but had not noticed that the figure representing *T* for toys in this alphabet book had on her hands puppets of the immensely popular Frog and Toad characters. That is, we did not notice them until a child pointed it out. Frog and Toad were made famous in Newbery and Caldecott Honor books created by Arnold Lobel—husband of Anita Lobel, who illustrated *On Market Street*. Children have shown us that the church tower clock in each illustration in *Anno's Counting Book* (Anno 1977) always points to the hour that corresponds with the number being presented. Gerald McDermott has observed that younger children, when reading *Arrow to the Sun* (McDermott 1974a), notice the sun symbol on the chest of the Sun God's child, an obvious visual link between father and son. However, McDermott (1974b) points out that older children tend not recognize the Pueblo boy's emblem.

Illustration in picture books is meant to delight, to capture attention, to tell a story or teach a concept, and to develop appreciation and awareness in children. Of course, appreciation is developed in part by consistent exposure to the wonderful varieties of art that are coupled with pleasing stories in today's picture books. Young children begin to sense something special in good art when they see lots of it. For example, Quincy had seen many fine picture books in his short six years. When he was listening to a new book, *17 Kings and 42 Elephants* (Mahy 1987), which has jewel-like batik on silk paintings by Patricia McCarthy, he suddenly interrupted to say, "Dad, these pictures are marvelous!" "Marvelous" was a bit unexpected coming from such a little body, but more amazing was his evaluative response to the artwork. Quincy didn't have the understanding or the words to analyze McCarthy's work, but he simply knew it was good stuff. How did he know? Because he'd seen so many picture books that he'd developed a level of appreciation that governed his taste in illustrations. Taste and appreciation come by comparison. Taste is broadened and cultivated by exposure; it is narrowed or allowed to lay fallow by restricting experience. Indeed, if all that children see in the world of art are Saturday morning cartoons, then such will be the standard of art for them.

FUNCTIONS OF ILLUSTRATIONS IN PICTURE BOOKS

"The function of art is to clarify, intensify, or otherwise enlarge our experience of life" (Canady 1980). This statement is as true for picture book illustrations as it is for gallery paintings, but picture book artwork also must operate in a manner unique to its special format. Because picture books are made up of a series of illustrations that typically tell a story, the art may function in one or more of the following ways:

ESTABLISH SETTING.   Art is a natural for creating the setting in an illustrated book. Time periods in historical stories or far-flung cultural settings can be brought to life through illustrations in ways words cannot do. Look at *The Fortune-Tellers* (Alexander 1992) as an example. This is a universal story that could have been set in any number of places and times, but Trina Schart Hyman's illustrations allow the story to spring suddenly into a certain place and time—the west African country of Cameroon in what Hyman calls "the fantastical present" (Hyman 1995). (See Illustration 1 in the color insert.)

DEFINE AND DEVELOP CHARACTERS.   Artists can give characters an extra fleshing out through illustrations. In *Ira Sleeps Over* (Waber 1972), for example, through the artwork we learn much about Ira's parents that is not revealed in the text. We see his parents' interesting and somewhat untraditional lifestyle, especially for the time when the book was published. For instance, in one illustration Ira's father is cooking dinner. *Frog Goes to Dinner* (Mayer 1974), a wordless picture book, relies completely on illustrations to define and develop the characters. Mayer is a marvel when it comes to using facial expressions to communicate what his characters are feeling. Note the double-page illustration of the angry family driving home after they had been thrown out of Fancy Restaurant. Each family member harbors an individual response to the disaster. (See Illustration 2.)

REINFORCE TEXT.   The primary function of some picture book illustrations is to reinforce the text. Nonfiction picture books often fall in this category, with the illustrations and diagrams restating visually what the words say. However, illustrations in a picture storybook may function primarily to reinforce the story. In the ever popular *Blueberries for Sal* (McCloskey 1948), for example, readers see what the text describes—the countryside in Maine as well as the characters who are out picking blueberries—but no major extensions to the text are evident.

PROVIDE A DIFFERING VIEWPOINT.   One of the most enjoyable ways in which illustrations may function in a picture book is that of telling a story different from the text or even being in opposition to the words. In *Rosie's Walk* (Hutchins 1968), the text says that Rosie the hen takes a peaceful stroll around the farm and gets "back in time for dinner." However, the illustrations tell another tale: A fox, never mentioned in the narrative, lurks behind Rosie every step of the way but is somehow frustrated every time it pounces forward to make Rosie its dinner. (See Illustration 3.) Peter Spier's (1978) *Oh, Were They Ever Happy* is an example of words and text that are humorously in opposition to one another. Children, inadvertently left alone for the day (the baby-sitter has her days confused and doesn't show), decide to do something nice for their parents—paint the house. The words say "Neat job" and "Pretty color!" while the illustrations show what a horrible mess the kids are making. They paint the bricks and window panes; they finish one color of paint and take up with another. Similarly, in Burningham's *Come Away from the Water, Shirley* (1977), the only words come from Shirley's parents, who nag her constantly to keep clean and stay safe during their day at the beach. In contrast, the illustrations show Shirley tuning out her parents' admonitions while her imagination takes her on a seaside adventure battling pirates.

PROVIDE INTERESTING ASIDES.   Sometimes picture book illustrations will be filled with interesting asides—subplots or details not necessarily related to the main story line. Many of Mitsumasa Anno's books employ this technique. In the wordless picture book *Anno's Journey* (Anno 1978), the main focus is a traveler whose journey takes him on horseback through the countryside, towns, and cities of historical Europe. A careful examination of the busy illustrations shows all sorts of wonderful surprises: fairy tale characters and famous historical figures blending into crowds of people, entertaining but brief human dramas such as a hotly contested foot race, and so on.

EXTEND OR DEVELOP THE PLOT.   The plot of a story may be advanced by illustrations. In wordless picture books, the whole plot is unfolded through pictures. Sometimes the plot is merely extended or rounded a little by the illustrations, as in

Stephen Gammell's art in *The Relatives Came* (Rylant 1985). Gammell shows that one family's journey to a family reunion is a bit perilous because Dad isn't such a good driver. Although Rylant's words say nothing about the driving, Dad levels the mailbox on the way out, loses suitcases, careens around mountain curves, and destroys their relatives' fence upon arrival. (See Illustration 4.)

ESTABLISH MOOD.   Illustrations are extremely effective in determining the mood of a picture storybook. *The Polar Express* (Van Allsburg 1985) is a Christmas story, and Christmas stories typically use a bright and cheery palette. The mood in Van Allsburg's story, however, is mysterious, and he uses dark colors to establish that mood. With muted reds and blues and even muted yellows along with plenty of black and brown, the artist creates an eerie feeling as a young boy watches a magical train steam its way into his front yard late Christmas Eve. The mood is maintained as the train whisks him and other children toward the North Pole, zipping past dark forests filled with wolves. (See Illustration 5.)

STYLE AND MEDIA IN PICTURE BOOK ILLUSTRATIONS

Artists are able to use a vast array of styles and media to create the illustrations in children's books today, partly because the technology of camera color separations makes reproducing sophisticated artwork feasible. In fact, some of the best and most varied artwork being done today appears in picture books. We know a professional artist who regularly checks the children's section at the public library to see what's new in picture books because he believes the best contemporary work is to be found there.

Excellent artwork can, of course, be rendered in various styles, ranging from extremely realistic to abstract. *Realism*, or *representational*, style is a faithful reproduction of nature, people, and objects as they actually appear. The illustrations in Zelinsky's (1986) *Rumpelstiltskin* are representational. (See Illustration 6.) *Surrealism* is realism skewed. It is an attempt to represent the working of the unconscious mind by creating a dreamlike state, as in Clément's (1989) *The Voice of the Wood*. (See Illustration 7.) *Expressionism*, which is an attempt to give objective expression to inner experience, often makes use of bright colors and figures that are a bit disproportionate. This stylized form is evident in Williams's (1982) *A Chair for My Mother*. (See Illustration 8.) Another popular style is *impressionism*, which emphasizes light, movement, and usually color over detail. A fine example of impressionism is Stevenson's art for Zolotow's (1980) *Say It!* (See Illustration 9.) *Naive* is a style that gives the appearance of being childlike, perhaps lacking perspective or a sense of proportion. Barbara Cooney used a naive style in her paintings for Hall's (1979) *Ox-Cart Man*. (See Illustration 10.) There are, of course, other artistic styles, including *cartoon art*, as found in James Stevenson's (1980) *That Terrible Halloween Night*. (See Illustration 11.)

The various styles artists use to create their artwork may be rendered in a variety of artistic media. There are basically two categories of media: painterly and graphic.

Painterly media include the most common art materials, such as paint, pencil, and ink. In *Rumpelstiltskin*, Zelinsky used *oil paints*, an opaque layering of colors. (See Illustration 6.) Watercolors, which are translucent, were the medium for Stevenson's paintings in *Say It!* (See Illustration 9.) Van Allsburg (1992) used *graphite*, or *pencil*, another painterly medium, in *The Widow's Broom*. (See Illustration 12.) Also in this category is *pen and ink*, which Isadora (1979) used in *Ben's Trumpet*. (See Illustration 13.) Other painterly media include *colored pencils*, *pastels* (chalk), *charcoal*, *crayons*, *felt-tip markers*, *gouache* and *tempera* (opaque water-based paints), and *acrylics* (plastic paints).

Artists apply the painterly media directly to canvas, paper, or some other surface. But when artists use *graphic media*, they generally create the artwork elsewhere before applying it to the final surface. With *woodcuts*, for instance, the artist carves images in relief into a block of wood. Then inks or paints are applied to the wood and transferred to a surface such as paper. Marcia Brown's (1961) illustrations for *Once a Mouse . . .* are woodcuts. (See Illustration 14.) *Linoleum cuts* are similar in technique to woodcuts, but they produce a cleaner line, as in Mary Wormell's (1996) *Hilda Hen's Scary Night*. (See Illustration 15.) *Collage*, another popular graphic technique, involves cutting and tearing shapes from paper or fabric and arranging them on the page, as in Keats's (1962) *The Snowy Day*. (See Illustration 16.) Collage may also include other objects that are attached to the surface, like the breakfast cereal and wire hangers in Diaz's (1994) illustrations for *Smoky Night*. David Wisniewski's (1996) dramatic illustrations in *The Golem*, created by overlaying intricate paper cutouts, are a sophisticated form of collage. (See Illustration 31.) *Stone lithography* is an engraving on stone that is printed on paper, such as the illustrations for the 1939 edition of *Abraham Lincoln* by Ingri and Edgar d'Aulaire. (See Illustration 17.) A graphic medium that looks a bit like pen and ink drawings is called *scratchboard*. A black ink coating is scratched away to show the white surface beneath; color may be added after the "drawing" is complete, as in *The Faithful Friend* (San Souci 1995), illustrated by Brian Pinkney. (See Illustration 18.) Even *photography* can be considered a graphic technique. Bruce McMillan's (1993) *Mouse Views: What the Class Pet Saw* uses color photography to give children a fresh look at their world. (See Illustration 19.) Also, artists will often mix media, using both graphic and painterly techniques together. A prime example is Molly Bang's (1985) *The Paper Crane*, which uses three-dimensional paper cutouts, traditional collage, and painterly techniques. Then each page was photographed to retain its three-dimensional quality. (See Illustration 20.)

VISUAL ELEMENTS

Like all artists, picture book illustrators incorporate several visual elements into the creation of their pictures that subtly affect the way we respond to the art. These elements are line, shape, color, texture, and composition.

LINES.   Lines in illustrations are either curved or straight. These lines may vary in thickness or length. They may run horizontally, diagonally, or vertically. They may be solid or broken. How line is used often plays an important role in what a picture communicates. For instance, diagonal lines suggest movement (slant of the road in Illustration 4 and of the keyboard in Illustration 13). The dominant vertical lines of the trees in Illustration 5, from Van Allsburg's *Polar Express,* create a static look, as if this scene were a photograph capturing and arresting a moment in the flow of action. On the other hand, horizontal lines may suggest order or tranquillity.

Artists also use line to direct the viewer's eye. Le Cain's use of line in *Thorn Rose* focuses the eye upon the ominous tower holding the only remaining spinning wheel. The lines created by a wall, row of windows, roof line, and balustrade lead to the upper right-hand corner and seem to converge at the tower. Even the fountain and the horizon point the way. In this manner, Le Cain guides our viewing of his painting. (See Illustration 26.)

SHAPE.   Shape is the two-dimensional form representing an object. Shapes may be simple or complex. The objects may be readily recognizable or so abstract as to be difficult to recognize. Curved shapes generally suggest things found in nature, and angular shapes depict objects built by humans. For example, the illustration from *Round Trip* by Ann Jonas shows from one perspective people sitting in a movie theater. Neither the theater nor the humans are clearly recognizable, only suggested by the shapes. The man-made items (seats, lights, screen) are angular forms, while the people are suggested by rounded forms representing heads. (See Illustration 28.)

COLOR.   Color is a visual element with these traits: hue, value, and saturation. Hue is simply the color itself (red, blue, yellow), and these hues are often categorized as being either cool (blue, green, violet) or warm (red, yellow, orange). The scene by James Stevenson (Illustration 9) uses blues and violets predominately to create the cool, crisp feel of autumn. Value is the lightness or darkness of the color (dark blue, light green), achieved by adding black or white to the hue. As discussed earlier in this chapter, the mood of a picture may be manipulated by value, as in the mysterious mood achieved by the dark palette Van Allsburg used in *Polar Express* (Illustration 5). Finally, saturation, or chroma, is the brightness or dullness of a color. For example, the brightness of the colors in the picture from *The Fortune-Tellers* (Illustration 1) creates a festive atmosphere, while the muted hues in Illustration 29 add an appropriately ancient feeling to the story of *Saint George and the Dragon.* Illustrations also may be achromatic, only rendered in black, white, and the various shades of gray in between. (See Illustrations 2 and 13.) Monochromatic illustrations use only one hue, such as the different values of brown in *The Widow's Broom* by Chris Van Allsburg (Illustration 12).

TEXTURE.   Texture is a tactile sensation communicated by the artist: rough, smooth, hard, soft, and so on. Collage, as discussed earlier, is the most obvious way of creating texture in illustrations because of its three-dimensional qualities. The cutout crane in Illustration 20, for instance, clearly has the sharp edges of a folded paper bird. However, illustrators most often create a sense of texture on a two-dimensional surface, as with the fabric of the automobile seats in Illustration 2. Mercer Mayer used cross-hatching (the crossing of lines) to produce the coarse texture of the material in both the seats and the boy's suit.

COMPOSITION.   Composition is the visual element that serves to unify all of the elements in an illustration.

> In arranging the elements on each page, including the printed type, the artist tries to obtain an effective balance between unity and variety and creates visual patterns that may be carried on from page to page. (Kiefer 1995, p. 129)

For example, an artist may balance objects in an illustration, either by distributing them evenly (symmetrically) or irregularly (asymmetrically). Another facet of composition concerns object dominance. Artists can ensure that certain shapes are dominant by making them larger or brighter in order to attract the eye. In Illustration 22, David Wiesner splits the picture evenly down the center from top to bottom. The backgrounds of both sides are balanced asymmetrically by the careful yet irregular placement of vehicles, people, and clouds. However, the police detective in the foreground is larger than any other individual and thus is the dominant figure. In this way, Wiesner directs the viewer's attention to the detective's actions.

FURTHER EVALUATING CHILDREN'S BOOK ILLUSTRATION

According to Cianciolo (1976, p. 9), in quality picture book art "something of significance is said." In inferior picture books, the art all begins to look the same—flat line and color washes, as in books like the Sesame Street titles and most things from Disney (Hearne 1990). In other words, quality picture book art is individual and unique. Stereotypical artwork denies individuality, both in the artistic rendering and in the characters and settings represented. It is more difficult to relate to the human experience and to get involved with the story when the art depicts generic or stereotypical people and places. For example, *I'm Glad I'm a Boy! I'm Glad I'm a Girl!* (Darrow 1970) shows insipid girls and powerful boys who are devoid of other personality traits. The generic, flat line illustrations accompany text such as "Boys invent things. Girls use what boys invent." Together, illustrations and text go beyond the uninspiring to drop negative stereotyping to a new low.

In better picture book illustrations, two basic elements tend to give individuality to the illustrations: action and detail. Action is important in picture storybooks in particular because the artwork moves the story along. Note the illustration from *Deep in the Forest* (Turkle 1976), a role reversal version of "Goldilocks and the Three Bears." (See Illustration 21.) This scene freezes the action at the climax, but the illustration is by no means static. The tilt of the human forms as they barrel forward in pursuit and the wild-eyed little bear with fully stretched body and churning legs create for us a true sense of the chaotic, frenzied chase. Sometimes action in illustrations is subtle but suggests a great deal of activity. For example, in *Tuesday* (Wiesner 1991) the police detective examines a lily pad suspended from a pencil, his quizzical look suggesting his mental activity. "Why and how?" he seems to ask himself, unable to fathom the hundreds of frogs who invaded the nighttime sanctity of his town on flying lily pads. (See Illustration 22.) One of the ways picture book artists create tension in their work is by using illustrations to anticipate or foreshadow action. Look at the illustration from *Rosie's Walk* (Hutchins 1968). (See Illustration 3.) Rosie, still unaware her life is in danger, is about to inadvertently foil another of the fox's attempts to capture her. The rope coiled about her leg shows us what is to come.

Certainly it is not difficult to see that details in illustrations tend to give the artwork depth and allow artists to assert their individuality. Even the power of a carefully placed line can make loosely drawn pictures say volumes. Consider the illustration from Glen Rounds's *Three Little Pigs and the Big Bad Wolf* (1992). (See Illustration 23.) Although the wolf is rather scratchily drawn, his raggedy appearance makes him look as if he's fallen on hard times. The flowing lines give the wolf a fluid, slinky sense of movement, which seems to say "vagabond."

Detail also may be evident in the use of perspective in many quality picture books. In Le Cain's version of the Grimm Brothers' (1975) *Thorn Rose or the Sleeping Beauty*, the artist shows a single scene from two very different perspectives. When everyone in the castle falls asleep, one illustration looks past the cook (who is about to box the kitchen boy's ears), out the kitchen door, and beyond horses sleeping in a stall. Later, when the prince finally arrives on the castle grounds, we are allowed to look past him, past the horses, and back into the kitchen to where the cook is slumped over a table. (See Illustrations 24 and 25.) This may seem a small thing, but such detail provides the setting with depth and makes it a believable place. Obviously, Le Cain envisioned this world carefully and translated his vision into illustrations that give us a sense of being there.

Le Cain also uses his illustrations in *Thorn Rose* to foreshadow most subtly the impending doom connected with the last spinning wheel to be found in the kingdom. In one painting, the artist shows Thorn Rose, now an adolescent, standing on a balcony walkway with a castle tower in the distance. The left side of the illustration is verdant; Thorn Rose is surrounded by flowering plants and peacocks, and the sky is bright. However, as one's eyes move across the painting toward the tower, the sky darkens ominously. The garden-like surroundings of the castle give way to a foreboding, craggy appearance. Even a great serpent, a symbol of evil, is wound about the parapet leading to the tower, which has a rather dragon-like look. Of course, the tower holds the accursed spinning wheel. This visual foreshadowing creates an unconscious feeling of tension in the reader.

Careful attention to detail often requires extensive research before an artist begins work on the illustrations. Depending on the book, illustrators may spend untold hours investigating the historical details of Ming Dynasty culture, the anatomy of wolves, or rain forest botany, for example. In Jarrell's retelling of *Snow-White and the Seven Dwarfs* (Grimm Brothers 1972), the artist, Nancy Ekholm Burkert, re-created the time period and cultural setting of the tale with accuracy. Even the illustration showing the evil queen's laboratory is stunning in its detail. The accoutrements of black magic are displayed on a workbench; each herb and root is authentic and poisonous. (See Illustration 27.) Trina Schart Hyman's illustrations for *Saint George and the Dragon* (Hodges 1984) include drawings, primarily in borders surrounding the text, of plants and flowers indigenous to Britain during those magical times. In researching his book *Make Way for Ducklings,* Robert McCloskey (1942) filled notebooks with artistic studies of ducks— sketches of wing extensions and so on (Schmidt 1990). He even had ducks swimming in his bathtub and walking about his apartment to use as ready references. McCloskey

(1965) points out that when he spends the time to examine a tree from twig to branch to trunk to root, the examination may not be apparent to the viewer of the artistically rendered tree, but the tree is better for his having thought of it in such detail.

Indeed, detail is often subtle. In fact, most artistic devices are like cosmetics; they must not be too noticeable or they are not doing their job. Makeup, for instance, must enhance so that we say, "What a gorgeous face," not "What great eye shadow." A device that Maurice Sendak (1963) used in *Where the Wild Things Are* is so subtle that most readers don't notice they are being influenced by it. As Max's anger grows, so do the illustrations, getting larger and larger until they fill a full double-page spread. Then as Max's anger cools, the illustrations begin to shrink.

Finally, the process of fine bookmaking gives us a few other evaluative considerations. The size and shape of books may match the story line, as in Janice Udry's (1956) *A Tree Is Nice*. Marc Simont's tall tree illustrations suggest the tall, thin format for the book. Other book design elements can set quality publications apart. For example, the rainbow trail, a significant recurring design on Pueblo Native American pottery and other art forms, becomes a unifying factor as it leads the reader through *Arrow to the Sun* (McDermott 1974a). Ann Jonas's (1983) *Round Trip* is designed to be read as a round trip. The illustrations are ingeniously created so that when we reach the end of the book, we flip it upside down and read it backward. All the illustrations suddenly transform into new pictures, an optical illusion of sorts. At the same time, the round-trip theme is a part of the story—a trip into the city and home again. (See Illustration 28.)

Even small details like decorated endpapers enhance the visual appeal of a picture book. The endpapers inside the cover of a book actually bind book to cover and are traditionally white. However, not only are endpapers often brightly colored in many of today's books, but they often are illustrated, sometimes with original pieces not found inside. Good examples are the two original paintings by Helen Oxenbury on the endpapers of Rosen's (1989) retelling of *We're Going on a Bear Hunt*. A deserted, daytime seashore scene appears on the front endpaper, and a nighttime seashore scene with a bear lumbering along in the surf is on the back.

Other illustrative techniques extend art beyond the traditional designs. Hyman's borders in *Saint George and the Dragon* (Hodges 1984) give the look of observing the story through an old-fashioned window. (See Illustration 29.) Brinton Turkle's (1976) inclusion of art on the title and copyright pages is an important part of the storytelling process in *Deep in the Forest*. These pages typically contain art only as embellishment or have none at all. Yet Turkle starts telling his story on the title page, where the bear cub steps out of his safe environment to begin an adventure. (See Illustration 30.)

All these elements of picture book creation and production are what make the visual storytelling and concept teaching process so successful. Children have available to them some of the best of the current artistic endeavor. As teachers and parents, we have the opportunity to help our children become visually literate through fine picture books, to curb the numbing effects of mindless television viewing. Our charge is to offer our children the best in picture and in word, to give them an arsenal for making judgments and developing taste.

For more on picture books, see Chapter 13.

REFERENCES

Alexander, Lloyd. 1992. *The Fortune-tellers*. Illustrated by Trina Schart Hyman. New York: Dutton.

Anno, Mitsumasa. 1977. *Anno's Counting Book*. New York: Crowell.

Anno, Mitsumasa. 1978. *Anno's Journey*. New York: Philomel.

Bang, Molly. 1985. *The Paper Crane*. New York: Greenwillow.

Brown, Marcia. 1961. *Once a Mouse . . . .* New York: Scribner's.

Bunting, Eve. 1994. *Smoky Night*. Illustrated by David Diaz. New York: Harcourt.

Burningham, John. 1977. *Come Away from the Water, Shirley*. New York: Harper.

Canady, John. 1980. *What Is Art?* New York: Knopf.

Cianciolo, Patricia. 1976. *Illustrations in Children's Books*. Dubuque, Iowa: W. C. Brown.

Clément, Claude. 1989. *The Voice of the Wood*. Illustrated by Frédéric Clément. New York: Dial.

Darrow, Whitney. 1970. *I'm Glad I'm a Boy! I'm Glad I'm a Girl!* New York: Windmill/Simon & Schuster.

d'Aulaire, Ingri, and Edgar d'Aulaire. 1939. *Abraham Lincoln*. New York: Doubleday.

Grimm Brothers. 1972. *Snow-White and the Seven Dwarfs*. Translated by Randall Jarrell. Illustrated by Nancy Ekholm Burkert. New York: Farrar, Straus and Giroux.

Grimm Brothers. 1975. *Thorn Rose or the Sleeping Beauty*. Illustrated by Errol Le Cain. New York: Bradbury.

Hall, Donald. 1979. *Ox-Cart Man*. Illustrated by Barbara Cooney. New York: Viking.

Hearne, Betsy. 1990. *Choosing Books for Children: A Commonsense Guide*. New York: Delacorte.

Hodges, Margaret. 1984. *Saint George and the Dragon*. Illustrated by Trina Schart Hyman. Boston: Little, Brown.

Hutchins, Pat. 1968. *Rosie's Walk*. New York: Macmillan.

Hyman, Trina Schart. 1995. Telephone interview with Elena Rockman. 27 January.

Isadora, Rachel. 1979. *Ben's Trumpet*. New York: Greenwillow.

Jonas, Ann. 1983. *Round Trip*. New York: Greenwillow.

Keats, Ezra Jack. 1962. *The Snowy Day*. New York: Viking.

Kiefer, Barbara Z. 1995. *The Potential of Picturebooks: From Visual Literacy to Aesthetic Understanding*. Upper Saddle River, N.J.: Merrill/Prentice Hall.

Lobel, Arnold. 1981. *On Market Street*. Illustrated by Anita Lobel. New York: Greenwillow.

Mahy, Margaret. 1987. *17 Kings and 42 Elephants*. Illustrated by Patricia McCarthy. New York: Dial.

Mayer, Mercer. 1974. *Frog Goes to Dinner*. New York: Dial.

McCloskey, Robert. 1942. *Make Way for Ducklings*. New York: Viking.

McCloskey, Robert. 1948. *Blueberries for Sal*. New York: Viking.

McCloskey, Robert. 1965. In *The Lively Art of Picture Books*. Videocassette. Weston, Conn.: Weston Woods.

McDermott, Gerald. 1974a. *Arrow to the Sun*. New York: Viking.

McDermott, Gerald. 1974b. "Image in Film and Picture Book." Speech at The University of Georgia, Athens, Georgia, September.

McMillan, Bruce. 1993. *Mouse Views: What the Class Pet Saw*. New York: Holiday House.

Rosen, Michael. 1989. *We're Going on a Bear Hunt*. Illustrated by Helen Oxenbury. New York: Macmillan.

Rounds, Glen. 1992. *Three Little Pigs and the Big Bad Wolf*. New York: Holiday House.

Rylant, Cynthia. 1985. *The Relatives Came*. Illustrated by Stephen Gammell. New York: Bradbury.

San Souci, Robert D. 1995. *The Faithful Friend*. Illustrated by Brian Pinkney. New York: Simon & Schuster.

Schmidt, Gary D. 1990. *Robert McCloskey*. Boston: Twayne.

Sendak, Maurice. 1963. *Where the Wild Things Are*. New York: Harper.

Spier, Peter. 1978. *Oh, Were They Ever Happy*. New York: Doubleday.

Stevenson, James. 1980. *That Terrible Halloween Night*. New York: Greenwillow.

Turkle, Brinton. 1976. *Deep in the Forest*. New York: Dutton.

Udry, Janice. 1956. *A Tree Is Nice*. Illustrated by Marc Simont. New York: Harper.

Van Allsburg, Chris. 1985. *The Polar Express*. Boston: Houghton Mifflin.

Van Allsburg, Chris. 1992. *The Widow's Broom*. Boston: Houghton Mifflin.

Waber, Bernard. 1972. *Ira Sleeps Over*. Boston: Houghton Mifflin.

Wiesner, David. 1991. *Tuesday*. New York: Clarion.

Williams, Vera B. 1982. *A Chair for My Mother*. New York: Greenwillow.

Wisniewski, David. 1996. *The Golem*. Clarion.

Wormell, Mary. 1996. *Hilda Hen's Scary Night*. Harcourt.

Zelinsky, Paul. 1986. *Rumpelstiltskin*. New York: Dutton.

Zolotow, Charlotte. 1980. *Say It!* Illustrated by James Stevenson. New York: Greenwillow.

What Is a Good Book?
The Pictures

The following illustrations are described in Chapter 4.

1. From *The Fortune-Tellers* by Lloyd Alexander, illustrated by Trina Schart Hyman.

2. From *Frog Goes to Dinner* by Mercer Mayer.

3. From *Rosie's Walk* by Pat Hutchins.

4. From *The Relatives Came* by Cynthia Rylant, illustrated by Stephen Gammell.

6. From *Rumplestiltskin* by Paul O. Zelinsky.

5. From *The Polar Express* by Chris Van Allsburg.

7. From *The Voice of the Wood* by Claude Clement, translated by Lenny Hort, illustrated by Frederic Clement.

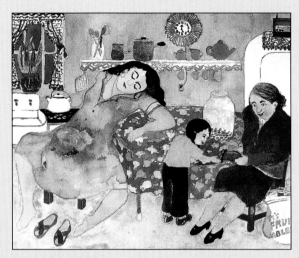

8. From *A Chair for Mother* by Vera Williams.

9. From *Say It!* by Charlotte Zolotow, illustrated by James Stevenson.

10. From *Ox-Cart Man* by Donald Hall, illustrated by Barbara Cooney.

11. From *That Terrible Halloween Night* by James Stevenson.

13. From *Ben's Trumpet* by Rachel Isadora.

about to be snatched up by a crow.

He hurried

12. From *The Widow's Broom* by Chris Van Allsburg.

14. From *Once Upon a Mouse* by Marcia Brown.

— a stick that was just right for smacking a snow-covered tree.

15. From *Hilda Hen's Scary Night* by Mary Wormell.

16. From *The Snowy Day* by Ezra Jack Keats.

17. From *Abraham Lincoln* by Ingri and Edgar d'Aulaire.

18. From *The Faithful Friend* by Robert D. San Souci, illustrated by Brian Pinkney.

19. From *Mouse Views: What the Class Pet Saw* by Bruce McMillan.

21. From *Deep in the Forest* by Brinton Turkle.

It happened just as the stranger had said. The owner had only to clap his hands and the paper crane became a living bird, flew down to the floor, and danced.

20. From *The Paper Crane* by Molly Bang.

22. From *Tuesday* by David Wiesner.

23. From *Three Little Pigs and the Big Bad Wolf* by Glen Rounds.

24. From *Thorn Rose; or, the Sleeping Beauty* by the Brothers Grimm, illustrated by Errol Le Cain.

25. From *Thorn Rose; or, the Sleeping Beauty* by the Brothers Grimm, illustrated by Errol Le Cain.

26. From *Thorn Rose; or, the Sleeping Beauty* by the Brothers Grimm, illustrated by Errol Le Cain.

27. From *Snow-White and the Seven Dwarfs* by the Brothers Grimm, translated by Randall Jarrell, illustrated by Nancy Ekholm Burkert.

28. From *Round Trip* by Ann Jonas.

29. From *Saint George and the Dragon*
by Margaret Hodges,
illustrated by Trina Schart Hyman.

30. From *Deep in the Forest* by Brinton Turkle.

31. From *Golem* by
David Wisniewski.

CHAPTER 5

Children's Books: History and Trends

The notion of childhood dawned late in the history of our Western world, not until the 17th century. The English philosopher John Locke influenced the prevailing attitudes about children as much as anyone in his time. Locke's book *Some Thoughts Concerning Education,* published in 1693, suggested gentler ways of raising children. He even suggested that children's books be made available, books that were easy and pleasant to read. However, *childhood* was a concept only among the affluent until well into the 20th century. As in the days before Locke, many children in both England and the United States continued to be treated as if they were small adults. Consider that child labor laws were not legislated until well into the 20th century in both countries. Kids dressed, worked, and lived like their adult counterparts, if that well. Therefore, for the general populace, the idea of special books for children was slow in coming.

Early Books for Children

As far back as the Middle Ages, books intended for youngsters existed in limited numbers in the form of handwritten texts for the extremely wealthy. However, because literature aimed at young readers has and always will reflect society's attitudes about children, these early books were meant to indoctrinate. The stories worth reading were available not in books but from the storytellers—fairy tales, myths, ballads, epics, and other stories from our oral tradition. Of course, these stories were not meant for children, although they were allowed to listen. Over time, these magical tales have become the property of childhood.

By the same token, books that were published in the early days of the printing press, books meant for adults, were also enjoyed and adopted by children. William Caxton, an English businessman and printer, produced several such books, including *Aesop's Fables* (1484), which was decorated with woodcut illustrations. From that time forward, children have claimed many books meant for adult audiences, including such well-known titles as Daniel Defoe's *Robinson Crusoe* (1719), Jonathan Swift's *Gulliver's Travels* (1726), Johann Wyss's *The Swiss Family Robinson* (1814), Walter Scott's *Ivanhoe* (1820), and J. R. R. Tolkien's *The Hobbit* (1937). (See Figure 5-1, later in Chapter 5, for a list including these and other significant publications in children's literature.)

Literature intended specifically for children and published from the 15th through the 17th centuries still was designed to indoctrinate. The so-called hornbooks, or lesson paddles, existed as reading material for children for more than two centuries, beginning in the 1440s. Generally made of wood, these small paddles (about 3 by 5 inches) had pasted to them pieces of parchment on which were printed the alphabet, verses from the Bible, or the like. The term *hornbook* comes from the thin, transparent sheet of cow horn that covered and protected the parchment. Hornbooks were particularly popular among the Puritans in Colonial America, who believed children to be basically wicked, like adults, and therefore in need of saving. This pious attitude is clearly evident in the first book published for American children, John Cotton's catechism called *Spiritual Milk for Boston Babes in Either England, Drawn from the Breasts of Both Testaments for Their Souls' Nourishment.* First published in England in 1646, it was revised and published in America in 1656.

Despite the preachy, often unpleasant nature of children's literature in the early days of printing, one especially bright spot appeared in 1657. Johann Amos Comenius, a Moravian teacher and bishop, wrote *Orbis Pictus (The World in Pictures)*, which is often called the first children's picture book. *Orbis Pictus* is filled with woodcut illustrations that work in harmony with the simple text to describe the wonders of the natural world.

In 1697 Charles Perrault, who had set about collecting the French fairy tales, published his enduring collection, *Tales of Mother Goose*, which included such old favorites as "The Sleeping Beauty" and "Cinderella." Here we find the first mention of Mother Goose, a figure popularized in many subsequent books and stories. Although Perrault's stories were popular with adults in the court of King Louis XIV, his fairy tale collection contains a frontispiece showing an old woman (presumably Mother Goose) telling stories to a group of children.

Even as early as the 16th century, a form of "underground" reading became popular. Called *chapbooks,* these crudely printed booklets were often sold by peddlers for pennies. Chapbooks became extremely popular in the 17th and 18th centuries and were the first real break from the oppressive, didactic, you-are-a-sinner books for children. Of course, the Puritans decried these tales of Robin Hood, King Arthur, and even an early rendition of "Froggie Went A-Courting." Yet, children and adults reveled in them, though often on the sly.

Chapbooks may have been indirectly responsible for what is perhaps the most important development in the history of children's literature—John Newbery's children's publishing house. Certainly Newbery was influenced by John Locke, who dared suggest that youngsters should enjoy reading, so it seems likely that he observed the popularity of chapbooks among children and decided that there was a market for true children's books. In any case, Newbery ushered in the age of children's books by beginning to publish exclusively for young readers. He released his first children's book in 1744. *A Pretty Little Pocket-Book* taught the alphabet not with catechism but with entertaining games, rhymes, and fables. Newbery published hundreds of titles (some of which he may have written himself), the most famous and enduring of which is *The History of Little Goody Two Shoes* (1765). So great was Newbery's contribution to children's publishing that the oldest of the world's children's book prizes bears his name, America's John Newbery Medal. Still, the moralistic tale continued to dominate much of children's literature, even in Newbery's books somewhat. Didacticism ruled well into the 19th century.

CHILDREN'S BOOKS COME OF AGE

The onset of the 19th century brought some of the most influential, honest, and lasting children's stories into print. Jacob and Wilhelm Grimm collected from oral sources the German variants of the folk and fairy tales and retold them in their *Household Tales*, which appeared in 1812 and included "Snow White" and "Rumpelstiltskin." Some of Hans Christian Andersen's original fairy tales were published in 1835 in a volume titled *Fairy Tales Told for Children*. The stories of this Danish author, such as "The Ugly Duckling" and "The Emperor's New Clothes," remain popular to this day.

One of the century's greatest contributions to verse for children came from England. Edward Lear's *A Book of Nonsense* (1846), a collection of outrageous limericks, became an immediate bestseller. Lear made the limerick famous, and it remains a favorite verse form among today's children. Robert Louis Stevenson's *A Child's Garden of Verses* (1885) is another poetry collection that children still love today.

A number of noteworthy books surfaced during the second half of the 19th century. Fantasy novels emerged with the publication of such greats as *The Water Babies* by Charles Kingsley in 1863 and, of course, Lewis Carroll's [Charles Dodgson] *Alice's Adventures in Wonderland* in 1865. Other noteworthy titles include *At the Back of the North Wind* (1871) by George MacDonald, *The Adventures of Pinocchio* (1881) by Carlo Collodi, and the novels of Jules Verne, which mark the advent of the science fiction genre. Beginning with *Journey to the Center of the Earth* in 1864, Jules Verne created stories meant for adults but happily embraced by young readers.

Stories about contemporary life were especially preachy and pious until a monumental children's novel made its debut in 1868. *Little Women* by Louisa May Alcott was like a breath of fresh air, with its lively characters, whose actions, words, and feelings reflected honest human experiences. The character of Jo March, for example, deviated radically from female characters of the past who were docile and certainly inferior to their male counterparts. In fact, Jo was something of a rebel (an early feminist), who railed constantly against what she considered the false set of standards dictated by the Victorian code of behavior. *Little Women* set the course for many realistic novels that immediately followed its publication, including several more from Alcott herself. A few years later came Mark Twain's (Samuel Clemens) *The Adventures of Tom Sawyer* (1876) and Robert Louis Stevenson's *Treasure Island* (serialized in the magazine *Young Folks*, then published as a book in 1883). The last decade of the 19th century gave us Rudyard Kipling's masterpiece, *The Jungle Books* (1894–95).

A number of magazines for children began publication during the 19th century. *St. Nicholas Magazine*, published in the United States starting in 1873, set standards of excellence in the world of children's literature. It was edited by Mary Mapes Dodge, author of *Hans Brinker, Or the Silver Skates* (1865). The best-known children's authors and illustrators contributed to *St. Nicholas*, and several novels appeared first in the magazine in serialized form, including *Jo's Boys* by Louisa May Alcott, *Sara Crewe* by Frances Hodgson Burnett, and *The Jungle Books* by Rudyard Kipling.

Children's book illustration also came of age during the 19th century. Illustrators gained increasing status as printing techniques improved and color illustrations became more common. Publishers enticed well-known artists, such as George Cruikshank, who illustrated *Grimm's Fairy Tales* in 1823, to produce work for children's books. The artwork by the immortal Victorian-age illustrators in Great Britain, such as Randolph Caldecott, Kate Greenaway, and Walter Crane, rival the fine work being done today, in spite of comparatively primitive color printing methods. So influential were these artists that two major awards for children's book illustration today bear their names: The Randolph Caldecott Medal in the United States and the Kate Greenaway Medal in Britain. Randolph Caldecott is often noted as the first illustrator to show action in pictures, as evidenced in *The Diverting History of John Gilpin* (1878), which has perhaps his best-remembered illustrations. In fact, the Caldecott Medal affixed to winning picture books is engraved with the most famous scene, John Gilpin's wild ride. American Howard Pyle also created stunning illustrations for classics like *The Merry Adventures of Robin Hood of Great Reknown* (1883), which he also wrote.

And so the domain of children's books was firmly established by the dawning of the 20th century. The century began with groundbreaking events, such as the birth of the modern picture storybook. Before Beatrix Potter wrote and illustrated her enduring story, *The Tale of Peter Rabbit* (1902), illustrations in books for children, beautiful as they were, were primarily decorations. Potter incorporated colored illustration with text, page for page, thus using the pictures as well as the words to tell the story. Therefore, Beatrix Potter is the mother of the modern picture storybook, and *Peter Rabbit* is the firstborn.

Another first that occurred early in the 20th century was the publishing of L. Frank Baum's *The Wonderful Wizard of Oz* in 1900. Modern fantasy had been primarily the domain of the Europeans, especially the British. *The Wonderful Wizard of Oz* was the first classic modern fantasy written by an American.

Many other enduring classics emerged in the first part of the century, such as J. M. Barrie's magical *Peter Pan in Kensington Gardens*, which was adapted in 1906 into a book from its original form as a play, and Lucy Maud Montgomery's Canadian classic featuring the spunky, red-headed Anne Shirley in *Anne of Green Gables* (1908). Also in 1908, the granddaddy of animal fantasies appeared. Kenneth Grahame's *The Wind in the Willows* became the standard for all subsequent animal fantasy stories. Another trend-setting fantasy, A. A. Milne's gentle story of *Winnie the Pooh*, was published in 1926.

While sterling illustrators like Arthur Rackham (*Mother Goose* 1913) were at work in Britain, America produced its counterpart to Beatrix Potter—Wanda Gág. Her *Millions of Cats* (1928) is credited as the first American picture storybook. Its descriptive pictures and rhythmic text have remained unforgettable: "Hundreds of cats, Thousands of cats, Millions and billions and trillions of cats." Other landmark picture books from the first half of the 20th century include American favorites such as *Goodnight Moon* (1939) by Margaret Wise Brown, which is still a champion bedtime story, and *Madeline*, Ludwig Bemelmans's 1939 story of the little, irrepressible Parisian girl and her boarding school experiences. Dr. Seuss (Theodor Geisel), who became the most widely known of American children's book authors and illustrators, began his work with *To Think I Saw It on Mulberry Street* in 1937. Another immortal name in the history of children's picture books, Robert McCloskey, published *Make Way for Ducklings*, which has become a modern classic, in 1941. This endearing tale of a spunky mother duck and her eight ducklings' dangerous trek through Boston to reach the Public Garden is loved by children today as much as ever.

Along with the many noteworthy books, a number of popular but lesser quality books appeared during the first half of the 20th century. The books published by the Stratemeyer Syndicate created a publishing phenomenon that has extended into current times. Beginning in the late 19th century, Edward Stratemeyer saw the potential profit in publishing a quickly produced fiction series for young readers. Certainly series books had been published and done well before Stratemeyer, but he created a machine that pumped out thousands of titles over the years. Typically, Stratemeyer would outline plots and then turn the writing over to a host of ghost writers. He published his series books under various pseudonyms, which many children still believe belong to real authors. Some of the Stratemeyer series titles include The Rover Boys, The Bobbsey Twins, Tom Swift, The Hardy Boys, and Nancy Drew. Today series books, such as the Animorphs and Goosebumps series, are, despite their mediocre literary quality, the best-selling children's books by a wide margin (Greenlee, Monson, and Taylor 1996; Chevannes, McEvoy, and Simson 1997; Saltman 1997).

In the latter half of the 20th century, a revolution in the world of children's books occurred. The 1950s were a stable time for children's publishing. Books still had predictable plots and contained the basic decency and restrained good fun that most adults expected. Some enduring modern classics were born during this decade, such as American E. B. White's *Charlotte's Web* (1952) and Britisher C. S. Lewis's *The Lion, the Witch, and the Wardrobe* (1950). In 1956 the major international award for children's writing, the Hans Christian Andersen Prize, was established by the International Board on Books for Young People.

The financial boom of the 1960s, which included large government grants to school libraries, helped make children's publishing big business. More books began to be published and sold, which is reflected by the rapid increase in the number of books chosen each year by the American Library Association as Notables. There were 19 Notable titles in 1956 and 62 Notables in 1964.

THE AGE OF NEW REALISM

Along with an increase in sales, the 1960s brought a revolution in writing and illustrating: the age of new realism. Long-standing taboos imposed on authors and illustrators began to break down as the social revolution of the '60s began to boil. Few books before this time dealt with topics like death, divorce, alcoholism, and child abuse. In fact, books did not even show children and parents at odds with one another. And there were almost no quality books for children written by and about minorities. Then, in the early '60s, daring new books began to emerge. A picture book, *Where the Wild Things Are* (1963) by Maurice Sendak, and a novel, *Harriet the Spy* (1964) by Louise Fitzhugh, are often credited with ushering in this age of new realism. Both were mildly controversial, partly because they showed children at odds with their parents. Max's mother in *Wild Things* loses her temper at his unruly behavior and sends him "to bed without eating anything." And Harriet's parents are aloof and too busy to be concerned with Harriet's day-to-day activities. Max's psychological fantasy, a vent for his frustration and for the anger he feels toward his mother, and Harriet's eventual need for psychotherapy were unsettling story elements for some adults.

The Snowy Day by Ezra Jack Keats, published in 1962, was the first picture book to show a black child as a protagonist without any vestiges of negative stereotyping. The book won the Caldecott Medal in 1963 and has remained a favorite.

Strong American high fantasy, rivaling the work of C. S. Lewis, also appeared in the 1960s, most notably the five books of The Prydain Chronicles by Lloyd Alexander, beginning with *The Book of Three* (1964). Also, an American emphasis on both international books and on books written and illustrated by African-Americans was encouraged by the establishment of two awards in the 1960s: the Mildred L. Batchelder Award for translated books and the Coretta Scott King Award, both administered by the American Library Association.

Federal monies for school libraries in the United States dwindled in the 1970s, and the market for children's books shifted toward a consumer, or bookstore, market. According to Jazan Higgins, vice president at William Morrow, today retail sales command about 35 percent of the children's book market at her publishing company, a significant rise over the 5 to 10 percent common before 1970. For companies who publish top-selling series paperbacks, as much as 70 percent of their sales may come through retail markets (Higgins 1997).

This change in marketplace brought about a change in the books. In an effort to attract adult retail consumers of children's books, editors shifted some of their emphases to books for younger audiences and to books more lavishly illustrated. Thus, baby/board books, virtually indestructible little books for babies and toddlers, invaded bookstores. There was also a proliferation of so-called toy books—pop-up, scratch-and-sniff, texture (touchy/feely) books—which are typically too fragile for library and school markets. Toy books in the 1990s often emphasized the toy more than the book. A book might be packaged with a stuffed animal, an inflatable globe, or even a full-blown kit for building a pyramid or planting a terrarium. Printing technologies also allowed for more affordable yet extremely sophisticated, full-color, camera-separated reproductions. Picture books became more colorful and the renderings increasingly showy, also a draw for bookstore patrons. Publishers further realized that the cheaper series books, published only in paperback, would sell quickly in bookstores, and so books like the Hardy Boys and a number of teenage romance series made a mammoth resurgence in the 1970s. The 1990s saw a proliferation of new paperback series titles—Goosebumps, Fear Street, Animorphs, Saddle Club, American Girls, Bailey School Kids, and so on—as well as the repackaging of older series such as the Boxcar Children and the Nancy Drew mysteries. Also, consumers began to find these books and other children's titles in stores not traditionally connected with bookselling: Walmart, Target, T.J. Maxx, Sam's Club, Cosco, and supermarket chains such as Stop & Shop (Rosen 1997).

However, during the same decade, new realism spread its wings. Divorce seemed to be at least an underlying theme in nearly every contemporary realistic novel. In fact, shockingly realistic novels and picture books became the mode as authors addressed serious taboos. For example, the novels of Judy Blume, such as her controversial yet extremely popular *Are You There God? It's Me, Margaret* (1970), and her even more explicit *Forever* (1975), treated physical maturation and sex candidly. Authors of historical novels also dared present to young readers varied and often unpopular viewpoints about our past. Books began to look at the American Revolution from perspectives other than that of a righteous rebellion, such as James Lincoln Collier and Christopher Collier's *My Brother Sam Is Dead* (1974). Some regarded these efforts to represent history more accurately as unpatriotic. Embarrassing annals from American history also began to appear more frequently in books for young readers, such as Yoshiko Uchida's book *Journey to Topaz* (1971), an autobiographical though fictionalized account of life in the Japanese-American internment camps during World War II.

It was also during the 1970s that African-Americans won the Newbery and Caldecott Awards for the first time. In 1975, Virginia Hamilton received the Newbery Medal for *M. C. Higgins the Great*, and in 1976 Leo Dillon won the Caldecott Medal (along with his wife, Diane, who is not African-American) for *Why Mosquitoes Buzz in People's Ears*.

The number of children's books published annually in the United States skyrocketed from approximately 2,500 in 1970 to about 5,000 in the 1990s (Bogart 1997, p. 506). A rise in institutional purchases of books was partly responsible for such growth. As teachers began to embrace literature-based reading philosophies and methodologies, schools began to purchase more and more trade books (books other than textbooks or reference books) for use in the classroom. Some school systems began to allot a percentage of the textbook budget for the acquisition of children's books, and sales from school paperback book clubs (Trumpet Club, Scholastic, Troll, Weekly Reader) leaped into the hundreds of millions of dollars. At the same time, publishers continued to do well in the retail market.

During the 1980s and '90s, colorful and skillfully illustrated picture books were the name of the game. Because children's publishers were doing well financially, the best illustrators were drawn to the field of picture book illustration. Both the money and the recognition were attractive. Even Wall Street had to pay attention when illustrator Chris Van Allsburg negotiated an $800,000 advance for the book *Swan Lake* (Helprin 1989). Of course, this sort of remuneration is an exception.

The 1980s saw the formation of publishing conglomerates. Larger corporations, often businesses having no relation to books, began purchasing publishing houses. Many long-standing American publishers became imprints of so-called umbrella companies or disappeared altogether. For example, the Macmillan Publishing Company purchased Atheneum, along with other publishing houses, until its children's book division comprised 11 imprints. Then Simon & Schuster bought Macmillan, and Paramount bought Simon & Schuster. Soon Viacom, the cable TV giant, snapped up Paramount. So children's book publishing became even bigger business.

In the mid-1990s, however, publishers began to experience the negative effects of growth. They had published more books than the demand required and were forced to downsize operations. As a partial result, the Simon & Schuster arm of Viacom was streamlined. Today the Macmillan name no longer is used as a children's book imprint. Also gone are many other imprints that were once a part of either Macmillan or Simon & Schuster, including Charles Scribner's Sons, Four Winds Press, Collier Books, and Bradbury Press. Fewer imprints mean the publication of fewer books and therefore a need for fewer editorial and marketing staff members—generally speaking, less overhead. As of this writing, Simon & Schuster has only three hardcover imprints: Simon & Schuster Books for Young Readers, Atheneum Books for Young Readers, and Margaret K. McElderry Books.

Although record numbers of books were being published, the number of books about minorities (diverse cultures) in America declined during the 1980s. Between the early 1970s and early '80s, the number of minority titles dropped by more than half, according to a list released by the New York Public Library (Rollock, 1989).

However, in the 1990s, the number of books with characters representing diverse cultures started to rise (Micklos 1996).

Historical novels, which waned during the 1970s, began a comeback in the next decade, and nonfiction (informational books) flourished. Although good informational books were available in earlier decades, an explosion of engaging, well-illustrated, and well-written nonfiction occurred. Informational books, which seldom appeared on Newbery Award lists, began to be honored more frequently. *Sugaring Time* (1983) by Kathryn Lasky, *Commodore Perry in the Land of the Shogun* (1985) by Rhoda Blumberg, *Volcano* (1986) by Patricia Lauber, *The Wright Brothers* (1991) and *Eleanor Roosevelt: A Life of Discovery* (1993) by Russell Freedman, and *The Great Fire* (1995) by Jim Murphy won Newbery Honors. *Lincoln: A Photobiography* by Russell Freedman, published in 1987, was awarded the Newbery Medal. One of the most exciting trends of the 1980s and '90s undoubtedly has been the increase in and emphasis on quality nonfiction for all age levels. Indeed, informational books are better as a whole than they ever have been. (See Chapter 12.) The first national award strictly for nonfiction writing was established by the National Council of Teachers of English in 1990 and appropriately named the *Orbis Pictus* Award in honor of the 17th-century picture book.

Expanding the emphasis on books for the very young in the 1970s, an increased number of quality "I can read," or beginning reader picture books, appeared in the 1980s and '90s. The trendsetters in this area emerged decades earlier with the 1957 publication of both *Little Bear* by Else Minarik and *Cat in the Hat* by Dr. Seuss. But the availability of large numbers of well-written books for fledgling readers occurred in the '80s. For example, HarperCollins publishes a series called "I Can Read Books," of which Minarik's *Little Bear* is a part. Fine authors who often have made a name by writing for older children have contributed to the series, which now offers parents, teachers, and children an exciting array of worthwhile beginning reader books.

Poetry also received more attention during the 1980s and '90s. Two books of poetry won Newbery Medals during this time: *A Visit to William Blake's Inn: Poems for Innocent and Experienced Travelers* (1981) by Nancy Willard and *Joyful Noise: Poems for Two Voices* (1988) by Paul Fleischman. In 1977, the National Council of Teachers of English established the Excellence in Poetry for Children Award, a lifetime achievement award honoring poets who write for young readers.

Today, books for young readers are more varied and engaging than they ever have been. Authors and illustrators of children's books continue to experiment with form and content. The rewards of this experimentation outweigh the obvious risks; many fine books are being published as a result. The risk requires that we accept the fact that many more weak books are being published, too. For instance, the 1990s became an age of politically correct standards for evaluation. Many books receiving stellar reviews suffered from this new brand of didacticism, which meant that from a literary standpoint weaker books sometimes received acclaim because of subject matter. Nevertheless, the latter part of the 20th century is a testament to the legacy of John Newbery—a golden age in the history of children's literature.

Figure 5–1 is a chronologic list of selected children's literature demonstrating significant historical developments and trends.

1440	Introduction of hornbooks
1484	*Aesop's Fables* published by William Caxton
1580	Introduction of chapbooks
1646	*Spiritual Milk for Boston Babes in Either England, Drawn from the Breasts of Both Testaments for Their Souls' Nourishment* by John Cotton
1657	*Orbis Pictus* by Johann Amos Comenius
1697	*Tales of Mother Goose* retold by Charles Perrault
1719	*Robinson Crusoe* by Daniel Defoe
1726	*Gulliver's Travels* by Jonathan Swift
1744	*A Pretty Little Pocket-Book* published by John Newbery
1765	*The History of Little Goody Two Shoes* published by John Newbery
1812	*Household Tales* retold by Jacob and Wilhelm Grimm
1814	*The Swiss Family Robinson* by Johann Wyss
1820	*Ivanhoe* by Walter Scott
1823	*Grimm's Fairy Tales* illustrated by George Cruikshank
1835	*Fairy Tales Told for Children* by Hans Christian Andersen
1846	*A Book of Nonsense* by Edward Lear
1863	*The Water Babies* by Charles Kingsley
1864	*Journey to the Center of the Earth* by Jules Verne
1865	*Alice's Adventures in Wonderland* by Lewis Carroll (Charles Dodgson), illustrated by John Tenniel
1865	*Hans Brinker, or the Silver Skates* by Mary Mapes Dodge
1868	*Little Women* by Louisa May Alcott
1871	*At the Back of the North Wind* by George MacDonald
1873	*St. Nicholas Magazine* begins publication
1876	*The Adventures of Tom Sawyer* by Mark Twain (Samuel Clemens)
1878	*The Diverting History of John Gilpin* illustrated by Randolph Caldecott
	Under the Window illustrated by Kate Greenaway
1881	*The Adventures of Pinocchio* by Carlo Collodi
1883	*Treasure Island* by Robert Louis Stevenson
	The Merry Adventures of Robin Hood of Great Reknown written and illustrated by Howard Pyle
1885	*A Child's Garden of Verses* by Robert Louis Stevenson
1894–95	*The Jungle Books* by Rudyard Kipling
1900	*The Wonderful Wizard of Oz* by L. Frank Baum
1902	*The Tale of Peter Rabbit* written and illustrated by Beatrix Potter
1906	*Peter Pan in Kensington Gardens* by J. M. Barrie, illustrated by Arthur Rackham
1908	*Anne of Green Gables* by Lucy Maud Montgomery
	The Wind in the Willows by Kenneth Grahame
1911	*The Secret Garden* by Frances Hodgson Burnett
1913	*Mother Goose* illustrated by Arthur Rackham

FIGURE 5–1

History and trends chronology.

1922	John Newbery Medal established
1926	*Winnie the Pooh* by A. A. Milne, illustrated by Ernest Shepard
1928	*Millions of Cats* written and illustrated by Wanda Gág
1937	*The Hobbit* by J. R. R. Tolkien
	To Think I Saw It on Mulberry Street written and illustrated by Dr. Seuss (Theodor Geisel)
1938	Randolph Caldecott Medal established
1939	*Goodnight Moon* by Margaret Wise Brown, illustrated by Clement Hurd
	Madeline written and illustrated by Ludwig Bemelmans
1941	*Make Way for Ducklings* written and illustrated by Robert McCloskey
1950	*The Lion, the Witch, and the Wardrobe* by C. S. Lewis
1952	*Charlotte's Web* by E. B. White, illustrated by Garth Williams
1956	Hans Christian Andersen Prize established
1957	*Little Bear* by Else Minarik, illustrated by Maurice Sendak
1957	*The Cat in the Hat* by Dr. Seuss
1959	*The Lantern Bearers* by Rosemary Sutcliff
1962	*The Snowy Day* written and illustrated by Ezra Jack Keats
1963	*Where the Wild Things Are* written and illustrated by Maurice Sendak
1964	*Harriet the Spy* by Louise Fitzhugh
	The Book of Three by Lloyd Alexander
1966	Mildred L. Batchelder Award established
1969	Coretta Scott King Award established
1970	*Are You There God? It's Me, Margaret* by Judy Blume
1971	*Journey to Topaz* by Yoshiko Uchida
1974	*My Brother Sam Is Dead* by James Lincoln and Christopher Collier
1975	*M. C. Higgins, the Great* by Virginia Hamilton
1976	*Why Mosquitoes Buzz in People's Ears* retold by Verna Aardema, illustrated by Leo and Diane Dillon
1977	NCTE Excellence in Poetry for Children Award established
1981	*A Visit to William Blake's Inn: Poems for Innocent and Experienced Travelers* by Nancy Willard, illustrated by Alice and Martin Provensen
1983	*Sugaring Time* by Kathryn Lasky, photographs by Christopher Knight
1985	*The Polar Express* written and illustrated by Chris Van Allsburg
1987	*Lincoln: A Photobiography* by Russell Freedman
1988	*Joyful Noise: Poems for Two Voices* by Paul Fleischman
1988	*The Way Things Work* by David Macaulay
1990	*Color Zoo* by Lois Ehlert
1990	*Orbis Pictus* Award established
1990	*Maniac Magee* by Jerry Spinelli
1992	*The Fortune-tellers* by Lloyd Alexander, illustrated by Trina Schart Hyman
1993	*The Giver* by Lois Lowry
1995	*Math Curse* by Jon Scieszka, illustrated by Lane Smith
1996	*Leonardo da Vinci* by Diane Stanley

FIGURE 5–1, *continued*

REFERENCES

Blumberg, Rhoda. 1985. *Commodore Perry in the Land of the Shogun.* New York: Lothrop.

Blume, Judy. 1975. *Forever.* New York: Bradbury.

Bogart, Dave, ed. 1997. *The Bowker Annual: Library and Book Trade Almanac.* 42nd ed. New Providence, N.J.: R. R. Bowker.

Chevannes, Ingrid, Dermot McEvoy, and Maria Simson. 1997. Big names top the charts. *Publishers Weekly* 244, no. 14 (7 April): 58–64.

Fleischman, Paul. 1988. *Joyful Noise: Poems for Two Voices.* New York: Harper.

Freedman, Russell. 1991. *The Wright Brothers.* New York: Holiday House.

Freedman, Russell. 1993. *Eleanor Roosevelt: A Life of Discovery.* New York: Clarion.

Greenlee, Adele A., Dianne L. Monson, and Barbara M. Taylor. 1996. The lure of series books: Does it affect appreciation for recommended literature? *The Reading Teacher* 50, no. 3 (November): 216–225.

Helprin, Mark. 1989. *Swan Lake.* Boston: Houghton Mifflin.

Higgins, Jazan. 1997. Telephone interview with Michael O. Tunnell, 15 September.

Lauber, Patricia. 1986. *Volcano.* New York: Bradbury.

Micklos, John, Jr. 1996. 30 years of minorities in children's books. *The Education Digest,* 62, no. 1 (September): 61–64.

Minarik, Else. 1957. *Little Bear.* Illustrated by Maurice Sendak. New York: Harper.

Murphy, Jim. 1995. *The Great Fire.* New York: Scholastic.

Rollock, Barbara. 1989. *Black Experience in Children's Books.* New York: New York Public Library.

Rosen, Judith. 1997. They're everywhere you look. *Publishers Weekly* 244, no. 29 (21 July): 120–123.

Saltman, Judith. 1997. Groaning under the weight of series books. *Emergency Librarian* 24, no. 5 (May/June): 23–25.

Seuss, Dr. 1975. *The Cat in the Hat.* New York: Random House.

PART TWO

The Content

CHAPTER 6

Categories of Children's Literature

The difficulty in covering the field of children's literature in one course is perhaps best understood by looking at a common undergraduate class for English majors, Shakespeare's Tragedies. The complete course focuses on one author, and only a part of what he wrote at that. On the other hand, the content of an introductory course in children's literature is every author of children's books and all the titles they have written. Considering the content, a solitary children's literature course makes only the briefest of introductions to the subject matter—one thread in the whole cloth.

Naturally, the teacher of children's literature must find an organized and digestible way of presenting such massive subject matter. One way of cutting up the literature pie (more than 100,000 books in print in America and about 5,000 new titles published each year) is to categorize books according to their format. Picture books and chapter books form the two largest areas, with the illustrated book (occasional pictures every few pages) as a much smaller third division. However, the line between picture book and chapter book is not always completely clear. Although most children's books are easily identified as either a picture book or a chapter book, some have characteristics of both, such as the separate chapters in fully illustrated beginning readers like the Frog and Toad series by Arnold Lobel.

Another way to view the field of children's literature is from the issues approach. Books are categorized by the issue or theme that drives the story: death, racism, family life, and so on. The categories of issues may be universal and timeless (family dynamics) or narrow and current (censorship and rock music lyrics). Because of the multitude of special interest issues, this approach to dealing with children's literature can become unwieldy.

The most common method of cutting children's literature into small bites is to group books by *genre*, a French word meaning "type" or "kind." Genre is a familiar term in many artistic areas: the genre of the detective film, or the genre of adult literature (novel, novella, short story, play, and poem). In children's literature, genre identifies a book according to content (see Figure 6–1).

All literature is either poetry or prose. To define poetry, the initial impulse might be to identify it as rhyming or shorter or more rhythmic than prose. Yet these obvious elements of poetry are not true distinctions. Some poetry does not rhyme. Some poetry is longer than some prose. Some poetry is less rhythmic than some prose. With all the forms poetry can take—haiku, sonnet, couplet, blank verse, limerick, narrative, cinquain, and free verse, to name a few—finding a definition that both identifies them all and distinguishes them from prose is next to impossible. It is easier and more practical to define poetry by saying what it is not. Poetry is not written in paragraphs; prose is. Poetry may appear on the page as a single line, thin column, or in the shape of a tree, but not in a paragraph. Beyond that difference in format, the function of the two literary forms is identical: Both poetry and prose explore the world, give insight into the human condition, or present the view of the writer.

The difference between fiction and nonfiction is documentation. Fiction springs largely from the author's imagination. An idea, question, or incident from the real world may give rise to a work of fiction, but the structure and details come from the workings of the mind. They cannot be verified elsewhere. Nonfiction, however, centers on a part of the universe that can be confirmed by other sources. The content of nonfiction exists. The evidence and facts presented in nonfiction books can be documented.

FIGURE 6–1
Genres of children's literature.

Nonfiction books are classified as biography and informational. Biography (and autobiography) tells the story of an actual person's life or at least part of that story. As with all nonfiction, reliable sources and documentation are imperative.

Informational books generally are called *nonfiction* in adult publishing. Children's libraries classify all books in one of ten categories (ranging by 100s from 000 to 900) in the Dewey Decimal System. All except the 800s (literature—fiction and poetry) are nonfiction. Anything in the world is grist for the nonfiction mill: building a violin, life in China, the history of the ball bearing, animals that hibernate, how governments work, and so on. No area of children's literature has changed so dramatically in recent years as has nonfiction. Although some excellent informational books were written decades ago, in recent times subject matter has broadened, the quality of writing and illustration has improved, and the number of books published has increased.

Realistic fiction and fantastic fiction have much in common. Both are invented stories, usually with invented characters, and they may take place in invented settings. Even when the setting is real, like Boston or Berlin, the exact neighborhood is often imagined. The difference between realism and fantasy lies in the laws of our universe. If an invented story takes place in the world as we know it—where dogs bark, trees are green, and gravity is everywhere—it is realistic fiction. The world where the story happens is real, even if the characters and events are invented. If a story has one or more elements not found in our world—if animals speak, magic is present, or time travel is involved—it is then called fantasy. The rest of the story might be absolutely realistic, but it is called fantasy if it contains any deviation from natural physical law.

The aim of both historical fiction and contemporary realistic fiction is to tell an interesting story about people in our world. The definitions are clear in the names of the genres. *Contemporary* identifies a story that takes place in today's world; *historical* indicates a tale that happened earlier, as in pioneer America or medieval England. At times, though, the difference between the two genres depends on the age of the reader. Some people classify a story that happened during the collapse of the Communist government in eastern Europe as contemporary; to others, it is clearly historical.

Like historical and contemporary fiction, the division between traditional fantasy and modern fantasy relates to antiquity. Some stories are as old as humanity. These ancient stories are called traditional because they are part of our human tradition. Their origin is oral; their authors unknown. Although they now have been preserved in print, those who first wrote them down, like the Brothers Grimm, were not authors but collectors. If a fantasy story has an identifiable author, and therefore originated in print, it is called modern fantasy. Thus, the tales of Hans Christian Andersen are classified as modern fantasy, even though the feel of the stories is often closer to traditional storytelling.

Science fiction, included under the modern fantasy heading, deals with scientific possibilities. Both modern fantasy and science fiction contain elements not found in the known universe, such as being able to change shapes or read another character's thoughts. In fantasy, those abilities just *are* or come about by magic—no questions asked. In science fiction, they result from an injection of distilled fluids discovered in the mucous membranes of a poisonous tree frog or from altering a person's brain chemistry using microlaser bursts. The otherworldly elements in science fiction are based on extrapolated scientific fact that is pushed into logical but unproven possibilities, such as cloning an entire human being from a DNA blueprint. Modern fantasy needs no such reasons: the character's double magically appears.

While knowing the genres can offer understanding in the field of children's literature, none of the definitions is watertight. The categories are not to be slavishly followed. It is possible to make a solid case that some books belong in more than one genre. For example, Esther Hautzig's *The Endless Steppe* (1968), a compelling tale of Esther and her Jewish family being routed from their home in Poland and sent to Siberia during World War II, can be classified as both biography and historical fiction. Ruth Heller's informational books about the parts of speech (*Many Luscious Lollipops*, 1989; *A Cache of Jewels, 1987; Kites Sail High, 1988;* etc.) are, at the same time, also books of poetry. The correct category for some titles depends not on immutable definition but on personal choice.

Although genre lines at times may blur, we have chosen the genre approach in this book as the most workable way of introducing and discussing the world of children's books—in part because genres are used most often by adults to define the field of children's literature. These categories are less important to children, however. Young readers usually do not care if a book belongs to a certain genre category. What they want is a good book, regardless of the classification. But adults can use the six categories of genre to help understand the field of children's literature more clearly, to draw upon a framework for discussing books, and to provide a yardstick for determining what holes exist in their own particular reading backgrounds. If a teacher never has read modern fantasy or science fiction, for instance, that becomes immediately apparent during a self-check and may provide direction to broaden personal reading and serve students better. However used, the genres of children's literature (Chapters 7–12) provide a road map for those interested in finding their way about.

After exploring the six genres, we have included chapters about two formats and two topics also important in children's literature. The two formats are so closely associated with categorizing books for children they have become pseudo-genres and, indeed, have their own headings in this book and the accompanying database: the picture book and poetry. The picture book (Chapter 13), still a mainstay of beginning reading and the primary grade classroom, has expanded its appeal to include older children and also to offer expanded information in nonfiction picture books. Because this format is so distinctive and is important to many teachers, we list it as a genre in the database, so picture book titles may be located. Poetry (Chapter 14), as with picture books, includes all the genres of literature. Poems may fall into any of the six genre categories, as do works of prose. Both are formats of literature. However, we choose to treat poetry as a separate genre because too few poems are available to study them under the same classifications we use for prose. If we were absolutely accurate, we would study "biographical prose" and also "biographical poetry;" "modern fantasy prose" as well as "modern fantasy poetry," and so on. Because of the relatively small number of published poems, we look at poetry as a whole and at the various forms of poetry instead of concentrating on the content.

In addition to the genres and the formats, we focus on two topics: (1) multicultural and international books and (2) controversial books. Multicultural and international books (Chapter 15) currently receive close attention because of their importance in helping us build human bridges among groups and nations. Controversial books (Chapter 16) always have been a part of the literary landscape and likely always will be, as topics and titles continue to fall in and out of favor.

REFERENCES

Heller, Ruth. 1987. *A Cache of Jewels*. New York: Grosset & Dunlap.

Heller, Ruth. 1988. *Kites Sail High*. New York: Grosset & Dunlap.

Heller, Ruth. 1989. *Many Luscious Lollipops*. New York: Grosset & Dunlap.

Hautzig, Esther. 1968. *The Endless Steppe*. New York: Crowell.

CHAPTER 7

Traditional Fantasy

Traditional tales had their beginnings around hearthside and campfire. The stories were almost always fantastic in nature, involving magic or talking animals. Originally, these tales provided entertainment for adults, who freely altered details as they told and retold the stories. As adults shared these stories with one another, children surely lounged about the fringes and listened. In modern times many of the tales have shifted from their origin with adults to being identified with children.

Because these stories were born in the oral tradition, no one knows who first told each tale and which is the original version. The definition of traditional fantasy is that the literature (1) originated orally and (2) has no author. Therefore, we often associate them with a collector or reteller. Jacob and Wilhelm Grimm collected, retold, and recorded in print the European variants of some of the best-known traditional tales in our Western cultures, such as "Cinderella," "Sleeping Beauty," and "Little Red Riding Hood." Other collectors include Charles Perrault, who preceded the Brothers Grimm in collecting many of the European tales. He filed away the hard edges of many of the tales so that they would be more acceptable to the genteel folk of the French court of Louis the XIV. Joseph Jacobs collected the British tales loved by young children, such as "The Three Little Pigs" and "The Little Red Hen." Peter Asbjørnsen and Jorgen Moe gathered the Scandinavian tales into a volume titled *East of the Sun and West of the Moon*, which included "The Three Billy Goats Gruff."

Tales from the oral tradition are part of the fabric of every culture. *The Arabian Nights*, including the story of "Aladdin," is a collection of Scheherazade's tales from the Middle East. Other collections of traditional tales from the Middle East include the Hodja stories from Turkey that tell of the wisdom of Nasredden Hodja and the Jataka stories from India that are centered on the lives of Buddha. The masterful storytelling of Isaac Bashevis Singer has preserved much of the folklore of Jewish tradition. Tales of Asian-, African-, and Native-American tradition abound and are available to children, most often in stunning picture book versions. (See the lists of "Picture books" at the conclusion of this chapter.)

Stories written by modern authors and patterned after traditional tales—such as the work of Hans Christian Andersen, as well as Rudyard Kipling's collection of *Just-So Stories*—are often confused with traditional tales that have no authors. However, these "literary tales" are modern fantasy stories, for they originated in written form.

PECULIARITIES OF TRADITIONAL FANTASY

Traditional stories differ in various ways from more modern writings and, therefore, are held to a different critical standard. For example, characters must be well developed in modern stories, but in traditional tales character development is lean and spare. Think of Cinderella, for example. How rounded is her character? We are given to know very little about her. How does she feel about her ill treatment? About her change in fortune? What are her interests? We don't even know much about her physical appearance. If listeners and readers are told about her personality or thoughts, it is only in general terms: "She wept at her mother's grave." The fact is that characters in traditional stories generally are archetypes; they are meant to be symbolic of certain basic human traits, such as good or evil. So, instead of the gradations of character in modern stories, where a character may reveal the mix of good and bad in all of us, in traditional tales we find single-faceted characters who typically do not change during the course of the story. Traditional tales, then, are stories of the human experience told in primary colors, the nuances of life stripped away in order to reveal the basic component parts: love, fear, greed, jealousy, mercy, and so on. Therefore, traditional stories from around the world are basically alike because fundamental human characteristics and motivations are universal.

Plots are also simple and direct in traditional fantasy. And because the tales generally were told by and among the common folk, they are often success stories that show the underdog making good—the youngest son or daughter, the little tailor, unwanted children, and so on. And success is often obtained against overwhelming odds, such as accomplishing an impossible task (spinning straw into gold, slaying invincible monsters).

These story lines are accompanied by typical themes, such as the rewards of mercy, kindness, and perseverance; justice, particularly the punishment of evil; and the power of love. Settings are quickly established and always in the distant past ("Once upon a time . . . "), and time passes quickly (Sleeping Beauty's 100 years of rest pass in a flash). Another hallmark of traditional stories is repeated patterns or elements. The magical number three appears frequently in tales: Rumpelstiltskin's three evenings of spinning straw into gold, Cinderella's three visits to the ball, Jack's three trips up the beanstalk. Or a refrain is repeated throughout the story: "Fee, fi, fo, fum. I smell the blood of an Englishman."

THE UNIVERSAL NATURE OF TRADITIONAL FANTASY

Although tales certainly vary from culture to culture, it is amazing how alike in form they are, how the basic sorts of literary elements are similar in Chinese stories, in stories from the Native-American tribes, and in stories from Europe (Frye 1964). Because traditional tales deal with such basic human experiences, stories like "Cinderella" surface in nearly every part of the world. The variants are certainly different in setting and detail, but a fascinating sameness still exists. "Cinderella" variants include *Yeh-Shen* (Chinese, 1990) retold by Ai-Ling Louie, *The Egyptian Cinderella* (Egypt, 1989) by Shirley Climo, *The Rough-Face Girl* (Native American, 1992) by Rafe Martin, and *Mufaro's Beautiful Daughters* (African, 1987) by John Steptoe, to mention a few.

Another example of the pervasiveness of traditional stories in modern literature (and conversation) is the almost constant use of allusions to traditional literature. Often we speak and write using a sort of old-tale shorthand. It is a part of the cultural cement that binds us together. We nod knowingly when someone says or writes, "Misery loves company," or "You are judged by the company you keep." Both maxims come from Aesop, who either collected most of his fables from more ancient oral sources or, as some scholars believe, did not exist at all. The Greek myths and European variants of the fairy tales are alluded to continually in novels written by Western culture authors. Note the distinct part Red Riding Hood plays in Lois Lowry's (1989) Newbery-winning historical novel, *Number the Stars*, which takes place during World War II. As

Anna makes her way through the woods with a basket of food containing a hidden packet of chemical designed to disarm the wolf's, or rather the guard dogs', ability to smell the Danish escapees, she suddenly feels as if she's walked this way before.

> The handle of the straw basket scratched her arm through her sweater. She shifted it and tried to run.
>
> She thought of a story she had often told to Kirsti as they cuddled in bed at night.
>
> "Once upon a time there was a little girl," she told herself silently, "who had a beautiful red cloak. . . . " (1989, pp. 106–108)

In fact, we are surrounded by such allusions. We write with Venus pencils; clean with Ajax cleanser; drive on Atlas tires; use words like *volcano, furious, cereal, music;* describe the human body and mind with terms like *Achilles tendon* and *Narcissus complex;* name the planets, the days of the week, and the cities of the world (*Mars, Saturday, Atlanta*)—all from Greek myths. Perhaps one of the clearest examples of the way the old tales provide a cultural cement is evident in newspaper and magazine cartoons. The political cartoon shown in Figure 7–1 was published in *The Chicago Tribune* when a number of day-care centers in the Chicago area were charged with child abuse and molestation. Because "Hansel and Gretel" is basic to our literary culture, the cartoon needs no caption.

However simple and straightforward traditional fantasy may seem, it is the mother of all literature. There are literally no character types, basic plots, or themes

FIGURE 7–1

Without our common knowledge of folktales, this cartoon has no meaning.

Reprinted by permission of Tribune Media Services.

that have not been explored in the oral tradition. Indeed, noted child psychologist Bruno Bettleheim (1977) believed that no other literature better prepares children to meet the complexities of adult life. Traditional fantasy is a wonderful metaphor for human existence, and because of its rich imagery and dreamlike quality, it speaks to us deeply. And, unless these stories have been dumbed down for printing in educational reading materials or oversimplified picture books, traditional tales are a blueprint for rich, masterful language (see the example from Randall Jarrell's translation of *Snow-White and the Seven Dwarfs* in Chapter 3).

THE VALUES OF FANTASY STORIES

Besides giving us modern readers a common ground for communicating, traditional fantasy—in fact, fantasy literature in general—offers us certain benefits that realistic fiction cannot do with quite the same power. Lloyd Alexander (1968), who had drawn liberally from the well of ancient stories to write his modern high-fantasy books, encapsulates these benefits into four notable points:

> First, on the very surface of it, the sheer delight of "let's pretend" and the eager suspension of disbelief; excitement, wonder, astonishment. There is an exuberance in good fantasy quite unlike the most exalted moments of realistic fiction. Both forms have similar goals; but realism walks where fantasy dances. . . .
>
> [Second, fantasy has the] ability to work on our emotions with the same vividness as a dream. The fantasy adventure seems always on a larger scale, the deeds bolder, the people brighter. Reading a fantasy, we never get disinterested bystanders. To get the most from it, we have to, in the best sense of the phrase, "lose our cool. . . ."
>
> Another value of fantasy [is its ability to develop a capacity for belief]. . . . In dealing with delinquency—I do not mean the delinquency that poverty breeds, but the kind of cold-hearted emptiness and apathy of "well-to-do," solid middle-class delinquents—one of the heart-breaking problems is interesting these young people in something. In anything. They value nothing because they have never had the experience of valuing anything. They have developed no *capacity* for believing anything to be really worthwhile.
>
> I emphasize the word *capacity* because, in a sense, the capacity to value, to believe, is separate from the values or beliefs themselves. Our values and beliefs can change. The capacity remains.
>
> Whether the object of value is Santa Claus or Sunday school, the Prophet Elijah or Arthur, the Once and Future King, does not make too much difference. Having once believed wholeheartedly in something, we seldom lose the ability to believe. . . .
>
> Perhaps, finally, the ability to hope is more important than the ability to believe. . . . Hope is one of the most precious human values fantasy can offer us—and offer us in abundance. Whatever the hardships of the journey, the days of despair, fantasy implicitly promises to lead us through them. Hope is an essential thread in the fabric of all fantasies, an Ariadne's thread to guide us out of the labyrinth, the last treasure in Pandora's box. . . .*

---

*Reprinted with permission of Lloyd Alexander from "Wishful Thinking—or Hopeful Dreaming." *The Horn Book* 44 (August 1968): 387–390.

TYPES OF TRADITIONAL FANTASY

Categories of any genre of literature never are cast in concrete. People never will agree on category names or on whether certain stories belong under certain category headings. Traditional fantasy is no different in this respect. However, we will present our view of what constitutes traditional stories, keeping in mind that this list is mostly a tool for introducing you to the stories themselves.

Folktales

Quite rightly, all traditional stories could be called folktales or stories of the people. We will use this heading to encompass a number of stories that are the most general or universal in nature. The most common kinds of folktales follow:

CUMULATIVE TALES.   These stories are "added upon" as the telling unfolds. Typically, the story is told up to a certain point, then begun again from near the beginning and told until a new segment is added. Then the teller starts again and again, each time adding a new wrinkle to the story, expanding a chain of events or a list of participants. Probably the best known example is the reasonably simple cumulative tale "The House That Jack Built."

POURQUOI TALES.   *Pourquoi* means "why" in French. These folktales answer questions or give explanations for the way things are, particularly in nature. Examples are "Why the Bear Is Stumpy-Tailed" or *Why Mosquitoes Buzz in People's Ears* (1975), as retold by Verna Aardema.

BEAST TALES.   Their distinction is simple: Beast tales are stories with animals as the principal players. The animals typically represent humans and are therefore anthropomorphized, such as animals in "The Three Little Pigs" and "The Three Billy Goats Gruff."

NOODLEHEAD, OR NUMBSKULL, TALES.   These humorous stories center on the escapades of characters who are not too bright. Sometimes they really make a mess of things with their incredibly stupid mistakes, as in the story "Epaminondas," in which a silly boy nearly destroys a number of items placed in his charge because he follows the wrong instructions for their care. For example, he is told to wrap butter in leaves and dip it in cool water to keep it in good shape. But then he uses those instructions with a puppy. In other stories, such as Grimm's "Hans in Luck," the simpleton stumbles merrily through life, coming out on top only because of providence.

TRICKSTER TALES.   Often a variety of beast tale, the trickster tale features a character who outsmarts everyone else in the story. Sometimes the trickster is sly and mischievous (B'rer Rabbit from the Uncle Remus stories). In other stories, the trickster is wise and helpful, as with some of the Anansi the Spider Man folktales from Africa (see *A Story, a Story,* 1970, by Gail Haley).

REALISTIC TALES.   Realistic tales seem to have their basis in an actual historical event or to feature an actual figure from history. These folktales have few, if any, elements of fantasy. "Dick Whittington and His Cat," a story with a main character who is supposed to have later become the mayor of London, is an example.

FAIRY TALES.   Of all the folktales, the fairy tale, or wonder tale, is the most magical. In fairy tales we see enchantments that go beyond talking animals to fairy godmothers, wicked witches, magical objects (mirrors, cloaks, swords, rings), and the like. (See Chapter 8 for a discussion of fantasy motifs.) Fairy tales are extremely popular with young listeners and readers. "Snow White," "Cinderella," "Sleeping Beauty," "Beauty and the Beast," and "Aladdin and His Wonderful Lamp" are a few examples of well-known fairy tales.

Tall Tales

Exaggeration is the major stylistic element in tall tales. Many tall tales grew out of the push to open the North American continent to settlement. Tall-tale characters, such as Paul Bunyan, Pecos Bill, Johnny Appleseed, John Henry, and Old Stormalong, were based either on actual people or on a composite of rough-and-tumble lumberjacks, sailors, or cowboys. Tall tales, of course, exist beyond our American culture. For instance, the Chinese tale, "The Seven [or Five] Chinese Brothers," tells of several brothers who use amazing talents, such as the ability to swallow an entire sea, to ward off the conquests of an evil emperor.

Fables

Fables are brief stories meant to teach a lesson, and they usually conclude with a moral such as "A bird in the hand is worth two in the bush" or "Haste makes waste." Besides the well-known collection of Aesop's fables from Greece, there are fables in ancient Egyptian culture, in the *Panchatantra* and the Jataka stories from India, plus a collection of fables by French poet Jean de La Fontaine.

Myths

Myths grew out of early people's need to understand and explain the world around them and their own existence, and therefore they recount the creation and tell of the gods and goddesses who control the fate of humans. Many myths are similar to pourquoi folktales because they explain nature. For example, the Greek myth of Apollo explains how and why the sun travels across the sky each day. Jane Yolen's retelling of *Sky Dogs* (1990) explains how horses came to one tribe of Native Americans. Every culture has its myths, although the Greek myths are perhaps the best known in the Western world. The international flavor of mythology is evident in Virginia Hamilton's collection of creation myths, *In the Beginning: Creation Stories from Around the World* (1988).

One variety of myth focuses on the heroic quest rather than on the mysteries of planet Earth. The hero myth, such as the story "Jason and the Argonauts," is a grand adventure that usually involves the intervention of heavenly beings. The hero myth is related to the epic.

Epics, Ballads, and Legends

The line separating epics, ballads, and legends tends to blur. The unifying feature is the hero tale, including hero myths, but epics, ballads, and legends also have distinguishing qualities.

- Epics are lengthy hero tales or even a series of tales focusing on a hero. Examples are the tales of the Trojan War (*The Iliad*) and the return of Odysseus (Ulysses) from Troy to his home in Ithaca (*The Odyssey*). Both of these epics are also steeped in the mythology of ancient Greece. *Beowulf*, the most famous piece of Old English literature, is another well-known epic.
- Ballads are typically hero stories in poetic form. Both *The Iliad* and *The Odyssey* are epic poems supposedly composed by the blind poet Homer, whose existence is doubted by some scholars, although others regard him as the recorder of a much retold set of tales. In Europe, the bards of old traveled from stronghold to stronghold, entertaining the people by singing ballads about local mythological and legendary heroes.
- The heroes in legends are rooted a bit more firmly in history. So, *The Iliad* could be considered an epic and legendary ballad. King Arthur also lives in epic, ballad, and legend. There are mythic stories of Arthur as well as historical accounts that indicate that he indeed existed and unified the British tribes around 500 A.D. Robin Hood, probably more thief than hero, is a character from ballad and legend. Of course, legendary characters also appear in the tall tales of North America (Mike Fink, Davy Crockett, Johnny Appleseed, John Henry, Casey Jones) and in realistic folktales.

Religious Stories

Classifying religious stories as traditional fantasy or as myths may bother many people, but *myth* in this sense can be broadly defined as the human's quest to discover and share with one another truth concerning the spiritual aspects of existence. Stories derived from the sacred writings of Buddhism, Christianity, Hinduism, Islam, and other religions of the world contribute to this arena of traditional literature.

Books and stories in this category include parables and Old Testament stories, including any number of legends or apocryphal tales with religious connections such as Ruth Robbins's *Baboushka and the Three Kings* (1960) or Tomie dePaola's *The Legend of Old Befana* (1980)—both variants of a Christmas story about an old woman too busy to follow the Three Wise Men. Other examples include *Buddha Stories*, the Jataka tales retold by Demi (1997), and a novel, *Rama: A Legend* (1994) by Jamake Highwater, based on a Hindu epic.

IN DEFENSE OF TRADITIONAL FANTASY

"About once every hundred years some wiseacre gets up and tries to banish the fairy tale. Perhaps I had better say a few words in its defence, as reading for children" (Lewis 1980, p. 213). These words by C. S. Lewis, who is known for his enduring fantasy series, the Narnia Chronicles, were written as part of his defense of traditional tales in 1952. Yet, in far less than 100 years—in fact, on a regular basis—"wiseacres" have been attempting to censor traditional stories. We have already discussed the importance of fairy and folktales but now wish to provide some responses to the major complaints voiced against traditional literature. These objections mainly fall into four categories: psychological fantasy, violence, frightening to young children, and waste of time (Tunnell 1994).

PSYCHOLOGICAL FANTASY

Some adults fear that fantasy stories will lead children to be somehow out of touch with reality, to suffer from fantasy in the clinical, psychological sense of the word. Psychological fantasy, the inability of the mind to distinguish what is real, does not result from reading literary fantasy. In fact, children who read stories that contain "unrealistic" elements—animals who talk, magical events, time travel—are actually less at risk of losing touch with the realities of daily life. Bruno Bettleheim (1977) confirmed this position when he said that fairy stories not only are safe for children but also necessary, and that children deprived of a rich fantasy life (which traditional tales provide) are more likely to seek a psychological escape through avenues like black magic, drugs, or astrology. Through fairy and folktales, children may vicariously vent the frustrations of being a child controlled by an adult world, for they subconsciously identify with the heroes of the stories who are often the youngest, smallest, least powerful characters (Hansel and Gretel, Cinderella, Aladdin). They also are given a sense of hope about their ultimate abilities to succeed in the world.

C. S. Lewis goes a step further, believing that certain realistic stories are far more likely to cause problems than good fantasy. He points to adult reading as an example:

> The dangerous fantasy is always superficially realistic. The real victim of wishful reverie
> . . . prefers stories about millionaires, irresistible beauties, posh hotels, palm beaches,
> and bedroom scenes—things that really might happen, that ought to happen, that

would have happened if the reader had had a fair chance. [T]here are two kinds of longing. The one is an askesis, a spiritual exercise, and the other is a disease. (1980, p. 215)

Violence

Critics suggest that violent acts in some traditional tales will breed violence in young children. The work of psychologist Ephraim Biblow shows how wrong-minded this sort of thinking is. In his experimental study, Biblow showed that children with rich fantasy lives responded to aggressive films with a significant decrease in aggressive behavior, while "low-fantasy" children showed a tendency toward increased aggression.

> The low fantasy child, as observed during play, presented himself as more motorically oriented, revealed much action and little thought in play activities. The high-fantasy child in contrast was more highly structured and creative and tended to be verbally rather than physically aggressive. (Biblow 1973, p. 128)

Much of the violence in fairy and folktales involves the punishment of truly evil villains. Children are concerned from an early age with the ramifications of good and bad behavior, which is represented in fundamental, archetypal ways in traditional stories. Lawrence Kohlberg's stages of moral development describe the young child as being in the "premoral stage" (up to about eight years), which basically means that "the child believes that evil behavior is likely to be punished and good behavior is based on obedience or avoidance of evil implicit in disobedience" (Lefrancois 1986, p. 446). According to Bettleheim (1977), the evil person in fairy tales who meets a well-deserved fate satisfies a child's deep need for justice to prevail. Sometimes this requires destroying the evil altogether.

Violence in movies and many books cannot be equated with the violence in fairy and folktales. Even in Grimm's version of "Cinderella," one of the bloodiest of fairy stories, the violent acts are surprisingly understated. Both truly wicked stepsisters mutilate themselves (a trimmed heel and a cut-off toe) to make the slipper fit and are revealed by the blood. Later, birds peck out their eyes as punishment for their treachery. Yet, the tale simply, compactly states the fact of each violent act. We don't read of viscous fluid streaming down faces or blood spurting on walls and floors. That's the stuff of slasher horror movies, sensationalism designed to shock or titillate, but not a careful comment on justice.

Frightening for Young Children

Many adults worry that some of the traditional tales will frighten children, causing nightmares and other sorts of distress. However, because dangerous story elements, such as wicked witches or dragons, are far removed in both time and place from the lives of children, they prove much less frightening than realistic stories of danger that focus on real-life fears (Smith 1989). Lewis felt that insulating a child completely from fear is a disservice. "Since it is so likely they will meet cruel enemies, let them at least have heard of brave knights and heroic courage. Otherwise you are making their destiny not bright but darker" (Lewis 1980, p. 216).

Fairy and folktales provide children a message of hope. No matter how bleak the outlook or how dark the path, these stories promise children that it is possible to make it through and come out on top. In fact, children who recoil from strong images of danger in fairy tales have the most to gain from the exposure (Smith 1989).

Some adults feel they can circumvent the problem of frightening children by choosing softened versions of fairy and folktales. This approach may have the opposite effect, causing children to become more distressed. Trousdale (1989) tells the story of a mother who used only the softened version of "The Three Little Pigs" with her young daughter. In this version the pigs are not eaten, and the wolf is not killed in boiling water. Instead, he comes down the chimney, burns his derriere, rockets up the chimney, and disappears into the sunset, never to been seen again. The little girl said, "He's gonna come back," and began to have nightmares. Trousdale (1989, p. 77) advised the child's mother to read the Joseph Jacobs version, in which the wolf dies; Trousdale soon received a letter that said, "Well, we put the Big Bad Wolf to rest." The evil was destroyed and thus the threat eliminated. The nightmares stopped.

Waste of Time

Perhaps the most insidious complaint is that traditional fantasy is a waste of time. Adults simply do not select fairy or folktales to use with children in favor of more substantial stories and books about the real world. However, no genre of literature better fosters creativity than fantasy (both modern and traditional). Recall that Biblow's study showed high-fantasy children to be "more highly structured and creative." Russian poet Kornei Chukovsky (1968, p. 17) felt that fantasy is "the most valuable attribute of the human mind and should be diligently nurtured from the earliest age." He even points out that great scientists have acknowledged this fact and quotes eminent British physicist John Tindale:

> Without the participation of fantasy . . . all our knowledge about nature would have been limited merely to the classification of obvious facts. The relation between cause and effect and their interaction would have gone unnoticed, thus stemming the progress of science itself, because it is the main function of science to establish the link between the different manifestations of nature, since creative fantasy is the ability to perceive more and more such links. (Chukovsky 1968, p. 124)

As the story goes, a woman with a mathematically gifted son asked Albert Einstein how she should best foster his talent. After a moment of thought, Einstein answered, "Read him the great myths of the past—stretch his imagination" (Huck 1982, p. 316). Teachers bemoan the lack of creative and critical thinking in today's students. How can we then not promote the very books and stories that cultivate imaginative thought?

REFERENCES

Aardema, Verna. 1975. *Why Mosquitoes Buzz in People's Ears*. New York: Dial.

Alexander, Lloyd. 1968. Wishful thinking—or hopeful dreaming. *The Horn Book* 44 (August): 382–390.

Bettleheim, Bruno. 1977. *The Uses of Enchantment: The Meaning and Importance of Fairy Tales*. New York: Vintage.

Biblow, Ephraim. 1973. Imaginative play and the control of aggressive behavior. In *The Child's World of Make-Believe*, edited by Jerome L. Singer. New York: Academic Press.

Chukovsky, Kornei. 1968. *From Two to Five*. Los Angeles: University of California Press.

Climo, Shirley. 1989. *The Egyptian Cinderella*. New York: Harper.

Demi. 1997. *Buddha Stories*. New York: Holt.

dePaola, Tomie. 1980. *The Legend of Old Befana*. New York: Harcourt.

Frye, Northrop. 1964. *The Educated Imagination*. Bloomington, Ind.: University of Indiana Press.

Haley, Gail. 1970. *A Story, A Story*. New York: Atheneum.

Hamilton, Virginia. 1988. *In the Beginning: Creation Stories from Around the World*. New York: Harcourt.

Highwater, Jamake. 1994. *Rama: A Legend*. New York: Harper.

Huck, Charlotte. 1982. I give you the end of a golden string. *Theory Into Practice* 12, no. 4 (Autumn): 315–325.

Lefrancois, Guy R. 1986. *Of Children*. Belmont, Calif.: Wadsworth.

Lewis, C. S. 1980. On three ways of writing for children. In *Only Connect*, edited by Sheila Egoff, G. T. Stubbs, and L. F. Ashley. New York: Oxford University Press.

Louie, Ai-Ling. 1990. *Yeh-Shen*. New York: Philomel.

Lowry, Lois. 1989. *Number the Stars*. Boston: Houghton Mifflin.

Martin, Rafe. 1992. *The Rough-Face Girl*. New York: Putnam.

Robbins, Ruth. 1960. *Baboushka and the Three Kings*. New York: Parnassus.

Smith, Charles A. 1989. *From Wonder to Wisdom*. New York: New American Library.

Steptoe, John. 1987. *Mufaro's Beautiful Daughters*. New York: Lothrop.

Trousdale, Ann. 1989. Who's afraid of the big bad wolf. *Children's Literature in Education* 20, no. 2 (June) 68–79.

Tunnell, Michael O. 1994. The double-edged sword: fantasy and censorship. *Language Arts* 71, no. 8: 606–612.

Yolen, Jane. *Sky Dogs*. 1990. Illustrated by Barry Moser. New York: Harcourt.

Traditional Fantasy Reading List

Ten of Our Favorites

Collections and Chapter Books

Dickinson, Peter. 1992. *City of Gold and Other Stories from the Old Testament*. Illustrated by Michael Foreman. Houghton. A retelling of 33 Old Testament narratives.

Hamilton, Virginia. 1988. *In the Beginning: Creation Stories from Around the World*. Illustrated by Barry Moser. Harcourt. An illustrated collection of 25 myths from various cultures explaining the creation of the world.

Harris, Joel Chandler (adapted by Van Dyke Parks and Malcolm Jones). 1986. *Jump! The Adventures of Brer Rabbit*. Illustrated by Barry Moser. Harcourt. A retelling of five folktales in which crafty Brer Rabbit tries to outsmart all the other creatures in the animal community.

Osborne, Mary Pope. 1998. *Favorite Medieval Tales*. Illustrated by Troy Howell. Scholastic. A collection of well-known tales from medieval Europe, including "Beowulf," "The Sword in the Stone," "The Song of Roland," and "Gudren and the Island of the Lost Children."

Sutcliff, Rosemary. 1981. *The Sword and the Circle*. Dutton. (See the other books in the King Arthur trilogy: *Light Beyond the Forest: The Quest for the Holy Grail* and *The Road to Camlann*.) Retells the adventures of King Arthur, Queen Guenevere, Sir Lancelot, and other knights of the Round Table.

Picture Books

Grimm Brothers (translated by Randall Jarrell). 1972. *Snow-White and the Seven Dwarfs*. Illustrated by Nancy Ekholm Burkert. Farrar. A beautifully illustrated rendition of the classic fairy tale. A Caldecott Honor Book.

Martin, Rafe. 1992. *The Rough-Face Girl*. Illustrated by David Shannon. Putnam. In this Algonquin Indian version of the Cinderella story, the Rough-Face girl and her two beautiful but heartless sisters compete for the affections of the Invisible Being.

McDermott, Gerald. 1975. *The Stonecutter: A Japanese Folk Tale*. Penguin. Not even the mightiest mountain is immune to a determined stonecutter.

Steptoe, John. 1987. *Mufaro's Beautiful Daughters: An African Tale*. Lothrop. Mufaro's two beautiful daughters, one bad-tempered, one kind and sweet, go before the king who is choosing a wife. An African variant of Cinderella. A Caldecott Honor Book.

Zelinsky, Paul O. 1997. *Rapunzel*. Dutton. The author melded several versions of the Rapunzel story in creating this unique telling. Caldecott Medal.

Others We Like

CHAPTER BOOKS AND COLLECTIONS

Evslin, Bernard. 1984. *Hercules*. Illustrated by Joseph A. Smith. Morrow.

Doherty, Berlie. 1998. *Tales of Wonder and Magic*. Illustrated by Juan Wijngaard. Candlewick.

Hamilton, Virginia. 1995. *Her Stories*. Scholastic (Blue Sky).

Low, Alice. 1985. *The Macmillan Book of Greek Gods and Heroes*. Illustrated by Arvis Stewart. Macmillan.

Osborne, Mary Pope. 1991. *American Tall Tales*. Illustrated by Michael McCurdy. Knopf.

Sutcliff, Rosemary. 1996. Illustrated by Alan Lee. *The Wanderings of Odysseus*. Delacorte.

PICTURE BOOKS

Aardema, Verna. 1975. *Why Mosquitoes Buzz in People's Ears*. Illustrated by Leo and Diane Dillon. Dial.

Aesop. 1981. *Aesop's Fables*. Illustrated by Heidi Holder. Viking.

Demi. 1994. *The Firebird*. Holt.

Fisher, Leonard. 1990. *Jason and the Golden Fleece*. Holiday House.

Goble, Paul. 1985. *The Girl Who Loved Wild Horses*. Bradbury.

Grimm Brothers. 1975. *Thorn Rose or the Sleeping Beauty*. Illustrated by Errol Le Cain. Bradbury.

Grimm Brothers. 1983. *Little Red Riding Hood*. Illustrated by Trina Schart Hyman. Holiday House.

Grimm Brothers (retold by Barbara Rogasky). 1986. *The Water of Life*. Illustrated by Trina Schart Hyman. Holiday House.

Haley, Gail. 1970. *A Story, a Story*. Atheneum.

Hasting, Selina. 1981. *Sir Gawain and the Loathly Lady*. Illustrated by Juan Wijngaard. Lothrop.

Hutton, Warwick. 1983. *Jonah and the Great Fish*. McElderry.

Isaacs, Anne. 1994. *Swamp Angel*. Illustrated by Paul O. Zelinsky. Dutton.

Kellogg, Stephen. 1986. *Pecos Bill*. Morrow.

Lester, Julius. 1994. *John Henry*. Illustrated by Jerry Pinkney. Dial.

Louie, Ai-Ling. 1982. *Yeh-Shen: A Cinderella Story from China*. Illustrated by Ed Young. Philomel.

Mayer, Marianna. 1978. *Beauty and the Beast*. Illustrated by Mercer Mayer. Four Winds.

Mayer, Mercer. 1978. *East of the Sun and West of the Moon*. Four Winds.

McDermott, Gerald. 1974. *Arrow to the Sun*. Viking.

McDermott, Gerald. 1997. *Musicians of the Sun*. Simon & Schuster.

Perrault, Charles (translated by Malcolm Arthur). 1990. *Puss in Boots*. Illustrated by Fred Marcellino. Farrar.

San Souci, Robert. 1989. *The Talking Eggs*. Illustrated by Jerry Pinkney. Dial.

Shannon, Mark. 1994. *Gawain and the Green Knight*. Illustrated by David Shannon. Putnam.

Stevens, Janet. 1995. *Tops & Bottoms*. Harcourt.

Wisniewski, David. 1996. *Golem*. Clarion.

Young, Ed. 1989. *Lon Po Po: A Red Riding Hood Story from China*. Philomel.

Notable Retellers and Illustrators of Traditional Stories

The names in this list include influential retellers and illustrators of traditional stories other than the pioneers who first preserved these tales in print (Brothers Grimm, Joseph Jacobs, Charles Perrault, and others).

Aardema, Verna: African folktales.

Bierhorst, John: Native-American folktales.

Brown, Marcia: Folktales from a variety of cultures.

Bruchac, Joseph: Native-American folktales.

Evslin, Bernard: Greek myths.

Fisher, Leonard Everett: Greek myths.

Hamilton, Virginia: Folktale collections, primarily African-American.

Hutton, Warwick: Bible stories.

Hyman, Trina Schart: European fairy tales.

Kimmel, Eric: Folktales from around the world.

McDermott, Gerald: Myths and folktales from various cultures.

Sutcliff, Rosemary: Arthurian and Greek myths and legends.

Young, Ed: Asian folklore.

Zelinsky, Paul O.: European fairy tales.

For a more complete list of traditional fantasy titles, consult the compact disc that accompanies this text.

CHAPTER 8

Modern Fantasy

And so they lived many happy years, and the promised tasks were accomplished. Yet long afterward, when all had passed away into distant memory, there were many who wondered whether King Taran, Queen Eilonwy, and their companions had indeed walked the earth, or whether they had been no more than dreams in a tale set down to beguile children. And, in time, only the bards knew the truth of it. (Alexander 1968a, p. 285)

Lloyd Alexander's epic five-book fantasy series called The Prydain Chronicles ends with these words in *The High King*. Those who have lived vicariously in the imaginary kingdom of Prydain and survived its trials with Taran and Eilonwy yearn to hold on to those golden, mythical times as surely as we reach out longingly to hold onto a pleasant dream. This is the legacy traditional fantasy gives to modern fantasy—a sense of the magical that extends back to our ancient roots. "Magic had its feet under the earth and its hair above the clouds. . . . [In] the beginning, Magic was everywhere and nowhere" (Colwell 1968, p. 178).

DEFINITION OF MODERN FANTASY

As with traditional fantasy, modern fantasy is distinguished from other genres by story elements that violate the natural, physical laws of our known world—events akin to magic. However, modern fantasy has known authors.

The application of these miraculous elements varies greatly in modern fantasy stories: talking animals, imaginary worlds, fanciful characters (hobbits, dwarves, giants), magical beings (witches, sorcerers, genies), and so on. However, quality fantasy stories do not employ fantastic elements casually. In fact, fantasy is probably the most difficult genre to write because an author must create a new set of physical laws and then conform unerringly to them. A tiny slip can destroy the credibility of a story. Lloyd Alexander recognizes the need for this sort of specialized internal consistency:

Once committed to his imaginary kingdom, the writer is not a monarch but a subject. Characters must appear plausible in their own setting, and the writer must go along with the inner logic. Happenings should have logical implications. Details should be tested for consistency. Shall animals speak? If so, do *all* animals speak? If not, then which—and how? Is it essential to the story, or lamely cute? Are there enchantments? How powerful? If an enchanter can perform such-and-such, can he not also do so-and-so? (1965, pp. 143–144)

Modern fantasy stories are not merely a matter of make-believe. Critics hold this genre to the same basic critical standards as they do other genres. For instance, modern fantasy must have strong, believable characters and should examine issues of the human condition, the universal truths found in well-written books.

CATEGORIES OF MODERN FANTASY

Modern fantasy stories are sometimes categorized by the type of fantastic story element employed. *Animal fantasy*, for example, is the tag often given to stories that depart from reality exclusively because of talking animals, such as E. B. White's (1952) immortal *Charlotte's Web* or Brian Jacques's popular Redwall series (see Jacques 1987). Other categories and a title that exemplifies each include the following:

- Toys and objects imbued with life; *Pinocchio* by Carlo Collodi (1904), *The Mennyms* by Sylvia Waugh (1994)
- Tiny humans; *The Borrowers* by Mary Norton (1953), *The Minpins* by Roald Dahl (1991)
- Peculiar characters and situations; *Mary Poppins* by P. L. Travers (1934), *Hob and the Goblins* by William Mayne (1994)
- Imaginary worlds; *Alice's Adventures in Wonderland* by Lewis Carroll (1865), *Talking to Dragons* by Patricia C. Wrede (1993)
- Magical powers; *The Chocolate Touch* by Patrick Catling (1979), *The Midnight Horse* by Sid Fleischman (1990)
- Supernatural tales; *Wait Till Helen Comes* by Mary Downing Hahn (1985), *Stonewords* by Pam Conrad (1990)
- Time-warp fantasies; *Tom's Midnight Garden* by Philippa Pearce (1958), *A Time for Andrew* by Mary Downing Hahn (1994)
- High fantasy; *The High King* by Lloyd Alexander (1968), *The Lion, the Witch, and the Wardrobe* by C. S. Lewis (1950)

Modern fairy and folktales round out this list. As discussed in the last chapter, modern fairy and folktales are written in the form of the ageless traditional tales, which were passed from generation to generation by word of mouth. Although a number of authors have written modern folktales—Oscar Wilde, George MacDonald, Rudyard Kipling, and Jane Yolen, to name a few—the stories of Hans Christian Andersen are perhaps the best known.

SIX BASIC FANTASY MOTIFS

Even though all modern fantasy stories contain some sort of magical element, some stories will have a higher fantasy quotient than others. Madsen (1976) determined that there are six basic fantasy motifs, and if a story contains all six, it is either a classic fairy tale or an example of modern high fantasy. However, if a story contains only the motif of magic, a necessary ingredient, it certainly is still classified as fantasy literature:

1. *Magic.* Magic is fantasy literature's most basic element. In fact, each of the following five motifs are tinged by magic to some degree. Magic is often a part of the setting, thus explaining otherwise unexplainable events. In Lloyd Alexander's (1968a) *The High King*, magic is evident in the very fabric of the mythical land of Prydain. Powerful wizards are able to harness the magic in Prydain's atmosphere, an oracular pig can foretell the future, and people try to use magical objects to manipulate their destinies. However, in White's (1952) *Charlotte's Web*, the only hint of magic is the ability of the barnyard animals to think and speak like humans. In fact, this is the only one of the six motifs that appears in the book.

2. *Other worlds (secondary worlds)*. In much of fantasy, a special geography or universe is established, a place wherein magic may freely operate. Sometimes these worlds are, as in the fairy tales, simply long, long ago. Of course, Alexander's Prydain is just this sort of other world, almost recognizable as the world we know but with a different set of governing rules. Other well-known fantasy worlds include the land of Oz (*The Wonderful Wizard of Oz* by L. Frank Baum 1900), Middle Earth (*The Hobbit* by J. R. R. Tolkien 1937), Narnia (*The Lion, the Witch, and the Wardrobe* by C. S. Lewis 1950), and Neverland (*Peter Pan* by J. M. Barrie 1906).

3. *Good versus evil*. The ancient, archetypal theme of good versus evil is what myth is all about, and modern fantasy stories often have a strong mythological base. "Fantasies are concerned with how good and evil manifest themselves in individuals" (Madsen 1976, p. 49). This basic theme, of course, gives rise to the conflict in a story, and, once again, without conflict there is no story. Fantasy readers usually have no trouble aligning characters on the sides of light and dark, as fantasy characters typically are not fence sitters.

4. *Heroism*. Natalie Babbitt (1987), drawing upon the writings of mythologist Joseph Campbell (1968), explains that the hero's quest will always follow an age-old pattern that is the backbone of many of today's fantasy stories. This "hero's round" is a circular journey, ending where it began. It is a time-honored template for various types of stories, though the hero's quest originated in traditional fantasy. The following six elements, drawn from Babbitt (1987), most commonly structure the hero's quest:

   a. *The hero is called to adventure by some sort of herald*. Taran in Alexander's Prydain Chronicles (see Alexander 1964) is lured to adventure by Hen Wen, a magical pig whom he follows on a wild chase much the same way Alice follows the white rabbit (*Alice's Adventures in Wonderland*). Heralds from other stories include Gandalf (*The Hobbit*), Toto (*The Wonderful Wizard of Oz*), and Mr. Tumnus (*The Lion, the Witch, and the Wardrobe*).

   b. *The hero crosses the threshold into the other world or into a place that is no longer safe and secure*. The hero leaves a place of relative safety and enters a world of danger. Sometimes he or she will pass from the familiar modern world into a forbidding secondary world, as when the children pass through the magical wardrobe into the land of Narnia (*The Lion, the Witch, and the Wardrobe*) or when Dorothy is whisked from Kansas to Oz (*The Wonderful Wizard of Oz*). In some stories, the hero already lives in an imaginary kingdom, as Bilbo Baggins does in *The Hobbit*, and is compelled to leave hearth and home to undertake a perilous journey.

   c. *The hero must survive various trials in his new environment*. Heroes often face both physical hardship and emotional setbacks. They may suffer the pain of long treks through bitter winter weather or the pain of having dear friends relinquish their lives for a noble cause. They likely will be driven to examine their own hearts. The quest becomes the hero's refining fire.

   d. *The hero is assisted by a protective figure*. Protective figures provide a sense of security in a tension-filled world. Older, wiser, and sometimes more powerful, the protective figure may serve as the hero's mentor. Readers will identify Dallben (The Prydain Chronicles), Gandalf (*The Hobbit*), Glinda, the Good Witch of the North (*The Wonderful Wizard of Oz*), and Aslan *(The Lion, the Witch, and the Wardrobe)* as protective figures.

   e. *The hero matures, becoming a "whole person."* Did Edmund change in *The Lion, the Witch, and the Wardrobe*? How about Dorothy in *The Wonderful Wizard of Oz*? Both of these characters matured significantly during the course of their quests. Taran from the Prydain books grows from a foolish boy to a man worthy of ascending to the High Kingship of Prydain. The hero motif involves the age-old rites-of-passage theme, wherein the young are initiated into the ranks of adulthood.

   f. *The hero returns home.* This step completes the hero's round. In each Prydain book, Taran returns to his home on Dallben's farm, and then symbolically finds "home" when he discovers his true destiny in the final book, *The High King*. In the high fantasy novels discussed in this section, all the young heroes return home as their quests draw to an end.

5. *Special character types.* Fantasies may include characters who either come from our legendary past or from an author's vivid imagination. These characters are rarely typical humans. Characters from our legendary past come from traditional tales: fairies, pixies, giants, wicked witches, ogres, vampires, wizards, dwarves, elves, and so on. Some special character types created in recent years by fantasy authors have become almost as well-known, such as Tolkien's hobbits, which appear in *The Hobbit* and the Lord of the Rings trilogy.

6. *Fantastic objects.* Characters in fantasy stories often employ magical props in accomplishing their heroic or evil deeds. These objects are imbued with power, such as magic cloaks, swords, staffs, cauldrons, and mirrors. Some well-known props are Dorothy's pearl slippers (*The Wonderful Wizard of Oz*), the White Witch's wand *(The Lion, the Witch, and the Wardrobe)*, and the dreadful ring that falls into Bilbo's hands (*The Hobbit*).

Some books operate strongly in only one of these six motifs, like *The Wind in the Willows* by Kenneth Grahame (1908) and White's *Charlotte's Web* (1952), where talking animals qualify as "magic." *Tuck Everlasting* (Babbitt 1975) arguably incorporates four of the six motifs: magic, good vs. evil, the hero's round, and fantastic objects. On the other hand, Baum's *The Wonderful Wizard of Oz* operates in all six of the motifs and is thus classified as a high fantasy.

SCIENCE FICTION

Science fiction generally appears in chapters about modern fantasy. However, it differs from the stories described to this point. "Science fiction differs from fantasy not in subject matter but in aim, and its unique aim is to suggest real hypotheses about mankind's future or about the nature of the universe"(Engdahl 1971, p. 450). However, there is a brand of science fiction that would be better labeled science fantasy.

Science fantasy stories play loosely with scientific fact, and the plots are often mixed with magical occurrences. The original Stars Wars films are examples of science fantasy and even incorporate the six fantasy motifs. The Animorphs, a popular paperback series, is another example of science fantasy. Several young people are endowed by a dying, benevolent alien with the power to "morph" into various animals in order to fight against an invasion of evil alien beings.

The magic of fantasy is unexplainable; it is just there, without source or reason. But the magic of true *science fiction* is rooted more firmly in scientific fact. Because "Cinderella" is fantasy, the fairy godmother simply has the power to turn the pumpkin into a coach. If it were science fiction, she would zap the pumpkin with a molecular rearranger (Alexander 1973).

Science fiction also concerns the way in which scientific possibilities might affect societies of human or alien beings, or both. Therefore, it is sometimes called *futuristic fiction*. This combination of scientific fact and scientific possibility is evident in such works as Nancy Farmer's (1994) *The Ear, the Eye, and the Arm*. Farmer starts with facts about the devastation of nuclear accidents and goes on to offer a view of how a society thus affected might look in the 22nd century. Then she extrapolates the scientific facts about the unusual effects radiation might have on human beings by creating three characters whose mutations have given them abnormal capabilities.

THE TRUTH IN FANTASY

Some adults dismiss all fantasy—whether traditional fantasy, modern fantasy, or even science fiction—as peripheral fluff. It is simply too whimsical for those who want reading for young people to be grounded firmly in reality. Yet these adults miss the point that good fantasy actually tells the truth about life. It clarifies the human condition and captures the essence of our deepest emotions, dreams, hopes, and fears. If fantasy does not do these things, it fails.

Fantasy casts light on the realities of life in much the same way a metaphor illustrates truth in general communication. On the evening news and in daily papers, fantasy language in the form of metaphor is common. Consider the italicized parts of the following: "County medics *see light at the end of the tunnel*." "Lawmakers *torpedo* peace plan." "During the inquiry, the congressman *played his cards close to his vest*." How can news writers get away with such wild statements when no tunnel was anywhere near the county medics, the lawmakers did not use a torpedo on the peace plan, and no cards were evident at the congressional inquiry? Because metaphor is an acceptable way of enhancing communication. In its broad definition, metaphor is figurative language and strengthens writing in at least three ways:

1. Metaphor speeds understanding. Metaphor makes the abstract become concrete by introducing an image, resulting in quicker comprehension of a situation. "County medics are confident their current troubles will be resolved in the near future" describes the situation adequately, but using the metaphor of the tunnel introduces the idea more quickly and with more power.

2. Metaphor creates interest. No one misunderstands "Lawmakers vote against peace plan," but "Lawmakers torpedo peace plan" is more precise, richer, and consequently more interesting. The image of "torpedo" makes the action more deliberate and more vigorous.
3. Metaphor adds emotional appeal. With the additional layer of meaning introduced by metaphor, the message goes beyond the intellect to act upon the emotions. Without the metaphor, we know the congressman involved in the inquiry was secretive and careful in his responses. The metaphor stirs the emotions with suggestions of "game playing," "calculating," and "intense personal interest."

Yet metaphor is more than the sum of these parts. It simply involves the reader more with the story or message, allowing for quicker learning, more precise understanding, and longer retention because of the image. And fantasy, which is a large, worked-out metaphor, illuminates the truths about life in the same way. Children can read directly about friendship, sacrifice, selfishness, the fear of death, and death itself, but the insight is somehow more meaningful when shown metaphorically through the lives of Wilbur the pig, Templeton the rat, and Charlotte the spider in *Charlotte's Web* (White 1952). Because Charlotte is a spider, she can embody all selflessness without losing credibility. On the other hand, if a character in realistic fiction were dedicated completely to doing good and had no flaw or foible, she would not be believable.

Compared with fantasy, straightforward informational writing does not do as good a job of dealing with topics like "the need for death." Although the argument certainly can be made—everyone has a time and season that must end; the earth would fill if death were to cease; living forever would hold unforeseen difficulties—such intellectual points do not convince the emotions that death ultimately is desirable. This issue is hard to explore even in realistic fiction. No human can honestly present the alternate view because all people from this world, including those in realistic fiction, are destined to die. Yet the fantasy story of Winnie Foster and the Tuck family in *Tuck Everlasting* (Babbitt 1975) allows the probing of this difficult concept. By listening to a family who has lost the ability to age or die, new light is shed on the appropriateness of an eventual death. Understanding the place of death, one of real life's greatest fears and challenges, is seen most clearly in the metaphor of fantasy.

The power of fantasy is reflected in the fact that many of the classic children's stories, those that have withstood the test of time, are fantasies: *Peter Pan* (Barrie 1906), *Winnie the Pooh* (A. A. Milne 1926), *The Wonderful Wizard of Oz* (Baum 1900), *The Wind in the Willows* (Grahame 1908) and *Mary Poppins (Travers* 1934). Certainly, good fantasy stories speak clearly and convincingly about real life, as author Lloyd Alexander observed (1968b, p. 386): "I suppose you might define realism as fantasy pretending to be true; and fantasy as reality pretending to be a dream."

REFERENCES

Alexander, Lloyd. 1964. *The Book of Three*. New York: Holt.

Alexander, Lloyd. 1965. The flat-heeled muse. *The Horn Book* 41 (April): 141–146.

Alexander, Lloyd. 1968a. *The High King*. New York: Holt.

Alexander, Lloyd. 1968b. Wishful thinking—or hopeful dreaming. *The Horn Book* 44 (August): 382–390.

Alexander, Lloyd. 1973. Letter to Shelton L. Root, Jr. 20 February.

Babbitt, Natalie. 1975. *Tuck Everlasting*. New York: Farrar, Straus & Giroux.

Babbitt, Natalie. 1987. Fantasy and the classic hero. *School Library Journal* 34 (October): 25–29.

Barrie, J. M. 1906. *Peter Pan*. New York: Scribner's.

Baum, L. Frank. 1900. *The Wonderful Wizard of Oz*. New York: G. M. Hill.

Campbell, Joseph. 1968. *The Hero with a Thousand Faces*. 2nd ed. Princeton, N.J.: Princeton University Press.

Carroll, Lewis. 1865. *Alice's Adventures in Wonderland*. London: Macmillan.

Catling, Patrick. 1979. *The Chocolate Touch*. New York: William Morrow.

Collodi, Carlo. 1904. *Pinocchio*. Boston: Ginn.

Colwell, Elizabeth. 1968. An oral tradition and an oral art: Folk literature. *Top of the News* 24 (January): 174–180.

Conrad, Pam. 1990. *Stonewords*. New York: HarperCollins.

Dahl, Roald. 1991. *The Minpins*. New York: Viking.

Engdahl, Sylvia Louise. 1971. The changing role of science fiction in children's literature. *The Horn Book* 47 (October): 449–455.

Farmer, Nancy. 1994. *The Ear, the Eye, and the Arm*. New York: Orchard.

Fleischman, Sid. 1990. *The Midnight Horse*. New York: Greenwillow.

Grahame, Kenneth. 1908. *The Wind in the Willows*. London: Methuen.

Hahn, Mary Downing. 1985. *Wait Till Helen Comes: A Ghost Story*. New York: Houghton Mifflin.

Hahn, Mary Downing. 1994. *A Time for Andrew*. New York: Clarion.

Jacques, Brian. 1987. *Redwall*. New York: Philomel.

Lewis, C. S. 1950. *The Lion, the Witch, and the Wardrobe*. New York: Macmillan.

Madsen, Linda Lee. 1976. Fantasy in children's literature: A generic study. Master's thesis, Utah State University.

Mayne, William. 1994. *Hob and the Goblins*. Boston: Houghton Mifflin.

Milne, A. A. 1926. *Winnie the Pooh*. New York: Dutton.

Norton, Mary. 1953. *The Borrowers*. New York: Harcourt, Brace.

Pearce, Philippa. 1958. *Tom's Midnight Garden*. New York: Lippincott.

Tolkien, J. R. R. 1937. *The Hobbit*. London: G. Allen and Unwin.

Travers, P. L. 1934. *Mary Poppins*. London: G. Howe.

Waugh, Sylvia. 1994. *The Mennyms*. New York: Greenwillow.

White, E. B. 1952. *Charlotte's Web*. New York: HarperCollins.

Wrede, Patricia. 1993. *Talking to Dragons*. New York: Harcourt Brace.

MODERN FANTASY READING LIST

Ten of Our Favorites

Alexander, Lloyd. 1964. *The Book of Three*. Holt. In the first book of The Prydain Chronicles, Taran, Assistant Pig Keeper at Caer Dallben, searches for the oracular pig Hen Wen while the forces of evil gather. (See the other four books in The Prydain Chronicles.)

Babbitt, Natalie. 1975. *Tuck Everlasting*. Farrar. The Tuck family is confronted with an agonizing situation when they discover that a 10-year-old girl and a malicious stranger now share their secret about the water from a spring that prevents people from ever growing any older.

Christopher, John. 1967. *The White Mountains*. Macmillan. (Science fiction.) A young boy and his companions make a perilous journey toward an outpost of freedom, where they hope to escape from the ruling tripod creatures who "cap" adult human beings with implanted metal skull plates that turn them into docile, obedient servants. (See the other three books in the White Mountains series.)

Conrad, Pam. 1990. *Stonewords*. Harper. Zoe's house is occupied by the ghost of an 11-year-old girl who died in 1870 and carries Zoe back to the day of her death to try to alter that tragic event.

Cooper, Susan. 1966. *Over Sea, Under Stone*. Harcourt. Three children on a holiday in Cornwall find an ancient manuscript that sends them on a dangerous quest for a grail that would reveal the true story of King Arthur. (See the other four books in the Dark Is Rising series.)

Hunter, Mollie. 1975. *A Stranger Came Ashore*. Harper. Twelve-year-old Robbie becomes convinced that the stranger befriended by his family is one of the Selkie Folk and tries to get help against his magical powers from the local wizard.

Lewis, C. S. 1950. *The Lion, the Witch, and the Wardrobe*. Macmillan. Four English schoolchildren find their way through the back of a wardrobe into the magic land of Narnia and assist Aslan, the golden lion, in triumphing over the White Witch, who has cursed the land with eternal winter. (See the other six books in the Narnia series.)

McKinley, Robin. 1978. *Beauty: A Retelling of the Story of Beauty and the Beast*. Harper. Kind Beauty grows to love the Beast, at whose castle she is compelled to stay. Through her love, she releases him from the spell that had turned him from a handsome prince into an ugly creature.

O'Brien, Robert C. 1975. *Z for Zachariah*. Atheneum. (Science fiction.) Seemingly the only person left alive after a nuclear holocaust, a young girl is relieved to see a man arrive into her valley until she realizes that he is a tyrant and that she must somehow escape.

White, E. B. 1952. *Charlotte's Web*. Harper. Wilbur, the pig, discovers that he is destined to be the farmer's Christmas dinner and is desolate until his spider friend, Charlotte, decides to help him. A Newbery Honor Book.

Others We Like

Alexander, Lloyd. 1997. *The Iron Ring*. Dutton.

Banks, Lynne Reid. 1981. *The Indian in the Cupboard*. Doubleday. (See others in the Indian in the Cupboard series.)

Barron, T. A. 1996. *The Lost Years of Merlin*. Philomel. (See others in The Lost Years of Merlin epic.)

Bellairs, John. 1973. *The House with a Clock in Its Walls*. Dial. (See others in the Lewis Barnavelt series.)

Dahl, Roald. 1988. *Matilda*. Viking Kestrel.

Dickinson, Peter. 1989. *Eva*. Delacorte. (Science fiction.)

Duncan, Lois. 1976. *Summer of Fear*. Little, Brown.

Engdahl, Sylvia Louise. 1970. *Enchantress from the Stars*. Atheneum. (Science fiction.)

Hahn, Mary Downing. 1986. *Wait Till Helen Comes: A Ghost Story*. Houghton Mifflin.

Hoover, H. M. 1977. *The Delikon*. Viking. (Science fiction.)

Jacques, Brian. 1987. *Redwall*. Philomel. (See others in the Redwall series.)

Le Guin, Ursula K. 1968. *A Wizard of Earthsea*. Parnassus. (See the other books in the Earthsea series.)

Lowry, Lois. 1993. *The Giver*. Houghton.

L' Engle, Madeleine. 1962. *A Wrinkle in Time*. Farrar. (See others in the Time series.)

Norton, Mary. 1953. *The Borrowers*. Harcourt. (See others in the Borrowers series.)

O'Brien, Robert C. 1971. *Mrs. Frisby and the Rats of NIMH*. Atheneum. (Science fiction.)

Pullman, Philip. 1995. *The Golden Compass*. Knopf. (See others in the His Dark Materials series.)

Rowling, J. K. 1998. *Harry Potter and the Sorcerer's Stone*. New York: Scholastic.

Smith, Sherwood. 1990. *Wren to the Rescue*. Harcourt. (See others in the Wren series.)

Waugh, Sylvia. 1994. *The Mennyms*. Greenwillow. (See others in the Mennyms series.)

Yolen, Jane. 1982. *Dragon's Blood*. Delacorte. (See others in the Dragon trilogy.)

Easier to Read

Brown, Jeff. 1964. *Flat Stanley*. Illustrated by Tomi Ungerer. Harper.

Catling, Patrick. 1979. *The Chocolate Touch*. Morrow.

Cleary, Beverly. 1965. *The Mouse and the Motorcycle*. Morrow.

Cuyler, Majorie. 1995. *Invisible in the Third Grade*. Illustrated by Mirko Gabler. Holt.

Fleischman, Sid. 1992. *Here Comes McBroom*. Greenwillow.

Howe, Deborah, and James Howe. 1983. *Bunnicula*. Atheneum.

Key, Alexander. 1965. *The Forgotten Door*. Westminster. (Science fiction.)

King-Smith, Dick. 1985. *Babe: The Gallant Pig*. Crown.

Scieszka, Jon. 1991. *Knights of the Kitchen Table*. Illustrated by Lane Smith. Viking. (See others in the Time Warp Trio series.)

Wright, Betty Ren. 1994. *The Ghost Comes Calling*. Scholastic.

Picture Books

Henkes, Kevin. 1996. *Lilly's Purple Plastic Purse*. Greenwillow.

Kellogg, Steven. 1977. *The Mysterious Tadpole*. Dial.

Meddaugh, Susan. 1992. *Martha Speaks*. Houghton.

Peet, Bill. 1987. *Jethro and Joel Were a Troll*. Houghton.

Rosenberg, Liz. 1993. *Monster Mama*. Illustrated by Stephen Gammell. Putnam.

Small, David. 1986. *Imogene's Antlers*. Crown.

Steig, William. 1990. *Shrek!* Farrar.

Van Allsburg, Chris. 1979. *The Garden of Abdul Gasazi*. Houghton.

Wood, Audrey. 1996. *The Bunyans*. Illustrated by David Shannon.

Yolen, Jane. 1989. *Dove Isabeau*. Illustrated by Dennis Nolan. Harcourt.

Notable Authors of Modern Fantasy

Listed after each name is the type of fantasy story for which each author is best known.

Alexander, Lloyd: High fantasy.

Bellairs, John: Supernatural.

Cooper, Susan: High fantasy.

Christopher, John: Science fiction.

Dahl, Roald: Peculiar characters/preposterous situations.

Duncan, Lois: Supernatural.

Hoover, H. M.: Science fiction.

Hughes, Monica: Science fiction.

Hunter, Mollie: Magical powers; supernatural.

Jacques, Brian: Animal fantasy.

King-Smith, Dick: Animal fantasy.

Lewis, C. S.: High fantasy.

McKinley, Robin: High fantasy.

Wright, Betty Ren: Supernatural.

Yolen, Jane: High fantasy.

For a more complete list of modern fantasy titles, consult the compact disc that accompanies this text.

CHAPTER 9

Contemporary Realistic Fiction

Contemporary realistic fiction tells a story that never happened but *could* happen. The events and the characters of contemporary realistic fiction flow from the author's imagination, just as they do in fantasy. Unlike fantasy, which includes at least one element not found in this world, everything in contemporary realistic fiction is possible on planet Earth.

IMPORTANCE OF STORY

W. Somerset Maugham disclosed the secret of writing an appealing book: "There are three rules for writing a good novel. Unfortunately, no one knows what they are" (Stephens 1990). While the exact recipe for solid writing does not exist—if it did, anyone privy to the formula could predictably crank out an award winner—all readers recognize one unfailing earmark of a good novel: It must tell a satisfying story. Every memorable work of fiction presents a conflict or problem that affects human beings, and how this obstacle is overcome *is* the story. Writers of contemporary realistic fiction draw on their own backgrounds or observe life around them to tell their stories.

IDENTIFYING WITH CONTEMPORARY REALISTIC FICTION

Of all the genres in children's literature, contemporary realistic fiction is the most popular. People are interested in their own lives, and this genre is about "my life." This is my world. This is how I live. This story is about a girl like me. Because the characters in contemporary realistic fiction are similar to people in my town, I get to know them quickly and feel as if I've known them a long time. The main character in particular becomes a kindred spirit. She experiences the same disappointments and hopes, rejections, and joys as the reader, who is amazed and thrilled to find someone who sees the world through similar glasses. Certainly, the reader can connect with the lives of those from the past and also with fantasy characters, but something about the here and now packs an additional emotional punch.

Books that deal with specific cultures, nationalities, minorities, and subgroups also provide a connection between each of those communities and the world. Almost all readers want to find at least an occasional title that reflects their lives, and it is the lack of books dealing with other cultures that can draw protest from members of a group who desire to read about something accurate and close to home. Because realistic fiction helps confirm our own membership in the human race, children's publishers and authors continue to represent the spectrum of minorities present in the United States—racial groups, different religions, stories from specific regions of the country—but not all bases have yet been covered. For instance, the half-million people in the United States who are Deaf (capitalized to indicate they belong to the Deaf culture, not just that they do not hear) are represented at the time of this writing in one picture storybook currently in print in America. A few informational picture books are available, detailing facts about sign language and what life is like for the nonhearing, but being represented by only one picture storybook leaves the Deaf without the confirmation of their lives and enrichment provided in a story about "someone like me." The lack of such books also means that others have less opportunity to get to know and understand the Deaf.

The importance of identifying with one's own life is a reason children's books have children as the protagonists. The age of the main character is approximately the age of the reader. For this reason, *The Endless Steppe,* Esther Hautzig's (1968) memoir about her World War II childhood in Poland and Russia, eventually was published as a children's book even though she did not have a child audience in mind as she wrote it. Because the main character is a young girl, its market and audience are the same—young readers. The rule of thumb is that children will read about characters who are slightly older than they are but are hesitant about reading books with characters who are younger.

A small but important type of contemporary realistic fiction does not fit the pattern where readers identify with the main character. Some main characters have little in common with young people, but their stories still offer enough humor, adventure, or entertainment to draw readers. Examples are Peggy Parish's (1963) Amelia Bedelia stories about the maid who takes too literally her employer's instructions (she ices the cake by topping it with ice cubes and sticking it in the freezer), and Sheila Burnford's (1961) *The Incredible Journey,* which chronicles the ordeal of two dogs and a cat as they travel 250 miles through the Canadian wilderness to reach their home.

Familiarity helps explain why many children who have not yet discovered the pleasure of books often find their first successful reading experiences with contemporary realistic fiction. Trying out a new book is a risk for the reader, and those not steeped in personal reading are less likely to take big chances. Contemporary realistic fiction offers less of a gamble because the book already contains familiar elements. When the reader meets a character who lives in a familiar world and who faces similar situations, a detailed introduction is less important. Much of the groundwork already exists for a relationship, or even a friendship, to develop between reader and character.

CONTEMPORARY REALISTIC FICTION AND SOCIETY

Contemporary realism reflects society and the child's place in it. Contemporary novels written in the 1920s provide a snapshot of the American scene during that time, and novels written and set in the 1990s do the same. The view of life in a realistic story reflects societal mores and attitudes of the time in which the tale is set. In books written around the time of World War I, for example, a pregnant woman would be identified as being "in a delicate condition," if she were identified at all. The word *pregnant* was rarely used in daily conversation and, consequently, rarely found in print. Life in the early 1900s definitely had pregnancies and other realities of human existence including crime, great injustice, and pockets of ugliness, but these aspects of life were not a part of books written for children, because social attitudes dictated that they were unsuitable for children and therefore unavailable for young readers.

Until the mid-1960s, the world in children's books typically was presented without negative or earthy aspects. Geoffrey Trease (1983) lists some of the generally accepted restrictions that applied to the writing of children's books before 1960: no budding love affairs, no liquor, no supernatural phenomenon, no undermining of authority, no parents with serious human weaknesses, no realistic working-class speech (including the mildest cursing). But then the face of American society took on a new look because of upheavals like the civil rights movement, Vietnam, and large cracks appearing in the traditional family structure. The effects were so widespread that children no longer could be kept in the dark (if they truly ever were). Evidence of the changes appeared on the front pages of newspapers, harsh realities were broadcast into the living rooms of the world on television newscasts, and no neighborhood was free from divorce.

A new attitude accompanied the shift toward facing problems previously ignored: Children were viewed as citizens with rights beyond those granted by their parents. Some voices called for children to have full access to information, and young people achieved a new prominence in society. Following tradition, contemporary realistic fiction chronicled the current scene, and the child as consumer/citizen began to appear in books for young readers.

Contemporary realistic fiction is most often the genre in which the taboos of literature are tested. Changes in the content of children's literature typically appear first in this genre and then spread to others. Louise Fitzhugh's *Harriet the Spy* was a pivotal book when it appeared in 1964. It tells about a nontraditional girl who dressed in a sweatshirt, spied on neighbors, was neglected by her well-to-do parents, and underwent psychotherapy. All of these elements signaled a shift in the acceptable literary content of the day.

Controversy over the realities in these and other books spread widely. These changes, beginning in the 1960s and flourishing in the '70s, came to be called *new realism* (see Chapter 5). The harsher parts of life simply had not been given center stage in books for young readers until then. When the taboos lifted, new books spewed forth problems and realities previously unseen in children's publishing. Topics like death, divorce, drugs, abuse in all its forms, profanity, nontraditional lifestyles, and single-parent families not only were mentioned in the books but also became major themes.

Society continued to change. New problems arose, such as anorexia nervosa, inner-city survival, AIDS, teen suicide, gang life, random shootings, and white supremacy. Those new problems sprouted in contemporary books for children, and still newer problems continue to surface in both society and writing for young readers.

Because of the immediacy of the problems in realistic fiction, it traditionally has been the genre that attracts the most controversy. When a book deals with the issue of cocaine in a modern middle school, the emotional impact of the problem tends to be stronger than in a story treating the consequences of opium addiction in 18th-century China. Society was affected as drastically by drugs 200 years ago as today, but the middle school setting is closer to home both emotionally and physically. That closeness is celebrated as relevant and helpful by some people and abhorred as too stark and unnecessary by others, and thus the debate begins. (For more on controversy and censorship, see Chapter 16.)

DIDACTICISM

If the problem or a social issue in a book becomes more important than the story, the book suffers. This is true whenever the author uses the book as a means to drive home a point or present a moral, no matter how worthy the cause or noble the intent. As soon as the story ceases to be an experience, it becomes didactic—a lesson instead of a discovery. Didactic fiction in the past often was used to define proper behavior and belief, as described in Chapter 5. Those earlier books lost their potential to become powerful reading experiences when they became vehicles for indoctrination. Yet in our enlightened modern times, current fiction can be equally as lopsided. Contemporary realistic fiction, which so often features modern problems, can be particularly prone to didacticism. When "problem novels" focus so narrowly on the problem—abuse, pregnancy, addiction—that they ignore the themes and issues raised by the situation, they generally offer a didactic quick-fix view of life.

Even when the social issue is largely agreed upon by readers as important, like protecting the environment, the book becomes second-rate as soon as that issue over-shadows the credibility of the characters and the believability of the plot. A book can be strengthened by its insights into contemporary issues and problems as long as those insights are secondary to the story. But using a book as a soapbox interferes with the impact of the reading experience, as in Chris Van Allsburg's *Just a Dream*, which is a thinly disguised lesson on ecology. Another example is Dr. Seuss's *Oh, the Places You'll Go*, which sacrifices story to present in greeting-card style the message that one's potential is limitless.

BIBLIOTHERAPY

In its broadest definition, bibliotherapy is any kind of emotional healing that comes from reading books. Therapy from books falls into at least three different categories: (1) the broad therapeutic feelings of recreation and gratification experienced by an individual reader, (2) the sense of connectedness felt by members of a group who read and share books together, and (3) the particular information and insight books can provide in dealing with specific personal problems (Chatton 1988).

The first two categories, recreation and connectedness, result naturally from reading. Those who have found compelling titles experience the first category as they discover the deep satisfaction, stimulation, and comfort that books can bring. The second category—connectedness—occurs when readers experience a book along with others, a new dimension to the group relationship. A teacher and classroom of children who read a book together are able to connect with one another in new ways when laughing, crying, or simply talking about their mutual experience.

It is in the third category—dealing with specific personal problems—where most difficulties arise. Because books can provide insight and comfort, adults sometimes are tempted to fix children's problems by insisting they read certain books to help them cope with those problems. If a boy is suffering because of his parents' divorce, for example, a well-meaning teacher might push him into a book about a child adjusting to life after a broken marriage. Because human beings are complex and unpredictable, the boy might not need or want to read about his own problem. He may be better served by a book that takes him far away from the painful reality at home. After all, "stories are not like mustard plasters to be applied for immediate relief where deep-seated problems of behavior, attitudes and values exist" (Heaton and Lewis 1955, p. 35). This sort of clinical bibliotherapy is, of course, best reserved for trained psychologists and psychotherapists, who can and do use books successfully in their practices. Other adults can serve children better simply by reading and recommending good books, and allowing personal insight, comfort, and the answering of troubling questions to come in their own natural and timely ways.

CATEGORIES OF CONTEMPORARY REALISTIC FICTION

Depending on who cuts up the realistic fiction pie, the pieces might be as few as six general categories: families, peers, adolescent issues, survival and adventure, persons with disabilities, and cultural diversity (Tomlinson and Lynch-Brown 1996). Or the genre can be divided into as many as the following 22 more specific categories:

1. Becoming one's own person: (a) living in a family, (b) family relationships, (c) extended families, (d) families in transition, (e) living with others, (f) finding peer acceptance, (g) making friends, (h) growing toward maturity, (i) developing sexuality, (j) finding one's self, (k) survival stories
2. Coping with problems of the human condition: (a) physical disabilities, (b) developmental and learning disabilities, (c) mental illness, (d) aging and death
3. Living in a diverse world: (a) appreciating racial and ethnic diversity, (b) African-American experiences in books for children, (c) books about other minorities, (d) understanding various world cultures (Huck et al. 1997)

Whichever of the limitless ways we may choose to organize these titles in contemporary fiction, one value of making categories is to provide adults, especially teachers, with a quick check to evaluate the breadth of our personal reading. Teachers ought to be familiar with a variety of titles in all genres, including the categories of contemporary realism, so that we may help satisfy the reading interests and needs of a diverse student body. We want to be sure that we don't allow our personal taste in reading to limit the breadth of titles we suggest to children.

A second value of these categories is that they may be used as a tool for organizing, presenting, and discussing the myriad of contemporary realistic fiction titles available. It is important to remember, however, that these categories are neither as exclusive nor as rigid as some students are led to believe. A single title may easily fall into several categories or may seem to defy definite assignment. In fact, if a teacher or parent needs a book dealing with an extremely focused topic, *The Bookfinder* (Dreyer 1995) can provide help. These five volumes organize books for children by hundreds of social topics as narrow as scoliosis, obesity, stealing, divorce, or bedwetting.

POPULAR TYPES OF CONTEMPORARY REALISTIC FICTION

Children do not ask a librarian, "Do you have another good book of contemporary realistic fiction?" But a child will zero in on a particular type of book found within that genre, wanting another good title about animals. Or sports. Or romance. Or survival. Or a good humorous book or mystery. Stories in these areas have a proven appeal. Mysteries, for instance, have been at the top of children's preference lists from the 1920s to the present, regardless of children's sex, ethnicity, or IQ (Haynes 1988; Tomlinson and Tunnell 1994). Teachers who prepare for the variety of students in an average classroom would do well to become familiar with some titles from each of these popular reading categories found within contemporary realistic fiction.

These categories—animals, humor, mysteries, sports, and survival—are represented in the recommended books section at the end of the chapter. Not all of the titles listed under these headings are strictly contemporary realistic fiction. The majority are realistic fiction, either contemporary or historical, but books that fall into such popular categories often cross genre lines. When a child likes mysteries, for example, it is important to find a good mystery. Whether the mystery has a fantasy component, such as the supernatural twist in Betty Ren Wright's (1983) *The Dollhouse Murders*, is of little consequence unless the child is searching specifically for a ghost story.

SERIES BOOKS

Books in series tend to be viewed unfavorably by literary critics but find continued popularity among readers. Series books tend to be formula fiction, written according to a recipe and suffering from predictable plots, relatively flat characters, and a writing style that tends toward the unimaginative. Strengths are that children may develop a familiarity with characters who appear in one book after another and also a comfortable feeling from a plot and setting that vary little in each story. When reading from a series, young readers take fewer risks because the books are reasonably predictable. Therefore, series books often have a special appeal for the hesitant reader who is not totally secure with books and who fears striking out into the unknown.

Old series are still popular, like The Hardy Boys and Nancy Drew. Recent series that have captured thousands of devoted readers include The Baby-Sitters Club (Ann Martin), California Diaries (Ann Martin), Sweet Valley Twins (Francine Pascal), Goosebumps (R. L. Stine), Saddle Club (Bonnie Bryant), Pony Pals (Jean Bethancourt), Adventures of the Bailey School Kids (Debbie Dady and Marsha Thornton Jones), Danger.Com (Jordan Cray), and the Anamorphs (K. A. Applegate). Even the early grades have series, like The Kids of Polk Street School (Patricia Reilly Giff) and The PeeWee Scouts (Judy Delton). With the possible exception of romance books, readers tend to immerse themselves in a particular series only until they reach a self-determined level of saturation or finish all the titles. As much as some teachers and librarians believe the weaker of the series books are somehow bad for a reader's literary health, no evidence exists to indicate that those who have indulged, even to extremes, tend to come to a bad end. However, the jury seems to be still out on romance books. Unlike other series, romance books appear under dozens of different imprints and names, each with its own identifiable label that accurately signals the degree of sexual involvement in that series. Young readers of romance stories make the easy transition to romance books for adults that flood wire book racks in endless waves. The number of romance titles and series continues to grow almost astronomically, with signs of continuing addiction detected in this series unlike any others.

The offerings of contemporary realistic fiction are as wide as life, helping explain today's people, problems, and places. In this popular genre young readers can find their own lives, recognize friends, and meet strangers who can show them different ways of living and thinking. Whether the appeal of a book lies in a skillful re-creation of current lifestyles or a comfortable pattern found in a series, the best of contemporary realistic fiction always will examine human beings facing and overcoming the challenges of living today.

REFERENCES

Burnford, Sheila. 1961. *The Incredible Journey.* Boston: Little, Brown.

Chatton, Barbara. 1988. Apply with caution: Bibliotherapy in the library. *Journal of Youth Services in Libraries* 1, 3 (Spring): 334–338.

Dreyer, Sharon Spredeman. 1981–1995. *The Bookfinder: A Guide to Children's Literature About the Needs and Problems of Youth Aged 2–15.* 5 volumes. Circle Pines, Minn.: American Guidance Service.

Fitzhugh, Louise. 1964. *Harriet the Spy.* New York: Harper.

Hautzig, Esther. 1968. *The Endless Steppe.* New York: Crowell.

Haynes, Carol. 1988. *The Explanatory Power of Content for Identifying Children's Literature Preferences.* Unpublished doctoral dissertation, Northern Illinois University, DeKalb, Ill.

Heaton, Margaret M., and Helen B. Lewis. 1955. *Reading Ladders for Human Relations.* Rev. ed. Washington, D.C.: American Council on Education.

Huck, Charlotte S., Susan Hepler, Janet Hickman, and Barbara Kiefer. 1997. *Children's Literature in the Elementary School.* New York: Harcourt.

Parrish, Peggy. 1963. *Amelia Bedelia.* New York: Harper

Stephens, Meic. 1990. *A Dictionary of Literary Quotations.* London: Routledge.

Tomlinson, Carl M., and Carol Lynch-Brown. 1996. *Essentials of Children's Literature.* Boston: Allyn and Bacon.

Tomlinson, Carl M., and Michael O. Tunnell. 1994. Children's Supernatural Stories: Popular but Persecuted. In *Censorship: A Threat to Reading, Learning Thinking,* edited by John S. Simmons. Newark, Del.: International Reading Association.

Trease, Geoffrey. 1983. Fifty years on: A writer looks back. *Children's Literature in Education* 14, no. 3 (Autumn): 21–28.

Wright, Betty Ren. 1983. *The Dollhouse Murders.* New York: Holiday House.

CONTEMPORARY REALISTIC FICTION READING LIST

Ten of Our Favorites

Hunt, Irene. 1976. *Lottery Rose*. Scribner's. A young victim of child abuse gradually overcomes his fears and suspicions when placed in a home with other boys.

Konigsburg, E. L. 1967. *From the Mixed-Up Files of Mrs. Basil E. Frankweiler*. Atheneum. Twelve-year-old Claudia is tired of her life of responsibility, so she and her little brother run away from home and hide in the Metropolitan Museum of Art. Winner of the Newbery Medal.

Lowry, Lois. 1977. *A Summer to Die*. Houghton Mifflin. Thirteen-year-old Meg envies her sister's beauty and popularity. Her feelings don't make it any easier for her to cope with Molly's strange illness and eventual death.

Paterson, Katherine. 1978. *The Great Gilly Hopkins*. Crowell. An 11-year-old foster child tries to cope with her longings and fears as she schemes against everyone who tries to be friendly. A Newbery Honor Book.

Paulsen, Gary. 1987. *Hatchet*. Bradbury. After a plane crash, 13-year-old Brian spends 54 days in the wilderness, learning to survive with only the aid of a hatchet given him by his mother and learning also to survive his parents' divorce. A Newbery Honor Book.

Pullman, Philip. 1988. *The Ruby in the Smoke*. Knopf. In 19th-century London, 16-year-old Sally, a recent orphan, becomes involved in a deadly search for a mysterious ruby.

Rawls, Wilson. 1961. *Where the Red Fern Grows*. Doubleday. A young boy living in the Ozarks achieves his heart's desire when he becomes the owner of two redbone hounds and teaches them to be hunters.

Robinson, Barbara. 1972. *The Best Christmas Pageant Ever*. Harper. The six mean Herdman kids lie, steal, smoke cigars (even the girls), and then become involved in the community Christmas pageant.

Slepian, Jan. 1990. *Risk n' Roses*. Philomel. In 1948, eleven-year-old Skip moves to the Bronx and longs to shed her responsibility for her mentally handicapped older sister and concentrate on her new friendship with the bold and daring girl who seems to run the neighborhood.

Spinelli, Jerry. 1990. *Maniac Magee*. Little, Brown. After his parents die, Jeffrey Lionel Magee's life becomes legendary, as he accomplishes athletic and other feats that awe his contemporaries. At the same time he searches in anguish for a place to call home. Winner of the Newbery Medal.

Others We Like

ANIMALS

Eckert, Allan. 1971. *Incident at Hawk's Hill*. Little, Brown.

Henry, Marguerite. 1990. *King of the Wind*. Macmillan. (Originally published by Rand 1947.)

Kjelgaard, Jim. 1945. *Big Red*. Holiday House.

Mowat, Farley. 1962. *Owls in the Family*. Little, Brown.

Naylor, Phyllis R. 1991. *Shiloh*. Atheneum.

North, Sterling. 1963. *Rascal*. Dutton.

HUMOR

Blume, Judy. 1972. *Tales of a Fourth Grade Nothing*. Dutton.

Cleary, Beverly. 1968. *Ramona the Pest*. Morrow.

Danziger, Paula. 1996. *Amber Brown Wants Extra Credit*. Putnam.

Korman, Gordon. 1991. *I Want to Go Home*. Scholastic.

Lowry, Lois. 1985. *Anastasia Krupnik*. Houghton.

Naylor, Phyllis Reynolds. 1989. *Alice in Rapture, Sort Of*. Atheneum.

See also riddle books and collections of jokes on the children's shelves at libraries and bookstores.

MYSTERIES

Duncan, Lois. 1973. *I Know What You Did Last Summer*. Little, Brown.

Nixon, Joan Lowry. 1986. *The Other Side of Dark*. Delacorte.

Raskin, Ellen. 1978. *The Westing Game*. Dutton.

Roberts, Willo Davis. 1975. *A View from the Cherry Tree*. Atheneum.

Stevenson, James. 1995. *The Bones in the Cliff*. Greenwillow.

Wright, Betty Ren. 1983. *The Dollhouse Murders*. Holiday.

PROBLEM NOVELS

Bauer, Marian Dane. 1986. *On My Honor*. Houghton Mifflin.

Blume, Judy. 1970. *Are You There, God? It's Me, Margaret*. Bradbury.

Byars, Betsy. 1977. *The Pinballs*. Harper.

Cole, Brock. 1987. *The Goats*. Farrar.

Staples, Suzanne Fisher. 1989. *Shabanu: Daughter of the Wind*. Knopf.

Williams, Carol Lynch. 1993. *Kelly & Me*. Delacorte.

SPORTS

Brooks, Bruce. 1984. *The Moves Make the Man*. Harper.

Christopher, Matt. 1988. *Tackle Without a Team*. Little, Brown.

Dygard, Thomas. 1993. *Game Plan*. Morrow.

Spinelli, Jerry. 1996. *Crash*. Knopf.

Slote, Alfred. 1973. *Hang Tough, Paul Mather*. Lippincott.

Slote, Alfred. 1990. *Trading Game*. Harper.

SURVIVAL

George, Jean Craighead. 1972. *Julie of the Wolves*. Harper.

Hobbs, Will. 1996. *Far North*. Morrow.

Holman, Felice. 1974. *Slake's Limbo*. Scribner's.

O'Dell, Scott. 1960. *Island of the Blue Dolphins*. Houghton Mifflin.

Sperry, Armstrong. 1940. *Call It Courage*. Macmillan.

White, Robb. 1972. *Deathwatch*. Doubleday.

Easier to Read

Bulla, Clyde Robert. 1975. *Shoeshine Girl*. Crowell. (Problem.)

Byars, Betsy. 1996. *Tornado*. Harper. (Humor.)

Cleary, Beverly. 1990. *Muggie Maggie*. Morrow. (Humor.)

Christopher, Matt. 1993. *The Dog That Stole Home*. Little, Brown. (Sports.)

Clements, Andrew. 1996. *Frindle*. Simon & Schuster. (Humor.)

Dahl, Roald. 1992. *The Vicar of Nibbleswicke*. Viking. (Humor.)

Giff, Patricia Reilly. 1996. *Good Luck, Ronald Morgan*. Viking. (Humor.)

Park, Barbara. 1982. *Skinnybones*. Knopf. (Humor.)

Peck, Robert Newton. 1974. *Soup*. Knopf. (Humor.)

Smith, Doris Buchanan. 1973. *A Taste of Blackberries*. Crowell. (Problem.)

Sobol, Donald. 1963. *Encyclopedia Brown, Boy Detective*. Nelson. (Mystery.)

Picture Books

Ammon, Richard. 1996. *An Amish Christmas*. Illustrated by Pamela Patrick. Atheneum.

Baylor, Byrd. 1994. *The Table Where Rich People Sit*. Illustrated by Peter Parnall. Scribner's.

Bunting, Eve. 1994. *Smoky Night*. Illustrated by David Diaz. Harcourt.

de Paola, Tomie. 1973. *Nana Upstairs & Nana Downstairs*. Viking.

Polacco, Patricia. 1992. *Chicken Sunday*. Philomel.

Say, Allen. 1997. *Allison*. Houghton Mifflin.

Schertle, Alice. 1995. *Down the Road*. Illustrated by E. B. Lewis. Browndeer/Harcourt.

Shannon, David. 1995. *The Amazing Christmas Extravaganza*. BlueSky/Scholastic.

Viorst, Judith. 1995. *Alexander, Who's Not (Do you hear me, I mean it!) Going to Move*. Illustrated by Robin Preiss Glasser. Atheneum.

Williams, Vera. 1990. *"More More More," Said the Baby*. Greenwillow.

Notable Authors of Contemporary Realistic Fiction

Blume, Judy: Teen and preteen problem novels.

Byars, Betsy: Preteen problem novels.

Cleary, Beverly: Primary and middle grade humor.

George, Jean Craighead: Ecological fiction.

Giff, Patricia Reilly: Primary and middle grade humor.

Hamilton, Virginia: African-American experience.

Henry, Marguerite: Horse stories.

Konigsburg, Elaine L.: Humorous childhood experiences, problem novels.

Lowry, Lois: Teen and preteen problem novels, middle grade humor.

Myers, Walter Dean: African-American experience.

Naylor, Phyllis R.: Mysteries, adolescent humor, animal stories.

Paterson, Katherine: Teen and preteen problem novels.

Paulsen, Gary: Survival and adventure fiction.

Voigt, Cynthia: Teen and preteen problem novels.

Yep, Laurence: Chinese-American experience.

For a more complete list of contemporary realistic fiction titles, consult the compact disc that accompanies this text.

CHAPTER 10

Historical Fiction

Primary grade curricula typically have not included the formal study of history because concepts of time develop slowly in children. How can youngsters to whom next week seems like an eternity, or who ask if grandpa was around when the Pilgrims arrived, possibly gain an appreciation of their historical heritage? However, we have learned that teaching history through narrative, or story, can provide "a temporal scaffolding for historical understanding that is accessible even to quite young children" (Downey and Levstik 1988, p. 338).

Humans tend to think in terms of narrative structures or story grammars, which basically involve characters formulating goals and then solving problems in order to achieve their goals. Children and adults are more likely to process and remember historical information when it comes in the form of a good story (Armbruster and Anderson 1984; Hidi, Baird, and Hildyard 1982; McGowan and Guzzetti, 1991). Therefore, teachers who share and encourage the reading of historical picture books and novels likely are helping students learn historical facts but more importantly are helping them see history as a vital and meaningful subject. Historical fiction can breathe life into what students may have considered irrelevant and dull, thus allowing them to see that their *present* is part of a *living past*, that people as real as themselves struggled with problems similar to their own, and that today's way of life is a result of what these people did in finding solutions.

HISTORY TEXTBOOKS VERSUS HISTORY TRADE BOOKS

History textbooks are *not* effective in helping children make meaningful, personal connections with the past. In fact, studies report that students at all grade levels name social studies (history) as their most boring class and point to their textbooks as one of the major reasons (Fischer 1997; Sewall 1988). As far back as 1893, the National Education Association declared, "When the facts are chosen with as little discrimination as in many school [history] textbooks, when they are mere lists of lifeless dates, details of military movements . . . [t]hey are repellent" (Ravitch 1985, p. 13).

The criticism from historians and educators today has not lessened (Loewen 1995). "[History] textbooks have relied more and more on broken text and pictorial flash to hold student interest. Efforts to render textbooks 'readable'—at least by the standards of readability formulas—have contributed to their arid prose" (Sewall 1988, p. 554).

History texts' biggest problems lie in the fact that they must cover so much material they cannot give justice to any event, person, or concept. For instance, Columbus is allowed only five paragraphs in Houghton Mifflin's fifth-grade history text (Bednarz et al. 1997), though the book also includes a brief excerpt from a historical novel about Columbus's first voyage. The Holocaust is covered in a single paragraph in the same textbook but is given five paragraphs (220 words) in Macmillan/McGraw Hill's book (Banks et al., 1997). Couple these short offerings with "arid prose," and you have a formidable product that separates young readers from "the story of ourselves" (Freedman 1993, p. 41).

If history is indeed the story of ourselves, then another weakness of history textbooks is glaringly evident: The people are missing! The best one-word definition of history is, in fact, "people." Without human beings, whose emotions and actions influence the times, there is no history. Ask anyone who has had a memorable history class to describe why it was good, and the reasons always include a focus on people, whether prominent or ordinary.

Jean Fritz, in her autobiographical novel *Homesick* (1982), recalls her first school experience with American history texts:

> Miss Crofts put a bunch of history books on the first desk of each row so they could be passed back, student to student. I was glad to see that we'd be studying the history of Pennsylvania. Since both my mother's and father's families had helped settle Washington County, I was interested to know how they and the other pioneers had fared. Opening the book to the first chapter, "From Forest to Farmland," I skimmed through the pages but I couldn't find any mention of people at all. There was talk about dates and square miles and cultivation and population growth and immigration and the Western movement, but it was as if the forest had lain down and given way to farmland without anyone being brave or scared or tired or sad, without babies being born, without people dying. Well, I thought, maybe that would come later. (p. 153)

But, it never did.

Not only are people missing in history texts but so are varying historical perspectives. "To present history in simple, one sided—almost moralistic—terms, is to teach nothing worth learning and to falsify the past in a way that provides worse than no help in understanding the present or in meeting the future" (Collier 1976, p. 138).

Indeed, history textbooks approach topics from single perspectives; they have space to do little else (Foster, Morris, and Davis 1996; Tunnell and Ammon 1996). For instance, the American Revolution typically has been reported from the Whig perspective, which depicts "simple, freedom-loving farmers marching in a crusade to fulfill God's plan for a rationally ordered society based on the principles of liberty and equality" (Collier 1976, p. 133). There are other points of view, however, such as the Imperialist view, which draws attention to the British perspective, and the Progressive view, which promotes economic reasons for the war above ideological or religious reasons. By the same token, Columbus is presented in elementary-school textbooks only from a Eurocentric perspective. Of course, the Native Americans have a defensible point of view that deglorifies Columbus, but this perspective is covertly censored (Shannon 1989) from textbook pages simply by not being mentioned.

So, "when a textbook is used as the only source of information, students tend to accept the author's statements without question" (Holmes and Ammon 1985, p. 366). But, once again, history never has a single side to its story, and children's literature in the form of historical fiction (and historical nonfiction) is more likely to invite "the reader to enter into a historical discussion that involves making judgments about issues of morality. . . . What was it like to be a person here? What was the nature of good and evil in that time and place, and with whom shall my sympathies lie?" (Levstik 1989, p. 137).

This sort of critical thinking about the story of ourselves involves examining conflicting viewpoints and making personal judgments. For example, several pieces of historical fiction for young readers approach the American Revolution from differing perspectives, books such as Esther Forbes's (1943) *Johnny Tremain*, a Whig treatment of the Revolution; James and Christopher Collier's (1974) *My Brother Sam Is Dead*, a combination of Whig and Progressive treatments; Avi's (1984) *The Fighting Ground*, wherein a boy changes from a flaming Patriot to wondering which side (if any) he is on; Scott O'Dell's (1980) *Sarah Bishop*, told through the eyes of a girl from a Loyalist, or Tory, family who is brutalized by the war; and the Colliers' (1981) *Jump Ship to Freedom*, an African-American perspective of the Revolution that tells of broken promises of liberty and justice for all. Read in combination, these titles provide the fodder for discussing, debating, and questioning the human motives behind the historical facts. Plus, historical fiction can be an engaging reading experience, which is perhaps the most important reason to involve its use in the classroom.

WHAT MAKES GOOD HISTORICAL FICTION?

Historical fiction must, of course, be set in the past. The main characters generally are fictional, though often they rub shoulders with historically prominent people. Sometimes the story's focus is not on events in history but rather on a wholly imaginary plot that is accurately set in a particular period and place from the past. An example is Wilson Rawls's (1961) immortal dog story, *Where the Red Fern Grows*, which is set in the Ozarks of Oklahoma in the 1920s. Other times the story's plot will involve the protagonist in famous historical events, such as the fictional Johnny Tremain's involvement in the Boston Tea Party and the Battles of Lexington and Concord (Forbes 1943). Sometimes it is difficult to decide whether certain books are contemporary or historical. Often the determining factor is the age of the reader; the Vietnam War may be contemporary for adult readers but ancient history to a fifth grader.

Historical fiction is judged by the same criteria as any other piece of fiction: strength of character development and plot, writing style, definition of setting, handling of theme. However, some considerations are peculiar to the genre.

HISTORY SHOULD NOT BE SUGAR-COATED.   When dealing with historical events, it is important to deal plainly with the truth. Several decades ago, some particularly unsettling truths were avoided or even revised in books written for children. The age of new realism in children's literature, which started in the mid-1960s, began a trend that dictated more honesty in the writing of realistic fiction. Topics that mostly had been avoided began to appear more frequently, such as the Japanese-American internment camps in the United States during World War II (*Journey to Topaz* by Yoshiko Uchida, 1971) or the frank treatment of the horrors of slavery (*Nightjohn,* by Gary Paulsen, 1993).

Kathryn Lasky (1990) explains that an author of historical fiction has the responsibility to preserve what she calls "the fabric of time" by remaining faithful to the historical context in which a story is set. Lasky (1983) herself confronted the difficulty some readers have with that honesty after publication of her book *Beyond the Divide*. In her research she learned that women in the Old West were constant targets of crime. They often were left alone and were vulnerable to rape and murder. And if they were raped, the women generally were ostracized, as happened with Serena Billings in *Beyond the Divide*. Lasky received a letter from an adult reader who was angry not so much because Serena was raped but because she was ostracized. The reader said, "[This] account did not set a good example for coping with the hurt and trauma that accompanies rape or for teaching young readers how they might cope with it" (Lasky 1990, p. 164). Lasky responded by saying, "As a writer of historical fiction, I have an obligation to remain faithful, to remain accountable in my story telling, to the manners and mores and the practices of the period" (1990, p. 165).

Indeed, much of our history is unsavory. But the lessons history has to teach us will go unlearned if we are forever softening the message. Understanding and being sickened by Serena's treatment help us become more aware of righting the mistakes of the past. In the immortal words of George Santayana, "Those who cannot remember the past are condemned to repeat it."

HISTORICAL ACCURACY IS REQUIRED. Because historical fiction is rooted in history, an infrastructure of accurate historical facts is necessary. When events are documented, they must not be altered. However, when fictionalizing history, authors may take some liberties. For example, they may create dialogue for famous individuals (but should not put words into their mouths that don't match with their known attitudes and personalities) or may patch in an invented character. To serve the purpose of storytelling, for instance, Esther Forbes (1943) created conversations between Johnny Tremain and many of the well-known Sons of Liberty. What Paul Revere said to Johnny is certainly not factual, although it reflects what Forbes knew about Revere's attitudes and personal life. The fictional Johnny serves as a vehicle to unite in an efficient way the major people and the complex events of the Boston Revolt, pulling fragmented occurrences together into a cohesive story. On the other hand, if Forbes had invented a surprise appearance of George Washington at the Boston Tea Party for dramatic effect, the reworking of the facts would have strained the story's historical credibility.

THE STORY MUST MAKE THE HISTORICAL PERIOD COME TO LIFE. A historical period is brought to life when the author re-creates the physical environment, patterns of daily living, and spirit of the times. What was it like to live from day to day in Boston in 1775? Or London in 1215? What did a servant eat? What diseases were feared? Who went to school and who didn't? Mollie Hunter (1976, p. 43), winner of Britain's Carnegie Award for her historical novel *The Stronghold* (1974), feels that this sort of realism can best be communicated in writing when authors have come to know the place and time so well that they "could walk undetected in the past," waking in the morning to know the sort of bed they'd be sleeping in or reaching in their pockets to grasp familiar coins. Creating this atmosphere in a novel also depends on avoiding modern terms. Joan Blos (1985), author of the Newbery Award-winning *A Gathering of Days* (1979), points out that authors of historical novels struggle with the compromises that must be made in maintaining strict historical validity and says sometimes the rules require bending to make a story readable. An overabundance of archaic speech in a story of the Middle Ages may derail a young reader. However, she says, "historical material and thought lack validity if expressed in modern phrases, idioms, or linguistic rhythms," as in this example relating to the American Revolution: "Peering out of her bedroom window, Deeny saw bunches of Hessians heading for the green" (1985, p. 39). "Bunches" to describe groups of people is an informal, modern use of the word that is out of place in a colonial American setting.

Re-creating the spirit of the times may be the most important and most difficult challenge an author faces. To understand the motivating factors that led individuals or groups of people to make decisions that altered the patterns of life or the course of political history is not a simple affair. What stirred the winds of change or suppressed them? The spirit of the times fueled the rebellion against the Crown or encouraged the acceptance of slavery, but as is true in today's world, not everyone was moved by the spirit in the same way. Tories resisted the American Revolution, and some southerners operated stations on the Underground Railroad. Yet, these varying perspectives that often led to the conflicts that initiated change are the very sort of spirit that should permeate good historical stories.

THE STORY USUALLY REVEALS HISTORY THROUGH THE EYES OF A YOUNG PROTAGONIST.   Although young main characters seem a requirement for most children's fiction, historical novels have an especially pressing need for them. Because young readers are accosted with a study of history that generally ignores the little people—people like themselves—almost no children are ever mentioned. Therefore, the gap between themselves and the dusty past widens. A young protagonist who is inserted into the tumultuous times of the Boston Revolt or the difficult period of the Great Depression allows young readers to experience history through the senses of someone who views life in a similar way—as a child.

Jane Yolen (1989) tells of being invited to talk to a group of eighth graders about the Holocaust. Horrified, the students asked her if she made "all that stuff up." The realities of Europe in the 1930s and '40s were so far outside their realms of experience that they thought this story of such massive human suffering was a joke. People couldn't do such things to one another. Yolen's answer to this problem is found in her novel *The Devil's Arithmetic* (1988), which uses a fantasy technique to transport a 14-year-old American Jewish girl of the 1980s back to World War II Poland. As a youngster disconnected with her own past, Hannah is allowed to experience personally the spirit of the times and ask questions such as "How could you be so dumb as to believe those Nazis when they say you are only being resettled?" Says Yolen, "Children are mired in the present. . . . [So, by] taking a child out of that *today* in a novel, [with] a child protagonist that the reader identifies fully with, and throwing the child backwards or forwards in time, the reader too is thrown into the slipstream of yesterday or tomorrow. The reader becomes part of that 'living and continuous process,' forced to acknowledge that we *are* our past just as we *are* our future" (1989, p. 248).

Whether bringing a modern child back in time or creating a young protagonist who is born to that time, authors of historical fiction thereby are able to give their young audience a sense of connecting with the past.

THE WRITING STYLE SHOULD AVOID GIVING TOO MUCH ATTENTION TO HISTORICAL DETAIL.   Telling a good story is still the essence of historical fiction.

Although authors may be tempted to cram in as many details from their historical research as possible, including too much historical detail may make the writing laborious and destroy the sense of story. Joan Blos (1985) notes two common ways an author may give in to this temptation. First, "the overstuffed sentence" (or paragraph or chapter) is loaded with far too many intrusive clauses of historical explanation:

> Zeke was eager to get to the corner. He wanted to be certain that when the procession came by he could see President Abraham Lincoln who, with his running mate, Senator Hannibal Hamlin of Maine. . . . (1985, p. 38)

Second, "the privy observed" involves a character who launches into inappropriate descriptions. Blos explains that a good test is to ask whether a contemporary character would carry on about a similar detail and gives this example:

> Sam's mother adjusted one of the four round dials that adorned the front of the white enamelled stove, turning it from High to Simmer, and waiting a minute to be sure that the heat had been reduced. (1985, pp. 38–39)

TYPES OF HISTORICAL FICTION

A STORY OF HISTORICAL EVENTS HAPPENING BEFORE THE LIFE OF THE AUTHOR.   Most historical stories are of the type that are set completely in the past, in a period the author has not personally experienced. This means that the author relies completely on historical research rather than personal experience in creating the story. An example of this common variety of historical novel is Paula Fox's Newbery Award-winning tale of the American slave trade, *The Slave Dancer* (1973).

A CONTEMPORARY NOVEL BECOMES HISTORICAL FICTION WITH THE PASSAGE OF TIME.   When Marie McSwigan (1942) wrote *Snow Treasure* during World War II, it was a contemporary novel based on the heroic true story of Norwegian children who smuggled gold bullion past Nazi guards in broad daylight on their sleds. They hid the gold in a snow cave, from which it was later secreted away by the British. Every one of today's schoolchildren and most of their teachers were not yet born when this event occurred. *Snow Treasure* is now most firmly in the realm of historical fiction.

AN AUTHOR CHRONICLES OWN LIFE STORY IN A FICTIONAL FORMAT. Another variety of historical fiction is unusual because the author recounts episodes from his or her own life. In other words, the story is a fictionalized account of the time period and events experienced by the author but often written years later. The Little House books (*The Little House in the Big Woods*, 1932; *Little House on the Prairie*, 1935; etc.) by Laura Ingalls Wilder are books of this type.

THE PROTAGONIST TRAVELS BACK INTO HISTORY.   Time travel, a feature of fantasy rather than realism, has been used as a mechanism to transport contemporary characters into the past and then later return them to their own time. Everything else in this type of historical novel conforms to the realistic nature of the genre. As mentioned earlier, Jane Yolen's *The Devil's Arithmetic* (1988) is an example of this type.

REVIEWING THE VALUES OF HISTORICAL FICTION

Historical fiction at its best is a good story and can be enjoyed as a read-aloud at home or school or as an exciting individual reading experience. Young readers may be influenced in developing lifelong positive reading behaviors by the power of story found in historical novels and picture books. Of course, historical fiction can quicken dry historical facts and breathe life into the people and events of the past. It may aid young children in developing a sense of time and of how they fit into the scheme of history. Indeed, children may connect, often for the first time, with their own heritage by reading "the story of ourselves" as offered in historical fiction.

REFERENCES

Armbruster, Bonnie B., and Thomas H. Anderson. 1984. Structures for explanation in history textbooks, or what if Governor Stanford missed the spike and hit the rail? In *Learning to Read in American Schools*, edited by Richard C. Anderson, Jean Osborn, and Robert J. Tierney. Hillsdale, N.J.: Earlbaum.

Avi. 1984. *The Fighting Ground*. Philadelphia: Lippincott.

Banks, J. A., B. K. Beyer, G. Contreras, J. Craven, G. Ladson-Billings, M. A. McFarland, and W. C. Parker. 1997. *United States: Adventures in Time and Place*. New York: Macmillan/McGraw-Hill.

Bednarz, S., C. Clinton, M. Hartoonian, A. Hernandez, P. L. Marshall, and M. P. Nickell. 1997. *Build Our Nation*. Atlanta: Houghton Mifflin.

Blos, Joan. 1979. *A Gathering of Days*. New York: Scribner's.

Blos, Joan. 1985. The overstuffed sentence and other means for assessing historical fiction for children. *School Library Journal* (November): 38–39.

Collier, Christopher. 1976. Johnny and Sam: Old and new approaches to the American Revolution. *The Horn Book 52* (April): 132–138.

Collier, James Lincoln, and Christopher Collier. 1974. *My Brother Sam Is Dead*. New York: Four Winds.

Collier, James Lincoln, and Christopher Collier. 1981. *Jump Ship to Freedom*. New York: Delacorte.

Downey, Mathew T., and Linda S. Levstik. 1988. Teaching and learning history: The research base. *Social Education* (September): 336–342.

Fischer, B., ed. 1997. The bottom line. *NEA Today*, 16, no. 4 (November): 9.

Forbes, Esther. 1943. *Johnny Tremain*. New York: Houghton Mifflin.

Foster, Stuart, J. W. Morris, and O. L. Davis. 1996. Prospects for teaching historical analysis and interpretation: National curriculum standards for history meet current history textbooks. *Journal of Curriculum and Supervision*, 11, no. 4 (Summer): 367–385.

Fox, Paula. 1973. *The Slave Dancer*. New York: Bradbury.

Freedman, Russell. 1993. Bring 'em back alive. In *The Story of Ourselves: Teaching History Through Children's Literature*, edited by M. O. Tunnell and R. Ammon. Portsmouth, N.H.: Heinemann.

Fritz, Jean. 1982. *Homesick: My Own Story*. New York: Putnam.

Hidi, Suzanne, W. Baird, and Angela Hildyard. 1982. That's important but is it interesting? Two factors in text processing. In *Discourse Processing*, edited by August Flammer and Walter Kintsch. Amsterdam: Elsevier-North Holland.

Holmes, Betty, and Richard Ammon. 1985. Teaching content with trade books: A strategy. *Childhood Education* 61, no. 5 (May/June): 366–370.

Hunter, M. 1976. Shoulder in the sky. In *Talent Is Not Enough*. New York: Harper.

Hunter, Mollie. 1974. *The Stronghold*. New York: Harper.

Lasky, Kathryn. 1983. *Beyond the Divide*. New York: Macmillan.

Lasky, Kathryn. 1990. The fiction of history: Or, what did Miss Kitty really do? *The New Advocate* 3, no. 3 (Summer): 157–166.

Levstik, Linda. 1989. A gift of time: Children's historical fiction. In *Children's Literature in the Classroom: Weaving Charlotte's Web*, edited by Janet Hickman and Bernice Cullinan. Needham Heights, Mass.: Christopher-Gordon.

Loewen, James. 1995. By the book. *The American School Board Journal* 182, no. 1 (January): 24–27.

McGowan, Tom, and Barabara Guzzetti. 1991. Promoting social studies understanding through literature-based instruction. *The Social Studies* 82, no. 1 (January/February): 16–21.

McSwigan, Marie. 1942. *Snow Treasure*. New York: Dutton.

O'Dell, Scott. 1980. *Sarah Bishop*. New York: Houghton Mifflin.

Ravitch, D. 1985. The precarious state of history. *American Educator* 9, no. 4 (Spring): 11–17.

Rawls, Wilson, 1961. *Where the Red Fern Grows*. Garden City, NY: Doubleday.

Sewall, G. T. 1988. American history textbooks: Where do we go from here? *Phi Delta Kappan* (April): 553–558.

Shannon, Patrick. 1989. Overt and covert censorship of children's books. *The New Advocate* 2, no. 2 (Spring): 97–104.

Tunnell, Michael O., and Richard Ammon. 1996. The story of ourselves: Fostering new perspectives. *Social Education* 60, no. 4 (April/May): 212–215.

Yolen, Jane. 1988. *The Devil's Arithmetic*. New York: Viking Penguin.

Yolen, Jane. 1989. An experiential act. *Language Arts* 66, no. 3 (March): 246–251.

Wilder, Laura Ingalls. 1932. *Little House in the Big Woods*. New York: Harper.

Wilder, Laura Ingalls. 1935. *Little House on the Prairie*. New York: Harper.

Historical Fiction Reading List

Ten of Our Favorites

Avi. 1984. *The Fighting Ground*. Lippincott. Thirteen-year-old Jonathan goes off to fight in the Revolutionary War and discovers the real war is being fought within himself.

Conrad, Pam. 1985. *Prairie Songs*. Harper. Louisa's life in a loving pioneer family on the Nebraska prairie is altered by the arrival of a new doctor and his beautiful, tragically frail wife.

Fleischman, Paul. 1993. *Bull Run*. Harper. Northerners, southerners, generals, couriers, dreaming boys, and worried sisters describe the glory, the horror, the thrill, and the disillusionment of the first land battle of the Civil War.

Lasky, Kathryn. 1983. *Beyond the Divide*. Macmillan. In 1849, a 14-year-old Amish girl defies convention by leaving her secure home in Pennsylvania to accompany her father across the continent by wagon train.

McCaffrey, Anne. 1996. *Black Horses for the King*. Harcourt. Galwyn, son of a Roman Celt, escapes from his tyrannical uncle and joins Lord Artos, later known as King Arthur, using his talent with languages and way with horses to help secure and care for the Libyan horses that Artos hopes to use in battle against the Saxons.

Speare, Elizabeth George. 1958. *The Witch of Blackbird Pond*. Houghton Mifflin. In 1687 in Connecticut, Kit Tyler—who feels out of place in the Puritan household of her aunt and befriends an old woman the community thinks is a witch—suddenly finds herself standing trial for witchcraft. Winner of the Newbery Medal.

Taylor, Mildred. 1976. *Roll of Thunder, Hear My Cry*. Dial. A black family living in the South during the 1930s is faced with discrimination. Because the family owns its own land and is uncharacteristically independent for the era, they have an unusually difficult time living with such prejudice. Winner of the Newbery Medal.

Sutcliff, Rosemary. 1995. (originally published 1955). *The Outcast*. Farrar, Straus. Exiled from his ancient British tribe, Beric is captured by the Romans and forced into slavery but harbors the hope of escaping to return to his homeland.

Watkins, Yoko Kawashima. 1986. *So Far From the Bamboo Grove*. Lothrop. A young Japanese girl, her older sister, and her mother struggle to escape the dangers of an angry Korea as World War II ends.

Yolen, Jane. 1988. *The Devil's Arithmetic*. Viking Penguin. Hannah resents the traditions of her Jewish heritage until time travel places her in the middle of a small Jewish village in Nazi-occupied Poland.

Others We Like

Armstrong, William. 1971. *Sour Land*. Harper.

Collier, James Lincoln, and Christopher Collier. 1974. *My Brother Sam Is Dead*. Four Winds.

Curtis, Paul Curtis. 1995. *The Watsons Go to Birmingham—1963*. Delacorte.

Choi, Sook Nyul. 1991. *Year of Impossible Goodbyes*. Houghton Mifflin.

Forbes, Esther. 1943. *Johnny Tremain*. Houghton Mifflin.

Fox, Paula. 1973. *The Slave Dancer*. Bradbury.

Greene, Bette. 1973. *The Summer of My German Soldier.* Dial.

Hunt, Irene. 1964. *Across Five Aprils*. Follett.

Lasky, Kathryn. 1994. *Beyond the Burning Time*. Scholastic (Blue Sky).

Lowry, Lois. 1989. *Number the Stars*. Houghton Mifflin.

MacLachlan, Patricia. 1985. *Sarah, Plain and Tall*. Harper.

McGraw, Eloise. 1961. *The Golden Goblet*. Coward.

Orlev, Uri. 1984. *The Island on Bird Street*. Houghton Mifflin.

O'Dell, Scott. 1986. *Streams to the River, River to the Sea: A Novel of Sacagawea*. Houghton Mifflin.

Paulsen, Gary. 1993. *Nightjohn*. Delacorte.

Richter, Hans Peter. 1970. *Friedrich*. Holt.

Rostkowski, Margaret I. 1986. *After the Dancing Days*. Harper.

Taylor, Theodore. 1969. *The Cay.* Doubleday.

Uchida, Yoshiko. 1971. *Journey to Topaz*. Scribner's.

Yep, Laurence. 1977. *Dragonwings*. Harper.

Easier to Read

Avi. 1979. *Night Journeys*. Morrow.

Bishop, Claire Huchet. 1980 (1952). *Ten and Twenty*. Penguin Puffin.

Bulla, Clyde Robert. 1956. *The Sword in the Tree*. Crowell.

Coerr, Eleanor. 1977. *Sadako and the Thousand Paper Cranes*. Putnam.

Fleischman, Sid. 1986. *The Whipping Boy*. Morrow.

Gardiner, John. 1980. *Stone Fox*. Crowell.

Herman, Charlotte. 1990. *The House on Walenska Street*. Dutton.

McSwigan, Marie. 1942. *Snow Treasure*. Dutton.

Turner, Ann. 1985. *Dakota Dugout*. Illustrated by Ronald Himler. Macmillan.

Wilder, Laura Ingalls. 1932. *Little House in the Big Woods*. Harper.

Picture Books

Bunting, Eve. 1990. *The Wall*. Illustrated by Ronald Himler. Houghton Mifflin.

Gauch, Patricia Lee. 1974. *This Time, Tempe Wick?* Illustrated by Margot Tomes. Coward.

Goble, Paul. 1987. *Death of the Iron Horse*. Bradbury.

McCully, Emily Arnold. 1996. *The Bobbin Girl*. Dial.

Polacco, Patricia. 1994. *Pink and Say*. Philomel.

Sewall, Marcia. 1986. *The Pilgrims of Plimoth*. Atheneum.

Tsuchiya, Yukio. 1988. *Faithful Elephants: A True Story of Animals, People and War*. Illustrated by Ted Lewin. Houghton Mifflin.

Uchida, Yoshiko. 1993. *The Bracelet*. Illustrated by Joanna Yardley. Philomel.

Winter, Jeanette. 1988. *Follow the Drinking Gourd*. Knopf.

Yolen, Jane. 1992. *Encounter*. Illustrated by David Shannon. Harcourt.

Notable Authors of Historical Fiction

Avi: American history.

Beatty, Patricia, and John Beatty: American Civil War and westward expansion.

Collier, James Lincoln, and Christopher Collier: American Revolution.

Haugaard, Erik Christian: European history.

Lasky, Kathryn: American history.

O'Dell, Scott: Native-American history, American West.

Orlev, Uri: Holocaust.

Rinaldi, Ann: American history.

Speare, Elizabeth George: Colonial America.

Sutcliff, Rosemary: Early history of Britain.

Taylor, Mildred: African-American history.

Uchida, Yoshiko: Japanese-American history.

Yep, Laurence: Chinese-American history.

Wilder, Laura Ingalls: Westward expansion.

For a more complete list of historical fiction titles, consult the compact disc that accompanies this text.

CHAPTER 11

Biography

"Dear Mr. Freedman," a young boy wrote in a letter, "I read your biography of Abraham Lincoln and liked it very much. Did you take the photographs yourself?" (Freedman 1993a, p. 41). Russell Freedman, whose book *Lincoln: A Photobiography* (1987b) won the Newbery Medal, explains that this fan letter expresses the highest praise a biographer can receive.

> Did you take the pictures yourself? he asks. That youngster came away from my book with the feeling that Abraham Lincoln was a real person who must have lived the day before yesterday. That's exactly the response I'm aiming for. After all, the goal of any biographer, any historian, is to make the past seem real, to breathe life and meaning into people and events that are dead and gone. (1993a, p. 41)

Of course, not all biographies are historical. Contemporary individuals are the topics of biographies and certainly autobiographies. Yet, the goal of the biographer ought to be the same—"to breathe life and meaning into people and events" (Freedman 1993a, p. 41).

The word *biography* renders its own definition: *bio* = life, *graphy* = writing. This specialized variety of nonfiction writing focuses on the lives of human beings, mostly people who are famous.

Typical Personalities in Biographies

Because famous personalities typically are the focus of adult as well as juvenile biographies, it is easy to organize biographies by either the careers of the individuals or some other factor responsible for their fame.

Scientists and inventors.   Perhaps Thomas Alva Edison is the most popular inventor in juvenile biographies. Other scientists and inventors popular in juvenile biographies include Albert Einstein, George Washington Carver, the Wright Brothers, Madame Curie, and Alexander Graham Bell.

Political leaders.   The category of political leaders includes presidents and senators as well as kings, queens, and other monarchs. The publishing of this type of biography can be influenced by current elections, coups, or other swings in power. On the eve of a presidential election, especially when no incumbent is running, some publishers will have biographies of both candidates ready for printing. When the results are announced, the winner's biography goes into production and the loser's into the incinerator.

There is fierce competition in the arena of current juvenile biographies. Of course, subjects like Abraham Lincoln are standard and lasting fare, as exemplified by Russell Freedman's *Lincoln: A Photobiography* (1987b), Carl Sandburg's *Abe Lincoln Grows Up* (1928), and many, many other biographies written about Lincoln over the years.

Artists, musicians, actors, authors, and other people from the arts.   The category of people in the arts also has its trendy facet. For example, many musicians and actors popular with young people do not really measure up over time and are soon forgotten, such as the rock group The Strawberry Alarm Clock. Yet, there is a market for quickly done, heavily illustrated with photographs, and reasonably brief biographies of figures in our popular culture. On the other hand, Mozart, the Beatles, and Glenn Miller are musicians who seem to warrant and get serious attention by biographers. Artists and authors are subjects that are less trendy for children. In fact, until recently few biographies of authors had been written for young readers. Now, many children's and young adult authors are writing their autobiographies. *Bill Peet: An Autobiography* is a Caldecott Honor Book about the popular picture book author and illustrator (Peet 1989), and *Homesick: My Own Story* is a Newbery Honor Book in which biographer Jean Fritz (1982) tells of her early years growing up in China.

SPORTS PERSONALITIES.   A few sports figures, like Babe Ruth, Jim Thorpe, Jackie Robinson, and Babe Didrickson Zaharias, withstand the test of time and appear in serious biographies for young readers. Others may be well-remembered in years to come, and yet others are forgotten except by the baseball, football, or basketball aficionado. Again, a trendy element exists in sports biography, almost to the point of dominating the subject. Watch for the slick, photograph-laden biographies that immediately appear after each Olympics, such as those for the reigning women's gymnast.

EXPLORERS AND FRONTIERSMEN.   As expected, a rash of Columbus biographies appeared during the quincentennial commemoration of his monumental voyage. They have provided broad coverage and varied perspectives on the motives for and impact of Columbus's mission. For example, Milton Meltzer's (1990) *Columbus and the World Around Him* is frank, perhaps even critical, about Columbus's shortcomings, and Kathy Pelta's (1991) *Discovering Christopher Columbus: How History Is Invented*, though more complimentary, examines how historian biases and the infusion of myth into history have slanted Columbus's story. Often we think of explorers as being from the past. Of course, our modern astronauts and oceanographers are no less intrepid in pushing back our remaining frontiers and are worthy subjects of current biographies.

HUMANITARIANS.   Jane Addams, Albert Schweitzer, Florence Nightingale, and Mother Teresa may be interesting subjects for young readers because of their daring and selfless deeds. The heroic qualities of humanitarians add special appeal to their stories.

PEOPLE WHO OVERCOME TREMENDOUS ODDS.   Biographies of people who overcome tremendous odds focus on a different sort of heroism. Many biographies have been published about Helen Keller (including her own autobiography), and her story of struggling to overcome nearly insurmountable physical difficulties continues to be popular reading for children and young adults.

VILLAINS.   Is there a place among children's biographies for history's truly wicked? Certainly, most biographies capture the lives of people who have admirable qualities. However, just as in fiction, villains are most interesting. Their stories also provide a contrast and a warning. Adolf Hitler is one of the villains many young readers find most horrific and yet fascinating, as portrayed in the biography *Hitler*, by Albert Marrin (1987).

ORDINARY PEOPLE.   A more recent trend in juvenile biography is the book that focuses on someone who is not famous. Examples are George Ancona's (1990) *Riverkeeper*, a photographic essay and partial biography about the work of John Cronin of the Hudson River Fisherman's Association; Bernard Wolf's (1978) *In This Proud Land: The Story of a Mexican American Family*, which traces a family's migration from the Rio Grande Valley to Minnesota; and Ryan White's (1991) *Ryan White: My Own Story*, a young boy's autobiographical account of his struggle with AIDS. This category includes lesser-known personalities from history, such as the photographer Solomon Butcher, who recorded in photographs the lives of pioneer families homesteading in Nebraska (see *Prairie Visions: The Life and Times of Solomon Butcher* by Pam Conrad, 1991). *Charlotte Forten: A Black Teacher in the Civil War*, by Peter Burchard (1995), is another example. Books like these give children the sense that everyone, not just the big names from history, has a story and can make a contribution.

TYPES OF BIOGRAPHIES

Until the Age of New Realism began to change the face of children's books in the 1960s (see Chapter 5), juvenile biographies generally were fictionalized, sometimes at the expense of honesty and accuracy. Publishers, librarians, and educators felt that children would not read a biography unless it looked and read like a novel. *Fictionalized biographies* are less common today. Instead, fictional treatments of a person's life are often classified as historical fiction. An example is *Upon the Head of the Goat*, Aranka Siegal's (1981) powerful autobiographical story of her family's Holocaust ordeal.

The *authentic biography*, written as true nonfiction, is today's trend in biographies for young readers. Although crafted in expository form rather than in narrative form (as with novels), authentic biographies can be as vigorous and entertaining as good fiction. Milton Meltzer, known for his biographies and informational books about history and social change, says, "I think I've used almost every technique fiction writers call on (except to invent the facts) in order to draw readers in, deepen their feeling for people whose lives may be remote from their own, and enrich their understanding of forces that shape the outcome of all our lives" (quoted in Donelson and Nilsen 1989, p. 259).

Note the stylistic flair Russell Freedman gives to these paragraphs in his Lincoln biography:

> Today it's hard to imagine Lincoln as he really was. And he never cared to reveal much about himself. In company he was witty and talkative, but he rarely betrayed his inner feelings. According to William Herndon, his law partner, he was "the most secretive—reticent—shut-mouthed man that ever lived."
>
> In his own time, Lincoln was never fully understood even by his closest friends. Since then, he had become as much a legend as a flesh-and-blood human being.

> While the legend is based on truth, it is only partly true. And it hides the man behind it like a disguise. (1987b, p. 2)

Fictionalized biographies are almost always *individual biographies*, which deal with the life of a single subject. Authentic biographies are either individual or collective. *Collective biographies* contain a number of short biographical pieces about subjects who have a common trait. For example, Russell Freedman's (1987a) *Indian Chiefs* looks at the lives of six prominent Native-American leaders, including Sitting Bull and Chief Joseph. Often collective biographies feature popular, current personalities, like sports heroes, actors, or rock stars. Although this sort of collective biography may not be well written, the interest level for many young readers is high.

The viewpoints in biographies also vary greatly. Subjectivity can't be avoided totally because authors are humans. For example, if an author is a Holocaust survivor, writing an objective biography of Adolf Hitler would be difficult. Or, a civil rights activist might have trouble writing an honest biography about Martin Luther King, Jr., a biography that would show King's weak points as well as his strong ones. As Newbery-winning author James Daugherty (1972) once said, "when you're writing biography you're also writing autobiography." In other words, how biographers feel about their subjects affects, at least subtly, how they portray them.

When people write about their own lives, the problem with objectivity is even more acute. However, *autobiography* provides the unique viewpoint of self-revelation. What writing about oneself loses in objectivity it gains in wholeness. No one has as complete a view of a life as the one who lives it. Biographers who write of others' lives can never get inside their subjects' heads and hearts, although this distance may allow for a more balanced and objective view.

The scope of a biography is often dictated by format, age of intended readers, and purpose, as indicated by the categories that follow.

PICTURE BOOK BIOGRAPHIES.   Picture book biographies, usually intended for very young readers, are brief and heavily illustrated. Generally 32 pages, the standard length for picture books, such biographies provide an overview, focusing on the highlights of the subject's life. A picture book biography series by David Adler is an example of the authentic, illustrated biographies in this category. Titles include *A Picture Book of Christopher Columbus* (1991a); *A Picture Book of Thomas Jefferson* (1990); *A Picture Book of Martin Luther King, Jr.* (1989); *A Picture Book of Thomas Edison* (1996); *A Picture Book of Eleanor Roosevelt* (1991b); and *A Picture Book of Anne Frank* (1993). Picture book biographies for a more sophisticated reader are created by Diane Stanley and Peter Vennema. Their titles, such as *The Bard of Avon: The Story of William Shakespeare* (1993), *Cleopatra* (1994), and *Shaka: King of the Zulus* (1988), have more text and are enjoyed by children in the middle and upper grades.

SIMPLIFIED BIOGRAPHIES.   Simplified biographies are aimed at newly independent readers and appear as picture books or as chapter books, typically with frequent illustrations. The Dell Yearling Biographies is a series of simplified biographies in paperback written by a variety of authors. David Adler also writes a series called A

First Biography, which includes many of the same subjects as his picture book biography series but for a slightly older audience. Viking's Women of Our Time series, written by a variety of well-known authors, focuses on influential women such as Sandra Day O'Connor, Margaret Mead, Laura Ingalls Wilder, and Mother Teresa. Jean Fritz's popular biographies of American Revolutionary War personalities are included in this category. Though heavily illustrated, these books emphasize the text rather than illustrations as Fritz recounts in lively prose the stories of the lives of Paul Revere, Samuel Adams, John Hancock, Benjamin Franklin, Patrick Henry, and King George III.

COMPLETE BIOGRAPHIES.   Although complete biographies may be in simplified, picture book, or lengthy chapter book format, their purpose is to span the entire life of a subject. Russell Freedman's work is a notable example. His complete biographies include three that appear on the Newbery list: *Lincoln: A Photobiography* (1987b), *The Wright Brothers: How They Invented the Airplane* (1991), and *Eleanor Roosevelt: A Life of Discovery* (1993b). Jean Fritz's complete biographies are also noteworthy. Titles include *The Great Little Madison* (1989), *Make Way for Sam Houston* (1986), *The Double Life of Pocahontas* (1983), and *Bully for You, Teddy Roosevelt!* (1991).

PARTIAL BIOGRAPHIES.   Partial biographies have a more focused purpose than complete biographies. They cover only a segment of the subject's life, as in Sandburg's (1928) *Abe Lincoln Grows Up*, which deals only with Lincoln's childhood, or Golenbock's (1990) *Teammates*, which focuses on the years that Jackie Robinson and Pee Wee Reese worked together to break the color barrier in major league baseball.

JUDGING BIOGRAPHIES FOR YOUNG READERS

Because biography is a brand of nonfiction, good biographies exhibit certain characteristics that vary from those in fiction. Naturally, the need for authenticity cannot be ignored. Authenticity involves several factors. First, and most basic, is that the facts in a biography are accurate. Often biographers will acknowledge their sources of information as a way of letting their readers know that plenty of research went into their writing. Also, authors of authentic biographies must take care with the use of direct quotes. Jean Fritz (1988) makes it clear that she does "not use quotation marks unless I have a source" (p. 759). For instance, in *Can't You Make Them Behave, King George?*, George's mother is quoted as saying, "Stand up straight, George. Kings don't slouch" (1977, p. 8). Although these words may sound fabricated, Fritz found them in *King George III* by John Brooke (1972). Of course, fictionalized biographies take greater liberties with the words spoken by the characters, which is why they often are classified as historical fiction today.

However, authenticity has its less exacting side. It is impossible for biographers to be totally objective. Their personal perspectives will always color the ways in which they present their subjects. Interpretation of events must be based soundly in fact, but, once again, there is always more than one side to a story. On the other hand, a biographer ought to avoid making blatant personal judgments and should allow the actions and words of the subject to speak for themselves. For example, Jean Fritz presents Christopher Columbus as an arrogant, egotistical individual in her brief biography *Where Do You Think You're Going, Christopher Columbus?* (1980). However, she does not state, "Christopher Columbus was a self-absorbed egomaniac." Instead, she allows the reader to come to that conclusion through Columbus's words and deeds, as when he robbed Rodrigo of the promised prize for spotting land first. "Columbus said no, he had, himself, sighted land when he'd seen a light at ten o'clock. How could it be otherwise? Surely God, who had gone to so much trouble to bring him here, meant him to have the honor" (Fritz 1980, p. 30).

One of the shortcomings of some juvenile biographies is to glorify the subjects, to turn them into idols or make them larger than life. This is another form of stereotyping that alienates readers from the subject of a biography instead of helping them know the subject as a real person. To present a balanced view means looking at the blemishes as well as the strong points. Instead of conveying the message, for instance, that Abraham Lincoln was born virtually perfect, a more positive and effective message for young readers is that Lincoln had many of the same human weaknesses as the rest of us, but he was able to rise above them to do great things.

Freedman's Lincoln biography provides a nice blend of blemishes and strong points. We see a Lincoln who was self-effacing, who stood bravely to sign the Emancipation Proclamation (though it was popular with nearly no other politicians), and who wrote the Gettysburg Address. But we also see the Lincoln whose law office was a colossal mess, who argued with his wife ("When Mary lost her temper, the neighbors would hear her furious explosions of anger." [Freedman 1987b, p. 41]), and who suffered from severe depression much of his life. We like this Lincoln better than the one on a pedestal because we recognize him as one of us. Note how human and vulnerable Lincoln appears when forced to end his courtship of Mary Todd:

> Early in 1841, Lincoln broke off the engagement. He had known bouts of depression before, but now he plunged into the worst emotional crisis of his life. For a week, he refused to leave his room. People around town said that he had thrown "two cat fits and a duck fit." He had gone "crazy for a week or two." To his law partner Stuart, who was serving a term in Congress, Lincoln wrote: "I am the most miserable man living. If what I feel were equally distributed to the whole human family, there would not be one cheerful face on earth." (Freedman 1987b, pp. 31–32)

Biographies should, of course, conform to the other standards of good writing. Facts are not enough; those may be obtained from an encyclopedia or biographical dictionary. Biographies must engage young readers with fresh prose and riveting perspective, bringing the subjects to life.

REFERENCES

Adler, David A. 1989. *A Picture Book of Martin Luther King, Jr.* New York: Holiday House.

Adler, David A. 1990. *A Picture Book of Thomas Jefferson.* New York: Holiday House.

Adler, David A. 1991a. *A Picture Book of Christopher Columbus*. New York: Holiday House.

Adler, David A. 1991b. *A Picture Book of Eleanor Roosevelt*. New York: Holiday House.

Adler, David A. 1993. *A Picture Book of Anne Frank*. New York: Holiday House.

Adler, David A. 1996. *A Picture Book of Thomas Edison*. New York: Holiday House.

Ancona, George. 1990. *Riverkeeper*. New York: Macmillan.

Brooke, John. 1972. *King George III*. New York: McGraw-Hill.

Burchard, Peter. 1995. *Charlotte Forten: A Black Teacher in the Civil War*. New York: Crown.

Conrad, Pam. 1991. *Prairie Visions: The Life and Times of Solomon Butcher*. New York: HarperCollins.

Daugherty, James. 1972. *James Daugherty*. Videocassette. Weston, Conn.: Weston Woods.

Donelson, K. L., and A. P. Nilsen. 1989. *Literature for Today's Young Adults*. Glenview, Ill.: Scott, Foresman.

Freedman, Russell. 1987a. *Indian Chiefs*. New York: Holiday House.

Freedman, Russell. 1987b. *Lincoln: A Photobiography*. New York: Clarion.

Freedman, Russell. 1991. *The Wright Brothers: How They Invented the Airplane*. New York: Holiday House.

Freedman, Russell. 1993a. Bring 'em back alive. In *The Story of Ourselves: Teaching History Through Children's Literature*, edited by Michael O. Tunnell and Richard Ammon. Portsmouth, N.H.: Heinemann.

Freedman, Russell. 1993b. *Eleanor Roosevelt: A Life of Discovery*. New York: Clarion.

Fritz, Jean. 1977. *Can't You Make Them Behave, King George*. New York: Coward, McCann & Geoghegan.

Fritz, Jean. 1980. *Where Do You Think You're Going, Christopher Columbus?* New York: Putnam.

Fritz, Jean. 1982. *Homesick: My Own Story*. New York: Putnam.

Fritz, Jean. 1983. *The Double Life of Pocahantas*. New York: Putnam.

Fritz, Jean. 1986. *Make Way for Sam Houston*. New York: Putnam.

Fritz, Jean. 1988. Biography: Readability plus responsibility. *The Horn Book* 64, no. 6 (November/December): 759–760.

Fritz, Jean. 1989. *The Great Little Madison*. New York: Putnam.

Fritz, Jean. 1991. *Bully for You, Teddy Roosevelt*. New York: Putnam.

Golenbock, Peter. 1990. *Teammates*. Illustrated by Paul Bacon. New York: Harcourt, Brace.

Marrin, Albert. 1987. *Hitler*. New York: Viking Kestrel.

Meltzer, Milton. 1990. *Columbus and the World Around Him*. New York: Watts.

Pelta, Kathy. 1991. *Discovering Christopher Columbus: How History Is Invented*. Minneapolis: Lerner.

Peet, Bill. 1989. *Bill Peet: An Autobiography*. New York: Houghton Mifflin.

Sandburg, Carl. 1928. *Abe Lincoln Grows Up*. New York: Harcourt Brace.

Siegal, Aranka. 1981. *Upon the Head of the Goat*. New York: Farrar, Straus and Giroux.

Stanley, Diane, and Peter Vennema. 1988. *Shaka: King of the Zulus*. New York: Morrow.

Stanley, Diane, and Peter Vennema. 1993. *The Bard of Avon: The Story of William Shakespeare*. New York: William Morrow.

Stanley, Diane, and Peter Vennema. 1994. *Cleopatra*. New York: William Morrow.

White, Ryan. 1991. *Ryan White: My Own Story*. New York: Dial.

Wolf, Bernard. 1978. *In This Proud Land: The Story of a Mexican American Family*. Philadelphia: Lippincott.

BIOGRAPHY READING LIST

Ten of Our Favorites

Conrad, Pam. 1991. *Prairie Visions: The Life and Times of Solomon Butcher*. Harper-Collins. A collection of photos and stories about photographer Solomon Butcher (who appears in Conrad's novel *Prairie Songs*) and 19th-century Nebraska.

Freedman, Russell. 1987. *Lincoln: A Photobiography*. Clarion. Photographs and text trace the life of the Civil War president. Winner of the Newbery Medal.

Freedman, Russell. 1993. *Eleanor Roosevelt: A Life of Discovery*. Clarion. A photobiography of the first wife of a president to have a public life and career of her own. A Newbery Honor Book.

Fritz, Jean. 1973. *And Then What Happened, Paul Revere?* Illustrated by Margot Tomes. Coward. A short, illustrated biography of this American Revolution hero. (See the other titles in Fritz's series about personalities from the American Revolution: *Can't You Make Them Behave, King George?*; *What's the Big Idea, Ben Franklin?*; *Where Was Patrick Henry on the 29th of May?*; *Why Don't You Get A Horse, Sam Adams?*; *Will You Sign Here, John Hancock?*)

Fritz, Jean. 1982. *Homesick: My Own Story*. Putnam. (Autobiography.) The author's fictionalized version, though all the events are true, of her childhood in China in the 1920s. A Newbery Honor Book.

Meltzer, Milton. 1990. *Columbus and the World Around Him*. Watts. Covers the voyages of Columbus, the terrible impact of the Spaniards on the Indians, and the ultimate cultural influence of the Native Americans on their white conquerors.

Paulsen, Gary. 1990. *Woodsong*. Bradbury. (Autobiography.) For a rugged outdoor man and his family, life in northern Minnesota is a wild experience involving wolves, deer, and sled dogs. Includes an account of the author's first Iditarod, a dogsled race across Alaska.

Peet, Bill. 1989. *Bill Peet: An Autobiography*. Houghton Mifflin. (Autobiography, picture book.) The well-known author and illustrator relates the story of his life and work, including his years at Disney Studios. A Caldecott Honor Book.

Stanley, Diane. 1997. *Leonardo da Vinci*. Morrow. (Picture book biography.) Follows the artistic and scientific careers of Italian Renaissance genius Leonardo da Vinci.

Stevenson, James. 1992. *Don't You Know There's a War On?* Greenwillow. (Autobiography, picture book.) The author recalls his childhood efforts to win the Second World War, including planting a victory garden, collecting tin foil, and looking for spies.

Others We Like

Burleigh, Robert. 1991. *Flight*. Illustrated by Mike Wimmer. Philomel. (Picture book biography.)

Fisher, Leonard Everett. 1995. *Gandhi*. Atheneum. (Picture book biography.)

Fleischman, Sid. 1996. *The Abracadabra Kid*. Greenwillow. (Autobiography.)

Freedman, Russell. 1990. *Franklin Delano Roosevelt*. Clarion.

Freedman, Russell. 1991. *The Wright Brothers: How They Invented the Airplane*. Holiday House.

Freedman, Russell. 1998. *Martha Graham: A Dancer's Life*. Clarion.

Fritz, Jean. 1991. *Bully for You, Teddy Roosevelt*. Putnam.

Fritz, Jean. 1995. *You Want Women to Vote, Lizzie Stanton?* Putnam.

Gerrard, Roy. 1988. *Sir Frances Drake: His Daring Deeds*. Farrar. (Picture book biography.)

Golenbock, Peter. 1990. *Teammates*. Illustrated by Paul Bacon. Harcourt. (Picture book biography.)

Hyman, Trina Schart. 1981. *Self-Portrait: Trina Schart Hyman*. Addison-Wesley. (Autobiography, picture book.)

Marrin, Albert. 1987. *Hitler*. Viking Kestrel.

Meltzer, Milton. 1993. *Lincoln: In His Own Words*. Illustrated by Stephen Alcorn. Harcourt.

Myers, Walter Dean. 1993. *Malcolm X: By Any Means Necessary*. Scholastic.

Parks, Rosa (with Jim Haskins). 1992. *Rosa Parks: My Story*. Dial. (Autobiography.)

Pelta, Kathy. 1991. *Discovering Christopher Columbus: How History Is Invented*. Lerner.

Szabo, Corinne. 1997. *Sky Pioneer: A Photobiography of Amelia Earhart*. National Geographic.

Severance, John. 1996. *Winston Churchill: Soldier, Statesman, Artist*. Clarion.

Stanley, Diane, and Peter Vennema. 1994. *Cleopatra*. Illustrated by Diane Stanley. Morrow. (Picture book biography.)

Uchida, Yoshiko. 1991. *The Invisible Thread*. Messner. (Autobiography.)

Young, Steve, and Greg Brown. 1996. *Forever Young*. Illustrated by Doug Keith. Taylor.

Collective Biographies

Cummings, Pat. 1992. *Talking with the Artists*. Bradbury.

Freedman, Russell. 1987. *Indian Chiefs*. Holiday House.

Jacobs, William J. 1996. *Great Lives: World Religions*. Atheneum. (See other titles in the Great Lives series.)

Krull, Kathleen. 1995. *Lives of the Artists: Masterpieces, Messes (and What the Neighbors Thought)*. Illustrated by Kathryn Hewitt. Harcourt Brace. (See other titles the Lives of . . . series.)

Leiner, Katherine. 1996. *First Children: Growing Up in the White House*. Tambourine.

Littlefield, Bill. 1993. *Champions: Stories of Ten Remarkable Athletes*. Illustrated by Bernie Fuchs. Little, Brown.

Meltzer, Milton. 1998. *Ten Queens: Portraits of Women of Power*. Dutton.

Provensen, Alice. 1995. *My Fellow Americans: A Family Album*. Browndeer/Harcourt. (Picture book biography.)

Rylant, Cynthia. 1996. *Margaret, Frank, and Andy: Three Writers' Stories*. Harcourt.

Turner, Glennette Tilley. 1989. *Take a Walk in Their Shoes*. Dutton.

Easier to Read

Adler, David A. 1990. *Thomas Alva Edison: Great Inventor*. Holiday House. (See the other titles in Adler's A First Biography series.)

Bulla, Clyde Robert. 1985. *A Grain of Wheat*. Godine. (Autobiography.)

Coerr, Eleanor. 1977. *Sadako and the Thousand Paper Cranes*. Putnam.

Freedman, Russell. 1997. *Out of the Darkness: The Story of Louis Braille*. Clarion.

Giblin, James Cross. 1992. *Edith Wilson: The Woman Who Ran the United States*. Viking. (See other books in the Women of Our Time series.)

Greenfield, Eloise. 1977. *Mary McLeod Bethune*. Illustrated by Jerry Pinkney. Harper.

Kramer, S. A. 1995. *Ty Cobb: Bad Boy of Baseball*. Random House.

Kraske, Robert. 1973. *Harry Houdini: Master of Magic*. Scholastic.

Meaderis, Angela Shelf. 1994. *Little Louis and the Jazz Band*. Lodestar/Dutton.

Osborne, Mary Pope. 1987. *The Story of Christopher Columbus, Admiral of the Ocean Sea*. Dell. (See other books in the Dell Yearling Biography series.)

Picture Books

Adler, David A. 1991. *A Picture Book of Eleanor Roosevelt*. Holiday House. (See the other titles in Adler's Picture Book of . . . series.)

Blos, Joan. 1991. *The Heroine of the Titanic: A Tale Both True and Otherwise of the Life of Molly Brown*. Illustrated by Tennessee Dixon. Morrow.

Cooney, Barbara. 1996. *Eleanor*. Viking.

Crews, Donald. 1991. *Bigmama's*. Greenwillow. (Autobiography.)

Demi. 1991. *Chingis Khan*. Holt.

Fisher, Leonard Everett. 1995. *Gandhi*. Atheneum.

Kellogg, Steven. 1988. *Johnny Appleseed*. Morrow.

Lasky, Kathryn. 1994. *The Librarian Who Measured the Earth*. Little, Brown.

Schroeder, Alan. 1996. *Minty: A Story of Young Harriet Tubman*. Illustrated by Jerry Pinkney. Dial.

Stanley, Diane, and Peter Vennema. 1993. *The Bard of Avon: The Story of William Shakespeare*. Illustrated by Diane Stanley. Morrow.

Notable Biographers

Adler, David: Picture book and simplified biographies.

Fisher, Leonard Everett: Picture book biography.

Freedman, Russell: Photobiographies.

Fritz, Jean: American history biographies.

Krull, Kathleen: Collective biographies.

Marrin, Albert: Biographies for middle school and junior high school readers.

Meltzer, Milton: Biographies and social histories.

Stanley, Diane: Picture book biographies for older readers.

For a more complete list of biography titles, consult the compact disc that accompanies this text.

CHAPTER 12

Informational Books

For 20 years we have asked college students majoring in elementary education for their immediate personal reaction to the term *informational books*. Only a few students in two decades have identified informational books as desirable or interesting. Most have responded negatively. Author Margery Facklam says many adults share this view. "Nonfiction is utilitarian—like underwear and hot water heaters—the kinds of things you *have* to buy when you'd really like caviar and cruisers. Libraries have to buy non-fiction so kids can write reports" (Facklam 1990). What are informational books, and what is it about them that lacks appeal for thousands of college students preparing to teach children and for many librarians?

PURPOSE

Informational books are nonfiction and present current and accurate knowledge about some part of the universe. The information in them is verifiable: sources in a library; letters or journals; or firsthand, observable fact. Expository writing—the form of language that explains and conveys information—is used for creating nonfiction.

Fiction, on the other hand, tells a story. Its purpose is not to present information but to engage readers in the lives of characters who are facing a dilemma. Fiction may be a total invention springing completely from the writer's imagination, but it also may contain accurate information from the world. If fiction does have verifiable fact, that information is always secondary to the story. Narrative writing—the form of language used to tell a story—is used for fiction.

Nonfiction books for children are divided into two main categories, biography (see Chapter 11) and informational books. The Dewey Decimal System, still used in most children's libraries, organizes all knowledge into 10 major categories, each labeled with a number from 000 to 900. Fiction is in the 800s. The rest of the numbers designate nonfiction. The content of this genre is endless: Everything about history, animals, space, technology, geography, music, sports, religion, jokes, folktales, geology, cooking, and so on until all topics and subjects known to humankind are listed.

If the contents of this genre include everything in this interesting and vibrant cosmos, why don't college students flock to informational books? At least three factors may help explain their largely negative responses.

1. *Informational books traditionally are not used for pleasure reading.* When a baby is born, parents who have learned that books can stimulate the intellect of their child and provide bonding experiences begin reading almost immediately to the newborn. Because of the high cost of picture books, they learn early to use the local library where appropriate titles have been collected on shelves labeled something like "First Books," "Beginning Books" or "Easy Reading."

What is the subject matter of these hundreds of books read for pleasure? Almost without exception, they come from the Dewey Decimal System 800s: fiction. All those desirable skills, attitudes, and memories that come from early reading typically are associated with fiction. Reading nonfiction aloud for pleasure generally does not happen.

2.   *Children's visits to the informational section of the library often are unrewarding.* Although some elementary school children discover that reading nonfiction is pleasurable, many of them go to the informational section only when they have been assigned a report. Most children want to find their information as quickly and with as little pain as possible, remembering to change a word in each paragraph so it doesn't have to be put in quotes. They often do not come away from writing a report with a conviction that informational reading is personally rewarding.

3.   *Informational books have a reputation for being boring.* To many college students, the benefit of reading a nonfiction book is to save money on sleeping pills. A lingering impression is that informational books are crammed with facts, have a few stiff drawings, and look more like old textbooks than anything else. It is true that informational books published years ago generally had less appeal than do those of today, but even then, notable exceptions delighted and rewarded readers. The good news is, a major transformation has occurred during the past 20 years. Attractive and appealing informational books are no longer the exception. In the past two decades, no other genre in children's literature has made such dramatic advances in gaining readers' attention.

So, the purpose of an informational book is not merely to present data but also to stir a reader's interest in the subject. When a reader already has an interest, virtually any book with new information about that topic will be appealing. If Frank loves motorcycles, he will embrace almost any book about motorcycles. However, if the reader knows nothing about a particular subject, the book must create an interest. For example, the title of *The I Hate Mathematics! Book* by Marilyn Burns (1975) immediately captures a reader's attention. Then the book itself feeds the reader's initial interest with a lively writing style, fascinating math games and puzzles, and unexpected connections between the young reader's world and math principles.

As with The *I Hate Mathematics! Book*, what makes a book appealing to the average reader generally is not the topic but how it is handled. In the right hands, any topic is potentially exciting. (The converse is also true: In the wrong hands, any topic can be deadly dull.) Fiction and nonfiction have much in common on this point. Skilled writers, regardless of genre, create interest by the smooth and artistic ways they shape their books.

But the writer of fiction and the writer of nonfiction approach their task from different viewpoints. Fiction writers create their world; nonfiction authors report on the real one.

> With fiction, you start with the embryo and build a person's life. You begin with, "What if?" and create a whole world. You work from the inside out. With nonfiction, you start with a complete life—or an invention, or an historical event, or an animal—and take it apart layer by layer to find out what made it happen, or what makes it work. You work from the outside in, like peeling away the layers of an onion. (Facklam 1990)

The writer of compelling nonfiction does not simply collect and display facts but weaves information and details into a vision that reveals the subject in a way readers find irresistible. How do adults recognize nonfiction books that will spark curiosity in elementary students? We can tell the potential of an informational book by picking it up and thumbing through it for no more than three minutes. If we are not "caught" before the time is up, the book ordinarily is not one that will grab younger readers. Usually the "catching" comes during the first minute and generally for one of the following five reasons: (1) attractive format and design, (2) compelling details, (3) fascinating comparisons, (4) unusual subjects or viewpoints, and (5) personalized content.

FINDING GOOD INFORMATIONAL BOOKS

Attractive Format and Design

Conventional wisdom cautions against making a hasty decision about books: "Don't judge a book by its cover." Yet, children pass over books that appear boring or unrewarding. Beverly Kobrin's motto is, "Say NO to ugly books" (Kobrin 1988, p. 59). An informational book may have solid and thoughtful content, but if it does not look interesting, it seldom gets the chance to work on a child unless someone else points out the strengths. Two elements that give a book that chance are color and design.

COLOR.   A common appeal of attractive books today comes from the extensive use of colored artwork and photographs. Recent technological developments in the printing process have resulted in color being less expensive than in the past. The result is a wealth of stunning illustrations and photographs that enrich nonfiction books as never before.

DESIGN.   In years past, nonfiction books looked more like textbooks than they do today. Books for older children were built of substantial chapters with information that seemed to drone on and on. Thinner informational picture books were brief and predictable. Although the content in earlier informational books was largely accurate and dependable, it did little to awaken interest or stir the imagination.

Currently, informational books for children are designed to catch the eye. Careful attention is given to making both the cover and the contents visually appealing. The increased use of illustrations and photographs has resulted in many new titles appearing in picture book format—large, slender volumes that skillfully mix text and illustration to make the content appealing. No longer the exclusive property of the very young, many contemporary picture books are geared for the upper elementary child, and even beyond, by presenting more sophisticated views of the subject matter and dealing with it in depth.

One successful approach to informational books was developed in the late 1970s when Usborne Books in England targeted older readers as an appropriate audience for picture books. In Usborne picture books, content is divided into distinct topics, each with its own focus or viewpoint treated fully on one double-page spread. *The Instant Answer Book of Countries* (Warrender 1978) for instance, presents information about the world. One double-page subject is weather: hot spots, cold spots, most rain, highest and lowest places. Turn the page and find a new point of focus, such as transportation: the country with the largest airline, most miles of roads, fewest cars, smallest street, and broadest highway. Every two-page spread can be read independently. The text is nonsequential, appearing in bite-size clusters near each illustration rather than in full paragraphs in columns. This format invites browsing and satisfies the reader, who can begin anywhere on the page and read as little or as much as desired—finishing only one sentence, skipping randomly throughout, or consuming the entire book.

Other publishers have adopted and sometimes extended this concept. Dorling Kindersley, another British publisher (known as DK Publishing in the United States), kept the double-page spread but uses photographs almost exclusively, varying the layout, and adding more white space. The photographs of each item, trimmed at the borders like paper-doll cutouts, are placed on a white background that highlights them dramatically. In addition, Dorling Kindersley added not only individual titles but also a number of distinct series: general information, art, science, and nature for younger readers.

With the right format and layout, books written even for the very young can capture the attention of adults. *Color Zoo* (Ehlert 1989) is a book of shapes aimed at preschoolers—one shape cut from the center of each heavy page. By overlaying three shapes at a time, Ehlert creates the face of an animal, which changes to a different animal as each page is lifted. Keeping the same set of eyes, the lion (turn page) becomes a mouse, which (turn page) becomes a fox. The young reader practices not only identifying the shapes but also seeing how different animal faces contain those shapes.

Compelling Details

Information becomes interesting when details are included. Details in nonfiction make the difference between showing and telling, just as they do in fiction, but in nonfiction that difference often accounts for a reader becoming interested in a new subject or ignoring it. Without sufficient details, it is difficult for the reader to be involved in a subject and experience a kinship with it. Details come in a variety of types, including quotations, anecdotes, and little-known facts.

QUOTATIONS.   *The Boys' War* (Murphy 1990) focuses on the Civil War from the viewpoint of boys age 16 and younger (estimated between 250,000 and 420,000) who served in that conflict. Imagining the glory of battle, young soldiers found instead fear and disillusionment, resulting in their loss of innocence, as illustrated in a letter written by Private Henry Graves:

> I saw a body of a man killed the previous day this morning and a horrible sight it was. Such sights do not effect [sic] me as they once did. I can not describe the change nor do I know when it took effect, yet I know that there is a change for I look on the carcass of a man with pretty much the same feeling as I would do were it a horse or dog. (1990, p. 75)

The words of the young soldier put a face on the weariness and desensitization described in a general way by the author.

Some informational books have no author's narrative, using only quoted material. Jill Krementz brings insight to young readers by interviewing children and teenagers who have experienced major challenges in their lives: adoption, a parent dying, divorce, or a life-threatening disease. In *How It Feels When Parents Divorce*, many children express the wish that their parents will marry each other again. One 16-year-old did not harbor that hope.

> When my parents were first getting divorced they used to have the most terrible fights on the phone which I can still remember vividly—they would have these violent conversations which were mostly about money. So, one thing you can be sure of is that I was never one of those "divorced kids" who kept hoping their parents would get back together, because when I saw the way they fought, I was just glad there was a phone line separating them. I didn't even want them in the same house. (Krementz 1984, p. 99)

ANECDOTES.   The power of anecdotes lies in the description of a person who has firsthand experience. Anecdotes can come from surprising sources. During the 1800s in the American South, slaves purposefully were kept illiterate and consequently did not keep many written records. Despite that unwritten law, some did learn to read and write, as did many blacks who were free. In Milton Meltzer's *The Black Americans: A History in Their Own Words*, we read the words of Solomon Northrup, a free black who was kidnapped in New York and taken to New Orleans, where he was sold on the auction block. Other blacks were auctioned the same day, including a woman named Eliza who had two children. One, the boy, was purchased separately.

> She kept on begging and beseeching them, most piteously, not to separate the three. Over and over again she told them how she loved her boy. A great many times she repeated her former promises—how very faithful and obedient she would be; how hard she would labor day and night, to the last moment of her life; if he would only buy them all together. But it was of no avail; the man could not afford it. The bargain was agreed upon, and Randall must go alone. Then Eliza ran to him; embraced him passionately; kissed him again and again; told him to remember her—all the while her tears falling in the boy's face like rain. . . .
>
> The planter from Baton Rouge, with his new purchase, was ready to depart.
>
> "Don't cry, mama. I will be a good boy. Don't cry," said Randall, looking back, as they passed out the door.
>
> What has become of the lad, God knows. It was a mournful scene indeed. I would have cried myself if I had dared. (1984, pp. 49–50)

The human drama in this heartbreaking scene, which must have been repeated thousands of times, has greater impact because it is recounted by one who was there.

LITTLE-KNOWN FACTS.   Little-known facts hold elements of both mystery and discovery. There seems to be a "wow" factor associated with this sort of trivia. When you read in *The Do-It Yourself Genius Kit* that "there is enough potassium in the human body to fire a small cannon" (Brandreth 1989), for example, you can't help but say "wow." Little-known facts also help breathe life into a certain historical period, a time of discovery, or an explanation of some phenomenon. They create interest in topics the reader often has not considered worth pursuing.

For example, *Stephen Biesty's Cross-Sections: Man of War* (Platt 1993) explores the little-known facts of life aboard a British warship during the Napoleonic era, when sailing ships ruled the world's oceans. Men on these vessels were at sea for long periods. With no refrigeration, the kinds of food were limited—salt pork, dried peas, salt beef, oatmeal, beer in sealed barrels, and hard, moldy cheese. Fresh bread was out of the question, but each ship had a store of unleavened bread called hardtack, which was something like very thick crackers. Unfortunately weevils and black-headed maggots liked hardtack, too. Sailors inadvertently chewed them up in their bites of hardtack. The sailors found "black-headed maggots were fat and cold, but not bitter . . . like weevils" (Platt 1993, p. 12). Weevils were impossible to dislodge, but the cook knew how to get rid of the black-headed maggots. He placed a raw fish on a plate on top of the hardtack. When it was completely covered with maggots, he threw the fish into the sea, replacing it as necessary until no more maggots appeared. The hardtack then was easier to eat.

The human face of the Holocaust is presented in *Smoke and Ashes* (Barbara Rogasky). Not only does Rogasky present a broad view of treatment of the Jews by the Nazis, but she also offers unusual insights and explanations such as how German children were taught to view Jews. The caption next to the photograph of a board game reads:

> Children were taught from the earliest years to stay away from "the evil Jew." Here is a popular children's game called "Get the Jews Out!" By throwing dice, the winner manages to get six Jews out of their homes and businesses—the circles—and on the road to Palestine. It sold over a million copies in 1938, when Nazi policy was forced Jewish emigration. (1988, p. 24)

Little-known facts create interest in familiar topics as well as new ones. *Amazing Mammals,* for example, describes a fox's unusual hearing. "A fox's ears are so sensitive it can hear a worm wriggling on the other side of a field" (Parsons 1990, p. 15). In the same volume, the sloth's lack of cleanliness is shown to have some merit. "Sloths don't clean their fur. After a while it grows a greenish scum and moths and beetles come to live in it. This is a good disguise—it makes the sloth look like a bunch of leaves" (Parsons 1990, p. 18).

Little-known facts have such an attraction that some books are devoted exclusively to them. *The Do-It-Yourself Genius Kit* (Brandreth 1989) is a slipcased set of four very small paperback books, each listing an assortment of odd bits of information, like the only place in the world where one can see the sun rise over the Pacific Ocean and set in the Atlantic.

Although the facts in these trivia books often appear in random order, a regular sprinkling of such information spices up the classroom by giving students things to think about, sending them to additional sources for verification or further information, and reminding everyone just how broad and interesting this world is.

Fascinating Comparisons

Human beings do not communicate well in the abstract or the complex. When we talk about any abstract or complex concept—kindness, the plight of endangered species, divorce, war, digestion, enormous numbers—we understand much more quickly and clearly when comparisons bring the fuzzy areas into sharp focus. Fascinating comparisons create instant and powerful images, working in much the same manner as metaphor or simile.

Seymour Simon, a former science teacher who has written over 100 informational books for young readers, frequently uses comparisons to clarify his content. In *Saturn*, he mentions that the ringed planet is much larger than Earth. How much larger? "If Saturn were hollow, about 750 planet Earths could fit inside" (1985, p. 5). Made of gases, Saturn is also lighter than Earth. How much lighter? "If you could find an ocean large enough, Saturn would float on the water" (p. 5). Large figures do not communicate well to the young mind; comparisons make the information instantly clear.

In *How Much Is a Million?*, David Schwartz (1985) uses comparisons to give readers a grasp of how the numbers million, billion, and trillion differ from each other by comparing how long it takes to count to each. To count to a million, saying each number completely and going nonstop, would take 23 days. To reach a billion would consume 95 years, and counting to a trillion over 200,000 years.

Fascinating comparisons can be found in the illustrations as well as the text. In *Giants of Land, Sea & Air*, David Peters (1986) shows and discusses huge animals from the past and the present. One animal is featured on each double-page spread. To help the reader understand how massive the beasts are, every picture also includes at the bottom an adult human in correct proportion to the size of the animal.

The digestive process becomes clearer in *Blood and Guts* (Linda Allison) by using a simile. After food leaves the stomach as "a mashed-up, milky liquid," it goes into the small intestine,

> a long, curly tube with a shaggy lining. It is equipped with its own set of digestive juices for final food breakdown. The walls of this tube hug and push the food along in an action called peristalsis (perry STAL sis).
> Peristalsis puts the squeeze on food muscles in the intestinal wall. They contract and relax, forcing the food around and through. It's the same way you might squeeze a tube of toothpaste. (1976, p. 76)

The wonder of food moving through intestines becomes clearer by comparing the process to moving toothpaste in a tube.

Unusual Subjects or Viewpoints

Some subjects are so unusual that they offer appeal simply by being presented. Often the title of the book treating an unusual subject or viewpoint is enough to entice readers to pick it up.

Kids/Shenanigans: Great Things to Do That Mom and Dad Will Just Barely Approve Of (Klutz Press Editors 1992)
Science Experiments You Can Eat (Cobb 1972)
Gold: The True Story of Why People Search for It, Mine It, Trade It, Steal It, Mint It, Hoard It, Shape It, Wear It, Fight and Kill for It (Meltzer 1993a)
Blood and Guts: A Working Guide to Your Insides (Allison 1976)

Books on unusual subjects generally appeal to a wide range of readers. *Arms and Armor* (Byam 1988) is a picture book study of selected weapons and protection against weapons humans have developed since earliest times. The photographs and text are simple enough to appeal to the middle grades and complete enough to satisfy adults. Stone axes are no surprise, nor are the variety of swords and knives used throughout history. But Byam presents some unusual inventions we have used, and continue to use, to hurt each other. The African throwing knife from Zaire is an odd arrangement of sharp edges and five irregularly placed points with one handle. "When thrown, the knife turns around its center of gravity so that it will inflict a wound on an opponent whatever its point of impact" (Byam 1988, p. 22). Another unusual weapon is the Apache pistol used around 1900 in Paris. It has a six-shot cylinder but no barrel, so it was accurate only at point-blank range. Instead of a barrel, it sports a folding dagger ideal for stabbing, and the pistol grip is a set of brass knuckles—three weapons in one.

The unusual topic allows books written for an adult audience to find their place in the elementary classroom. *Alaska Bear Tales* (Kaniut 1983) is a collection of more than 100 encounters between bears and humans in Alaska that have been taken from magazines, newspapers, and personal interviews. The variety is enormous—in length, humor, violence and tension. In these encounters some people were killed, some maimed, and some left unscathed, with the same true for the bears. For example,

> One of the most unusual bear escapes and deaths I've heard about took place near Wainwright. A woman was walking along the beach across the bay from Wainwright. She was gathering coal when she saw a bear approaching. She searched her brain for some means of escape, realizing that she couldn't outrun Nanook. It seemed futile, and as the bear shuffled up to her, it opened its mouth just inches from her. As a last resort, she shoved her fur-mittened fist down its throat and withdrew her arm before it could bite her, leaving the mitten in its throat. The bear instantly started choking, and forgot about its victim. Within minutes it lay suffocated at her feet. (Kaniut 1983, p. 219)

And that is the only incident of a mitten-killed brown bear on record.

Another adult author also successful with children is David Feldman, who asks questions and finds answers about why the world is as it is. His series of 11 books (for example, *How Do Astronauts Scratch an Itch?* Feldman 1996) explores what he calls "imponderables," and during the exploring, teaches children as a by-product how to observe, question, and discover. For example:

• Why do some ice cubes come out cloudy and others come out clear?
• Why don't birds tip over when they sleep on a telephone wire?

- How does the Campbell Soup Company determine which letters to put in their alphabet soup? Are there an equal number of each letter? Or are the letters randomly inserted in the can?
- Why don't crickets get chapped legs from rubbing their legs together? If crickets' legs are naturally lubricated, how do they make that sound?
- What flavor is bubble gum supposed to be? Why is bubble gum usually pink?
- Why do we have to close our eyes when we sneeze?

Personalized Content

A good informational book is not a bucket of facts but a personal tour of a subject. The format and design, the details, the comparisons, and even the topics reflect the individuality of the author and illustrator. What we have not mentioned is that authors of good informational books teach the same way good classroom teachers teach: They examine a subject, think about things, make discoveries, and then share a personal view about what they have learned. Skilled authors of informational books personalize content using the techniques already described, but they also may provide readers with a new, personal perspective on old subjects and may take readers along on an eyewitness journey.

NEW PERSPECTIVE.   When subjects have been around a while, particularly as a part of the curriculum, they sometimes take on a familiarity that produces yawns. Quality informational books prove those prejudices groundless, reminding us it is not the subject that is dull but the presentation. For instance, the eight parts of speech are still taught in most classrooms, although learning about them generally does not rivet students to their seats. Ruth Heller has created a number of picture books to present the parts of speech, using polished meter and stunning illustrations to introduce them in a fresh way. The following text comes from the first 10 pages of *A Cache of Jewels and Other Collective Nouns* (1987)*

A word that means a collection of things,
like a
CACHE
of jewels
for the crowns of kings . . .

or a BATCH of bread all warm and brown,

is always called a COLLECTIVE NOUN.

a SCHOOL of fish

a GAM of whales

From *A Cache of Jewels and Other Collective Nouns* by Ruth Heller. Copyright © 1987 by Grosset & Dunlap. Reprinted by permission of the publisher.

a FLEET of ships
with
purple sails . . .

In *Round Buildings, Square Buildings & Buildings That Wiggle Like a Fish*, Philip Isaacson (1988) looks at dozens of structures including the Brooklyn Bridge. After a brief discussion of the French and Egyptian influences in its stone towers, he mentions the thin cables that support the road and how he sees those massive towers and spidery cables contrasting and interacting with each other.

> Most bridges are made of concrete and steel and tell us about the power of engineering. The Brooklyn Bridge is not like them; it tells us about the shapes of grand old buildings. It will always be a wonder because of a friendly game it seems to play. Its designers wove webs of light wires and cables and hung them from the towers to hold the bridge's roadways and paths. The fat towers make the webs look silky, and the silky webs make the towers seem even heavier than they are. This game of tag will go on forever. (Isaacson 1988, p. 14)

The interplay of towers and cables adds to the beauty of the Brooklyn Bridge.

From *Round Buildings, Square Buildings & Buildings That Wiggle Like a Fish* by Philip M. Isaacson. Copyright © 1988 by Philip M. Isaacson. Reprinted by permission of Alfred A. Knopf, Inc.

The human body is the same today as it has been for thousands of years, but Jonathan Miller's (1993) views in *The Human Body* show its characteristics in a new light. Opening the pop-up book, the front of a skull snaps into shape about five inches off the page, the left half showing bone and the right half a variety of muscles. Anatomically accurate but looking slightly macabre, the jaw moves up and down when the cover is wiggled, and readers can peer down from the open top of the skull to locate the brain. Using pull tabs, slides, and folds, additional pages show how sounds vibrate the bones in the ear, demonstrate how fibers slide over one another when muscles flex, and allow readers to lift all torso muscles to reveal the stomach and ribs, raise the ribs to expose the lungs, and fold back the lungs to show the heart.

FIRST-PERSON ACCOUNTS.   Another form of personalized content is the first-person account. When the author actually experiences something and then writes about it, the resulting book often has the feel of a personal tour. It is not a recounting of information but an experience where reader and author seem to discover together. For instance, we watch Bianca Lavies as she tries to improve the soil in her home garden by making a compost pile. But what is garbage to Bianca Lavies becomes a banquet for a host of organisms from microscopic bacteria to earthworms and snails, an army of new guests she photographs and describes in *Compost Critters* (1993). The human element and progressive changes she witnesses in her compost pile personalize the way nature creates rich soil.

The same power of personal story is in *Buried in Ice: The Mystery of a Lost Arctic Expedition* (Beattie and Geiger 1992). The authors take the reader on their journey to discover what happened to two ships chasing after the Northwest Passage in 1845. From a frozen and perfectly preserved crewman buried on an island in the Canadian Arctic, the authors determined the fate of the ships and their crews. The reader is present as the mystery slowly unravels, and the authors discover that the crew may have perished from lead poisoning due to a newly developed canning process for preserving rations in the mid-1800s.

The Search for the Right Whale (Kraus and Mallory 1993) documents in text and photographs the work of a team of scientists from the New England Aquarium in Boston in determining migration patterns of a small species of whales called right whales. Using a ship and helicopter, they followed a pod of whales they could identify by their individual markings caused by whale lice. The marine biologists successfully determined when and where the whales traveled, and the reader is present for all the discoveries.

ACCURACY

The basis of all informational books is accuracy. The books exist to introduce the reader to the world or to present something particular about it, so the content must be factual and dependable. But in the past, authors and editors seemed not to be as concerned about absolute accuracy as they are today—factual liberties in informational books for children were winked at. In the name of the readers' immaturity or the need to capture interest, elements were allowed in nonfiction that technically were not accurate. Most compromises involved making animals and objects more human-like. Wild animals in a life-cycle book might have been given names, for instance, making them seem more like pets than denizens of their own world. Or motives were attributed to animals that made them seem human (anthropomorphism): "The deer *wondered* when the snow would melt so he could find grass to eat." Today's nonfiction books for young readers are less likely to take liberties with the facts, and yet, because of their artistry, they retain enormous appeal.

Readers often can recognize the accuracy of an informational book by looking at the author's notes, references, acknowledgments, or appendices. However, footnotes generally are not used in the text because they intrude on the reading and learning experience. The truth is that the average reader, even an adult reader, doesn't know if all the facts are correct in a children's informational book. And taking time to check the accuracy with other sources is laborious. We are, after all, reading the book to learn this information. Today we trust the author to have done appropriate home-work, and we rely on the publisher to have facts checked. Occasionally mistakes do slip through. Certainly, inaccuracies cannot be excused or overlooked, but we main-tain the same position as with books for adults: We take the word of the author until other evidence shows us we should not.

TYPES OF INFORMATIONAL BOOKS

Focused, One-Subject Books

The bulk of children's informational books straightforwardly introduce or explain one subject: animal noses (*Bizarre & Beautiful Noses* by The Santa Fe Writer's Group 1993), plagues (*When Plague Strikes: The Black Death, Smallpox, AIDS* by James Cross Giblin 1995), prehistoric cave paintings (*Painters of the Caves* by Patricia Lauber 1998), tracking whale migrations (*The Search for the Right Whale* by Scott Kraus and Ken Mallory 1993), and superstitions (*Cross Your Fingers, Spit in Your Hat* by Alvin Schwartz 1974). The depth of detail varies according to the format (picture book or chapter book) and target audience (toddler through adolescent), which allows for a picture book of 32 pages to deal with birds in general (*What Makes a Bird a Bird?* by May Garelick 1995) while one species of bird gets an entire chapter book (*The Ameri-can Prairie Chicken* by Mary Adrian 1968).

While all types of informational books tend to keep focused and stick to one sub-ject, similar approaches, presentation, or treatments occur frequently enough that cat-egories emerge. Some books seem to defy description; others carry earmarks that allow them to be labeled. And in labeling them, we realize the breadth of the subject matter. The following categories of informational books can appear in either picture book or chapter book format: activity books (craft, how-to, experiment), concept books, journals and interviews, photo essays, pop-ups, reference books, series, social histories, and survey books.

Activity Books

Activity books include any books that invite the reader to engage in a specific activity beyond the reading. Classic types of activity books include science experiments; how-to, craft, and cookbooks; and art activities, such as Joan Irvine's (1992) *How to Make Super Pop-Ups*. By following clear directions, children are able to create their own three-dimensional pop-ups for cards or books. *Make Believe: A Book of Costume and Fantasy* (Klutz Press Editors 1993) comes with a plastic box of costume jewelry and invites readers to become their own heroes, sports stars, ballerinas, monsters, and meanies easily and inexpensively. *Balloon Science* (Etta Kaner 1989) shows the reader how to use the 50 balloons that accompany the book to learn principles about electricity, air, water, and physics. *Super Flyers* (Neil Frances 1988) teaches how to make paper airplanes, kites, helicopters, parachutes, and gliders, while explaining the aerodynamics that allow both the paper models and their genuine counterparts to fly. Principles of flight are learned as they are applied. In *Fun with Hieroglyphics* (Roehrig 1990), young readers learn about hieroglyphics as they use the chart and 24 rubber stamps accompanying the book to write their own names, make crossword puzzles, and construct messages. *Making Books That Fly, Fold, Wrap, Hide, Pop Up, Twist, and Turn: Books for Kids to Make* (Diehn, 1998) provides the history of various kinds of books plus instructions for making them: a magic carpet book from the Far East, which unfolds one piece at a time until the whole is exposed; a travel journal with a secret middle page for private messages; and a traveling museum book with places to collect bits of information found in field study. Today's offerings in activity books seem practically unlimited.

Concept Books

The first type of informational book a child sees is usually a concept book (discussed at length in Chapter 13), a simplified picture book that presents basic knowledge about one topic in a way both understandable and interesting for a small child learning basic information about the world. Concept books often invite the young reader to engage in some activity to reinforce the idea being presented, such as picking out which object is small and which is large in Margaret Miller's (1998) *Big and Little* or identifying the circles and squares from familiar surroundings in Tana Hoban's (1998) *So Many Circles, So Many Squares.*

Journals and Interviews

Journals and interviews are the two most common kinds of books based on primary sources. *I, Columbus: My Journal 1492–3* (Peter Roop and Connie Roop 1990) offers edited but accurate selections from the log of Columbus's first voyage. Milton Meltzer uses journals from more than one person to paint a specialized picture of an era or event. *Voices from the Civil War* (Meltzer 1989) is a mosaic created from the journals of those who participated in or were affected by America's bloodiest conflict. Interviews, like journals, offer information directly to the reader with only a minimum of author manipulation. Examples include the Jill Krementz books mentioned earlier, such as *How It Feels When a Parent Dies* (1981).

Photo Essays

Photo essays employ photographs in a journalistic fashion to capture emotion and to verify information. Photographs accompany the text on almost every page in a photo essay, as in *Volcano* (Patricia Lauber 1986), the story of the devastating eruption of Mount St. Helens and its recovery from fire, ash, and shifted landmass. But the pictures do more than merely illustrate; they create in the reader a sense of the massive devastation and then kindle emotions associated with recovery as they show nature healing itself. The photographs in Kathryn Lasky's (1998) *Shadows in the Dawn: The Lemurs of Madagascar* perform the same function of extending the information in the text by showing how lemurs move, relate to one another in their society, and respond to the death of an infant lemur.

Pop-Ups

Once pop-up books were largely for entertainment, but today a number of excellent informational books appear in pop-up format. *Nature's Deadly Creatures* (Frances Jones 1992) jump off the page, like the cobra with flickering tongue. Scorpion, black widow, and gila monster all appear in three dimensions along with fold-out information and photos. Ron Van der Meer's series of seven pop-up titles presents overviews of a variety of subjects: art, music, architecture, the brain, math, rock music, and earth (*The Architecture Pack*, 1997; *Music Pack*, 1994; and so on). Sailing ships, castles, the universe, and modes of transportation are a few other subjects that are treated seriously in this format.

Reference Books

Although some children may spend time browsing in reference books or occasionally reading them from beginning to end, young readers generally go to reference books for isolated bits of knowledge. The current trend to make reference books attractive and readable adds a new dimension: reference books as recreational reading. The Eyewitness series, published by DK Publishing and Knopf and often labeled as identification books, is an example of the new generation of colorful, engaging reference tools.

Series

School libraries traditionally have informational books in series, partly because subject areas studied in school provide ready-made topics. For example, elementary schools frequently have a series of books about America, one title per state, which students use mostly for doing reports. Although the information in traditional series is generally acceptable, their appeal is usually low. Often information is neatly stacked in unexciting lines of text that do little to reach out to the reader.

Fortunately, some series have been conceived and executed by those who go beyond simply listing information to seeing inside it. Their views are accurate, and the books convey excitement about the topics. Some examples of series that readers find interesting are listed at the end of this chapter.

Social Histories

A look at an event, era, or prevailing attitude in the past is sometimes called social history. In *The Boys' War*, described earlier, Jim Murphy (1990) shows the Civil War from the point of view of participants under the age of 16. *Children of the Dust Bowl: The True Story of the School at Weedpatch Camp* (Stanley 1992) documents the plight of migrant workers who came to California during the Depression. *Immigrant Kids* (Freedman 1980) shows what life was like for those who left their homes to find new lives in America. Social histories can be narrative accounts or a collection of documentary accounts. Whatever the format, the goal is best expressed by Milton Meltzer: "To meld eyewitness accounts with my narrative to create a dramatic history that will illuminate fundamental issues and bring to life the people who shape them" (1993b, p. 27).

Survey Books

Survey books present an overview of a broad subject. Even when in picture book format, they often are thicker than most other informational children's books because they cover so much material. Although reminiscent of an encyclopedia, survey books are usually far more captivating. For example, *The Smithsonian Book of Flight for Young People* (Boyne 1988) presents a fascinating pictorial history of flight from the Montgolfier brothers' hot air balloon to present-day space travel.

As never before, informational books provide sources for accurate and practical classroom instruction. Evidence that these books are finding their place in the world of children's literature includes the establishment of the Orbis Pictus Award in 1989, the prize given by the National Council of Teachers of English for the outstanding nonfiction book published each year. The Orbis Pictus Award is an indication of what teachers and children have discovered about today's informational books: They not only teach us about the world but also make pleasurable reading.

REFERENCES

Adrian, Mary. 1968. *The American Prairie Chicken*. New York: Hastings House.

Allison, Linda. 1976. *Blood and Guts*. Boston: Little, Brown.

Beattie, Owen, and John Geiger. 1992. *Buried in Ice: The Mystery of a Lost Arctic Expedition*. New York: Scholastic.

Boyne, Walter. 1988. *The Smithsonian Book of Flight for Young People*. New York: Atheneum.

Brandreth, Gyles. 1989. *The Do-It-Yourself Genius Kit*. New York: Penguin.

Burns, Marilyn. 1975. *The I Hate Mathematics! Book*. Boston: Little, Brown.

Byam, Michelle. 1988. *Arms and Armor*. New York: Knopf.

Cobb, Vicki. 1972. *Science Experiments You Can Eat*. Philadelphia: Lippincott.

Diehn, Gwen. 1998. *Making Books That Fly, Fold, Wrap, Hide, Pop Up, Twist, and Turn: Books for Kids to Make*. Ashville, N.C.: Lark Books.

Ehlert, Lois. 1989. *Color Zoo*. New York: Lippincott.

Facklam, Margery. 1990. "Writing nonfiction." Speech at the Highlights Writer's Conference, Chautauqua, New York, 12 July.

Feldman, David. 1996. *How Do Astronauts Scratch an Itch?* New York: Harper.

Frances, Neil. 1988. *Super Flyers*. Reading, Mass.: Addison-Wesley.

Freedman, Russell. 1980. Immigrant Kids. New York: Dutton.

Garelick, May. 1995. *What Makes a Bird a Bird?* Greenvale, NY: Mondo.

Giblin, James Cross. 1995. *When Plague Strikes: The Black Death, Smallpox, AIDs*. New York: HarperCollins.

Heller, Ruth. 1987. *A Cache of Jewels and Other Collective Nouns*. New York: Grosset & Dunlap.

Hoban, Tana. 1998. *So Many Circles, So Many Squares*. New York: Greenwillow.

Irvine, Joan. 1992. *How to Make Super Pop-Ups*. New York: Morrow.

Isaacson, Philip M. 1988. *Round Buildings, Square Buildings, & Buildings That Wiggle Like a Fish*. New York: Knopf.

Jones, Frances. 1992. *Nature's Deadly Creatures*. New York: Dial.

Kaner, Etta. 1989. *Balloon Science*. Reading, Mass.: Addison-Wesley.

Kaniut, Larry. 1983. *Alaska Bear Tales*. Bothell, Wash.: Alaska Northwest Books.

Klutz Press Editors. 1992. *Kids/Shenanigans: Great Things to Do That Mom and Dad Will Just Barely Approve Of*. Palo Alto, Calif.: Klutz Press.

Klutz Press Editors. 1993. *Make Believe: A Book of Costume and Fantasy*. Palo Alto, Calif.: Klutz Press.

Kobrin, Beverly. 1988. *Eyeopeners!* New York: Viking.

Kraus, Scott, and Ken Mallory. 1993. *The Search for the Right Whale*. New York: Crown.

Krementz, Jill. 1981. *How It Feels When a Parent Dies*. New York: Knopf.

Krementz, Jill. 1984. *How It Feels When Parents Divorce*. New York: Knopf.

Lasky, Kathryn. 1998. *Shadows in the Dawn: The Lemurs of Madagascar*. Photographs by Christopher G. Knight. San Diego, CA: Harcourt Brace.

Lauber, Patricia. 1986. *Volcano: The Eruption and Healing of Mount St. Helens*. New York: Bradbury.

Lauber, Patricia. 1998. *Painters of the Caves*. Washington, D.C.: National Geographic Society.

Lavies, Bianca. 1993. *Compost Critters*. New York: Dutton.

Meltzer, Milton. 1984. *The Black Americans: A History in Their Own Words*. New York: Crowell.

Meltzer, Milton. 1989. *Voices from the Civil War*. New York: Crowell.

Meltzer, Milton. 1993a. *Gold: The True Story of Why People Search for It, Mine It, Trade It, Steal It, Mint It, Horde It, Shape It, Wear It, Fight and Kill for It*. New York: HarperCollins.

Meltzer, Milton. 1993b. Voices from the past. In *The Story of Ourselves: Teaching History through Children's Literature*, edited by Michael O. Tunnell and Richard Ammon. Portsmouth, NH: Heinemann.

Miller, Jonathan. 1993. *The Human Body*. New York: Viking.

Miller, Margaret. 1998. *Big and Little*. New York: Greenwillow.

Murphy, Jim. 1990. *The Boys' War*. New York: Clarion.

Parsons, Alexandra. 1990. *Amazing Mammals*. New York: Dorling Kindersley.

Peters, David. 1986. *Giants of Land, Sea & Air: Past and Present*. New York: Knopf.

Platt, Richard. 1993. *Stephen Biesty's Cross-Sections: Man of War*. New York: Dorling Kindersley.

Roehrig, Catharine. 1990. *Fun with Hieroglyphics*. New York: Viking.

Rogasky, Barbara. 1988. *Smoke and Ashes*. New York: Holiday House.

Roop, Peter, and Connie Roop. 1990. *I, Columbus: My Journal, 1492–3*. New York: Walker.

Santa Fe Writer's Group. 1993. *Bizarre & Beautiful Noses*. Santa Fe, NM: John Muir.

Schwartz, Alvin. 1974. *Cross Your Fingers, Spit in Your Hat: Superstitions and Other Beliefs*. Philadelphia: Lippincott.

Schwartz, David. 1985. *How Much Is a Million?* New York: Lothrop.

Simon, Seymour. 1985. *Saturn*. New York: Morrow.

Stanley, Jerry. 1992. *Children of the Dust Bowl: The True Story of the School at Weedpatch Camp*. New York: Crown.

Van der Meer, Ron. 1994. *Music Pack*. New York: Knopf.

Van der Meer, Ron, and Deyan Sudjic. 1997. *The Architecture Pack*. New York: Knopf.

Warrender, Annabel. 1978. *The Instant Answer Book of Countries*. London: Usborne.

INFORMATIONAL BOOK READING LIST

Ten of Our Favorites

Allison, Linda. 1976. *Blood and Guts*. Little, Brown. Discusses the elements and workings of the human body. Includes suggestions for related experiments and projects.

Cobb, Vicki, and Kathy Darling. 1980. *Bet You Can't: Science Impossibilities to Fool You*. Lothrop. A science experiment book that uses tricks as a medium for teaching science principles.

Freedman, Russell. 1994. *Kids at Work: Lewis Hine and the Crusade Against Child Labor*. Photographs by Lewis Hine. Clarion. A photoessay filled with many of the photographs Lewis Hine secretly took in order to expose the cruelties of child labor in the United States during the early 20th century.

Giblin, James Cross. 1987. *From Hand to Mouth, Or, How We Invented Knives, Forks, Spoons, and Chopsticks & the Table Manners to Go with Them*. Crowell. A history of the eating utensils and table manners of various cultures from the Stone Age to the present day.

Isaacson, Philip M. 1993. *A Short Walk Around the Pyramids & Through the World of Art*. Knopf. Introduces tangible and abstract components of art and the many forms art can take, including sculpture, pottery, painting, photographs, and even furniture and cities.

Murphy, Jim. 1990. *The Boys' War*. Clarion. Documents the lives of the young boys who actually fought in the American Civil War. Illustrated with archival photographs.

Rogasky, Barbara. 1988. *Smoke and Ashes*. Holiday House. Examines thoroughly and in a manner appropriate for young readers the Jewish Holocaust of World War II. Illustrated with archival photographs.

Schwartz, Alvin. 1974. *Cross Your Fingers, Spit in Your Hat: Superstitions and Other Beliefs*. Lippincott. Superstitions collected into 23 categories such as love and marriage, money, ailments, travel, weather, school, and death.

Simon, Seymour. 1997 (1980). *Strange Mysteries*. Morrow. Describes nine strange phenomena and possible explanations for them, including the day it rained frogs, an atomic explosion that occurred 40 years before the atom bomb, and an eerie crystal skull.

Stanley, Jerry. 1992. *Children of the Dust Bowl: The True Story of the School at Weedpatch Camp*. Crown. Describes the plight of the migrant workers who traveled from the Dust Bowl to California during the Depression and were forced to live in a federal labor camp and then focuses on the marvelous school that was built for their children.

Others We Like

Arnosky, Jim. 1988 (1977). *I Was Born in a Tree and Raised by the Bees*. Bradbury.

Bauer, Marion Dane. 1992. *What's Your Story?* Clarion.

Blumberg, Rhoda. 1985. *Commodore Perry in the Land of the Shogun*. Lothrop.

Cohn, Amy L., compiler. 1993. *From Sea to Shining Sea: A Treasury of American Folklore and Folk Songs*. Illustrated by eleven Caldecott Medal and four Caldecott Honor Book artists. Scholastic.

Cone, Molly. 1992. *Come Back, Salmon*. Photographs by Sidnee Wheelwright. Sierra Club.

Fleischman, Paul. 1996. *Dateline: Troy*. Illustrated by Gwen Frankfeldt and Glen Morrow. Candlewick.

Giblin, James Cross. 1990. *The Riddle of the Rosetta Stone*. Crowell.

Irvine, Joan. 1992. *How to Make Super Pop-Ups*. Beech Tree.

Jackson, Donna M. 1996. *The Bone Detectives: How Forensic Anthropologists Solve Crimes and Uncover Mysteries of the Dead*. Photographs by Charlie Fellenbaum. Little, Brown.

Jones, Charlotte Foltz. 1996. *Accidents May Happen: Fifty Inventions Discovered by Mistake*. Delacorte.

Kaniut, Larry. 1983. *Alaska Bear Tales*. Alaska Northwest Books.

Lasky, Kathryn. 1998. *Shadows in the Dawn: The Lemurs of Madagascar*. Photographs by Christopher Knight. Harcourt.

Lauber, Patricia. 1989. *The News about Dinosaurs*. Bradbury.

Lauber, Patricia. 1998. *Painters of the Caves*. National Geographic.

Macaulay, David. 1988. *The Way Things Work*. Houghton.

McKissack, Patricia, and Fredrick L. McKissack. 1994. *Christmas in the Big House, Christmas in the Quarters*. Illustrated by John Thompson. Scholastic.

Meltzer, Milton. 1993. *Gold: The True Story of Why People Search for It, Mine It, Trade It, Steal It, Mint It, Horde It, Shape It, Wear It, Fight and Kill for It*. Harper.

Patterson, Francine. 1985. *Koko's Kitten*. Scholastic.

Platt, Richard. 1993. *Stephen Biesty's Cross-Sections: Man of War*. Dorling Kindersley.

Roehrig, Catharine. 1990. *Fun with Hieroglyphics*. Viking.

Rosenthal, Paul. 1992. *Where on Earth: A Geografunny Guide to the Globe*. Knopf.

Simon, Seymour. 1979. *Pets in a Jar*. Puffin.

Swanson, Diane. 1994. *Safari Beneath the Sea: The Wonder World of the North Pacific Coast*. Photographs by the Royal British Columbia Museum. Sierra Club.

Tunnell, Michael O., and George W. Chilcoat. 1996. *The Children of Topaz: The Story of a Japanese-American Internment Camp Based on a Classroom Diary*. Holiday House.

Walker, Barbara M. 1979. *The Little House Cookbook: Frontier Foods from Laura Ingalls Wilder's Classic Stories*. Illustrated by Garth Williams. Harper.

Zotti, Ed. 1993. *Know It All! The Fun Stuff You Never Learned in School*. Ballantine.

Easier to Read

Bare, Colleen Stanley. 1989. *Never Kiss an Alligator*. Dutton.

Brandreth, Gyles. 1989. *The Do-It-Yourself Genius Kit*. Penguin.

Fritz, Jean. 1987. *Shh! We're Writing the Constitution*. Illustrated by Tomie dePaola. Putnam.

Getz, David. 1994. *Frozen Man*. Illustrated by Peter McCarty. Holt.

Grover, Wayne. 1993. *Dolphin Adventure*. Greenwillow.

Lavies, Bianca. 1993. *Compost Critters*. Dutton.

Martin, James. 1993. *Tentacles*. Crown.

Simon, Seymour. 1979. *Animal Fact/Animal Fable*. Illustrated by Diane de Groat. Crown.

Snedden, Robert. 1996. *Yuck!: A Big Book of Little Horrors—Micromarvels In, On, and Around You!* Simon & Schuster.

Sobol, Donald J., and Rose Sobol. 1991. *Encyclopedia Brown's Book of Strange but True Crimes*. Illustrated by John Zielinski. Scholastic.

Picture Books

Aliki. 1979. *Mummies Made in Egypt*. Harper.

Appelbaum, Diana. 1993. *Giants in the Land*. Illustrated by Michael McCurdy. Houghton Mifflin.

Burleigh, Robert. 1991. *Flight: The Journey of Charles Lindbergh*. Illustrated by Mike Wimmer. Philomel.

Heller, Ruth. 1995. *Behind the Mask: A Book About Prepositions*. Grosset & Dunlap.

Hirst, Robin, and Sally Hirst. 1990. *My Place in Space*. Illustrated by Roland Harvey with Joe Levine. Orchard.

Macaulay, David. 1975. *Pyramid*. Houghton, Mifflin.

Miller, Jonathan. 1983. *The Human Body*. Viking.

Parsons, Alexandra. 1990. *Amazing Mammals*. Dorling Kindersley.

Schwartz, David. 1985. *How Much Is a Million?* Lothrop.

Spier, Peter. 1980. *People*. Doubleday.

PUBLISHERS OF INFORMATIONAL BOOKS

Three publishers of nonfiction books for young readers merit special notice. Each produces such interesting books and so many titles that consulting their catalogs is perhaps the easiest way to find books appropriate for individual libraries and classrooms.

- **Usborne Books** pioneered the now-popular format of presenting one aspect of a subject on a double-page spread, complete with many illustrations and snippets of text. Turn the page, and find another focus. Usborne now has over 100 different nonfiction series for children of different ages and interests. Catalog: EDC Publishing, P.O. Box 470663, Tulsa, OK 74147-0663. Phone: (800) 475-4522.
- **DK Publishing, Inc.** (formerly Dorling Kindersley) has more than 20 informational series for young readers plus a wealth of single titles as well as some fiction. DK is noted for fine photography, appealing layout, and information that is intriguing as well as accurate. Catalog: DK Publishing, Inc., 95 Madison Avenue, New York, NY 10016. Phone: (212) 213-4800 ext. 291.
- **Eyewitness Books and Eyewitness Junior Books** are series from DK Publishing but more than 100 titles of these series were published only by Knopf/Random House and not listed or sold by DK (the contract was made before DK had a U.S. office). Catalog: Random House Publishing, 400 Hahn Road, Westminster, MD 21157. Phone: (800) 733-3000.
- **Klutz Press** specializes in the zany, clever, and innovative—in both format and subject. Many of the 71 books published for children come with some sort of manipulative, like the hair bows, ribbons, and clips that accompany *Hair: A Book of Braiding and Styles* (Johnson 1995) and the eight bricks of different-colored clay that are a part of *The Incredible Clay Book: How to Make and Bake Zillions of Permanent Clay Creations* (Sherri Haab and Laura Torres 1994). Catalog: Klutz Press, 455 Portage Avenue, Palo Alto, CA 94306. Phone: (650) 857-0888.

INFORMATIONAL SERIES

For each series of informational books mentioned next, two sample titles are included. The number in parentheses indicates how many titles were in that series as of summer 1998. That number naturally will change with time but provides a general idea of the series size.

Brown Paper School Books (19 titles). Hands-on activities and compelling views of both traditional and nontraditional subjects.

Booth, Jerry. 1988. *The Big Beast Book.* Little, Brown.

Burns, Marilyn. 1976. *The Book of Think (or How to Solve a Problem Twice Your Size).* Little, Brown.

Extremely Weird (16 titles) and *Bizarre & Beautiful* (5 titles). Illustrated with lavish photographs, each title in these two similar series presents unusual animals or strange physical characteristics of animals.

Lovett, Sarah. 1993. *Extremely Weird Snakes.* John Muir.

Santa Fe Writers Group. 1993. *Bizarre & Beautiful Noses.* John Muir.

Imponderables (11 titles). Explanations of events, traditions, and happenings in every-day life. Written for adults; devoured by children.

Feldman, David. 1996. *How Do Astronauts Scratch an Itch?* Harper.

Feldman, David. 1993. *How Does Aspirin Find a Headache?* Harper.

Inside Story (15 titles). Detailed cutaway views of the building and function of histori-cal structures and other engineering marvels.

MacDonald, Fiona. 1996. *The Roman Colosseum*. Peter Bedrick.

Steedman, Scott. 1993. *A Frontier Fort on the Oregon Trail*. Peter Bedrick.

Let's Read-and-Find-Out Science (77 titles—24 Stage 1 [preschool and kindergarten]; 53 Stage 2 [grades 1–3]). Science concepts for preschool through third grade.

Esbensen, Barbara Juster. 1993. *Sponges Are Skeletons*. Illustrated by Holly Keller. Harper. (Stage 2.)

Otto, Carolyn. 1996. *What Color Is Camouflage?* Illustrated by Megan Lloyd. Harper. (Stage 1.)

Magic School Bus (10 titles—plus 6 more based on separate episodes from the ani-mated TV series). Ms. Frizzle takes her class on field trips in a special bus that can change size and function as it travels through various parts of the universe—the human digestive system, the earth's crust, a hurricane, the solar system, and the gener-ators and electric wires that bring power to a town.

Cole, Joanna. 1997. *The Magic School Bus and the Electric Field Trip*. Illustrated by Bruce Degen. Scholastic.

Cole, Joanna. 1996. *The Magic School Bus Inside a Beehive*. Illustrated by Bruce Degen. Scholastic.

Time Quest Books (8 titles). In-depth looks at disasters and historical mysteries.

Reeves, Nicholas. 1992. *Into the Mummy's Tomb: The Real-life Discovery of Tutankhamen's Treasures*. Scholastic.

Tanaka, Shelley. 1996. *On Board the Titanic: What It Was Like When the Great Liner Sank*. Scholastic.

What Makes a . . . a . . . ? (10 titles). Each title focuses on the style, subject matter, and contribution of one famous artist.

Mühlberger, Richard. 1993. *What Makes a Monet a Monet?* Viking.

Mühlberger, Richard. 1994. *What Makes a Picasso a Picasso?* Viking.

Notable Authors and Illustrators of Informational Books

Aliki: Informational picture books for younger readers.

Ancona, George: Photographer and author of photoessays.

Arnosky, Jim: Illustrator and author of nature books.

Blumberg, Rhoda: History—transcontinental railroad, California gold rush, Louisiana Purchase, Commodore Perry in Japan.

Burns, Marilyn: Math topics, primarily hands-on math activities.

Cobb, Vicki: Hands-on science books.

Cole, Joanna: Science topics, notably the Magic School Bus series.

Fisher, Leonard Everett: Illustrator and author of books on a variety of topics—architecture, historical figures and events, social history.

Gibbons, Gail: Informational picture books for preschool and primary grades on a vast variety of topics.

Giblin, James Cross: Informational chapter books about unique subjects—scarecrows; histories of chairs, windows, and eating utensils; plagues; Rosetta Stone; chimney sweeps.

Heller, Ruth: Illustrator and author of brilliantly colored picture books about the individual parts of speech and about plants and animals.

Lasky, Kathryn, and Christopher Knight: Wife (author) and husband (photographer) team; photoessays, primarily about nature topics.

Lauber, Patricia: Physical and natural science topics.

McKissack, Patricia, and Fredrick McKissack: Wife and husband team; books primarily about African-American history.

Meltzer, Milton: Social histories; known particularly for presenting history using the words of those people who lived through it.

Murphy, James: U.S. social histories—immigrant train, Chicago fire, Civil War.

Pringle, Laurence: Natural and physical science books.

Schwartz, Alvin: Specialist in American folk culture; collects superstitions, legends and true stories, scary stories, tongue-twisters.

Simon, Seymour: Physical and natural science topics.

For a more complete list of informational book titles, consult the compact disc that accompanies this text.

CHAPTER 13

Picture Books

Picture books are defined by their format rather than their content. Picture books may be of any genre, including poetry. They are unique because illustrations and text share the job of telling the story or teaching content. No other type of literature works in the same manner.

Picture books often are considered to be only for the very young. Yet, picture books—from rugged board books for babies to the mysterious tales of Chris Van Allsburg, which adults appreciate wholeheartedly—exist for a wide a range of readers. In today's publishing world, the picture book has ascended to a true art form. As full-color printing processes have improved and the demand for quality picture books has increased, some of our best artists and authors spend at least part of their creative lives expressing themselves in the picture book form. (See Chapters 4 and 5 for details about picture book art and about the history and trends in picture book publishing.)

CATEGORIES OF PICTURE BOOKS

Several basic picture book categories may serve as a vehicle for discussing the variety of picture books available. Once again, it is important to remember that these divisions are not mutually exclusive. A single book may fall into several of these categories.

ABC Books

Alphabet books were one of the earliest varieties of illustrated books for children, and artists and authors continue to devise inventive ways of introducing the ABCs to children. In Suse MacDonald's (1986) Caldecott Honor Book *Alphabatics*, for example, MacDonald shows each letter going through an amazing acrobatic metamorphosis: *E* tips, and turns, and mutates until it becomes the legs of an elephant. The alphabet may also be used as a vehicle to introduce or categorize information or concepts for older children. For example, *Illuminations* by Jonathan Hunt (1989) is an ABC introduction to the Middle Ages: *A* is for Alchemist, *B* is for Black Death, and so on (with a paragraph or two of explanation for each term).

One of the most inventive ABC books in recent years is Cathi Hepworth's (1992) *Antics! An Alphabetical Anthology*. Hepworth paints humanlike ants, whose personality traits represent words that begin with each letter of the alphabet and have the letters *a-n-t* embedded in them. For the letter *B*, Hepworth shows an Albert Einstein-type ant labeled "Brilli**ant**," and for *I*, the illustration shows forlorn, turn-of-the-century "Immigr**ant**s" huddled nervously on the deck of a ship.

Another example of a creative approach to the ABC book is *Tomorrow's Alphabet* by George Shannon (1996, illustrated by Donald Crews). It works this way: "A is for seed . . . tomorrow's apple."

One word of caution about ABC books: Most alphabet books are not well suited to teaching the ABCs along with their phonic generalizations, and they are not intended to serve such a purpose. They are meant to introduce fascinating words and interesting concepts and to entertain. However, if a teacher or parent insists on using an ABC book as a medium for teaching the alphabet and its sounds, then care must be exercised to find some of the extremely rare books that conform to this task. Three criteria help to define this type of ABC book (Criscoe 1988, p. 233).

1. Words used to represent each letter must begin with the common sound generally associated with that letter. In other words, blends, digraphs, and silent letters should be avoided. MacDonald's *Alphabatics* violates this principle in its use of *ark* for *A*, *elephant* for *E*, and *owl* for *O*.
2. Illustrations must represent each letter using only one or two objects that are easily identifiable by and meaningful to young children. Once again, *Alphabatics* often violates this rule. For instance, the word *insect* is used for the letter *I*, and the illustration shows an insect along with a large, bright yellow flower. A young child's attention may be drawn to the flower, thus "I" is for "flower."
3. Illustrations must represent objects that do not have several correct names, thus confusing young readers. *Alphabatics* uses *quail* for *Q*, which would certainly be identified as bird by a child. Even the insect in the preceding example would likely be called a bee, a fly, or a bug.

Counting Books

Counting books were also one of the earlier types of picture books for children. Numbers and letters have always been considered the rudiments of early education. However, unlike ABC books, counting books usually do help children learn basic numbers and give them practice counting, typically from 1 to 10.

The simplest form of the counting book provides a printed Arabic number accompanied by the same number of like objects:

However, the better counting books allow for personal discovery and are beautifully illustrated. *Anno's Counting Book* by Mitsumasa Anno (1982) is a fine example.

Anno begins with an important concept generally ignored in counting books: zero. Teachers who work with older elementary children can attest that many of them do not understand how zero works and therefore have problems with place value. So, Anno wisely introduces the idea of zero to children just beginning to learn numbers. The first double-page spread shows a barren snow-covered landscape. The Arabic number "0" is on the right side of the book, and an empty counting stick partitioned into 10 squares is on the left.

Each succeeding double-page spread shows the same scene, only buildings, people, trees, animals, and other objects are added. For example, on the spread for seven, Anno has the Arabic numeral on the right and seven different-colored cubes stacked in front of the counting stick on the left. Also, the once-barren landscape now has sets of seven of a variety of objects: seven buildings, seven children, seven adults, seven evergreen trees, seven deciduous trees, seven colors in the rainbow, seven windows in one of the houses, seven pieces of laundry on the line, and so on. So much can be discovered in each scene that older children who have mastered counting long ago still search the pictures to find all the sets of six, seven, or eight. Even the clock in the church tower always shows the hour of the number in question!

Besides the variety and opportunity for discovery, Anno also offers fledgling mathematicians one final boon: He does not stop at 10. Anno wisely chooses to go on to 11 and 12, two transitional numbers that do not conform to the usual pattern (oneteen and twoteen?). Anno also has applied the twelve numbers to other concepts. The seasons change throughout the scenes and correspond to the twelve months of the year. Twelve hours are, of course, on the face of the clock. As a whole package, *Anno's Counting Book* is a marvel: beautiful naive-style paintings, sound teaching processes, and pure entertainment.

Concept Books

Concept books introduce single, focused concepts to young children. Some typical topics include colors, the idea of opposites (over, under; outside, inside), and the basic geometric shapes. ABC and counting books are usually considered concept books as well. Picture books that deal with topics in greater depth are sometimes called *informational picture books* (see Chapter 12), although the lines between concept and informational picture books may blur. For instance, *How Much Is a Million?* by David Schwartz (1985, illustrated by Steven Kellogg) deals with the concept of large numbers, but the more complex idea may not be for younger children.

Tana Hoban is well known for her classic concept books that are usually wordless and are illustrated with crisp, clear photographs. *Is It Red? Is It Yellow? Is It Blue?* (1978) has become a concept book classic that reinforces a child's knowledge of colors. Quality concept books tend to help children think about ideas, and Hoban accomplishes this by providing a brilliant color photograph of a city or home scene and then placing colored circles below each photo. The young reader is drawn back and forth between circles and photographs to find the matching colors.

Participation Books

A number of picture books are designed to involve children in a physical activity that goes beyond the reading of the text, such as finding hidden objects in an illustration (*Where's Waldo?* by Martin Handford 1987), manipulating the flaps and tabs of a pop-up book (*The Wheels on the Bus* by Paul Zelinsky, 1990), or chiming in with a refrain ("Hundreds of cats, Thousands of cats, Millions and billions and trillions of cats" from *Millions of Cats* by Wanda Gág 1928). *Anno's Counting Book* (Anno 1982) becomes a participation book when children search for and discover the sets of objects representing each number. Another classic participation book is Janet and Allan

Ahlberg's (1979) *Each Peach Pear Plum*, a marvelous romp through the land of fairy tales and nursery rhymes. It is an "I Spy" book wherein small children search for a familiar character hidden in each illustration: "Cinderella on the stairs, I spy the Three Bears." Cinderella, partially hidden in the previous picture, is now in full view, while the Three Bears are difficult to spot as they peek into the cottage through a window.

Of course, participation books also typically fall into other categories. Counting books, for instance, usually demand a child's physical participation, and refrains that invite listeners to chime in often appear in picture storybooks.

Wordless Picture Books

Books without words may seem a contradiction in terms to some parents and teachers. "How can kids learn to read by just looking at pictures?" they ask. But young children reinforce much of what they know about what books are and how books work as they "read" by themselves (left-to-right/top-to-bottom orientations, the grammar of story, personal pleasure of reading). Also, teachers may find that wordless picture books are a vehicle for practicing the language experience approach. For example, children may create their own text for an action-packed wordless book, such as *Frog Goes to Dinner* by Mercer Mayer (1974) or *Tuesday* by David Wiesner (1992). The teacher records the students' dictated text, and the children then read and reread their new, worded version of the picture book. Older children may try their hand at writing the words for a wordless picture book as a creative and meaningful writing experience.

Wordless picture books are meant, above all, to be enjoyed like any other book. They may tell stories or teach concepts, and many of today's offerings are stunning lessons in art. Mercer Mayer is credited with popularizing the wordless picture book, beginning in 1967 with the publication of *A Boy, a Dog, and a Frog*. Mayer's skill at telling a story and creating characters through illustrations is remarkable: Facial expressions speak with the power of words, visual actions foreshadow events, and the story line flows seamlessly. On the other hand, the wordless concept books of Tana Hoban (*Is It Red? Is It Yellow? Is It Blue? 1978*; *Exactly the Opposite, 1990*; *Shapes, Shapes, Shapes,* 1986) teach with economy and clarity, and David Wiesner's work has been awarded the most prestigious U.S. prize for picture book art: a Caldecott Honor Medal in 1989 for *Free Fall* and the Caldecott Medal in 1992 for *Tuesday*. Indeed, wordless picture books have much to offer.

Predictable Books

As young children begin to read, predictable books, sometimes called pattern books, often can be their bridge into the world of independent reading. These picture books are characterized by repeated language patterns, story patterns, or other familiar sequences. However, creating a lifeless, stilted, and uninteresting predictable book is an easy trap to fall into if an author focuses on pattern at the expense of good writing and good story. The best of the predictable books are lively, use interesting words, and invite children to chime in. Bill Martin's *Brown Bear, Brown Bear, What Do You See?* (1964/1992) is a favorite in kindergartens everywhere:

> Brown Bear, Brown Bear, what do you see?
> I see a redbird looking at me.
> Redbird, redbird, what do you see?
> I see a yellow duck looking at me.
> Yellow duck . . . *

Predictable books may use a repeated story pattern, often found in fairy and folktales such as "The Three Billy Goats Gruff" or "The Little Red Hen." Cumulative tales provide even greater repetition, as in "The House That Jack Built." Sometimes a song or verse is predictable because of its familiarity as well as its repetitive language patterns, such as "There Was an Old Lady Who Swallowed a Fly," which has appeared variously in picture book form (see Simms Taback's 1998 Caldecott Honor Book version; Taback, 1997). Even familiar sequences such as numbers or days of the week can make for easily recognized patterns. Eric Carle's (1969) *The Very Hungry Caterpillar* follows an unconventional caterpillar through each day of the week as he eats one, then two, then three of certain foods not meant for caterpillar consumption. The familiarity of numbers and days helps children "read" this well-loved predictable picture book.

Beginning Reader Picture Books

The beginning reader picture book is designed to give fledgling independent readers well-written yet easy-to-read materials. Both Dr. Seuss (Theodor Geisel) and Else Minarik put the beginning reader picture book on the map in 1957 with the publication of Seuss's *Cat in the Hat* and Minarik's *Little Bear*. Minarik's several Little Bear titles became part of Harper's I Can Read Book series, which has continued to be one of the best collections of beginning reader picture books. The series represents all genres, including poetry, and often the books are written and illustrated by some of the best-known names in children's publishing, such as Arnold Lobel and his Frog and Toad books. In fact, *Frog and Toad Are Friends* (1970) was chosen as a Caldecott Honor Book, and *Frog and Toad Together* (1972) as a Newbery Honor Book. Harper also publishes the My First I Can Read Book series, with books that have few words yet tell strong stories. Usually the Harper I Can Read Books are divided into three to five short chapters to give young readers an early introduction to the format of longer books. However, each page is illustrated so that a picture book format is maintained.

Many other beginning reader series have been developed by other publishers in recent years: Dutton's Easy Reader, Random House's Stepping Stone, Simon &

---

*From BROWN BEAR, BROWN BEAR, WHAT DO YOU SEE? by Bill Martin, Jr., © 1967, 1970 by Harcourt Brace & Company, © 1995 by Bill Martin, Jr. Reprinted by permission of Henry Holt and Company, Inc.

Schuster's Ready-to-Read, Dial's Easy-to-Read, Grosset & Dunlap's All Aboard Reading, Scholastic's Hello Reader!, Candlewick's Giggle Club, Dell's Yearling First Choice Chapter Book, the Holiday House Readers, Harcourt's Green Light Readers, and the Dino Easy Readers from Little, Brown. Newbery-winner Cynthia Rylant has created a series of easy-to-read picture books featuring Henry and his dog Mudge (such as *Henry and Mudge and the Happy Cat*, 1990; *Henry and Mudge and the Best Day of All*, 1995; *Henry and Mudge and the Sneaky Crackers, 1998*), as well as the easy reader series about Poppleton the pig and Mr. Putter and Tabby. Not all beginning reader picture books are part of a series. Excellent individual titles may pop up on many publishers' lists.

Adults often will choose any controlled vocabulary picture book for their children merely because the words are overly simplified and seem easy to read. However, many of these titles offer little more than vocabulary practice and are of limited interest to children (see Chapter 3). Strong story and a fresh and lively writing style coupled with a wise control of vocabulary make for easier reading. Beginning reader picture books that are stilted and contrived, that follow the unnatural language patterns evident in the old-style Dick and Jane basal readers, are actually more difficult for young readers (Goodman 1988).

Picture Storybooks

The origin of the picture storybook goes back to the publication in 1902 of Beatrix Potter's *The Tale of Peter Rabbit* (see Chapter 5). What set Potter's book apart from other illustrated books of the time, including books illustrated by Randolph Caldecott and Kate Greenaway, was the true marriage of illustration and story (see Chapter 4). The hallmark of the picture storybook is that text and illustrations work together on each page to tell a story.

Picture storybooks are the most plentiful and the most popular variety of picture book. Most of the Caldecott winners are picture storybooks, and picture storybooks are the most likely choice for parents and children who read together before bedtime. Such books are read to young children long before they are able to read them on their own, and yet these books often hold the best-loved stories from our childhoods and are the foundations of our literacy training. Children typically learn their favorite picture storybooks by heart, thus beginning a process that eventually becomes full-fledged reading. The rich vocabulary and sparkling illustrations help broaden language horizons and develop taste in art.

Engineered Books

The category of engineered books is one of physical structure rather than format or content. In fact, engineered books will always fall into at least one of the other categories previously listed. Paper engineering involves the cutting, folding, or otherwise restructuring of the normal printed or illustrated page. Pop-up books are likely the best-known variety of the engineered book. Jan Pieńkowski has a long-standing reputation for unique pop-up books, such as *Dinnertime* (Carter 1981), *Haunted House* (1979) and *ABC Dinosaurs* (1993). In the 1990s, Robert Sabuda's pop-up books (*The Christmas Alphabet*, 1994; *Cookie Count*, 1997) are also noteworthy.

Often pop-ups include pull-tabs, cardboard wheels to be turned, or flaps to be lifted, thus allowing children to manipulate the pages. In *Haunted House*, for example, pull-tabs cause a skeleton to jump from a wardrobe and ducks in a wallpaper pattern to come to life and flap their wings. Paul Zelinsky's (1990) *The Wheels on the Bus* animates the familiar song with the use of similar manipulatives: Bus doors swing open and a rider steps out, riders bounce as the bus goes over bumps, windshield wipers swish back and forth, and babies' mouths open and close as they bawl.

Some engineered books rely completely on lifting flaps to reveal concept or story elements. Others provide a tactile experience, such as the classic *Pat the Bunny* by Dorothy Kunhardt (1940), which allows children to pet a fuzzy little rabbit. The die-cut book, with pages that have shapes cut away, became the first type of engineered book to be recognized by a Caldecott committee, when *Color Zoo* by Lois Ehlert (1989) received a Caldecott Honor Medal in 1990. Ehlert incorporates die-cuts to teach geometric shapes while creating the figures of animals (see Chapter 12).

Baby/Board Books

Baby books, especially the board book variety, were firmly established as a distinct type of picture book in the early 1980s with the publication of Helen Oxenbury's (1981) books (*Dressing, Family, Friends, Playing, Working*). These comparatively armor-clad books are made from thick cardboard with clear plasticized coatings. They are meant to withstand the buffetings, dunkings, and suckings of babies and toddlers. Many of these baby books are wordless, and each page depicts a single object, such as a shoe or a spoon, that is common in a baby's environment. Sometimes single words or short phrases accompany illustrations. However, Rosemary Wells's Max books are a bit more sophisticated. For example, in *Max's First Word* (1979), big sister Ruby is trying to teach her little bunny brother how to talk, but Max's only word is "BANG!" No matter how she prompts him, "bang" is his only response—that is, until Ruby gives him an apple and says, "APPLE, Max. Say, APPLE." Max's final response: "Delicious."

A picture book trend evident in the last decade is the reissuing of regular format picture books in smaller, board book form. Examples include *The Snowy Day* (Keats 1962), *Strega Nona* (dePaola 1975), and *Freight Train* (Crews 1978)—all Caldecott or Caldecott Honor titles.

Picture books are an abundant resource for initiating children into the worlds of literacy and image. Never before have we had such choices. Today's books are some of the finest ever made available for young readers. Nevertheless, substandard books are still being published, and in great quantity. Parents, teachers, and librarians must make a dedicated effort to share the best picture books with children, for it is the best books that make the most profound impressions on young minds.

REFERENCES

Ahlberg, Janet, and Allan Alhberg. 1979. *Each Peach Pear Plum*. New York: Viking.

Anno, Mitsumasa. 1982. *Anno's Counting Book*. New York: Philomel.

Carle, Eric. 1969. *The Very Hungry Caterpillar.* New York: Philomel.

Carter, Anne. 1981. *Dinnertime*. Los Angeles: Price Stern Sloan.

Crews, Donald. 1978. *Freight Train*. New York: Greenwillow.

Criscoe, Betty. 1988. A pleasant reminder: There is an established criteria for writing alphabet books. *Reading Horizons* 28, no. 4 (Summer): 232–234.

dePaola, Tomie. 1975. *Strega Nona*. Upper Saddle River, NJ: Prentice Hall.

Ehlert, Lois. 1989. *Color Zoo*. New York: Lippincott.

Gàg, Wanda. 1928. *Millions of Cats*. New York: Putnam.

Goodman, Kenneth. 1988. Look what they've done to Judy Blume!: The basalization of children's literature. *The New Advocate* 1, no. 1 (Fall): 29–41.

Handford, Martin. 1987. *Where's Waldo?* Boston: Little, Brown.

Hepworth, Cathy. 1992. *Antics! An Alphabetical Anthology*. New York: Putnam.

Hoban, Tana. 1978. *Is It Red? Is It Yellow? Is It Blue?* New York: Greenwillow.

Hoban, Tana. 1990. *Exactly the Opposite*. New York: Greenwillow.

Hoban, Tana. 1986. *Shapes, Shapes, Shapes*. New York: Greenwillow.

Hunt, Jonathan. 1989. *Illuminations*. New York: Bradbury.

Keats, Ezra Jack. 1962. *The Snowy Day*. New York: Viking.

Kunhardt, Dorothy. 1940. *Pat the Bunny*. Racine, Wisc.: Western.

Lobel, Arnold. 1970. *Frog and Toad Are Friends*. New York: Harper & Row.

Lobel, Arnold. 1972. *Frog and Toad Together.* New York: Harper & Row.

MacDonald, Suse. 1986. *Alphabatics*. New York: Bradbury.

Martin, Bill, Jr. 1964. *Brown Bear, Brown Bear, What Do You See?* New York: Holt, Rinehart & Winston.

Mayer, Mercer. 1967. *A Boy, a Dog, and a Frog*. New York: Dial.

Mayer, Mercer. 1974. *Frog Goes to Dinner.* New York: Dial.

Minarik, Else. 1957. *Little Bear.* New York: Harper & Row.

Oxenbury, Helen. 1981. *Dressing*. New York: Wanderer Books.

Oxenbury, Helen. 1981. *Family*. New York: Wanderer Books.

Oxenbury, Helen. 1981. *Friends*. New York: Wanderer Books.

Oxenbury, Helen. 1981. *Playing*. New York: Wanderer Books.

Oxenbury, Helen. 1981. *Working*. New York: Wanderer Books.

Pieńkowski, Jan. 1979. *Haunted House*. New York: Dutton.

Pieńkowski, Jan. 1993. *ABC Dinosaurs*. New York: Dutton.

Potter, Beatrix. 1902. *The Tale of Peter Rabbit*. New York: Warne.

Rylant, Cynthia. 1990. *Henry and Mudge and the Happy Cat*. Illustrated by Susie Stevenson. New York: Bradbury.

Rylant, Cynthia. 1995. *Henry and Mudge and the Best Day of All*. New York: Bradbury.

Rylant, Cynthia. 1998. *Henry and Mudge and the Sneaky Crackers*. New York: Simon & Schuster.

Sabuda, Robert. 1994. *The Christmas Alphabet*. New York: Orchard.

Sabuda, Robert. 1997. *Cookie Count*. New York: Little Simon.

Schwartz, David. 1985. *How Much Is a Million?* Illustrated by Steven Kellogg. New York: Lothrop.

Seuss, Dr. 1957. *The Cat in the Hat*. New York: Random House.

Shannon, George. 1996. *Tomorrow's Alphabet*. Illustrated Donald Crews. New York: Greenwillow.

Taback, Simms. 1997. *There Was an Old Lady Who Swallowed a Fly*. New York: Viking.

Wells, Rosemary. 1979. *Max's First Word*. New York: Dial.

Wiesner, David. 1992. *Tuesday*. New York: Clarion.

Wiesner, David. 1988. *Free Fall*. New York: Lothrop.

Zelinsky, Paul O. 1990. *The Wheels on the Bus*. New York: Dutton.

PICTURE BOOK READING LIST

Fifteen of Our Favorites

Alexander, Lloyd. 1992. *The Fortune-tellers*. Illustrated by Trina Schart Hyman. Dutton. (Picture story.) A carpenter goes to a fortune-teller and finds the predictions about his future come true in an unusual way.

Anno, Mitsumasa. 1977. *Anno's Counting Book*. Crowell. (Counting.) A counting book depicting the growth in a village and surrounding countryside during 12 months.

Carter, Anne. 1981. *Dinnertime*. Illustrated by Jan Pieńkowski. Paper engineering by Marcin Stajewski and James Roger Diaz. Price Stern Sloan. (Engineered.) Frog, vulture, gorilla, tiger, crocodile, and shark open pop-up mouths, accompanying a story in which each animal is eaten by the next.

Crews, Donald. 1978. *Freight Train*. Greenwillow. (Concept.) Colors and the names of the cars on a freight train are introduced with sparse but rhythmic text and brilliantly colored illustrations. A Caldecott Honor Book.

Henkes, Kevin. 1990. *Julius, the Baby of the World*. Greenwillow. (Picture story.) Lilly is convinced that the arrival of her new baby brother is the worst thing that has happened in their house, until Cousin Garland comes to visit.

Hepworth, Cathi. 1992. *Antics! An Alphabetical Anthology*. Putnam. (ABC.) Alphabet entries from A to Z all have an "ant" somewhere in the word, such as *E* for Enchanter, *P* for Pantaloons, *S* for Santa Claus, and *Y* for Your Ant Yetta.

Mayer, Mercer. 1974. *Frog Goes to Dinner*. Dial. (Wordless.) Having stowed away in a pocket, Frog wreaks havoc and disgraces his human family at the posh restaurant where they are having dinner.

Parish, Peggy. 1963. *Amelia Bedelia*. Illustrated by Fritz Siebel. Harper. (Beginning reader.) A literal-minded housekeeper causes a ruckus in the household when she attempts to make sense of some instructions.

Peet, Bill. 1982. *Big Bad Bruce*. Houghton Mifflin. (Picture story.) Bruce, a bear bully, never picks on anyone his own size until he is diminished in more ways than one by a small but very independent witch.

Sendak, Maurice. 1963. *Where the Wild Things Are*. Harper. (Picture story.) A naughty little boy, sent to bed without his supper, sails to the land of the Wild Things, where he becomes their king. Winner of the Caldecott Medal.

Steig, William. 1982. *Doctor DeSoto*. Farrar. (Picture story.) A clever mouse dentist outwits his wicked fox patient. A Newbery Honor Book.

Turkle, Brinton. 1981. *Do Not Open*. Dutton. (Picture story.) Following a storm, Miss Moody and her cat find an intriguing bottle washed up on the beach. Should they ignore its "Do not open" warning?

Van Allsburg, Chris. 1981. *Jumanji*. Houghton Mifflin. (Picture story.) Left on their own for an afternoon, two bored and restless children find more excitement than they bargain for in a mysterious and mystical jungle adventure board game. Winner of the Caldecott Medal.

Waber, Bernard. 1972. *Ira Sleeps Over*. Houghton Mifflin. (Picture story.) A little boy is excited at the prospect of spending the night at his friend's house but worries about how he'll get along without his teddy bear.

Wells, Rosemary. 1979. *Max's First Word*. Dial. (Baby/board.) It seems Max can say only one word, no matter how hard his older sister tries to teach him others.

Others We Like

ABC

Aylesworth, Jim. 1992. *Old Black Fly*. Illustrated by Stephen Gammell. Holt.

Azarian, Mary. 1981. *A Farmer's Alphabet*. Godine.

Ehlert, Lois. 1989. *Eating the Alphabet*. Harcourt.

Fisher, Leonard Everett. 1991. *The ABC Exhibit*. Macmillan.

Garten, Jan. 1994 (1964). *Alphabet Tale*. Illustrated by Muriel Batherman. Greenwillow.

Harrison, Ted. 1989. *A Northern Alphabet*. Tundra.

Hoban, Tana. 1982. *A, B, See!* Greenwillow.

Johnson, Stephen T. 1995. *Alphabet City*. Viking.

Jonas, Ann. 1990. *Aardvarks, Disembark!* Greenwillow.

Kitchen, Bert. 1984. *Animal Alphabet*. Dial.

Lobel, Anita. 1990. *Allison's Zinnia*. Greenwillow.

Lobel, Arnold. 1981. *On Market Street*. Illustrated by Anita Lobel. Greenwillow.

MacDonald, Suse. 1986. *Alphabatics*. Bradbury.

Martin, Bill, Jr., and John Archambault. 1989. *Chicka Chicka Boom Boom*. Illustrated by Lois Ehlert. Holt.

Provensen, Alice, and Martin Provensen. 1978. *A Peaceable Kingdom: The Shaker Abecedarius*. Viking.

Shannon, George. 1996. *Tomorrow's Alphabet*. Illustrated by Donald Crews. Greenwillow.

Van Allsburg, Chris. 1987. *The Z Was Zapped: A Play in Twenty-Six Acts*. Houghton Mifflin.

COUNTING

Anno, Mitsumasa. 1982. *Anno's Counting House*. Philomel.

Bourke, Linda. 1995. *Eye Count: A Book of Counting Puzzles*. Chronicle.

Fleming, Denise. 1992. *Count!* Holt.

Geisert, Arthur. 1992. *Pigs from 1 to 10*. Houghton Mifflin.

Giganti, Paul, Jr. 1992. *Each Orange Had 8 Slices: A Counting Book*. Illustrated by Donald Crews. Greenwillow.

Grossman, Virginia. 1991. *Ten Little Rabbits*. Illustrated by Sylvia Long. Chronicle.

Hoban, Tana. 1985. *1, 2, 3*. Greenwillow.

Hutchins, Pat. 1982. *1 Hunter*. Greenwillow.

Kitchen, Bert. 1987. *Animal Numbers*. Dial.

Merriam, Eve. 1993. *12 Ways to Get to 11*. Illustrated by Bernie Karlin. Simon & Schuster.

Pacovská, Kveta. 1990. *One, Five, Many*. Clarion.

Scott, Ann Herbert. 1990. *One Good Horse: A Cowpuncher's Counting Book*. Illustrated by Lynn Sweat. Greenwillow.

Sloat, Teri. 1991. *From One to One Hundred*. Dutton.

Walsh, Ellen Stoll. 1991. *Mouse Count*. Harcourt.

CONCEPT

Barton, Byron. 1986. *Trains*. Crowell.

Davis, Lee. 1994. *The Lifesize Animal Opposites Book*. Dorling Kindersley.

Ehlert, Lois. 1989. *Color Zoo*. Lippincott.

Jonas, Ann. 1989. *Color Dance*. Greenwillow.

Hoban, Tana. 1978. *Is It Red? Is It Yellow? Is It Blue?* Greenwillow.

Hoban, Tana. 1990. *Exactly the Opposite*. Greenwillow.

Koch, Michelle. 1991. *Hoot, Howl, Hiss*. Greenwillow.

McMillan, Bruce. 1991. *Eating Fractions*. Scholastic.

Micklethwait, Lucy. 1993. *A Child's Book of Art: Great Pictures, First Words*. Dorling Kindersley.

Micklethwait, Lucy. 1995. *Spot a Dog*. Dorling Kindersley.

Scieszka, Jon. 1995. *Math Curse*. Illustrated by Lane Smith. Viking.

Serfozo, Mary. 1988. *Who Said Red?* Illustrated by Keiko Narahashi. McElderry.

Walsh, Ellen Stoll. 1989. *Mouse Paint*. Harcourt.

PARTICIPATION

Ahlberg, Janet, and Allan Ahlberg. 1979. *Each Peach Pear Plum*. Viking.

Anno, Mitsumasa. 1983. *Anno's U.S.A.* Philomel.

Burton, Marilee Robin. 1988. *Tail Toes Eyes Ears Nose*. Harper.

Carlstrom, Nancy. 1986. *Jesse Bear, What Will You Wear?* Macmillan.

Gág, Wanda. 1928. *Millions of Cats*. Putnam.

Handford, Martin. 1987. *Where's Waldo?* Little, Brown.

Hill, Eric. 1980. *Where's Spot?* Putnam.

Martin, Bill, Jr. 1993. *Old Devil Wind*. Illustrated by Barry Root. Harcourt.

Marzollo, Jean. 1997. *I Spy Super Challenger: A Book of Picture Riddles*. Photographs by Walter Wick. Scholastic.

Yoshi. 1987. *Who's Hiding Here?* Picture Book Studio.

WORDLESS

Baker, Jeannie. 1991. *Window*. Greenwillow.

Briggs, Raymond. 1978. *The Snowman*. Random.

Day, Alexandra. 1985. *Good Dog, Carl*. Green Tiger.

Hutchins, Pat. 1971. *Changes, Changes*. Macmillan.

Goodall, John. 1988. *Little Red Riding Hood*. McElderry.

McCully, Emily Arnold. 1988. *The Christmas Gift*. Harper.

Spier, Peter. 1977. *Noah's Ark*. Doubleday.

Spier, Peter. 1982. *Rain*. Doubleday.

Rohmann, Eric. 1994. *Time Flies*. Crown.

Wiesner, David. 1988. *Free Fall*. Lothrop.

Wiesner, David. 1991. *Tuesday*. Clarion.

Wouters, Anne. 1992. *This Book Is Too Small*. Dutton.

PREDICTABLE

Brown, Margaret Wise. 1947. *Goodnight Moon*. Harper.

Brown, Ruth. 1981. *A Dark Dark Tale*. Dial.

Carlstrom, Nancy White. 1986. *Jesse Bear, What Will You Wear?* Illustrated by Bruce Degen. Macmillan.

Carle, Eric. 1969. *The Very Hungry Caterpillar*. Philomel.

Carle, Eric. 1990. *The Very Quiet Cricket*. Philomel.

Emberley, Barbara. 1967. *Drummer Hoff*. Illustrated by Ed Emberley. Prentice Hall.

Fox, Mem. 1988. *Hattie and the Fox*. Illustrated by Patricia Mullins. Bradbury.

Martin, Bill, Jr. 1964. *Brown Bear, Brown Bear, What Do You See?* Illustrated by Eric Carle. Holt.

Numeroff, Laura Joffe. 1985. *If You Give a Mouse a Cookie*. Illustrated by Felicia Bond. Harper.

Rosen, Michael. 1989. *We're Going on a Bear Hunt*. Illustrated by Helen Oxenbury. McElderry.

Sendak, Maurice. 1962. *Chicken Soup with Rice*. Harper.

Shaw, Nancy. 1986. *Sheep in a Jeep*. Illustrated by Margot Shaw. Houghton Mifflin.

Slobodkina, Esphyr. 1947. *Caps for Sale*. Addison-Wesley.

Taback, Simms. 1997. *There Was an Old Lady Who Swallowed a Fly*. Viking.

Waddell, Martin. 1992. *Farmer Duck*. Illustrated by Helen Oxenbury. Candlewick.

Wood, Audrey. 1984. *The Napping House*. Illustrated by Don Wood. Harcourt.

BEGINNING READER

Baker, Barbara. 1988. *Digby and Kate*. Illustrated by Marsha Winborn. Dutton.

Bulla, Clyde Robert. 1987. *The Chalk Box Kid*. Illustrated by Thomas B. Allen. Random.

Byars, Betsy. 1990. *Hooray for the Golly Sisters!* Illustrated by Sue Truesdell. Harper.

Cohen, Miriam. 1990. *First Grade Takes a Test*. Illustrated by Lillian Hoban. Greenwillow.

Lobel, Arnold. 1970. *Frog and Toad Are Friends*. Harper.

Lobel, Arnold. 1981. *Uncle Elephant*. Harper.

Minarik, Elsa. 1957. *Little Bear*. Illustrated by Maurice Sendak. Harper.

Rylant, Cynthia. 1990. *Henry and Mudge and the Happy Cat*. Illustrated by Suçie Stevenson. Bradbury.

Rylant, Cynthia. 1997. *Poppleton*. Illustrated by Mark Teague. Blue Sky (Scholastic).

Sharmat, Marjorie Weinman. 1992. *Nate the Great and the Stolen Base*. Illustrated by Marc Simont. Coward.

Seuss, Dr. 1957. *The Cat in the Hat*. Houghton Mifflin.

Van Leeuwen, Jean. 1990. *Oliver Pig at School*. Illustrated by Ann Schweninger. Dial.

PICTURE STORY

Ackerman, Karen. 1988. *Song and Dance Man*. Illustrated by Stephen Gammell. Knopf.

Agee, Jon. 1988. *The Incredible Painting of Felix Clousseau*. Farrar.

Allard, Harry. 1977. *Miss Nelson Is Missing*. Illustrated by James Marshall. Houghton Mifflin.

Bemelmans, Ludwig. 1939. *Madeline*. Viking.

Bunting, Eve. 1989. *The Wednesday Surprise*. Illustrated by Donald Carrick. Clarion.

Burningham, John. 1985. *Grandpa*. Crown.

Carle, Eric. 1989. *The Very Busy Spider*. Philomel.

Cooney, Barbara. 1982. *Miss Rumphius*. Viking.

Crowe, Robert. 1976. *Clyde Monster*. Illustrated by Kay Chorao. Dutton.

Day, Alexandra. 1990. *Frank and Ernest Play Ball*. Scholastic.

Demi. 1997. *One Grain of Rice: A Mathematical Folktale*. Scholastic.

dePaola, Tomie. 1975. *Strega Nona*. Prentice Hall.

Fox, Mem. *Possum Magic*. 1990. Illustrated by Julie Vivas. Harcourt.

Hoban, Russell. 1964. *Bread and Jam for Frances*. Illustrated by Lillian Hoban. Harper.

Keats, Ezra Jack. 1971. *Apt. 3*. Macmillan.

Kellogg, Steven. 1979. *Pinkerton, Behave!* Dial.

Lionni, Leo. 1967. *Frederick*. Knopf.

Mayer, Mercer. 1968. *There's a Nightmare in My Closet*. Dial.

McCloskey, Robert. 1948. *Blueberries for Sal*. Viking.

Meddaugh, Susan. 1994. *Martha Calling*. Houghton Mifflin.

Peet, Bill. 1983. *Buford the Little Bighorn*. Houghton Mifflin.

Rathmann, Peggy. 1995. *Officer Buckle and Gloria*. Putnam.

Rylant, Cynthia. 1985. *The Relatives Came*. Illustrated by Stephen Gammell. Bradbury.

Schwartz, Amy. 1988. *Anabelle Swift, Kindergartner*. Orchard.

Scieszka, Jon. 1989. *The True Story of the Three Little Pigs!* Illustrated by Lane Smith. Viking.

Seuss, Dr. (Theodore Geisel). 1938. *The 500 Hats of Bartholomew Cubbins*. Vanguard.

Small, David. 1985. *Imogene's Antlers*. Crown.

Stevens, Janet. 1995. *Tops and Bottoms*. Harcourt.

Stevenson, James. 1977. *Could Be Worse!* Greenwillow.

Tunnell, Michael O. 1997. *Mailing May*. Illustrated by Ted Rand. Tambourine/Greenwillow.

Van Allsburg, Chris. 1992. *The Widow's Broom*. Houghton Mifflin.

Viorst, Judith. 1972. *Alexander and the Terrible, Horrible, No Good, Very Bad Day*. Illustrated by Ray Cruz. Atheneum.

Wisniewski, David. 1996. *The Golem*. Clarion.

Wood, Audrey. 1987. *Heckedy Peg*. Illustrated by Don Wood. Harcourt.

Yolen, Jane. 1987. *Owl Moon*. Illustrated by John Schoenherr. Putnam.

ENGINEERED

Ahlberg, Janet, and Allan Ahlberg. 1986. *The Jolly Postman or Other People's Letters*. Little, Brown.

Carle, Eric. 1986. *My Very First Book of Sounds*. Crowell.

Carter, Noelle, and David Carter. 1990. *I'm a Little Mouse: A Touch & Feel Book*. Holt.

Ehlert, Lois. 1990. *Color Farm*. Lippincott.

Goodall, John. 1988. *Little Red Riding Hood*. McElderry.

Hill, Eric. 1991. *Spot Goes to the Park*. Putnam.

Milne, A. A. 1987. *Pooh and Some Bees (Pooh Carousel Book)*. Illustrated by Ernest H. Shepard. Paper engineering by Paulette Petrovsky. Dutton.

Monfried, Lucia. 1989. *Dishes All Done*. Illustrated by Jon Agee. Dutton.

Pieńkowski, Jan. 1979. *Haunted House*. Paper engineering by Tor Lokvig. Dutton.

Pieńkowski, Jan. 1993. *ABC Dinosaurs*. Paper engineering by Rodger Smith and Helen Balmer. Dutton.

Sabuda, Robert. 1994. *The Christmas Alphabet*. Orchard.

Sabuda, Robert. 1997. *Cookie Count*. Little Simon.

Zelinsky, Paul O. 1990. *The Wheels on the Bus*. Paper engineering by Rodger Smith. Dutton.

BABY/BOARD

Bohdal, Susi. 1986. *Bobby the Bear*. North-South Books.

Boynton, Sandra. 1995. *Blue Hat, Green Hat*. Little Simon.

Dickens, Lucy. 1991. *At the Beach*. Viking.

Duke, Kate. 1986. *What Bounces?* Dutton.

Hill, Eric. 1985. *Spot at Play*. Putnam.

Hoban, Tana. 1985. *What Is It?* Greenwillow.

Oxenbury, Helen. 1981. *Dressing*. Simon & Schuster.

Oxenbury, Helen. 1982. *Mother's Helper*. Dial.

Oxenbury, Helen. 1986. *I Can*. Random.

Pfister, Martin. 1996 (1992). *The Rainbow Fish*. North-South Books.

Tafuri, Nancy. 1987. *My Friends*. Greenwillow.

Notable Authors and Illustrators of Picture Books

Anno, Mitsumasa: Wordless concept books.

Brown, Marcia: Appears on the Caldecott list nine times; illustrates in a variety of artistic styles.

Cooney, Barbara: Varied subject matter including picture book biographies, folktales, realistic and historical fiction.

Crews, Donald: Concept books rendered in graphic arts style.

dePaola, Tomie: Prolific illustrator of more than 200 books; trademark style using pastel colors.

Dillon, Leo, and Diane Dillon: Many books on African themes.

Gammel, Stephen: Airy illustration style created with colored pencil and graphite.

Jeffers, Susan: Best known for illustrated folktales.

Hyman, Trina Schart: Lavish illustrations accompanying classic fairy-tale retellings.

Keats, Ezra Jack: Stories of the inner city for primary grades.

Kellogg, Steven: Humorous stories often involving animals; tall-tale retellings.

Lobel, Arnold: Popularized beginning reader picture books with the Frog and Toad series.

McCloskey, Robert: Picture books set in New England, mostly on the coast of Maine.

McDermott, Gerald: Folktales and myths rendered in an abstract artistic style.

Peet, Bill: Animal fantasies written in lively prose and verse; former Disney animator.

Pinkney, Jerry: Watercolor specialist; mostly African-American themes.

Potter, Beatrix: Mother of the modern picture storybook in English, *The Tale of Peter Rabbit*.

Say, Allen: Asian-American stories reflecting family themes.

Sendak, Maurice: Fantasy stories, most notably *Where the Wild Things Are*.

Steig, William: Sketchy artistic style and Newbery-award winning picture book prose.

Seuss, Dr.: Pioneered the beginning reader picture book with his zany, nonsensical stories.

Van Allsburg, Chris: Fantasy stories for older readers.

Wiesner, David: Wordless fantasy stories.

Young, Ed: Mostly Chinese folktale variants.

Zelinsky, Paul O.: Traditional tales in classical artistic style.

For a more complete list of picture book titles, consult the compact disc that accompanies this text.

CHAPTER 14

Poetry

Unfortunately, poetry does not receive the same attention in our elementary and secondary schools as do other literary forms. Several years of informal polls of our undergraduate preservice elementary teachers continue to affirm that a large percentage of these students enter teacher training with an ambivalence toward or a distinct dislike for poetry. From one- to two-thirds of each class admit such negative attitudes. Is the alarming frequency of these attitudes due to teaching practices that alienate children from poetry or simply the absence of poetry in the curriculum? Whatever the reason, the fact remains that if many of our young teachers enter the field with an ambivalence toward poetry—or worse—then it is likely that a similar feeling will be passed to our children.

WHY CHILDREN MAY LEARN TO DISLIKE POETRY

Children have a natural affinity for poetry, which is exhibited before they enter school by their love for nursery rhymes, jingles, and childhood songs. Sometime during the course of their schooling, a great number of these children seem to change their minds about the appeal of poetry. Indeed, some of our teaching practices may be responsible. When asked what sorts of poetry-related school activities they found distasteful, our undergraduate students invariably listed these: memorizing and reciting, writing poetry, and heavy-duty analyzing of a poem's structure and meaning. Many students reported a distaste for playing the "I know the true meaning of this poem; it's your job to discover it" game with their teachers.

Too often teachers, who themselves do not appreciate poetry and tend to ignore it in their daily routine, ask children to write or memorize poetry during a two-week poetry unit that appears in the language arts textbook. In a mechanistic manner, poetry is dealt with by teaching a few forms, giving practice in those forms by having the students write some poems (which are illustrated and posted on the bulletin board), memorizing and reciting some poetry, and then moving on to the next unit, never to return to poetry again during the school year. Haiku, a Japanese poetry form, is commonly the form most abused in this manner. It is a seemingly quick and simple form to teach and write, having only seventeen syllables (a line of five syllables, a line of seven syllables, and another line of five syllables) that traditionally express something about nature:

> Take the butterfly:
> Nature works to produce him.
> Why doesn't he last?
>
> *David McCord*

Haiku may be short, but it is not simple. Because it is a rather abstract form, children actually require some experience and maturity to understand and appreciate haiku. Thus, as the studies of children's poetry preferences indicate, generations of children have been taught to despise haiku (Fisher and Natarella 1982; Kutiper and

Wilson 1993; Terry 1974). With proper instructional techniques, however, children can and do learn to appreciate this elegant verse form.

Obviously, teachers who dislike poetry may have negative effects on children's poetry attitudes. However, the overzealous teacher who dearly loves poetry may cause problems, too, by rushing headlong into the sophisticated poems rendered by the traditional poets. Children may be overwhelmed by the complicated structures and intense imagery and figurative language. When pushed at an early age to analyze and discover deeply couched meanings, their excitement about poetry wanes.

Studies of children's poetry preferences reveal children's common dislikes about poetry. The results of several of the best-known studies were summarized by Kutiper and Wilson (1993, p. 29):

1. The narrative form of poetry [and limericks] was popular with readers of all ages, while free verse and haiku were the most disliked forms.
2. Students preferred poems that contain rhyme, rhythm, and sound.
3. Children most enjoyed poetry that contained humor, familiar experiences, and animals. [Disliked poems about nature.]
4. Younger students (elementary and middle school/junior high age) preferred contemporary poems.
5. Students disliked poems that contained visual imagery or figurative language.

What students like about poetry relates to their early childhood love for poems that are heavily rhymed and straightforward in meaning. What they dislike frequently identifies teaching practices: the abuse of haiku (which also surfaces in the dislike for nature poems), a lack of connection with the more abstract form of free verse, and the distaste for figurative language. Sometimes in elementary schools and middle schools, we seem to know and teach only personification, simile, and metaphor. After innumerable exercises wherein students are asked to find, circle, and label in a poem (or story) examples of simile, metaphor, and personification, it is little wonder that figurative language seems a burden.

Bernard Lonsdale and Helen Mackintosh best express how we should approach poetry in the elementary schools:

PEANUTS® by Charles M. Schultz

PEANUTS reprinted by permission of UFS, Inc.

Experiences with poetry should be pleasurable and should never be associated with work. Teachers defeat their own purpose if they attempt to analyze the structure or form of the poem other than to show whether it rhymes; what the verse pattern is; and whether it is a ballad, a limerick, a lyric poem, or perhaps haiku. Children in elementary schools should be asked questions of preference and of feeling rather than of knowing. (1973, p. 213)

Children have less opportunity for preference and feeling when the teacher makes all the decisions about poetry and its use in the classroom. If the teacher selects one poem for the entire class to memorize, fewer children will respond positively than if each is allowed to choose a favorite poem for memorization. If the teacher presents one form of poetry and afterward insists that everyone write a poem in that style, the overall response is less enthusiastic than waiting until two or three forms have been introduced and permitting students to select the type they wish to write. Or insightful teachers can help students see that their poems may be free of form yet extremely personal and powerful. (See *A Celebration of Bees: Helping Children Write Poetry* by Barbara Juster Esbensen 1995.) The principle of allowing children to make choices, whenever possible, is closely associated with success in presenting poetry in the elementary classroom.

BUILDING APPRECIATION FOR POETRY

Children who have learned a dislike for poetry can be lured back by teachers who capitalize on the winning power of light, humorous verse. No collection of light verse has done more to attract children to poetry than Shel Silverstein's (1974) *Where the Sidewalk Ends*. Young readers hungrily latch onto Silverstein's lighthearted, sometimes irreverent, poems about contemporary childhood. Jack Prelutsky's poems are similar to Silverstein's, but they are more numerous and more varied in theme. Prelutsky's collection *The New Kid on the Block* (1984) actually edged out *Where the Sidewalk Ends* as the most circulated poetry book in the libraries of schools selected for a poetry preference study (Kutiper and Wilson 1993). Here is the poem that opens the collection:

THE NEW KID ON THE BLOCK
There's a new kid on the block,
and boy, that kid is tough,
that new kid punches hard,
that new kid plays real rough,
that new kid's big and strong,
with muscles everywhere,
that new kid tweaked my arm,
that new kid pulled my hair.

That new kid likes to fight,
and picks on all the guys,

that new kid scares me some,
(that new kid's twice my size),
that new kid stomped my toes,
that new kid swiped my ball,
that new kid's really bad,
I don't care for her at all.

As Kutiper and Wilson (1993) point out, the light verse that children tend to prefer must not remain their only poetry diet. Wise teachers will use the rhythmic, humorous verse to build appreciation for poetry in general and use it as a bridge to more sophisticated contemporary and traditional poetry written for children and adults. Teachers who share poems daily, with no ulterior motive other than to build appreciation, help create students (and future teachers) who will have a lifelong interest in poetry. Share a poem as children wait in the lunch line, sit down after recess, or as a way to begin each school day. One teacher simply wrote a new poem on the chalkboard each day without reading or referring to it. Soon students were commenting on the poem and some began writing down the ones they liked. Poetry may fit nicely into a social studies or science unit—in fact, into any area of the curriculum. In language arts, Ruth Heller's beautifully illustrated poems present the parts of speech (*Many Luscious Lollipops: A Book About Adjectives,* 1989, and *Up, Up and Away: A Book About Adverbs, 1991*). The key is consistent, unfettered exposure to poetry by an enthusiastic teacher who begins mixing light verse and more artistic poetry.

As poetry really is meant to be heard more than read silently, the avenue to poetry appreciation for many students is the oral highway. Therefore, teachers should read poems aloud—fresh selections as well as old favorites—on a regular, even daily, basis. And for older, hard-core poetry haters, music is often the road to recovery. Students tend not to associate the lyrics of songs they know and love with poetry. Teachers of older children have changed students' negative attitudes toward poetry by duplicating the lyrics of popular tunes and distributing them as poems. Often barriers will tumble down, clearing the way for sharing other sorts of poetry.

Choral speaking is another oral/aural method for sharing poetry. Through choral speaking, children get the opportunity to play with words and their sounds—to both hear and manipulate the language. For example, free verse (noted by children as one of their least favorite forms) can spring to life when performed as a choral reading. Here is a free verse poem by Harold Munro, divided into speaking parts by a teacher, that has proven to be an icebreaker with upper elementary students:

OVERHEARD ON A SALT MARSH
by Harold Munro

(May be divided as light voices and dark voices, or girls as the goblins
and boys as the water nymphs.)

Boys: NYMPH, NYMPH, WHAT ARE YOUR BEADS?
Girls: Green glass, goblin. Why do you stare at them?

Boys: GIVE THEM ME.
Girls: NO.
Boys: GIVE THEM ME.
    GIVE THEM ME.
Girls: NO.
Boys: THEN I WILL HOWL ALL NIGHT IN THE REEDS,
    LIE IN THE MUD AND HOWL FOR THEM.
Girls: Goblin, why do you love them so?
Boys: THEY ARE BETTER THAN STARS OR WATER,
    BETTER THAN VOICES OF WINDS THAT SING,
    BETTER THAN ANY MAN'S FAIR DAUGHTER,
    YOUR GREEN GLASS BEADS ON A SILVER STRING.
Girls: Hush, I stole them out of the moon.
Boys: GIVE ME YOUR BEADS, I WANT THEM.
Girls: NO.
Boys: I WILL HOWL IN A DEEP LAGOON
    FOR YOUR GREEN GLASS BEADS,
    I LOVE THEM SO.
    GIVE THEM ME. GIVE THEM.
Girls: NO.

From *Overheard on a Salt Marsh* by Harold Munro. Reprinted by permission of Gerald Duckworth and Co. Ltd.

Teachers do much to convince children of the worth of poetry when they share what is personally delightful. They are always more successful when presenting poems they honestly like. A folder with readily accessible favorite poems or a shelf holding favorite poetry volumes makes the job easier. If a teacher does not have a collection of personal favorites, it is only because she has not read enough poems. The pleasure of writing poetry should be modeled in a similar way. We recall a sixth-grade teacher who genuinely enjoyed writing limericks for his students, who soon became so enamored with limericks they chose to stay in during recess to write poems!

THE NCTE POETRY AWARD

To encourage the sharing of poetry with children and to raise the awareness of teachers about the quality of the poetry available, the National Council of Teachers of English established an award to recognize a living poet whose body of work for children ages 3 to 13 is deemed exceptional. The NCTE Award for Excellence in Poetry for Children was presented annually from 1977 until 1982, when the council began giving it every three years.

The works of the poets who have won the NCTE Poetry Award are certainly not as well known among children as the poems of Silverstein and Prelutsky, but they provide teachers a reservoir of fine poetry that is both very accessible to children and of better artistic quality than the popular lighter verse. (See *A Jar of Tiny Stars: Poems by*

NCTE Award-Winning Poets edited by Bernice E. Cullinan 1996.) Here are the names of the award-winning poets, the dates of their awards, and a sample of their poetry:

DAVID McCORD, 1977

SONG OF THE TRAIN

Clickety-clack,
Wheels on the track,
This is the way
They begin the attack:
Click-ety-clack,
Click-ety-clack,
Click-ety, *clack*-ety,
Click-ety
Clack.

Clickety-clack,
Over the crack,
Faster and faster
The song of the track:
Clickety-clack,
Clickety, clack
Clickety, clackety,
Clackety
Clack.

Riding in front,
Riding in back,
Everyone hears
The song of the track:
Clickety-clack,
Clickety-clack,
Clickety, *clickety*,
Clackety
Clack.

AILEEN FISHER, 1978

I LIKE IT WHEN IT'S MIZZLY

I like it when it's mizzly
and just a little drizzly
so everything looks far away
and make-believe and frizzly.

I like it when it's foggy
and sounding very froggy.
I even like it when it rains

on streets and weepy windowpanes
and catkins in the poplar tree
and *me*.

KARLA KUSKIN, 1979

FULL OF THE MOON

It's full of the moon
The dogs dance out
Through brush and bush and bramble.
They howl and yowl
And growl and prowl.
They amble, ramble, scramble.
They rush through brush.
They push through bush.
They yip and yap and hurr.
They lark around and bark around
With prickles in their fur.
They two-step in the meadow.
They polka on the lawn.
Tonight's the night
The dogs dance out
And chase their tails till dawn.

MYRA COHN LIVINGSTON, 1980

MY BOX

Nobody knows what's there but me,
knows where I keep my silver key
and my baseball cards
and my water gun
and my wind-up car that doesn't run,
and a stone I found with a hole clear through
and a blue-jay feather that's *mostly* blue,
and a note that I wrote to the guy next door
and never gave him—and lots, lots more
of important things that I'll never show
to anyone, *anyone* else I know.

EVE MERRIAM, 1981

TV

In the house
of Mr. and Mrs. Spouse
he and she
would watch TV
and never a word
between them spoken

until the day
the set was broken.

Then "How do you do?"
said he to she.
"I don't believe
that we've
met
yet.
Spouse is my name.
What's yours?" he asked.

"Why, mine's the same!"
said she to he,
"Do you suppose that we could be—?"

But the set came suddenly right about,
and so they never did find out.

JOHN CIARDI (*CHAR*-DEE), 1982

HOW TO TELL THE TOP OF A HILL

The top of a hill
Is not until
The bottom is below.
And you have to stop
When you reach the top
For there's no more UP to go.

To make it plain
Let me explain:
The one *most* reason why
You have to stop
When you reach the top—is:
The next step up is sky.

LILIAN MOORE, 1985

PIGEONS

Pigeons are city folk
content
to live with concrete
and cement.

They seldom
try
the sky.

A pigeon never sings
of hill
and flowering hedge,
but busily commutes
from sidewalk
to his ledge.

Oh pigeon, what a waste of wings!

ARNOLD ADOFF, 1988

LOVE SONG

great goblets of pudding   powder in milk
hot with marshmallows on a winter afternoon
syrup on vanilla ice cream   frosting on cake
a kind of cake   dripping to dry on warm
doughnuts fresh from the oven   candy
                                       candy bars
bars   chunks   thick and broken pieces   squares
spoons and pots   and lots
                              before brushing
fudge and milk
        and german and sour cream
light and dark and bitter sweet and
                                       even
                                       white

you are no good
                for me
you are no good

you are so good

Chocolate
Chocolate
            i
love
    you so
            i
want
        to
marry
        you
        and
live
    forever
            in the

                    flavor
of your
        brown

VALERIE WORTH, 1991
STOCKINGS (FROM AT CHRISTMASTIME)

Long ago, we
Hung up my
Mother's old

Nylons, and
Woke to find
Them swollen

With beige
Unnatural bulges,
Thigh to toe.

Nowadays, there
Are velvety
Crimson boots,

Brighter, and
Shapelier—but
A lot shorter.

BARBARA ESBENSEN, 1994
PENCILS

The rooms in a pencil
are narrow
but elephants   castles and watermelons
fit in

In a pencil
noisy words yell for attention
and quiet words wait their turn

How did they slip
into such a tight place?
Who
gives them their
lunch?

From a broken pencil
an unbroken poem will come!
There is a long story living

in the shortest pencil

Every word in your
pencil
is fearless   ready to walk
the blue tightrope lines
Ready
to teeter and smile
down   Ready to come right out
and show you
thinking!

ELOISE GREENFIELD, 1997

KEEPSAKE

Before Mrs. Williams died
She told Mr. Williams
When he gets home
To get a nickel out of her
Navy blue pocketbook
And give it to her
Sweet little gingerbread girl
That's me

I ain't never going to spend it

FORMS OF POETRY

Poetry is distinguishable from prose primarily because of its distinct patterns or forms. The variety of patterns, in turn, distinguishes one form of poetry from another. Here are a few of the forms teachers commonly use in elementary school.

NARRATIVE POEMS.   Narrative poems tell stories. Children usually enjoy narrative poetry because it is easy to understand and because they are naturally attuned to stories. A classic example is Henry Wadsworth Longfellow's "Paul Revere's Ride," available in a picture book version handsomely illustrated by Ted Rand (1990). Ballads are narrative poems adapted for singing or to create a musical effect, such as the popular American ballad "On Top of Old Smoky."

LYRIC POEMS.   Lyric poetry is melodic or songlike. Generally, it is descriptive, focusing on personal moments, feelings, or image-laden scenes. John Ciardi's (1982) poem "How to Tell the Top of a Hill" is an example of a lyric poem.

LIMERICKS.   Limericks are humorous poems that were popularized in 1846 with the publication of Edward Lear's *Book of Nonsense*. The rhyming scheme and verse pattern of limericks are familiar to most children:

A thrifty young fellow of Shoreham
Made brown paper trousers and woreham;
  He looked nice and neat
  Till he bent in the street
To pick up a pin; then he toreham.

Anonymous

HAIKU.   As described earlier in this chapter, haiku has a total of seventeen syllables (a line of five syllables, a line of seven syllables, and another line of five syllables). Refer to "Why Children May Dislike Poetry," earlier in this chapter, for an example and further description.

CONCRETE POEMS.   A concrete poem is written or printed on the page in a shape representing the poem's subject. It is a form of poetry that is meant to be seen even more than heard and often does not have a rhyming scheme or a particular rhythm:

J. Patrick Lewis

FREE VERSE.   Free verse, though relying on rhythm and cadence for its poetic form, is mostly unrhymed and lacks a consistent rhythm. Its topics are typically quite philosophical or abstract—but intriguing. The poems presented in this chapter by Harold Munro and Valerie Worth are examples of free verse.

BUILDING A POETRY COLLECTION

Select poems that meet the needs of children who are in the process of developing an appreciation of poetry. This means building a collection filled with a variety of poems to match differing tastes and levels of sophistication: light and humorous verse, poems that create vivid images or express our hard-to-communicate feelings, story poems, or poetry that plays with the sounds of language.

Do not rely on textbooks to supply poetry for your classroom. For one thing, basal readers simply do not have enough poetry. Also, because poems (and other literary works) are protected by copyright laws for the author's lifetime plus 50 years, textbook companies and other anthologizers find it less expensive to choose poems that are in the public domain. In other words, the poet has been dead long enough that one does not have to pay a permission fee to reprint the poem. As a result, basals and anthologies may be heavily weighted toward older poetry. Although some old poems appeal to modern children, contemporary poetry—found largely in single, thin volumes or specific collections—generally has a stronger draw for today's reader.

The world of children's books offers teachers an almost endless supply of poetry. The reading list at the end of this chapter is representative of the excellent collections available that provide a broad range of poetry to meet every need. Many books of poetry are collections of a single poet's work (note collections by the NCTE Poetry Award winners). However, some fine general anthologies are also listed, such as *The Random House Book of Poetry* (selector, Jack Prelutsky 1983) and *Sing a Song of Popcorn* (selector, Beatrice Schenk de Regniers 1988). Both books have themed sections, such as a collection of weather poems or animal poems, and provide a balance of modern and traditional poets. *The Random House Book of Poetry* contains 579 poems, and although *Sing a Song of Popcorn* has considerably less poetry, it is illustrated by nine Caldecott-winning artists.

A number of specialized anthologies appear in the reading list as well. These collections contain poems about a particular topic and by a variety of poets in one book. Myra Cohn Livingston, an NCTE Poetry Award winner, is also known for the many specialized collections she has published, such as *Cat Poems* (1987), *Poems for Mothers* (1988), *Birthday Poems* (1989), *Halloween Poems* (1989), *Valentine Poems* (1987), *Poems for Jewish Holidays* (1986).

The single-poem picture book is another variety of poetry book that is particularly useful for giving children a taste of the more traditional and sometimes more sophisticated poet. For example, Susan Jeffers has illustrated a stunning picture book version of *Stopping by Woods on a Snowy Evening* by Robert Frost (1978), which will attract the most reluctant poetry reader.

Teachers who do not know the world of children's poetry have a responsibility not only to discover the bounty that awaits them but also to use it to help stem the tide of ambivalence toward poetry among their students. A well-rounded classroom and school library poetry collection can have something for everyone. By sharing and enjoying poetry frequently, teachers and children together will build a lifelong appreciation, as the following poem by Eloise Greenfield expresses.

THINGS
Went to the corner
Walked in the store
Bought me some candy
Ain't got it no more
Ain't got it no more

Went to the beach
Played on the shore
Built me a sandhouse
Ain't got it no more
Ain't got it no more

Went to the kitchen
Lay down on the floor
Made me a poem
Still got it
Still got it

REFERENCES

Cullinan, Bernice E., ed. 1996. *A Jar of Tiny Stars: Poems by NCTE Award-Winning Poets.* Honesdale, Pa.: Wordsong/Boyds Mills.

de Regniers, Beatrice Schenk, Eva Moore, Mary Michaels White, and Jean Carr, compilers. 1988. *Sing a Song of Popcorn.* New York: Scholastic.

Esbensen, Barbara Juster. 1995. *A Celebration of Bees: Helping Children Write Poetry.* New York: Holt.

Fisher, Carol J., and Margaret A. Natarella. 1982. Young children's preferences in poetry: A national survey of first, second and third graders. *Research in the Teaching of English* 16, no. 4: 339–354.

Frost, Robert. 1978. *Stopping by Wood on a Snowy Evening.* Illustrated by Susan Jeffers. New York: Dutton.

Heller, Ruth. 1989. *Many Luscious Lollipops: A Book about Adjectives.* New York: Grosset & Dunlap.

Heller, Ruth. 1991. *Up, Up and Away: A Book about Adverbs*. New York: Grosset & Dunlap.

Kutiper, Karen, and Patricia Wilson. 1993. Updating poetry preferences: A look at the poetry children really like. *The Reading Teacher* 47, no. 1 (September): 28–35.

Livingston, Myra Cohn. 1986. *Poems for Jewish Holidays*.

Livingston, Myra Cohn. 1987. *Cat Poems*. New York: Holiday House.

Livingston, Myra Cohn. 1987. *Valentine Poems*. New York: Holiday House.

Livingston, Myra Cohn. 1988. *Poems for Mothers*. New York: Holiday House.

Livingston, Myra Cohn. 1989. *Birthday Poems*. New York: Holiday House.

Livingston, Myra Cohn. 1989. *Halloween Poems*. New York: Holiday House.

Longfellow, Henry Wadsworth. 1990. *Paul Revere's Ride*. Illustrated by Ted Rand. New York: Dutton.

Lonsdale, Bernard J., and Helen K. Mackintosh. 1973. *Children Experience Literature*. New York: Random House.

Prelutsky, Jack, ed. 1983. *The Random House Book of Poetry*. Illustrated by Arnold Lobel. New York: Random House.

Prelutsky, Jack. 1984. *The New Kid on the Block*. Illustrated by James Stevenson. New York: Greenwillow.

Silverstein, Shel. 1974. *Where the Sidewalk Ends*. New York: Harper.

Terry, Ann C. 1974. *Children's Poetry Preferences*. Urbana, Ill.: NCTE Research Report No. 16.

POETRY READING LIST

Ten of Our Favorites

Adoff, Arnold. 1973. *Black is Brown is Tan*. Illustrated by Emily Arnold McCully. Harper. Describes in verse the life of brown-skinned mama, white-skinned daddy, their children, and assorted relatives.

Ciardi, John. 1962. *You Read to Me, I'll Read to You*. Illustrated by Edward Gorey. Lippincott. Designed so that the child reads the poem on one page and the adult reads the poem on the next page. A collection mostly of humorous verse.

de Regniers, Beatrice Schenk, Eva Moore, Mary Michaels White, and Jean Carr, compilers. 1988. *Sing a Song of Popcorn*. Illustrated by nine Caldecott Award-winning artists. Scholastic. A collection of poems by a variety of well-known poets with illustrations by nine Caldecott medalists.

Esbensen, Barbara. 1992. *Who Shrank My Grandmother's House?* Illustrated by Eric Beddows. Harper. A collection of poems about childhood discoveries concerning everyday objects and things.

Fleischman, Paul. 1988. *Joyful Noise: Poems for Two Voices*. Illustrated by Eric Beddows. Harper. A collection of poems (divided into two columns to be read together by two people) describing the characteristics and activities of a variety of insects. Winner of the Newbery Medal.

Kuskin, Karla. 1980. *Dogs & Dragons, Trees & Dreams: A Collection of Poems*. Harper. A representative collection of Karla Kuskin's poetry with introductory notes on poetry writing and appreciation.

Merriam, Eve. 1987. *Halloween ABC*. Illustrated by Lane Smith. Macmillan. Each letter of the alphabet introduces a different, spooky aspect of Halloween.

Prelutsky, Jack, ed. 1983. *The Random House Book of Poetry for Children*. Illustrated by Arnold Lobel. Random House. More than 550 poems by American, English, and anonymous authors.

Prelutsky, Jack. 1984. *The New Kid on the Block*. Illustrated by James Stevenson. Greenwillow. Humorous poems about such strange creatures and people as Baloney Belly Billy and the Gloopy Gloopers.

Silverstein, Shel. 1974. *Where the Sidewalk Ends*. Harper. An extremely popular collection of humorous, somewhat irreverent poems written for children.

Others We Like

Cassedy, Sylvia. 1987. *Roomrimes*. Illustrated by Michele Chessare. Crowell.

Chandra, Deborah. 1990. *Balloons and Other Poems*. Illustrated by Leslie Bowman. Farrar.

Cullinan, Bernice E., ed. 1996. *A Jar Tiny of Stars: Poems by NCTE Award-Winning Poets*. Illustrated by Andi MacLeod and Marc Nadel. Wordsong/Boyds Mills.

Florian, Douglas. 1997. *Insectlopedia: Poems and Paintings*. Harcourt.

Greenfield, Eloise. 1978. *Honey, I Love and Other Poems*. Illustrated by Leo and Diane Dillon. Harper.

Kennedy, X. J. 1986. *Brats*. Illustrated by James Watt. Atheneum.

Lansky, Bruce, ed. 1991. *Kids Pick the Funniest Poems*. Illustrated by Stephen Carpenter. Meadowbrook.

Larrick, Nancy, ed. 1968. *Piping Down the Valleys Wild*. Illustrated by Ellen Raskin. Delacorte.

Lewis, J. Patrick. 1990. *A Hippopotamusn't*. Illustrated by Victoria Chess. Dial.

Livingston, Myra Cohn. 1985. *Celebrations*. Illustrated by Leonard Everett Fisher. Holiday.

McCord, David. 1977. *One at a Time*. Little, Brown.

Merriam, Eve. 1986. *Fresh Paint*. Illustrated by David Frampton. Macmillan.

Moore, Lilian. 1982. *Something New Begins*. Illustrated by Mary J. Dunton. Atheneum.

Nash, Ogden. 1980. *Custard & Company*. Illustrated by Quentin Blake. Little, Brown.

Opie, Iona, ed. 1996. *My Very First Mother Goose*. Illustrated by Rosemary Wells. Candlewick.

Philip, Neil. 1995. *Singing America*. Illustrated by Michael McCurdy. Viking.

Prelutsky, Jack. 1976. *Nightmares: Poems to Trouble Your Sleep*. Illustrated by Arnold Lobel. Greenwillow.

Sierra, Judy. 1998. *Antarctic Antics: A Book of Penguin Poems*. Illustrated by Jose Aruego and Ariane Dewey. Harcourt.

Thomas, Carol Joyce. 1993. *Brown Honey in Broomwheat Tea*. Illustrated by Floyd Cooper. Harper.

Volavkova, H., ed. 1994. . . . *I Never Saw Another Butterfly: Children's Drawings and Poems from Terezin Concentration Camp, 1942–1944*. Random.

Worth, Valerie. 1987. *All the Small Poems*. Illustrated by Natalie Babbitt. Farrar.

Picture Books

Baylor, Byrd. 1986. *I'm in Charge of Celebrations*. Illustrated by Peter Parnall. Scribner's.

Esbensen, Barbara Juster. 1995. *Dance with Me*. Illustrated by Megan Lloyd. Harper.

Frost, Robert. 1978. *Stopping by Woods on a Snowy Evening*. Illustrated by Susan Jeffers. Dutton.

Hoberman, Mary Ann. 1978. *A House Is a House for Me*. Illustrated Betty Fraser. Viking.

Longfellow, Henry Wadsworth. 1983. *Song of Hiawatha*. Illustrated by Susan Jeffers. Dial.

Longfellow, Henry Wadsworth. 1990. *Paul Revere's Ride*. Illustrated by Ted Rand. Dutton.

Schertle, Alice. 1996. *Keepers*. Illustrated by Ted Rand. Lothrop.

Service, Robert W. 1987. *The Cremation of Sam McGee*. Illustrated by Ted Harrison. Greenwillow.

Siebert, Diane. 1989. *Heartland*. Illustrated by Wendell Minor. Crowell.

Thayer, Lawrence Ernest. 1995. *Casey at the Bat*. Illustrated by Gerald Fitzgerald. Atheneum.

Easy to Read

Brown, Marc, ed. 1987. *Play Rhymes*. Dutton.

Calmenson, Stephanie. 1989. *What Am I? Very First Riddles*. Illustrated by Karen Gundersheimer. Harper.

Greenfield, Eloise. 1995. *On My Horse*. Illustrated by Jan Spivey Gilchrist. Harper.

Hopkins, Lee Bennett, ed. 1987. *More Surprises*. Illustrated by Megan Lloyd. Harper.

Hopkins, Lee Bennett, ed. 1994. *Weather: Poems for All Seasons*. Illustrated by Melanie Hall. Harper.

Kuskin, Karla. 1992. *Soap Soup and Other Verses*. Harper.

Livingston, Myra Cohn. 1990. *My Head Is Red and Other Riddle Rhymes*. Illustrated by Tere LoPrete. Dutton.

Livingston, Myra Cohn, ed. 1989. *Dilly Dilly Piccalilli: Poems for the Very Young*. Illustrated by Eileen Christelow. McElderry.

Prelutsky, Jack. 1980. *Rolling Harvey Down the Hill*. Illustrated by Victoria Chess. Greenwillow.

Prelutsky, Jack. 1983. *It's Valentine's Day*. Illustrated by Yossi Abolafia. Greenwillow.

Notable Children's Poets

Adoff, Arnold

Ciardi, John

Esbensen, Barbara Juster

Fisher, Aileen

Fleischman, Paul

Greenfield, Eloise

Kennedy, X. J.

Kuskin, Karla

Livingston, Myra Cohn

McCord, David

Merriam, Eve

Moore, Lilian

Prelutsky, Jack

Silverstein, Shel

Worth, Valerie

For a more complete list of poetry titles, consult the compact disc that accompanies this text.

CHAPTER 15

Multicultural and International Books

Multicultural and international books offer positive experiences to young readers in at least three ways. Books about specific cultures and nations can

- Foster an awareness, understanding, and appreciation of people who seem at first glance different from the reader.
- Present a positive and reassuring representation of a reader's own cultural group.
- Introduce readers to the literary traditions of different world cultures or cultural groups in America.

Well-written books that express multicultural themes or are international in their origins may have a profound effect on readers, prompting a global outlook as well as an understanding that members of the human family have more similarities than differences.

MULTICULTURAL LITERATURE

Multicultural (diverse cultures) children's books typically focus on so-called parallel cultures. Fiction involves main characters from minority groups; nonfiction focuses on the lives of real people from parallel cultures. Multicultural literature has often been equated with books about people of color, especially within the United States and Canada: African Americans, Native Americans, Asian Americans, Hispanics/Latinos. However, this definition is far too narrow. Our diverse population includes a variety of cultural groups that often cross color lines, such as religious groups. Jews, Catholics, Moslems, Mormons, and the Amish all have their own subcultures and often have been misunderstood and even persecuted for their beliefs. As an example of books promoting understanding among religious factions, many Jewish students have expressed both interest and pleasure in reading Barbara Robinson's (1972) *The Best Christmas Pageant Ever*. Some students said they had always wondered about the Christian Christmas tradition of the pageant and Robinson's book made understandable what was strange to them—the story helped to bridge a cultural gap. Individuals with intellectual or physical challenges also deserve books that represent them in honest, positive ways. For example, some deaf individuals consider themselves part of the Deaf culture and are concerned about how the rest of society misunderstands them.

The labels and terms we use to talk about diverse cultures are sometimes self-created and sometimes created by external forces, such as government agencies. As cultural groups continue clarifying their status and worth, they create newer terms and labels to identify themselves. Therefore, it may be difficult to keep up with the currently acceptable words to describe or identify cultures. In this chapter, we have tried to employ the terms that are most prevalent in the current literature.

The Need for Multicultural Books

Xenophobia, the mistrust or fear of people who are strangers or foreigners, is the root of our worldwide inability to live together in peace. Parents and society may purposely or inadvertently program children to mistrust, fear, or even hate certain groups of people who are unlike them. Teaching children at an early age "about the [positive] differences and similarities between people will not singularly ensure a more gentle and tolerant society, but might act as a prerequisite to one" (Sobol 1990, p. 30). Candy Dawson Boyd (1990) makes it clear that we cannot begin too early to give our children a multicultural perspective:

> We know that . . . a substantial body of research on the development of racial consciousness [began] in 1929, and what does it tell us? It tells us that children develop negative attitudes towards other people as they take on the culture of their parents. It tells us that by age three, racial awareness is evident. *Three*. And that by age ten, racial attitudes have crystallized.

Yet, children in early adolescence "are not too old for significant attitudinal change. Counteraction is therefore possible . . . " (Sonnenschein 1988, p. 265).

Literature can be one of the most powerful tools for combating the ignorance that breeds xenophobic behavior. "For decades experienced educators have reported success stories about using children's literature to broaden attitudes toward people from a variety of cultures" (Hansen-Krening 1992, p. 126). Rudine Sims Bishop (1992, p. 40), who has long been a champion of the well-written multicultural book, believes that "literature is one of the most powerful components of a multicultural education curriculum, the underlying purpose of which is to help make the society a more equitable one." In support of this view, she quotes James Baldwin: "Literature is indispensable to the world. . . . The world changes according to the way people see it, and if you alter, even by a millimeter, the way a person looks at reality, then you can change it" (Sims 1982, p. 1). Indeed, studies have indicated that students' prejudices have been reduced because of their involvement with good multicultural books (Pate 1988).

Certainly, children of minority cultural groups need books that bolster self-esteem and pride in their heritage (Nieto, 1996). And children of all groups, especially majority children, need books that sensitize them to people from cultural groups different from their own.

Judging Multicultural Literature

As with all books, multicultural books ought to measure up to the criteria used to judge literature in general (see Chapters 2 to 4). However, additional criteria focusing on the multicultural themes and content are also necessary to consider.

Racial or cultural stereotyping must be avoided. Stereotypes are alienating because they perpetuate a simplified, biased, and often negative view of groups of people: All African Americans are poor, all Hispanics are lazy, all Asians are secretive and sly, all Jews are born entrepreneurs. Though common elements often link the lives and daily practices of members of a cultural group, it is important to communicate that every group is made up of individuals who have their own sets of personal values, attitudes, and beliefs. In books written for children, characters who are cultural minorities need to be represented as true individuals, and a positive image needs to be presented. However, this still leaves room for showing both positive and negative behaviors in minority as well as majority group characters. For instance, in the New-bery-winning novel *Roll of Thunder, Hear My Cry*, a story of racial prejudice in Missis-sippi of the 1930s, Mildred Taylor (1976) creates African-American characters who represent a broad spectrum of human characteristics. Cassie Logan is proud and hon-orable, though a bit stubborn. T. J. is weak and dishonest. By the same token, Taylor does not make all whites racial bigots.

Cultural details need to be represented accurately in literature. These may include the use of dialects or idioms; descriptions of ethnic foods, customs, and clothing; and infor-mation about religious beliefs and practices. Of course, sensitivity to subcultures within a group is also important. For example, customs vary among the different factions of Judaism; Hasidic Jews are strictly orthodox, as evidenced by dress codes and other identi-fiable practices, but Reform Jews are much less bound by religious law. In the same way, customs and lifestyles vary greatly among the many Native-American tribes.

Cultural authenticity, a sensitive issue in children's literature today, means that those from within a culture feel that a book has accurately and honestly reflected their experi-ences and viewpoints. However, many people feel that books examining a specific cul-ture should not be written by someone who is an outsider. For instance, the Newbery-winning novel *Sounder* by William Armstrong (1969) portrays the lives of a poor family of African-American sharecroppers. Armstrong is not an African American, and critics charge that there is no way he could understand the nuances of living in this culture. "Someone who does not share the specifics of a culture remains an outsider, no matter how astute a student or how well-meaning their intentions" (Wilson 1990, p. A25). Worse yet, some critics maintain that many multicultural books written by outsiders provide a distorted view because the author is biased or culturally prejudiced.

At the same time, others believe that if outsiders make concentrated efforts not only to understand but also to inhabit a different cultural world, then they may indeed be able to write with cultural authenticity. Of course, some rare authors seem to have a particular gift for "imagining other's lives" (Horn 1993, p. 78). For instance, Miriam Horn makes a case for Eudora Welty's uncanny ability:

> "Miss Eudora" could . . . enter into the stolid, exhausted body of an old black woman or let loose with a bluesy tale as full of tumbles and howls as a Fats Waller jam. Before she was 30, she could feel the frantic loneliness of a middle-aged traveling sales-man. . . . She could even, on the hot night in 1963 that civil-rights leader Medgar Evers was killed, transform her own soft, lilting voice into the bitter ranting of a hate-filled assassin. Of the story she wrote that night in the voice of the murderer she says: "You have to give any human being the right to have you use your imagination about them." (Horn 1993, p. 78)

Whoever the author, it is of great importance to have books for young readers that are culturally authentic.

Awareness about the types of multicultural books that exist may be helpful in judg-ing and selecting books for libraries and classrooms. Certainly, they include folktales, biographies, historical novels, informational books, fantasy, picture books, and contemporary realistic novels. However, Rudine Sims Bishop (1992) suggests there are three general categories of books about people of color: neutral, generic, and specific. In many instances, these categories also could be applied to other cultural groups.

Culturally neutral children's books include characters from cultural minorities but are essentially about other topics. Sims (1992) says that this variety is mostly made up of picture books and gives the example of a book about medical examinations wherein "a Japanese-American child might be shown visiting the doctor, who might be an African-American female" (p. 46). Neutral books randomly place multicultural faces among the pages in order to make a statement about the value of diversity.

Generic books focus on characters representing a cultural group, but few specific details are included that aid in developing a cultural persona. Instead, these characters are functioning in the books as regular people existing in a large common culture, such as American culture. A classic example is the Caldecott-winning *The Snowy Day* by Ezra Jack Keats (1962), which features an African-American family living in an inner city. The book shows a black child enjoying newly fallen snow, just as any child might. Although this book is noted as one of the first books to have an African-American child as a protagonist, some critics feel that the child's mother is presented as a stereotypical black woman—the large, loving Negro mammy image. Despite the fact that this variety of multicultural book contains little culturally specific material, readers concerned about multicultural issues still scrutinize these books hoping to find characters with realistic, nonstereotypical qualities.

Culturally specific children's books incorporate specific cultural details that help define characters. Cultural themes are evident if not prevailing in fictional plots or nonfiction content. Of course, in picture books the artwork will express many of these cultural details. It is in this category of multicultural literature that cultural authenticity is particularly important. The recommended reading list at the conclusion of this chapter is organized by cultural divisions and presents books considered by many to be both quality literature and culturally authentic.

The Growth of Multicultural Literature

Children's books in the past generally treated minority groups badly or ignored them completely. However, when African-American author Arna Bontemps (1948) won a Newbery Honor Award in 1949 for *Story of the Negro* and became the first African American to appear on the Newbery list, he ushered in the real beginnings of change for all cultural groups. Though few other minority authors or illustrators appeared on award lists during the next two decades, more of their work was being produced. Also, books by majority culture authors that presented less stereotypical images of minority cultures appeared and received awards: *Song of the Swallows* by Leo Politi (1949) won the Caldecott Award in 1950 and was the first Caldecott winner with a Hispanic-American protagonist. Then *Amos Fortune, Free Man* by Elizabeth Yates (1950), *Secret of the Andes* by Ann Nolan Clark (1952), and . . . *And Now Miguel,* by Joseph Krumgold (1953) won the Newbery Award in 1951, 1953, and 1954, respectively. *The Snowy Day* by Ezra Jack Keats won the Caldecott in 1963.

As the civil rights movement gained momentum in the 1960s, awareness of and sensitivity toward minorities increased. In 1965 the literary world was awakened by the publication of a startling article titled "The All White World of Children's Books." Printed in the *Saturday Review* and written by Nancy Larrick, this article reported that almost no African Americans appeared in any of America's children's books. The publishing and library worlds took notice, and efforts to include more African Americans in children's books eventually blossomed to include other racial minorities, women, people with physical and mental disadvantages, and other groups.

In 1966 the Council on Interracial Books for Children (CIBC) was founded. Its publication pointed to racial stereotypes still appearing in children's books, and its efforts with publishers helped promote and get into print the works of authors and illustrators of color, particularly African Americans. In fact, for a number of years the CIBC sponsored an annual contest for unpublished writers and illustrators of color and saw to it that the winners' works were published. The authors and illustrators who were given their start by the CIBC are some of the best-known today in the world of multicultural children's literature: African-American authors Mildred Taylor and Walter Dean Myers, Native-American author Virginia Driving Hawk Sneve, and Asian-American writers Ai-Ling Louie and Minfong Ho.

In 1969 the American Library Association (ALA) established the Coretta Scott King Award to recognize the distinguished work of African-American writers and illustrators. Soon after, in 1974, the National Council for the Social Studies created the Carter G. Woodson Award for the most distinguished children's books that treat topics related to ethnic minorities and race relations.

As books by and about diverse cultures and minority populations began to receive more attention, writers and illustrators of color also began to receive the major U.S. literature awards. In 1975, Virginia Hamilton won the Newbery Award for *M. C. Higgins the Great* (1974), the first African American to be so honored. The next year Leo Dillon became the first African American to win the Caldecott Medal, an award he shared with his wife, Diane, for their illustrations in *Why Mosquitoes Buzz in People's Ears* (1975) written by Verna Aardema. Then in 1990, Ed Young became the first Chinese American to win the Caldecott Medal (*Lon Po Po: A Red Riding Hood Story from China,* 1989) and in 1994 Allen Say the first Japanese American (*Grandfather's Journey,* 1993). It was not until 1995 that a person of Hispanic background was awarded one of the ALA's major children's book prizes. David Diaz won the Caldecott for his illustrations in *Smoky Night* (1994), written by Eve Bunting. Since that time, the ALA has established the Pura Belpré Award (1996) to honor the work of Latino/Latina writers and illustrators.

Since the 1960s, more authors from minority cultural and racial groups have been writing for children and appear consistently on best-books lists and awards lists. Still, there is much room for growth in this area of publishing. More minority titles and writers are needed, particularly Hispanic and Native American, and books representing the intellectually and physically disabled cultures. However, the call has been issued, and in time we hope that the void will be filled.

INTERNATIONAL BOOKS

Just as multicultural books dealing with American society assist in creating a bridge of understanding, international books can help children gain an appreciation and understanding of our global society. The history and culture of other countries as well as their literary traditions are illuminated through books that have their origins outside the United States.

The most common international books in the United States are English-language titles written and published in another English-speaking country, such as England, Canada, Australia, and New Zealand. Because these books need no translation, they can be acquired and marketed readily by American publishers. (See Appendix F for the names of foreign, English-language book awards.)

Although translated books are less plentiful in the United States, this area of publishing is growing. These foreign-language books originally are written and printed in other countries. American companies then acquire the rights to publish them, and they are translated into English. A very limited number of foreign-language children's books from other countries are released in the United States in untranslated form.

One consideration when judging translated books is the quality of the translation. Though the flavor of the country needs to be retained, the English text must be fluent and readable, yet not too "Americanized." Often a few foreign words and phrases may be left in to provide readers a feel for the culture and language, but too many can be troublesome for children.

There is an ever-increasing exchange of children's books among countries, but most of the international books published in the United States come from Europe. Each year since 1966, publishers from around the world have attended an international children's book fair in Bologna, Italy, where they share their books with one another and work out agreements for publishing them in other countries.

Since World War II, a number of organizations, publications, and awards have been established to promote the idea of an international world of children's books. In 1949, the International Youth Library was founded in Munich, Germany. It has become a world center for the study of children's literature. In 1953, the International Board on Books for Young People (IBBY) was established, and soon after, in 1956, this organization created the first international children's book award. The Hans Christian Andersen Medal is given every two years to an author whose lifetime contribution to the world of children's literature is considered outstanding. In 1966, a separate award for illustration was added to the Hans Christian Medal, and IBBY also began publishing *Bookbird*, a journal linking those interested in international children's books. In 1968 in the United States, the ALA began presenting the Mildred Batchelder Award to the American publisher of the most noteworthy translated children's book of the year.

With the increased emphasis on well-written multicultural and international children's books, teachers and parents have an additional means by which they may help children avoid the pitfalls of ignorance that breed intolerance, hatred, and conflict. In an atomic age, we certainly cannot afford the increasingly deadly outcomes sparked by xenophobic behaviors.

REFERENCES

Aardema, Verna. 1975. *Why Mosquitoes Buzz in People's Ears*. New York: Dial.

Armstrong, William. 1969. *Sounder.* New York: Harper & Row.

Bishop, Rudine Sims. 1992. Multicultural literature for children: Making informed choices. In *Teaching Multicultural Literature in Grades K–8*, edited by Violet J. Harris. Norwood, Mass: Christopher-Gordon.

Bontemps, Arna. 1948. *Story of the Negro*. New York: Knopf.

Boyd, Candy Dawson. 1990. Presentation given at The American Bookseller's Association Convention and Trade Exhibit, Las Vegas, Nevada, 5 June (cassette recording).

Bunting, Eve. 1994. *Smoky Night*. New York: Harcourt.

Clark, Ann Nolan. 1952. *Secret of the Andes*. New York: Viking.

Hamilton, Virginia. 1974. *M. C. Higgins the Great*. New York: Macmillan.

Hansen-Krening, Nancy. 1992. Authors of color: A multicultural perspective. *Journal of Reading* 36, no. 2 (October): 124–129.

Horn, Miriam. 1993. Imagining other's lives. *U.S. News and World Report* 114, no. 6 (February 15): 78–81.

Keats, Ezra Jack. 1962. *The Snowy Day*. New York: Viking.

Krumgold, Joseph. 1953. *And Now Miguel*. New York: Crowell.

Larrick, Nancy. 1965. The all white world of children's books. *Saturday Review,* 11 September, pp. 63–65, 84–85.

Nieto, Sonia. 1996. *Affirming Diversity*. 2nd ed. White Plains, N.Y.: Longman.

Pate, Glenn S. 1988. Research on reducing prejudice. *Social Education* 52, no. 4 (April/May): 287–291.

Politi, Leo. 1949. *Song of the Swallows*. New York: Scribner's.

Robinson, Barbara. 1972. *The Best Christmas Pageant Ever.* New York: Harper & Row.

Say, Allen. 1993. *Grandfather's Journey*. New York: Houghton Mifflin.

Sims, Rudine. 1982. *Shadow and Substance: Afro-American Experience in Contemporary Children's Fiction*. Urbana, Ill.: National Council of Teachers of English.

Sobol, Thomas. 1990. Understanding diversity. *Educational Leadership* 48, no. 3 (November): 27–30.

Sonnenschein, Frances M. 1988. Countering prejudiced beliefs and behaviors: The role of the social studies professional. *Social Education* 52, no. 4 (April/May): 264–266.

Taylor, Mildred. 1976. *Roll of Thunder, Hear My Cry*. New York: Dial.

Wilson, August. 1990. I want a black director. *The New York Times*, 26 September, p. A25.

Yates, Elizabeth. 1950. *Amos Fortune, Free Man*. New York: Dutton.

Young, Ed. 1989. *Lon Po Po: A Red Riding Hood Story from China*. New York: Philomel.

MULTICULTURAL BOOKS READING LIST

Many fine multicultural and international titles, indeed many of our favorites, have been included in the other reading lists in this book. For the most part, they have not been repeated here.

African American

Curtis, Christopher Paul. 1995. *The Watsons Go to Birmingham—1963*. Delacorte.

Draper, Sharon M. 1997. *Forged by Fire*. Atheneum.

Hamilton, Virginia. 1995. *Her Stories: African American Folktales, Fairy Tales, and True Tales*. Illustrated by Leo Dillon and Diane Dillon. Blue Sky/Scholastic.

Haskins, James. 1995. *Black Eagles: African Americans in Aviation*. Scholastic.

Hoffman, Mary. 1991. *Amazing Grace*. Illustrated by Caroline Binch. Dial.

McKissack, Patricia. 1988. *Mirandy and Brother Wind*. Illustrated by Jerry Pinkney. Holt.

Meltzer, Milton. 1984. *The Black Americans: A History in Their Own Words, 1619–1983*. Crowell.

Myers, Walter Dean. 1991. *Now Is Your Time: The African-American Struggle for Freedom*. Harper.

Myers, Walter Dean. 1997. *Harlem*. Illustrated by Christopher Myers. Scholastic.

Schroeder, Alan. 1996. *Minty: A Story of Harriet Tubman*. Illustrated by Jerry Pinkney. Dial.

Taylor, Mildred. 1990. *Road to Memphis*. Dial.

Asian American

Brown, Tricia. 1991. *Lee Ann: The Story of a Vietnamese-American Girl*. Putnam.

Choi, Sook Nyul. 1997. *Yunmi and Halmoni's Trip*. Houghton.

Lord, Bette Bao. 1984. *In the Year of the Boar and Jackie Robinson*. Harper.

Mochizuki, Ken. 1993. *Baseball Saved Us*. Illustrated by Dom Lee. Lee and Low.

Morey, Janet Nomura, and Wendy Dunn. 1992. *Famous Asian Americans*. Dutton.

Salisbury, Graham. 1994. *Under the Blood-Red Sun*. Delacorte.

Say, Allen. 1993. *Grandfather's Journey*. Houghton Mifflin.

Uchida, Yoshiko. 1981. *A Jar of Dreams*. McElderry.

Yee, Paul. 1990. *Tales from Gold Mountain: Stories of the Chinese in the New World*. Macmillan.

Yep, Laurence. 1977. *Child of the Owl*. Harper.

Yep, Laurence. 1998. *The Cook's Family*. Putnam.

Hispanic American (Latino)

Ancona, George. 1993. *Pablo Remembers: The Fiesta of the Day of the Dead*. Lothrop.

Anderson, Joan. 1989. *Spanish Pioneers of the Southwest*. Dutton.

Buss, Fran Leeper. 1991. *Journey of the Sparrows*. Lodestar.

Carlson, Lori M. 1994. *Cool Salsa: Bilingual Poems on Growing Up Latino in the United States*. Holt.

Cofer, Judith Ortiz. 1995. *An Island Like You: Stories of the Barrio*. Orchard.

Dorros, Arthur. 1991. *Abuela*. Illustrated by Elisa Kleven. Dutton.

Lomas Garza, Carmen. 1996. *In My Family/En mi familia*. Children's Book Press.

Martinez, Floyd. 1997. *Spiritis of the High Mesa*. Arte Público Press.

Meltzer, Milton. 1982. *The Hispanic Americans*. Harper.

Soto, Gary. 1990. *Baseball in April and Other Stories*. Harcourt.

Soto, Gary. 1997. *Snapshots from the Wedding*. Putnam.

Native American

Begay, Shonto. 1992. *Ma'ii and Cousin Horned Toad: A Traditional Navajo Story*. Scholastic.

Bruchac, Joseph, and Jonathan London. 1992. *Thirteen Moons on Turtle's Back: A Native American Year of Moons*. Illustrated by Thomas Locker. Philomel.

Bruchac, Joseph. 1996. *Legends of Native American Sacred Places*. Dial.

Cohen, Carol. 1988. *The Mud Pony*. Illustrated by Shonto Begay. Scholastic.

Dorris, Michael. 1996. *Sees Behind Trees*. Hyperion.

Ekoomiak, Normee. 1988. *Arctic Memories*. Holt.

Freedman, Russell. 1992. *Indian Winter*. Illustrated by Karl Bodmer. Holiday House.

Highwater, Jamake. 1977. *Anpao: An American Indian Odyssey*. Lippincott.

O'Dell, Scott. 1970. *Sing Down the Moon*. Houghton Mifflin.

Sneve, Virginia Driving Hawk, ed. 1989. *Dancing Teepees: Poems of American Indian Youth*. Illustrated by Stephen Gammell. Holiday House.

Religious Cultures

Ammon, Richard. 1989. *Growing Up Amish*. Atheneum. (Christian–Amish.)

Barrie, Barbara. 1990. *Lone Star*. Delacorte. (Jewish.)

Cormier, Robert. 1990. *Other Bells for Us to Ring*. Delacorte. (Christian–Catholic.)

Demi. 1996. *Buddha*. Holt. (Buddhist.)

Dickinson, Peter. 1979. *Tulka*. Dutton. (Buddhist.)

Highwater, Jamake. 1994. *Rama: A Legend*. Holt. (Hindu.)

Meltzer, Milton. 1982. *The Jewish Americans: A History in Their Own Words, 1650–1950*. Harper. (Jewish.)

Oppenheim, Shulamith Levey. 1994. *Iblis: An Islamic Tale*. Illustrated by Ed Young. Harcourt. (Islam.)

Osborne, Mary Pope. 1996. *One World, Many Religions: The Ways We Worship*. Knopf.

Rylant, Cynthia. 1986. *A Fine White Dust*. Bradbury. (Christian–Protestant.)

Cultures of the Physically and Mentally Challenged

Bezzant, Pat. 1994. *Angie*. Fawcett/Juniper.

Bloor, Edward. 1997. *Tangerine*. Harcourt.

Charlip, Remy, and Mary Beth Miller. 1987. *Handtalk Birthday: A Number and Story Book in Sign Language*. Photographs by George Ancona. Four Winds. (See other books in the Handtalk series.)

Little, Jean. 1991. *Listen for the Singing*. Harper.

Maguire, Gregory. 1994. *Missing Sisters*. McElderry.

McKenzie, Ellen Kindt. 1990. *Stargone John*. Illustrated by William Low. Holt.

Morpurgo, Michael. 1996. *The Ghost of Grania O'Malley*. Viking.

Shreve, Susan. 1991. *The Gift of the Girl Who Couldn't Hear*. Tambourine.

St. George, Judith. 1992. *Dear Dr. Bell . . . Your Friend, Helen Keller*. Putnam.

Sutcliff, Rosemary. 1970. *The Witch's Brat*. Walck.

Wolff, Virginia Euwer. 1988. *Probably Still Nick Swansen*. Holt.

Women

(Because women historically have had minority status, we have included some of the recent titles dealing with women's rights and accomplishments.)

Colman, Penny. 1995. *Rosie the Riveter: Women Working on the Home Front in World War II*. Crown.

Cushman, Karen. 1994. *Catherine, Called Birdy*. Clarion.

Dash, Joan. 1996. *We Shall Not Be Moved: The Women's Factory Strike of 1909*. Scholastic.

Fritz, Jean. 1995. *You Want Women to Vote, Lizzie Stanton?* Putnam.

Gherman, Beverly. 1991. *Sandra Day O'Connor: Justice for All*. Illustrated by Robert Masheris. Viking. (See other titles in the Women of Our Time series.)

Hodges, Margaret. 1989. *Making a Difference: The Story of an American Family*. Scribner's.

Keenan, Sheila. 1996. *Scholastic Encyclopedia of Women in the United States*. Scholastic.

Lauber, Patricia. 1988. *Lost Star: The Story of Amelia Earhart*. Scholastic.

Macy, Sue. 1996. *Winning Ways: A Photobiography of American Women in Sports*. Holt.

Oneal, Zibby. 1990. *A Long Way to Go*. Viking.

Rappaport, Doreen, ed. 1990. *American Women: Their Lives in Their Words*. Harper.

INTERNATIONAL BOOKS READING LIST

English Language Books

Aiken, Joan. 1995. *Cold Shoulder Road*. Delacorte. (U.K.)

Fine, Anne. 1996. *Step by Wicked Step*. Little, Brown. (U.K.)

Fox, Mem. 1987. *Possum Magic*. Illustrated by Julie Vivas. Abington. (Australia.)

Harrison, Ted. 1993. *O Canada*. Ticknor, 1993. (Canada.)

Hughes, Monica. 1995. *The Golden Aquarians*. Simon & Schuster. (Canada.)

Lunn, Janet. 1987. *Shadow in Hawthorne Bay*. Scribner's. (Canada.)

Mahy, Margaret. 1995. *The Other Side of Silence*. Viking. (New Zealand.)

Naidoo, Beverly. 1990. *Chain of Fire*. Lippincott. (South Africa.)

Park, Ruth. 1980. *Playing the Beatie Bow*. Macmillan. (Australia.)

Sutcliff, Rosemary. 1990. *The Shining Company*. Farrar. (U.K.)

Westall, Robert. 1991. *The Kingdom by the Sea*. Farrar. (U.K.)

Translated Books

Björk, Christina. 1987. *Linnea in Monet's Garden*. Illustrated by Lena Anderson. R & S Books. (Sweden.)

Gallaz, Christopher. 1985. *Rose Blanche*. Illustrated by Roberto Innocenti. Creative Education. (France.)

Heine, Helme. 1989. *Prince Bear*. McElderry. (Germany.)

Lindgren, Astrid. 1983. *Ronia, the Robber's Daughter*. Viking. (Sweden.)

Llorente, Molina. 1993. *The Apprentice*. Farrar. (Spain.)

Maruki, Toshi. 1982. *Hiroshima No Pika*. Lothrop. (Japan.)

Orlev, Uri. 1991. *The Man from the Other Side*. Houghton Mifflin. (Israel.)

Orlev, Uri. 1995. *The Lady with the Hat*. Houghton. (Israel.)

Reuter, Bjarne. 1994. *The Boys from St. Petri*. Dutton. (Denmark.)

Richter, Hans Peter. 1972. *I Was There*. Holt. (Germany.)

Zei, Aldi. 1979. *The Sound of Dragon's Feet*. Dutton. (Greece.)

For a more complete list of multicultural titles, consult the compact disc that accompanies this text.

CHAPTER 16

Controversial Books

Books are dangerous. They can undermine morals, fuel revolutions, and indoctrinate our children. Hitler certainly believed in the power of print and saw to it that publications challenging Nazi policy or written by anyone he deemed an enemy of the state (which, of course, included books by all Jewish authors) were banned or, worse yet, burned. No doubt there are books that we, as individuals, would find offensive or that would challenge our way of thinking and make us uncomfortable. But danger exists far less in these books than in the people who would usurp the power and authority to decide for the rest of us what is fit to be read.

Our First Amendment rights are under constant attack by those who consider paramount their personal agendas, sets of standards, or brands of special interest. The more radical or fanatical the group objecting to certain printed materials—and extremists come from both the political right and left—the more control they seek over individual freedom of choice. Give them the power, and they will decide for us what is best, as Hitler so self-righteously did for his people. Supreme Court Justice William Brennan eloquently expressed this idea when he said, concerning the censorship case Texas v. Johnson, "If there is a bedrock principle underlying the First Amendment, it is that the Government may not prohibit the expression of an idea simply because society finds the idea itself offensive or disagreeable" (American Library Association, 1998).

This is not to say that individuals should not have the right to make decisions about the personal acceptability of books. We have not only the right but also the responsibility to make choices for ourselves and to help our children make wise choices. And if we find a book particularly offensive or dangerous, we should express that opinion without seeking to destroy the book.

In today's diverse society, what may seem clearly offensive to one group of people may be viewed as beautiful and uplifting by another. An example of this dichotomy occurred not long ago in Rockford, Illinois. Parents of a particular religious sect felt that reading Greek myths in the public schools was an evil practice. Believing strongly in the truth of their Christian faith, they considered the Greek myths pagan theology that threatened to undermine the faith of their children. Of course, many others, Christians and non-Christians alike, viewed the Greek myths as remarkable literature that illuminates the history of our world and fosters an understanding of cultures unlike our own. The controversy in Illinois is, unfortunately, not an isolated incident of this sort of censorship aimed at public schools and libraries.

We do not wish to give the impression that any and all books should be available without considering the ages of the children or the prevailing community standards. For example, in virtually every community excessively pornographic books are unacceptable materials for school and public libraries and even for bookstores. We use the term *excessive* here because even pornography does not seem to have clearly defined borders. Some adults consider Judy Blume's (1970) *Are You There God? It's Me, Margaret* to be a form of pornography because it includes sexual topics. Others would consider laughable the labeling of this book as pornographic. Nonetheless, a fine line often must be trod by school librarians and teachers when it comes to preserving intellectual freedoms and students' right to read. In some instances, certain titles are kept in closed areas to be circulated only with parental permission. Sex education books often are hidden on these restricted shelves, especially in elementary schools.

As school and library personnel know, sex and bad language in books for young readers predictably generate controversy anywhere in the country. Other topics may be volatile in particular communities, such as violence, the occult, racism, or religion; but sex and bad language in children's books seem to alienate adults generally. For example, Katherine Paterson's (1978) Newbery Honor Book, *The Great Gilly Hopkins,* has a number of potentially controversial elements. Gilly racially slanders her black teacher. She steals without conscience from the blind man next door, who is also black. She is cruel to her foster brother. Yet, as Paterson (1989) explains, the vast amount of mail she has received from adults complains only about the so-called rough language Gilly uses in the story. When it comes to children's reading, adults seem particularly sensitive to this issue.

Because controversies about sexual content or bad language in books are predictable, teachers and librarians know that if they use certain books they must be prepared to weather the inevitable storm of complaints. Unpredictable controversies, on the other hand, take educators by surprise. They can feel extremely vulnerable and even defenseless against unexpected censorship attacks for which they have prepared neither intellectually nor emotionally. Here are several surprising examples of unpredictable controversy occurring within the last few decades:

- The 1970 Caldecott winner, William Steig's (1969) *Sylvester and the Magic Pebble,* seemed an innocuous animal fantasy until someone pointed out that the policemen in the book were depicted as pigs. The book was published during the era of Vietnam War protests, when policemen often were branded as "pigs" by demonstrators. "No wonder that the children and some adults have no respect for the law enforcement officer . . . we demand the book be removed," said the International Conference of Police Associations (Harvey 1971).
- A public librarian reported an objection about a children's Halloween book raised by a woman who claimed to be a witch. She "felt the book was anti-witch and presented an unfair and unfavorable picture" (Chu 1982, p. 7).
- A poem in Shel Silverstein's (1981) popular collection *A Light in the Attic* tells of a girl who tries to make a milkshake by shaking a cow and is accompanied by a pen-and-ink drawing that shows her in action. The Eagle Forum, a politically conservative organization, charged that the illustration was "an example of subliminal suggestion of 'sex with animals' " (Haferd 1988).
- Dr. Seuss (1971), who is an American institution, found his book *The Lorax* in hot water in Laytonville, California, a single-industry lumber town. *The Lorax* tells of a "little creature who loses his forest home when greedy Once-lers cut down all the Truffula trees." Residents saw this as "a flagrant attack on the livelihood" of the town and on the lumbering industry in general and demanded that the book be removed from the second-grade required reading list (Arias and McNeil 1989, pp. 67–68).
- The Newbery Award-winning book *Bridge to Terabithia* by Katherine Paterson (1977) consistently shows up on the American Library Association's (ALA)(1998) yearly banned books list. Not surprisingly, many complaints center around the theme of death or the use of bad language, but a 1996 com-

plaint accuses the book of creating "an elaborate fantasy world that might lead to confusion."

- Ed Young's 1993 Caldecott Honor Book, *Seven Blind Mice* (1992) is a variant of the story of the three blind men and the elephant. Each mouse, a different and brilliant color, incorrectly identifies the object (elephant) they have encountered until the white mouse solves the riddle. A host of critics surfaced, complaining that representing the white mouse as the "savior" perpetuates the racist viewpoint of white supremacy.

Controversy about children's books may spring from anywhere, and the challenge may be about almost anything. So, how should we as teachers and school librarians proceed in our selection and use of books? First, we need to affirm our personal commitment to individual choice by examining how we view books. If we view books strictly as mirrors that must reflect our particular mores, lifestyles, or standards, then our problem is a difficult one. Whose standards or beliefs are the books to model? The answer could mean the difference between Greek myths or no Greek myths. If, instead, we view books as windows to the world, we have determined that literature is designed to celebrate diversity and that we accept the risks that may accompany such a stance.

If we indeed view books as windows, we then will be less inclined to exercise control over other readers. The diagram in Figure 16–1 represents the domains of control in which all of us may choose to function. The smallest sphere is the domain of self. No one would disagree that we each have the responsibility to decide what we personally will or will not read and, as the circle widens, that parents have the right to at least influence the reading of their minor children. It is the people who view books strictly as mirrors who more likely will choose to operate in the expanded spheres of control by seeking to control reading materials in their community or, if they had the power, in the entire world. The International Conference of Police Associations wished to exercise this sort of far-reaching control by demanding that *Sylvester and the Magic Pebble* (Steig, 1969) be removed from all libraries.

Professional organizations such as the ALA, the International Reading Association, and the National Council of Teachers of English have adopted statements of philosophy concerning intellectual freedom and our right to read. Organizations that actually assist teachers and librarians who need help in fighting censorship attacks include the ALA's Freedom to Read Foundation (phone: 800-545-2433 ext. 4226), the National Coalition Against Censorship (phone: 212-807-6222), and People for the American Way (phone: 800-326-7329). But even with this sort of support network, teachers and librarians may wish to exercise some caution, especially in selecting books to read aloud to children or to be required classroom reading. Whenever children are captive audiences, book watchdogs are more strident. Therefore, a few touchstones may help us to understand and talk about potentially controversial books.

ASSIGNED BOOKS VERSUS AVAILABLE BOOKS. There is a difference, within a school setting, between a book that is assigned reading and a book that is merely available on school or classroom library shelves. When a book is compulsory reading for students, the likelihood of parental complaints is higher. Teachers should consider

FIGURE 16–1
Domains of control.

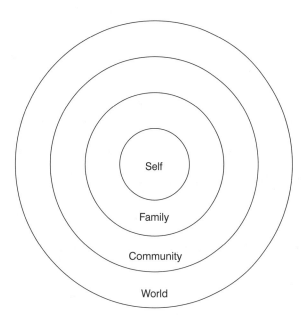

carefully whether or not a book they plan to use as an assigned title is one they would be willing to defend.

POSITIVE LEARNING CAN COME FROM NEGATIVE PORTRAYALS. It is not unusual that books with negative content are dismissed out-of-hand. For example, some adults do not want their children reading a novel that involves drug abuse, because they feel it may plant a suggestion that could lead to trouble. However, if the story illustrates the negative consequences of drug abuse, the book actually may be desirable. That drug use appears in a book does not automatically condemn the title; its presence may serve positive ends.

Even religious literature includes negative episodes for positive purposes. In the Bible, King David's story involves lust, adultery, deceit, and even murder in an illustration of how indulgence and becoming self-serving can lead to undesirable ends.

Avoiding the harsh and often unsavory realities of life does not make them go away. In fact, a child may be more susceptible to the effects of controversial material by being totally unprepared. As Jane Smiley (1994) says, "A child who is protected from all controversial ideas . . . is as vulnerable as a child who is protected from every germ. The infection, when it comes, and it will come, may overwhelm the system, be that the immune system or the belief system."

BOOKS SHOULD BE JUDGED HOLISTICALLY. It is impossible and unfair to judge a book simply by the subject. All books showing drug abuse, all books that deal with sexual topics, and all books containing swear words are not automatically bad.

Nor are they automatically good. The light in which these subjects are presented makes the difference.

If uncomfortable subject matter offers insight, helps develop attitudes and skills for dealing successfully with life, and fosters resolution or hope, the book may be a worthwhile addition to a recommended list. For instance, in *Dear Mr. Henshaw* by Beverly Cleary (1983), the main character, Leigh Botts, is torn by his parents' divorce. Living with his mother and longing for his parents to get back together, he suffers from two common misconceptions held by children of divorce: (1) It's my fault my parents are divorcing, and (2) if I behave the right way I can bring them back together. Leigh struggles with these perceptions, but by the conclusion of the book he has come to grips with the fact that not only was he not to blame for the breakup but also that he can do nothing to change things. With this resolved, he finally is able to go forward with his life. Resolution provides hope. Hopeful books are easier to defend.

AMOUNT AND DEGREE OF REALISTIC DETAIL CAN BE A REASON FOR NOT RECOMMENDING A BOOK. Some exposure to life's harshness can prepare children for difficult times; too much exposure can traumatize them. With literature we hope to sensitize children to important issues of the human experience. If details are too explicit, however, children may be traumatized instead of sensitized. The age of the children will make a difference—what may work with twelve-year-olds may not work with five-year-olds. Also, individual differences in children of the same age can be significant. Adults need to know both the books and the children to make this judgment call. In any case, it is a literary weakness to resort to sensationalistic details that merely titillate or shock.

An example of a book that sensitizes young readers to an issue without an excess of raw detail is Paula Fox's (1973) Newbery-winner *The Slave Dancer*. She goes just far enough in this story of the American slave trade to show people's inhumanity without becoming too explicit. By comparison, the adult book *Roots by* Alex Haley (1976), which was published about the same time as *The Slave Dancer*, covers the same basic material in far more complete and explicit detail.

HANDLING BOOK CHALLENGES

Because controversy about books is so unpredictable, almost any book sitting on the library shelf or being shared in the classroom may be challenged by parents and other adults. Therefore, we may find ourselves defending our choice of books. If a parent comes in to complain, remember that reaching an understanding is possible and even probable. Sometimes the problem may be a simple misunderstanding that can be cleared up once teacher and parent communicate. For example, parents may hear about a troublesome book but then discover they have been misinformed. However, if a serious challenge surfaces, teachers and librarians need to have a plan in place to control a potentially explosive situation.

The first rule of thumb when potential censors challenge materials is to deal with *only* one book at a time. Allowing complainants to challenge several books at once or all books by one author makes for an uncontrollable situation. To keep the situation under control, each library system, school, or school district must have policies and procedures that will govern censorship cases. Consider the following three guidelines for handling book challenges: (1) materials selection policy, (2) grievance procedure, (3) steps to reduce emotional tension.

Materials Selection Policy

Have a materials selection policy at your school or library. A selection policy will guide the process of choosing books and other media for libraries and classroom use. Often, guidelines and procedures outlined in a selection policy will include the ALA's "Library Bill of Rights" or other "right to read" statements that confirm the institution's support of First Amendment rights and intellectual freedom. Also, selection policies will suggest the use of nationally recognized review journals in helping to make selections. Generally a selection committee with teacher representatives from various grade levels or disciplines and sometimes from parent groups such as the Parent/Teacher Association (PTA) is named to make final selection recommendations. Policy statements also may specify the standards of all materials used in a school setting, even personal books that a teacher may bring to read to students.

Grievance Procedure

Each library system, school, or school district must have a formal grievance procedure in place, either as a section of the materials selection policy or as a separate document. This procedure dictates the process by which an individual may request that the library or school reconsider a book. It always includes a formal complaint form that must be filled out and signed by the complainant (see Figure 16–2). Some people who challenge books are reluctant to sign a formal complaint. Unless a complainant is willing to file a formal complaint that bears his or her signature, the school or library need no longer consider the challenge to the book. However, if the form is filed, the grievance procedure dictates further action by the library system or school district. Generally a committee, which may be the same as the selection committee, is convened to consider the complaint. It is wise to include community representation on such a committee. The decision of the committee is then passed on to the school or library board, which usually makes the final decision based on committee recommendation. It is possible the censors may take their case into the court system if they are not pleased with a board's decision. However, the fact that the complaint was given a fair and carefully prescribed hearing can only strengthen a school or library system's case.

Steps to Reduce Emotional Tension

With policies in place, teachers and librarians can breathe easier. Still, when the time comes to face someone who is challenging a book, two other guidelines are helpful. First, we must make a supreme effort to keep conversation with an upset parent or

Citizen's Request for Reconsideration of a Book

Paperback_____

Author_____ Hardcover _____

Title_____

Publisher (if known)_____

Request initiated by_____

Telephone _____ Address _____

City_____ Zip Code _____

Complainant represents:
_____ Himself/herself
_____ Organization (Name) _____
_____ Other group (Identify) _____

1. To what in the book do you object? (Please be specific; cite pages.)_____
_____
_____

2. What do you feel might be the result of reading this book?_____
_____
_____

3. For what age group would you recommend this book?_____
_____
_____

4. Is there anything positive about this book?_____
_____
_____

5. Did you read the entire book?_____ What parts? _____
_____
_____

6. Are you aware of the judgment of this book by literary critics?_____
_____
_____

7. What would you like the library/school to do about this book?
_____ Withdraw it.
_____ Return it to the selection committee/department for reconsideration.
_____ Do not assign or lend it to my child.
_____ Other. (Please explain.)_____
_____

8. In its place, what book would you recommend that would convey as valuable a picture and perspective of the subject treated?_____
_____
_____

_____   _____
Signature of Complainant   Date

FIGURE 16–2

Example of a citizen's request for reconsideration of a book.

library patron on a rational level rather than an emotional one. Having the complainant *fill out the form* is one way to reduce emotions and provide more focused discussion. Another way is simply to *listen to the complaint*. This may not be as easy as it sounds, for often teachers and librarians feel attacked, and their natural response is to be defensive. If angry words rule, however, the chances are that the book will not be as big an issue as the escalating distaste for one another. So, we need to hold our tongues and listen, which allows us to determine if the complaint is a product of a misunderstanding or if we need to channel the complainant peacefully into the formal grievance procedure.

Along with listening calmly to the complainant, we also ought to *get someone else to listen:* another librarian, the teacher from across the hall, the principal. Having someone else present helps to keep everyone honest and serves to reduce tension. We are always more careful of our words when others are there to hear.

Cynthia Robinson (1998), from the ALA's Office for Intellectual Freedom, says that censorship cases reported during the 1990s to the ALA have numbered between 500 and 700 annually. However, Judith Krug (1998), director of the Office for Intellectual Freedom, makes it clear that these numbers represent only about 20 to 25 percent of the challenges; the others go unreported. According to children's book editor Phyllis J. Fogleman, censorship letters received by publishers in the 1970s and '80s mostly complained about sexuality, "but now censors are broadening their scope . . . " (West 1988, p. 111). Though she points particularly to complaints about anything that seems even remotely anti-Christian, the prickly world of political correctness also has fueled the censorship fires, as exemplified by the criticism of *Seven Blind Mice* (Young, 1992).

Of the top ten challenged titles of 1997, six were children's books (Robinson, 1998). Two of those six were not single titles but entire series, which greatly increases the number of challenged children's titles on the top-ten list (American Library Association, 1998). These figures are indicative of the particular attention adult censors give to children's books. As we have seen earlier in this chapter, these challenges are spawned by a vast variety of special interests that may or may not represent mainstream thought. And even if mainstream opinion is supported by a successful censorship attempt, then certain voices from our pluralistic society will be silenced. Ultimately, those of us who love books and cherish the right to choose must actively stand on the side of individual choice and intellectual freedom.

REFERENCES

Amercian Library Association. 10 March, 1998. Internet website: Office of Intellectual Freedom http://www.ala.org/oif.html; Challenged and Banned Books http://www.ala.org/bbooks/challeng.html

Arias, Ron, and Liz McNeil. 1989. A boy sides with Dr. Seuss, and puts a town at loggerheads. *People Weekly* 32, no. 17 (23 October): 67–68.

Blume, Judy. 1970. *Are You There God? It's Me, Margaret.* New York: Bradbury.

Chu, Nancy. 1982. Some thoughts concerning censorship. *The Dragon Lode* 3, no. 2 (March): 6–10.

Cleary, Beverly. 1983. *Dear Mr. Henshaw.* New York: Morrow.

Fox, Paula. 1973. *The Slave Dancer.* New York: Bradbury.

Haferd, Laura. 1988. Activist leads fight against "subliminals." *The Akron (Ohio) Beacon Journal,* 23 April.

Haley, Alex. 1976. *Roots.* New York: Doubleday.

Harvey, James S. 1971. *Newsletter on Intellectual Freedom* (March): 44–45.

Krug, Judith. 1998. Telephone interview with Michael Tunnell, 9 March.

Paterson, Katherine. 1977. *Bridge to Terabithia.* New York: Crowell.

Paterson, Katherine. 1978. *The Great Gilly Hopkins.* New York: Crowell.

Paterson, Katherine. 1989. Tale of a reluctant dragon. *The New Advocate* 2, no. 1 (Winter): 1–8.

Robinson, Cynthia. 1998. Telephone interview with Michael Tunnell, 10 March.

Seuss, Dr. 1971. *The Lorax.* New York: Random House.

Silverstein, Shel. 1981. *A Light in the Attic.* New York: Harper & Row.

Steig, William. 1969. *Sylvester and the Magic Pebble.* New York: Windmill/Simon & Schuster.

Smiley, Jane. 1994. Censorship in a world of fantasy. *Chicago Tribune,* February 15, Section 1, p. 19.

West, M. I. 1988. *Trust Your Children: Voices against Censorship.* New York: Neal-Schuman.

Young, Ed. 1992. *Seven Blind Mice.* New York: Philomel.

PART THREE

The Classroom

CHAPTER 17

The Teacher as Reader

THE POWER OF EXAMPLE

When it comes to teaching reading, the central principle of this chapter is the most important in the book: Teachers must *be* readers before they can help children become readers. That premise is the bedrock of successful reading education. In the educational quagmire of getting children to read—how to teach children to read, which assignments to give, what to do with class time, and how to evaluate their reading—nothing in the entire school has a greater impact on convincing children that books are worthwhile than teachers' reading habits (Perez 1986, p. 9). To witness and participate in real, engaged reading with an adult does more good than any educational program.

The United States Office of Education (USOE) underscores the importance of providing a model of a real reader. In an overview of reading instruction commissioned by the USOE, ten principles and ideas were identified that would heighten literacy learning. One of the ten is teacher modeling (Sweet 1993, p. 6).

Albert Schweitzer knew that nothing is more important than modeling in effecting change in people, including the students we teach. He noted that "example is not the main thing in influencing others. It is the only thing" (quoted in Simpson 1997, p. 388).

An experiment with a preschool class demonstrated the power of example. As the teacher talked with the children who were seated on a rug, she walked to a table behind her and took a piece of candy from a bowl. Putting it in her mouth, she paused and then said to no one in particular, but in a voice loud enough the children could hear, "M-m-m-m. I like this candy. It tastes good to me." The morning discussion continued, but within a minute she took the candy from her mouth and put it on a napkin on the table behind her. After more conversation, she again went to the table, this time to a bowl holding different candy. Taking a piece, she put it in her mouth, made an unpleasant face, and said, "Oh. I don't like this candy. It doesn't taste good to me." But she kept it in her mouth until she'd eaten it. When the discussion was finished, she told the children they could go to one bowl or the other and take a piece of candy. Most of the children made a beeline for the second bowl, the one she said was not good but she ate (Larson 1994). Her *actions* determined theirs; her words were empty.

A serious enemy of real learning is the kind of educational duplicity in the candy example. We adults influence children more by what we do than what we say, and teachers who speak one way but live another introduce an artificiality into education. They erroneously think children can be tricked into valuing what the teacher says instead of what the teacher believes and does. The insincerity of such teaching often results in student boredom and teacher burnout. Until teachers find a personal interest and excitement in what they teach, they never will teach it well.

People taught by excellent, energetic teachers who love their subjects know that the power felt in those classrooms came only in part from the accumulation of new knowledge. When students become excited about learning, the reason is not the subject matter but the teacher who has breathed life into it.

BENEFITS TO TEACHERS WHO READ

The miracle of education always has been the teacher: the human being who is first a learner and second a guide who enthusiastically leads others to learning. Teachers weak in their areas of instruction or not personally committed to a subject can make assignments and ask students to fill out worksheets, but those activities are not the kind that touch lives. Stimulation and enlightenment, which entice students to become involved in subject matter, come from people who are stimulated and enlightened. Teachers cannot successfully give away attitudes and ideas they do not own, particularly attitudes about books and reading.

Three solid benefits come to teachers who read.

1. *Teachers who read gain new knowledge constantly.* Teachers who read keep growing intellectually, realizing ever anew how broad and interesting the world is and how little of it can be squeezed into the formal curriculum. From reading they learn how life began on Surtsey, the newest island in the world, coughed up from a volcano near Iceland. How thermometers work. How Columbus is viewed as both hero and villain or somewhere in between.

Teachers who read also discover endless new ways to extend their subject areas: In science they discover that air pressure can be revealed dramatically by boiling a spoonful of water in a soft drink can, then turning it quickly upside down and plunging it into an inch of water where it loudly and satisfyingly implodes. In social studies they learn that Harriet Tubman's work to free slaves is even more heroic in light of the headaches and sleeping fits she suffered all her life, the result of having her skull broken when a storekeeper threw a fist-size scale weight at someone else and accidentally hit her.

2. *Teachers who read understand education better.* The range of information that comes to teachers who read broadly from trade books can help them develop and keep a wider view of what real learning is. Only interested learners can become interesting teachers. Teachers who read continue to challenge themselves in a broader arena than the school halls and curriculum. They have an easier time remembering the significance of their profession and keeping a true educational perspective, as pointed out by John W. Gardner (1981):

> The ultimate goal of the educational system is to shift to the individual the burden of pursuing his own education. This will not be a widely shared pursuit until we get over our odd conviction that education is what goes on in school buildings and nowhere else. Not only does education continue when schooling ends, but it is not confined to what may be studied in adult education courses. The world is an incomparable classroom, and life is a memorable teacher for those who aren't afraid of her. (pp. 11–12)

When our learning experiences are limited to the school classroom, we have more difficulty remembering the world classroom. But reading books other than those traditionally associated with school helps us remember that life is a memorable teacher.

Teachers who know that life is a memorable teacher find it less difficult to take risks. Having learned not to be afraid of life, they can accept the inevitable difficulty and fumbling that accompany learning. Max Plank referred to this when he was awarded the Nobel Prize:

> Looking back . . . over the long and labyrinthine path which finally led to the discovery [of the quantum theory], I am vividly reminded of Goethe's saying that men will always be making mistakes as long as they are striving after something. (Beveridge 1957, p. 60)

And teachers who are continuing learners also can abandon more easily the false notion that they must be The Answer Person. When they see themselves as joint learners with their students, facing a question for which they have no answer loses much of its threat. For example, when a teacher shared with her class the picture book *Thorn Rose or the Sleeping Beauty* (Grimm 1975), the story mentioned that not just the princess fell asleep for 100 years but that everything in the kingdom fell asleep, including the flies in the kitchen. As the teacher showed the illustration of the prince entering Sleeping Beauty's bedchamber, a child spied spider webs attached to her hair and promptly asked, "If everything's asleep, where did the spider webs come from?" The teacher, a learner at heart, replied, "I don't know. How can *you* explain this?"

By gaining new knowledge and a better understanding of education, teachers are less apt to suffer burnout. Teachers who continually are learning new content and who continually are aware of the processes of learning have more to draw on in teaching their students, are more enthusiastic, and are swayed less by the inevitable political winds that blow through the school district. Their vision tends to be broader, and they seem more able to cope with the unavoidable complexities, and even messiness, of education and life.

3.   *Teachers who read influence students to become readers.* It is too simplistic to say that a teacher needs only to read in order to influence students to become true learners. Yet the effects of reading can help teachers become the kind of people who make a positive difference in the lives of students. By being readers, teachers offer students a living model of the positive results of spending time with books: natural enthusiasm for the printed page, ease in handling differing viewpoints, confidence in knowing how to find new information, and ready knowledge at their fingertips, to name a few. Teaching and learning with a teacher who is a reader become much more than completing a set of worksheets or prepared learning activities. A teacher who is genuinely rewarded by personal reading, and willingly shares this enthusiasm with students, will influence them in a host of unpredictable, positive ways. Teachers who are lifelong readers create students who are lifelong readers.

So what kind of reading model do you currently offer students? The self-assessment in Figure 17–1 may help you take stock of your standing as a positive model of lifelong reading behaviors for the children you teach.

How Good a Reading Model Am I?

Personal Model

1. I read in a book for personal pleasure at least two different days per week.   Yes   No
2. Two of my favorite authors for children are _____.
3. One of my favorite illustrators of children's books is _____.
4. The title of a picture book published during the past three years is _____.
5. The title of a children's chapter book published during the past three years is _____.
6. I have a personal library of more than forty children's trade books.   Yes   No
7. The book I am going to read next is _____.
8. During the past three months, I found myself showing an interesting book to someone else or mentioning it in conversation. The title is _____.
9. My favorite genre or type of book is _____.
10. Two of my favorite authors for adults are _____.

Classroom Model

1. At least twice weekly I engage in personal reading where my students can see me with a book. Yes   No
2. My students can identify at least one type of book I like or dislike.   Yes   No
3. I have a growing classroom library of trade books.   Yes   No
4. I introduce or "book talk" books with my students at least twice a week.   Yes   No
5. I read aloud a picture book or from a chapter book to my class at least once every day.   Yes   No
6. I read aloud something other than books to my class daily.   Yes   No
7. Sustained Silent Reading (SSR) is a part of our daily schedule.   Yes   No
8. I always read in my own book during SSR.   Yes   No
9. I require my children to read regularly on their own outside of class.   Yes   No
10. I run a regular book club program or encourage children to buy books and help make that possible.   Yes   No

Scoring

Personal Model. Each questions counts 2 points.
1. Yes = 2 points. If teachers aren't reading, they can't deliver an honest love of books to students.
2. 1 point for each author. Teachers who read children's books will respond more to some authors than others and need to recognize they have favorites.
3. 2 points for completion. Even die-hard upper elementary teachers need to be familiar with picture books.
4. 2 points for completion. If a teacher knows only old books, chances for reaching children are more limited.
5. 2 points for completion. See number 4.

FIGURE 17–1
Reading model self-assessment for teachers.

6. One point for every 20 children's trade books you own (2 points maximum).
7. 2 points for completion. If you don't have an idea of what to read next, chances are you're not reading much.
8. 2 points for completion. If teachers never talk about the books they read, their influence will be limited.
9. 2 points for completion. Identifying a favorite type of book or genre is important self-knowledge.
10. 1 point for each author. Teachers who are readers generally will have a broader interest than just children's books.

Classroom Model. Each "yes" response receives 2 points.
1. Yes = 2 points. Adults who are most successful in turning children into readers do not hide their own reading. This is as true at home as in the classroom. One of our graduate students read regularly, yet none of her four children valued books. Further conversation revealed she read only in the bathtub and in bed after the children were asleep. Because she never talked to them or in front of them about her reading, they had no idea at all she liked books.
2. Yes = 2 points. If you emphasize personal reading with children, they need to learn about your personal reading, which includes the types of books you like and those that are not as appealing to you. Children deserve a teacher with identified favorites.
3. Yes = 2 points. We have a difficult time convincing children that books are worthwhile if none are at hand.
4. Yes = 2 points. Sharing titles consistently will give children needed and welcome reading options.
5. Yes = 2 points. Hearing books being read aloud is the most important classroom activity for turning children into readers.
6. Yes = 2 points. The more we immerse students in "real" reading (see Chapter 1), the better chance we have that they will become readers.
7. Yes = 2 points. SSR is the second most important classroom activity for turning children into readers.
8. Yes = 2 points. The key to a successful SSR program is seeing the teacher read.
9. Yes = 2 points. This is the most important out-of-class activity for turning children into readers.
10. Yes = 2 points. Book ownership is a mark of a truly literate person.

Each quiz has a maximum of 20 points. Scores and rating for each quiz, and both combined, are as follows:

Personal or Classroom Score	Total Score	Rating
16–20	32–40	Stupendous. You're a fine model.
12–15	24–31	Very good. You're better than most.
8–11	16–23	Okay, but you need work.
4–7	8–15	Weak. Quick—get books into your life.
0–3	0–7	Don't have children or teach school just yet.

FIGURE 17–1, *continued*

PRACTICAL HINTS FOR BECOMING A BETTER READING MODEL

If you scored lower on the self-assessment form (Figure 17–1) than you would like, all is not lost. It is never too late to adopt new reading practices and attitudes. Some helpful suggestions follow:

1. *Make reading easy in your life*. Imagine two people who sing the praises of reading, say they love books, and consider the time they spend with a good paperback absolutely delicious. Both are sincere, completely honest, and will stay up most of the night to finish a book that has captured them. Yet one of the people reads a good deal more than the other. Their responses to one question often can identify the frequent reader from the infrequent one: "What are you going to read next?" Infrequent readers usually have difficulty coming up with a title. They stare at the ceiling for a while and do a fair amount of throat clearing before finally mentioning a book—if they name one at all. Most of the frequent readers, on the other hand, immediately identify a title. Frequent readers have made getting to the next book a natural, easy process in their lives and usually have a stack next to their beds, on a shelf, or in their nightstands, so when they finish their current book they slide into the next title without missing a beat. Every infrequent reader personally has to solve the problem of where the next book is coming from—book clubs, library visits, bookstore browsing, bestseller lists, or friends' recommendations—but frequent readers already have worked out a system for getting easily to that next new title.

2. *Model reader response*. Tell people about the books you read. Share your experiences with print. Talk with your students and others about your reading, reflecting the honest devotion, rejection, pleasure, frustration, admiration, analysis, or admiration that you feel for what you have read. Introduce to your students favorite books and characters. Copy from a book a passage or sentence that has meaning for you, and tack it up where others can see. Read a section that has personal significance, and tell the class why. In short, show students how you feel about books, encouraging them to respond with the same honesty. Ask them for their feelings about what they are reading. And accept the feelings of the reader, regardless of your own.

3. *Remember to walk two reading paths simultaneously*. Every teacher should identify and feed personal reading interests. You ought to read books from favorite authors and subject areas, both for children and adults, with no thought to professional preparation. At the same time, you need to read children's books beyond areas of personal interest to prepare for the variety of student interest that is in every class. These books do not have to be read with the same devotion, but your being familiar with titles outside your normal reading can make an enormous difference to your students.

4. *View books as shared experiences rather than test fodder*. Children and adults experience the same emotions. The fear, joy, peace, jealousy, anger, and love an adult feels are the same feelings children experience. When it comes to personal reading, which deals largely with emotions, children are our peers and not our clones. Let children teach us as well. Sharing a book with children is much like visiting Disneyland with

them. At the end of the day, the adult does not return to the motel to administer a quiz about the activities and rides. Participants relive the experience with each other.

A brief scene in an old black-and-white movie captures the essence of this chapter. The title of the film and names of actors are long forgotten, but in it a couple returned from a date and the man was pressuring the woman for a kiss. (This was a *very* old movie.) She resisted. He persisted. And so it went. In desperation, he finally said, "What if I simply steal a kiss and enjoy it without your permission?" Speaking slowly she responded, "If *I* don't enjoy it, you *can't* enjoy it." The same is surely true for the classroom teacher who wishes to lead children to a love of books.

REFERENCES

Beveridge, W. I. B. 1957. *The Art of Scientific Investigation.* New York: Norton.

Gardner, John W. 1981. *Self-Renewal.* New York: Norton.

Grimm Brothers. 1975. *Thorn Rose or the Sleeping Beauty.* Illustrated by Errol Le Cain. New York: Bradbury.

Larson, Jean. 1994. Personal interview in Provo, Utah. 9 September.

Perez, Samuel A. 1986. Children see, children do: Teachers as reading models. *The Reading Teacher* 40 (October): 8–11.

Schweitzer, Albert. 1997. In *Simpson's Contemporary Quotations,* edited by James B. Simpson. New York: HarperCollins.

Sweet, Anne P. 1993. *Transforming Ideas for Teaching and Learning to Read.* Washington, D.C.: U.S. Department of Education.

CHAPTER 18

Motivating Students to Read

When T. H. Bell served as U.S. Secretary of Education, he traveled the country observing schools to find ways to make them better. His experiences led him to identify three areas where change must take place if education is to improve (Bell 1982). "The first," he said, "is student motivation." He explained that nothing of any consequence is learned without the consent and involvement of the learner. Students have to *want* to know something in order to acquire it genuinely rather than temporarily, say, to pass a test. If teachers are to make a difference in current educational practice, they must pay more attention to students' attitudes. He then identified the second area as "student motivation." And the third area of needed change: "Student motivation." In short, he said nothing is as important in improving schools as motivating students.

But in practice, motivation in educational circles often means carefully planning an activity so the students appear to choose it when actually the whole thing is the teacher's idea. That definition comes closer to manipulation. Genuine motivation is a personal decision and comes from the heart.

There is never a guarantee that a teacher's most sincere efforts will motivate anyone. The best we can do is offer, sincerely and continually, and hope that students will resonate to what they see and hear. No one can predictably orchestrate real motivation in another human being, but speaking with honest passion and genuine enthusiasm increases the odds that we can influence others.

HELPING STUDENTS FIND BOOKS THEY LIKE

Perhaps the most common way to motivate a child to read is to identify the child's interests and then locate books on those subjects. Although this method largely works well, it has two drawbacks: (1) In a regular library, all the books on that topic soon are exhausted, so the teacher still needs to know how to get children interested in other areas. More important, (2) some children do not know what they are interested in and tend to fall between the cracks. Unfortunately, such children usually are the ones who need books the most. Teachers can create the desire to read in both types of students—those who would benefit from expanding their areas of interest and those who have none—when they introduce and read from a variety of children's books they personally like.

Choosing personal favorites to recommend to children is at least as successful as any other way of selecting titles. No source or method is foolproof. Even picking books exclusively from lists of award winners like the Caldecott and Newbery carries no guarantee children will respond positively to them. When teachers introduce and read from books they genuinely like, students are more likely to be motivated for two reasons.

1. Those books generally are better books. They usually are more solidly crafted and contain more levels where children can make connections.
2. When teachers recommend books that are personally meaningful, a genuine and irresistible enthusiasm accompanies their words. When people talk about books they like, those who listen often are influenced by their sincerity and conviction.

Nothing we offer children is more important than an adult who reads. As mentioned in Chapter 17, children end up doing what we do, not what we say, and all the admonitions about the importance of reading in their lives fall on deaf ears if they view us as people who do not take our own advice. When we speak from experience, however, our words are more honest and persuasive. We can't convince children of the beauty of mathematics unless that vision comes from our own hearts and minds. We can't paint a believable picture of how appealing life is in the desert unless we have lived there and loved it. And we largely waste our time singing the virtues of reading when the last book we read was five years ago.

> In summary, teachers have a choice in motivating children to become lifelong readers. They can either preach on the joys of reading, or they can model for the youngsters what a reader who enjoys reading does. And what teachers do ultimately will depend on how much they truly believe in the importance of reading. (Perez 1986, p. 11)

LEARNING FROM MOTIVATED READERS

A group of college-age Americans was living in Germany, trying to learn German but making slow progress. An old hand offered a piece of advice that made an enormous difference: "If you want to speak like the Germans, listen to the way Germans speak." Embarrassingly simple and obvious, it changed the course of their learning, which until then had been too formal and academic.

We adapt that advice for this chapter: "If we want students to be motivated readers, look at how motivated readers read." Teachers sometimes believe that students need careful preparation to read a book or that they have to be bribed or prodded into reading. Yet some children jump right into books, reading without the benefit of preparatory steps or the intervention of either a carrot or a whip. Two principles underlie the motivation of these eager readers: (1) Reading is personal. (2) Reading is a natural process. The following common characteristics of motivated readers reflect these two principles:

1. Motivated readers read not for others but for their own purposes. They read what is important to them and know real reading is not to answer someone else's questions or fill out a worksheet.
2. Motivated readers have personal and identifiable likes and dislikes in books: subject matter, authors, illustrators, formats, styles, and so on.
3. Motivated readers feel rewarded during the reading process. They find immediate pleasure in the book and don't read because they will need the information next year.
4. Motivated readers do not feel trapped by a book. They can put it down without guilt when it no longer meets their needs.
5. Motivated readers feel free to talk about what they read from their own point of view. They are not hesitant about passing judgment on a book.
6. Motivated readers read at their own rate. They skip, scan, linger, and reread as is necessary or desirable.

7. Motivated readers don't feel obligated to remember everything they read. They find reading worthwhile even if they can't recall every concept or idea, and they allow themselves to skip over words they don't know as long as they understand the idea or story.
8. Motivated readers read broadly, narrowly, or in-between, depending on how they feel.
9. Motivated readers develop a personal attachment to books they like.
10. Motivated readers find time to read regularly.

Motivated readers don't look over their shoulders as they read. They are in charge. We adults shouldn't get excited when they put down books without finishing them, when they devour what we think are worthless books, when their taste does not reflect our own, or when they read very narrowly.

Yet teachers with the best of intentions can interfere with motivated readers. Often the most difficult hurdle is simply getting out of their way. Whatever an adult does that keeps the child from becoming involved with the book is something to be avoided. It is easy to spot mind-numbing exercises that treat the book as merely a repository of facts to be mined, and those practices should be avoided.

Yet even the right principles can be followed with too much fervor, as is evident in the following two examples:

Rose Napoli is an experienced, dedicated teacher who became enthusiastic about trade books and their classroom use during a summer institute. She returned to her teaching inflamed with ideas about allowing students to choose their own books, providing time for them to read, and initiating discussions based on their personal responses. The trouble was that her enthusiasm had become so strong, she simply overpowered the children. She jumped immediately into questions about their involvement with the stories and so peppered them with requests for their feelings that even those children who initially responded began to keep quiet. Only when she began to let students talk from their own perspectives, and sincerely listened to them, did the children start to respond honestly. In time, the simplistic but honest comments became more complex and perceptive, and Rose eventually found the kind of student involvement she earlier had tried to force (Calkins 1986, pp. 243–249).

Gordon Whiting, a professor at Brigham Young University, prided himself on allowing his nine-year-old daughter adequate rein in selecting the books she would read. He was pleased to see her choose The Little House series and was not bothered when she finished them all and began immediately to reread the seven titles in the slipcase. She read them a third time, then a fourth. When she began a fifth reading, he wondered if she wouldn't be served better by reading something else but said nothing. As she started the sixth time, he had to hold his tongue. When she picked up the first book to begin a seventh reading, he could keep his peace no longer. He did not forbid her to read them again but insisted she read one different book before returning to the series. Result? She quit reading altogether. Chances are good that she would have moved to other titles in her own time, but clearly she was getting something from the series that caused her to read the books again and again. We simply don't know what goes on in the heads of children when they are immersed in a book. If they are to become motivated readers, we must allow them to be in charge.

GET STUDENTS QUICKLY INTO BOOKS

We learn a useful lesson about reading from TV. Why do people watch it so much? Because it is so good? No, because watching TV is so easy. It is in a central place in the home, highly visible, and simple to use. If the TV were stored in a basement closet, we might bring it out on weekends but would likely find something else to do instead of hauling it upstairs every time we wanted to see a program.

When we make reading easier, we find more children reading. We need to make books as accessible as TV. We need to use them. Have them handy. Hold them up. Read passages. Get students to see what is inside. We need to handle children and books like we handle children and basketball: provide them a hoop and a ball and let them play. No need to recite the history of the game, learn about the manufacturing of basketballs, or study the specifications of different backboards. Give them the ball, and let them on the court. (Not that a little discussion during reading can't give added depth to the experience, like wise coaching can improve the play on a basketball court.) An interesting book does not need elaborate introductions or preparations any more than an appealing movie needs a narrator to set the stage for the viewer. We open the cover and read.

READING INCENTIVE PROGRAMS

To focus on individual reading in the classroom and inspire students to spend time with books, teachers sometimes provide an incentive by using a chart or other visual record of each child's reading. Often thematic, the chart may be called "Shoot for the Moon" with a rocket ship for each child lined up at the bottom and a moon at the top. For every book read, the rocket ship advances an inch. Or paper ice cream cones may line the back wall. Every time a child reads a book, the title is written on a paper ice cream scoop and placed on the cone. When every cone has ten scoops, the class has an ice cream party.

Incentive programs often revolve around prizes as well as charts. Some are generated by teachers, like the ice cream party, and others come from businesses, such as coupons good for a pizza. Despite being conceived and carried out with the best of intentions, some research shows that extrinsic rewards actually can hinder the development of intrinsic motivation to read (Lepper, Greene, and Nisbett 1973). Yet other research reports that extrinsic rewards do not necessarily have a negative impact on intrinsic motivation to read, at least in the areas of attitude, time on task, and performance (Cameron and Pierce 1994). Teachers need to be aware, however, that when they offer a prize as a reward for reading, they must to be able to determine when the prize overshadows the book. Teachers should ask, "How can I know if the student is reading for the prize or for the love of the book?" If they are not sure of the answer, then teachers should examine the situation more closely to know if the reward is getting in the way. As soon as the prize becomes more important than the reading, the incentive program is no longer a friend but has become the enemy. If teachers are sure students are motivated primarily by the books, then nothing is wrong with cashing in on the free pizzas. But one reward, and one reward only, keeps people reading over time: the reading itself. Over the long haul, people turn to books because the books are worthwhile.

An example of an incentive program going astray was clear when a male student came up after class to tell about the contest sponsored by his school when he was in the third grade. Whoever read the most books over three months would win a bicycle. This student burned with the idea of owning the bike and read during every free moment at school and home. He read more than any of the fourth, fifth, or sixth graders. And he won the bicycle. During the schoolwide assembly when the principal presented him the prize, his fine example was held up to the rest of the students as stellar and enviable. Finishing the story, he said, "Since winning the bike, I have not read one book except those required by my classes." The reading champion of the school never was a reader. To win a bicycle, he simply engaged in a competitive activity involving books.

One problem with the moon shot and the ice cream cones is that these programs do not help those who need them most. We never have seen a reading chart without finding a few race cars still at the starting line or bookworms waiting for additional body segments. These belong to the children in every class who need books the most. They do not read easily, are not doing well in school, and receive little or no encouragement at home. And because they are not doing well at school, the chart meant to inspire instead condemns, revealing at a glance the names of those children who are failures and who, yet again, have blown it.

At the other end of the spectrum are the handful of achievers whose rockets take off in a blinding blast. They shoot to the moon, continue beyond the mark to the top of the wall, and then make a turn at the ceiling toward the opposite wall. These competitive types can't stand to lose. Like the boy who won the bike, their compulsion to win often overshadows the pleasures of reading, and they tend to zoom through book after book at home with thoughts like "I'll get that Ruthie! I'll bet I'm reading more pages tonight than she is." As if possessed, these readers exhibit the same drive whether the contest is skipping rope or gathering leaves. Born to win, they sail through stacks of books with little benefit.

The majority of the children, the regular kids, go along with a reading incentive plan for a while. Then they are inclined to drift away from the chart, particularly after an initial goal is met or teacher support wanes. Except in rare cases, these three groups—nonreaders, the cut-throat competitors, and regular kids—tend to be served badly by a system that places the game before the book.

Group motivation and record keeping are another matter. The teacher who requires students to keep records of their personal reading (see Chapter 21) can tally each week's reading and then display the increasing total, perhaps in a thermometer where the temperature rises with continued reading or simply in a growing line that snakes around the top of the walls. These visual summaries provide bragging rights to everyone in the class, as opposed to the individual successes offered by the race car or ice cream charts. When a goal is reached, everyone participates in the victory, even those kids who have read few or no books. No one except the teacher is aware of the amount each child reads, so no additional stigma is placed on those who are not performing. The teacher now has the opportunity to work individually with those students who need extra time and attention.

Organizing the Classroom to Get Children into Books

Teachers who desire to make reading a natural part of the educational landscape will want to plan their classrooms so books fit smoothly and easily into the school day and their children's lives. Six areas to consider when organizing the ideal reading classroom are teacher example, providing books, making time, creating a reading atmosphere, working with parents, and choosing meaningful activities.

First: Teacher Example

In motivating children to read, the most important element of education is a teacher who reads. The power of a teacher's example, as described earlier in this chapter and covered more thoroughly in Chapter 17, appears here as a reminder. "The key to developing a personal love of books is a teacher who communicates enthusiasm and an appreciation of literature through his attitudes and examples" (Wilson and Hall 1972, p. 341).

Second: Providing Books

The love of reading cannot be taught generally; it depends on contact with specific titles, certain subjects, and particular authors. To catch students, an enormously wide variety of books of different formats and levels of difficulty need to be available in the elementary classroom. All grades need fiction, nonfiction, and poetry. Every lower grade needs some chapter books. Every upper grade needs some picture books. The most sincere and devoted intentions to help children become readers turn to dust if books are not handy for teachers to read aloud and introduce to the class and for students to pick over for silent reading time. (Chapter 19 suggests specific ways to acquire books and build a classroom library. Appendix B lists some appealing current magazines.)

Third: Making Time for Books

Put books on the agenda. If reading for its own sake does not appear on the daily schedule, the message to students is clear: "We do not value personal reading in this classroom." Four useful ways to structure time for books are (1) reading aloud, (2) silent reading, (3) introducing books to children, and (4) going to the library.

READING ALOUD.   Good experiences reading aloud don't just happen. They occur when certain principles are followed.

1. You should honestly like the books you read aloud. The difference in reading aloud a book only because it is handy and reading aloud a book because it is loved is enormous.
2. Don't read aloud unfamiliar books. The temptation is great to learn the book as you share it with the class, but too many drawbacks can occur:
   • You may not like the book.
   • The book may have unpleasant surprises—words you are not comfortable saying aloud, a character with negative traits who shares a name with a child in your class, or something in the plot you wish you had known about earlier.
   • You can't dramatize or emphasize highlights because you don't know about them.
   • Most important, your enthusiasm for the story probably will be weak because you are learning at the same time as the children.
3. Teachers should do the oral reading themselves. Even if a child is skilled enough to read the book aloud, teacher participation carries a message: Our teacher *wants* to be a part of this activity; it must be important. In addition, students get to see a teacher's personal involvement in books that, through time, generally will include both laughter and tears. Children learn much more than the story when an adult reads aloud.
4. Don't expect all students to like every book. Tell your class, "We will read many books in here this year. No one will like them all. I expect that everyone will find some they do like."
5. Establish your own rules for read-aloud time. Some teachers allow students to draw; others don't. Some are not concerned when children fall asleep; others are. If anything bothers a teacher, it must be fixed, or the distraction will weaken the reading experience.

SILENT READING.   Students need time at school to read in books of their own choosing. Commonly called SSR (*s*ustained *s*ilent *r*eading), DEAR (*d*rop *e*verything *a*nd *r*ead), or SQUIRT (*s*tudents' *q*uiet *uni*nterrupted *r*eading *t*ime), this portion of the daily schedule is reserved for personal reading. The rules are easy: for the allotted time, everyone reads—including the teacher. SSR is not an automatic success. To make it work, these are the essentials:

1. The teacher reads. When a number of SSR programs were evaluated, findings indicated the program failed when the teacher did not participate (McCracken 1978, pp. 406–408). If the teacher does not read, the message to the students is clear: "This is only a school assignment, important for you but not for me." One of the best parts about SSR is the time it provides the teacher to catch up on new children's books, but her reading does not have to

be limited to titles appropriate for children. Anything personally interesting is fair game. However, when a student recommends a book and the teacher actually reads it, the positive results are overwhelming.

2. If someone starts a book and gets into it without being interested, finishing is not required.

3. The teacher makes no assignments for the books read during SSR. Students may choose to use a book they read during SSR for an assigned activity, but they are not required to report on SSR books.

4. Anticipate possible distractions or interruptions, and let students know what to do about them. Fine tuning the activity is inevitable—you can't consider every possible difficulty beforehand—but being clear on as many points as possible makes for a smoother reading time. For example:

   • What does a student do who finishes a book in the middle of a reading period? (Be sure to have at least one additional book in your desk, particularly when you are getting to the end of the one you're reading.)

   • Do children have to stay in their seats during the entire reading time? (Some teachers have trained students to get up quietly and find another book; others do not allow them to wander about for any reason.)

   • What happens if they took their book home last night and forgot to bring it back today? (Have a box or plastic carton of short books or magazines available so appealing reading material is not difficult to locate.)

   • What if a student has a pressing question during SSR? (It can wait until the reading period is over. This time is also for the teacher who does not want to be interrupted.)

INTRODUCING BOOKS TO CHILDREN.   Simply releasing children into a world filled with books does not make them readers. If they have no interest in books, no reading habit, and nothing they are looking for, children can easily ignore a wealth of superb titles. It is up to the teacher to bridge the gap between book and child, and one successful way is for the teacher to introduce new titles to the students.

There are many ways to introduce books. Holding up the book so students can see what it looks like while telling them something about it is all that is necessary. Teachers are most successful when introducing books they have read and liked, but it is possible to introduce books the teacher does not yet know. By reading the blurb on the back of paperbacks or on the inside flap of hardbacks, enough information is available to present the book to the class. In addition, you may want to turn on the PBS book-introduction programs *Reading Rainbow* or *Cover to Cover*.

A book-introduction time should be on the schedule, but the number of books presented to the students can vary during that period. For the first week or two of the school year, you may want to introduce as many as five or more per day to ensure that enough books are known to get the students started. After that, a book or two every day is fine. The point is to provide students with some titles they can look forward to trying out.

GOING TO THE LIBRARY.   If the elementary school has a library, teachers should plan to get their children there regularly. Some teachers elect not to sign up the entire class but after a few introductory visits make a schedule for students so they may use the library singly or in pairs before and after school, at lunch, or during the school day. If you visit as a class, always stay in the library and circulate among the students, helping them find good books. The more titles they know and the more excitement generated for books, the more successful the library visit will be.

Even with your presence in the library, be prepared to have students wander aimlessly and make small disturbances. Giving them specific directions before entering can help eliminate trouble and streamline the process. These three directions from a teacher to the students work as well as any:

1. *Try 'em on.* Your job is to find books that fit you. One way to pick a good chapter book is to turn somewhere near the middle and start reading. If you read three or four pages and find the story interesting, this could be a good choice.
2. *Check 'em out.* Check out the books that appeal to you.
3. *Read 'em.* Sit down and read your books until we all are ready to go back to class.

Fourth: Creating a Reading Atmosphere

A classroom where reading is valued will have an atmosphere that gives evidence books are important. That message may be delivered in a number of ways:

1. Make the emotional climate safe but exciting. Students' reactions to books will be accepted and not belittled. The teacher hopes students will reflect her involvement with print but will not expect them to mirror her taste. And the emphasis will be on making personal connections and new discoveries.
2. Promote the idea of a community of readers. A focus will be on developing a group attitude of reading as a pleasurable way of making discoveries about the world in fiction as well as nonfiction. Everyone in the community will have the chance to select reading materials that reflect personal choices and interests.
3. Liven up that room. Ask for old displays or posters from bookstores. Tack up children's drawings inspired by books. Display books or book jackets. Write publishers for their free, attractive materials—posters, postcards, bookmarks—to decorate the walls. (Check publisher offerings in the *CBC Features* brochure from the Children's Book Council, mentioned in Appendix A.)
4. Keep the classroom library visible, not behind locked cabinet doors. Have books become a part of the classroom's interior decoration scheme.
5. As the teacher's personality and classroom space permit, allow students to do their free reading in places other than their desks. You may want a reading center—a place designated for pleasure reading that may have pillows, a comfortable chair or couch, or other homey furnishings. But make sure everyone gets to use the reading center. If it becomes the domain of those who finish their work first, those who need it most never get the chance.

Fifth: Working with Parents

Except for the often painfully polite back-to-school evenings, parents and teachers usually have contact only when there is trouble. As a result, teachers and parents have a natural hesitancy to communicate, much to the delight of many children who prefer keeping their two worlds separate. The teacher who decides to bridge this traditional gap between school and home can do so with relative ease and much positive effect on children and their reading.

Teachers need to initiate the contact, either through a letter or a meeting with each child's parents. To gain support for your approach to reading, that contact should deal with two points: communicating with parents and requesting their support.

COMMUNICATE WITH PARENTS. You should communicate to the parents the benefits of regular, yearlong reading (both in school and at home) for their child. Include your own views on the advantages of daily reading, and you could also cite research that supports those ideas (see Chapter 20).

REQUEST PARENTAL SUPPORT. You should request parental support for each child's personal reading at home. Parents can help their child in the following ways:

- Encourage their child to read regularly at home. Setting aside a certain time is helpful. (If you require children to read daily outside of school, mention that and ask for parental support.)
- Talk with the child about the books being read.
- Read with and to the child.
- Buy books for birthdays and holidays, and allow the child to buy from school-sponsored book clubs when possible.
- Help the child create a place in the bedroom to keep personal books.
- Read where the child can see them with a book.
- Periodically tell the child about what they are reading.
- Volunteer to come to the classroom and assist children in their reading.

Sixth: Choosing Meaningful Activities/Assignments

The purpose of having children engage in an activity after reading a book is to enhance their experience, not check their reading or evaluate their comprehension. Chapter 21 describes activities, but the idea is noted here as one of the six areas to consider when organizing a classroom to highlight reading.

The ideas in this chapter come from years of classroom experience, both ours and others. Unfortunately, following them to the letter will not guarantee that every child will become a reader. No reading approach, person, or program has a 100 percent conversion rate with children. Simply expect that some tough nuts to crack will not fall in love with books, no matter what you do. Implementing these ideas, however, will increase the odds that children will read more and read better.

REFERENCES

Bell, T. H. 1982. Speech to faculty of College of Education at Brigham Young University, Provo, Utah, 21 October.

Calkins, Lucy McCormick. 1986. *The Art of Teaching Writing*. Portsmouth, N.H.: Heinemann.

Cameron, J., and W. D. Pierce. 1994. Reinforcement, reward, and intrinsic motivation: a meta-analysis. *Review of Educational Research* 64: 363–423.

Lepper, M. R., D. Greene, and R. E. Nisbett. 1973. Undermining children's intrinsic interest with extrinsic rewards: A test of the "overjustification" hypothesis. *Journal of Personality and Social Psychology* 28: 129–137.

McCracken, R. A., and M. J. McCracken. 1978. Modeling is the key to sustained silent reading. *The Reading Teacher* 31 (January): 406–407.

Perez, Samuel A. 1986. Children see, children do: Teachers as reading models. *The Reading Teacher* 40 (October): 8–11.

Wilson, Robert, and Mary Ann Hall. 1972. *Reading and the Elementary School Child*. New York: Van Nostrand Reinhold.

CHAPTER 19

Building a
Classroom Library

Every classroom needs its own library. Even if the school has a fine offering of books in an attractive central library or media center, each classroom should have a collection of conspicuously displayed titles. Two main reasons underscore the need for classroom libraries, one practical and one philosophical. The practical reason is that if books are present and prominent, they can be found easily and used for sustained silent reading, for browsing, or for answering personal questions as well as those arising from classroom discussions. The philosophical reason is that the presence of trade books in a classroom speaks volumes about their central place in the learning process. Simply by being there, shelves of real books—not textbooks—give evidence to the teacher's commitment to immediate and lifelong learning. If a teacher talks about the importance of reading, but only a few books are visible, the message rings hollow to young ears.

A love of reading can't be taught in the abstract any more than a love of good food can be taught through the lecture method. Until we hold the books in our own hands, or slide the steaming forkful of chicken Kiev between our own open lips, we can't truly know the reward of either print or entrée. Hence, we need the books close at hand—right there in the classroom—to sample and respond to. The obvious truth is that we don't love the act of reading. If we did, any page filled with words would thrill us. We would be equally delighted by random IRS directives, last year's text on quantum mechanics, a current issue of *Guns and Ammo*, and directions for Danish cross stitching. What we do love is a particular book. Perhaps the writings of a particular author. Maybe a particular subject. Since a book holds no attraction simply because it is filled with words, we need enough titles within arm's length to appeal to a wide audience.

How many books do we need so children in our classrooms can feast on the titles, authors, or subjects they love? One third-grade teacher reported he had 25 books or so—"More than I could use." Then he began using trade books in his reading program and boosted the classroom library to over 400—"Not nearly enough." How many are enough? The multimillionaire John D. Rockefeller reportedly was asked how much money was enough. His reply: "Just a little bit more." Teachers who seek to expand their classroom libraries tend to respond similarly.

The greatest obstacle to building a classroom library is impatience. Once convinced of the value in having books close at hand, most teachers want their collections to mushroom *right now*. The enthusiasm and desire are understandable but sometimes harmful. It simply takes time, usually years, to get the kinds and numbers of books a teacher wants. The point is to begin building the collection and learning to resist the natural feelings of discouragement because it doesn't grow faster.

Imagine you recently signed your first teaching contract and just arrived at your new school. After meeting the principal, you find your classroom, which is stark and empty, and then look for the library. The school does not have one. You are fresh out of college and own fifteen trade books. What next?

The greatest strength of good teachers is a willingness to persevere no matter the odds. Good teachers make do. If services or materials are lacking, they use what is available and make it work. If no money is in the supply budget, they still find some way to give students what they need. Good teachers enter the profession because they want to make a difference and will not be stopped because conditions are below par. This make-do attitude is a blessing to the profession and the lives of children.

When confronted with a shortage of trade books, however, you must go against the tradition of good teachers who accept substandard situations and do their best. If a lack of trade books in the classroom is viewed without alarm—"I guess I'll have to get along without books"—the make-do attitude is a curse instead of a blessing. Finding books is imperative. A teacher who accepts empty bookshelves as a given, making no attempt to fill them, deprives children of the most powerful classroom tool for convincing them of the value of reading. To become readers, children must have constant access to books. And teachers must find ways to provide those titles.

Having decided to fill the shelves, a teacher needs to concentrate on two areas: finding free books and finding money to buy books. Even in tight economic times, both are possible.

ACQUIRING FREE BOOKS

With ingenuity and grit, a teacher can bring books into the classroom from a variety of sources, like the following. Note the pluses (+) and minuses (–) of each.

SCHOOL LIBRARY. The easiest and fastest way to get books on classroom shelves is to borrow them from the school library or media center. Regulations vary, but teachers generally can check out large numbers of books for classroom use. Some teachers do not allow these library books to go home, but others develop a checkout system.

+ Effortless way to get many books into the classroom. Good selection of titles.
– Books need to be returned to the library. Teacher is responsible for lost books.

PUBLIC LIBRARY. Another quick way to get books on the shelf is to visit the public library and borrow as many titles as allowed. Many libraries have special arrangements for classroom teachers, which often include a longer checkout time and an easier checkout system. If your town has no local library, you generally are served by some other library—in a neighboring town, a county system, a bookmobile, or the state library.

+ Wide selection of materials. Immediate availability.
– Transporting books back and forth. Teacher is responsible for lost books. Usually a six-week maximum checkout time.

ASK STUDENTS TO BRING BOOKS FROM HOME. Many children in the classroom have books at home that are appropriate for classroom reading. Often, they are willing to share these books with others for the year. Before they bring their personal books, ask students to write their names in each book in at least two places. Tell them to leave treasured books at home because they can be damaged or lost even when students take pains to treat them carefully. During the final week of the school year, these books are to be returned to their owners.

+ Less work for the teacher than any other method. Students feel ownership in their library and like to recommend their personal titles to others.
– Inevitably some books will be damaged or will disappear.

BONUS TITLES FROM BOOK CLUBS.   When students order from a book club (Trumpet, Scholastic, Troll, Weekly Reader), the teacher receives points that can be used to order free books. Regularly using a book club not only helps students by focusing on book reading and ownership but also by adding substantially to the classroom library with the bonus books. Some clubs even have extra teacher catalogs offering Big Books, classroom sets, recommended packages of preselected books, or individual titles for good reading.

+ Bonus books are often attractive and always new.
– Somewhat limited selection.

BIRTHDAY BOOKS.   If it is a classroom custom for parents to provide a treat on their child's birthday, the teacher can request that a book be donated to the classroom library instead. Inscribing the child's name and birth date inside the front cover helps personalize the gift and make it more noteworthy. Be sure parents do not think they need to spend a great deal. Paperbacks are perfectly acceptable as birthday books. These birthday books might be placed on a special shelf.

+ Encourage parents to participate in building the library. Children leave a legacy for others.
– Can introduce a small degree of competitiveness.

LIBRARY DISCARDS.   All libraries undergo a periodic weeding process. The titles taken from the shelves are usually sold for a dollar or less. It is possible that a library will donate these discards to a school. Ask the library director.

+ Little or no cost. Immediate delivery.
– Many titles are discarded for a good reason; be selective in your choices.

BOOK DRIVE.   A book drive is an organized request for people to donate their unwanted books to your classroom or school. Book drives normally yield hundreds of books appropriate for the classroom and also raise money for purchasing new books. Although they take some planning and also demand energy for sorting and disposing of books, the rewards of a book drive make the time and effort worthwhile.

Plan the book drive for a Saturday morning from 9:00 to noon. About six weeks before, talk to the class about the need for books and the idea of having people donate their unwanted titles. Secure or draw a large map of the area around your school or the areas your students will canvass. Organize the students into pairs, and assign each pair to cover a certain part of the neighborhood. Write a flyer explaining the book drive, and have each pair deliver it about three weeks before the actual drive. Have them deliver a reminder flyer on the Thursday or Friday immediately before the book drive.

Sign up a parent volunteer to oversee each pair of students during the flyer deliveries and during the book drive itself so students can take the books to a car. Begin no earlier than 9:00 A.M.

When all the books are in your classroom, your task is to divide them into two piles: keep and not keep. The books you don't wish to keep may be turned into capital for buying more titles.

Trade the unwanted books at a used bookstore for titles you would like. Or speak to the manager of a thrift store about a 2-for-1 deal. If you have 600 books, offer to donate them for 300 of your choosing, and everyone wins. If the store doesn't have 300 you want, take a credit for the remainder, which you will pick up over time.

Books also can be sold many ways, but the object is to get rid of the books as quickly and easily as possible. Resist tedious and cumbersome methods like yard sales, flea markets, back-to-school-night sales, and classified ads. One of the most efficient ways is to sell them to a used bookstore. The drawback is that you will not get top dollar. Another efficient way yields more money. After getting permission, sell them outside a mall or large grocery store on a Saturday morning, charging one price for paperbacks and one for hardcover books. When business slows down, sell by the pound or line them as you would on a shelf and sell by the inch. Naturally students handle all the transactions, having practiced selling (and weighing and measuring, when necessary) and making change. If the students are too young, simply have people pick the books they like and pay the students what they think is appropriate for such a worthy cause as the education of the town's children.

+ Boxes of free books. Money for purchasing additional titles. Students practice skills in map reading, talking to adults, selling, measuring, weighing, and making change.
− A good deal of planning and labor involved.

RAISING MONEY FOR BOOKS

All requests for raising money need to be cleared with the principal. Sometimes you may be unaware of conditions or rules that affect your plans. To ensure maximum success, the principal must support your efforts for soliciting funds.

ASK THE PRINCIPAL.   Resist the urge to think this is senseless, even though the principal just asked the faculty to cut back on copier paper because money is tight this year. Schools are budgeted organizations and have to keep some money in reserve for unforeseen problems. Usually some funds remain near the end of the fiscal year. Because budgeted monies are spent instead of returned, a worthy project has a high chance of getting funded at that time.

To increase the chance for support from the principal, acknowledge that money is short, look at the expenditures made for your classroom, and identify purchases you can do without. If you are allotted $600 for basal materials, for example, you may not need to spend the whole amount because you plan on using trade books to teach some of your reading program. Perhaps you can get by without a basal workbook. That amounts to a savings of $240 (30 students times $8 per book) that could be used to buy children's books. Or commit to using ten fewer reams of copier paper (and stick to that). Principals often are edgy about requests for money because so many teachers simply ask. When your idea is stated clearly in writing *and* accompanied by your willingness to cut present expenses, your chances of getting the money are greatly improved.

SOLICIT DONATIONS FROM LOCAL BUSINESSES.   Businesses generally are supportive of community needs, particularly when they receive publicity for their support. Plan with the children how to provide publicity for businesses, such as

- Insert bookplates naming the contributing business inside the front cover of each book.
- Submit before-and-after articles to the local newspaper, mentioning the names of all who contributed.
- Identify the business in a detailed article to appear in the school newsletter, which goes to each home and encourages parents to patronize those who have donated to the program.
- Make printed thank-you cards that can be posted on the wall of the business.
- Create a classy certificate to present to each donor. Put the certificate in a frame, suitable for immediate hanging.
- List all contributors on a permanent plaque to hang in your school.

Then create several donating options that the children can present to businesses when they visit. Adapt your options to fit local conditions. For donations up to $25, for example, a business will be mentioned in a newspaper article, in the school newsletter, and will receive a thank-you card. A donation up to $50 adds a bookplate for each title bought with that money and a place on the permanent plaque. Up to $75 includes the certificate, and up to $100, a framed certificate with an official seal identifying maximum contribution.

Identify the most likely businesses. Have children practice long and well their sales approach with the samples of bookplates and certificates before meeting with the owners. A child should call to ask for an appointment. Have the children do the asking in pairs or threes. It is much harder to turn down nine-year-old brown eyes than to say no to an adult teacher.

ASK THE PTA/PTSA.   The Parent/Teacher Association is committed to improving the school and generally hosts some kind of fund-raiser as a part of its duties. Write a plan that shows how you will strengthen teaching and learning by using more trade books in the curriculum. You are likely to merit closer consideration if you propose the idea along with other teachers, showing how all of you can share or rotate the books to get maximum use from them.

HOST A BOOK FAIR.   Bringing tables full of new books to the school for student browsing and buying is called a book fair. Usually book fairs run a number of days with each class visiting the buying area twice—once to look around and another time to buy the books. The plus of a book fair is that a percentage of the total sales goes to the school, generally from 20 to 40 percent, depending on the volume. Books are available from local bookstores (it's always nice to have a local bookstore support the project and bring a salesperson), local news distributors (check the Yellow Pages under "Magazines—Distributors"), and national companies. Three of the large national book fair companies are Scholastic Book Fairs (phone: 800-325-6149 for the number of the your local representative), Troll Book Fairs (phone: 800-446-3194), and Trumpet Book Fairs (phone: 800-347-3080).

ASK LOCAL SERVICE CLUBS. Service organizations like Rotary, Kiwanis, Sertoma, Lions, Eagles, and B.P.O.E. are interested in being a part of and improving the community. Requesting $200 to $300 for a specific improvement in a school is reasonable. Follow the group's specific procedures. If invited to a meeting, prepare the children so they make the bulk of the presentation.

GRANTS. Ask about district and state programs for improving instruction. Develop an approach that genuinely fits your personality and curriculum goals. For instance, if you are particularly fond of social studies, or feel a need to strengthen your social studies instruction, propose a plan that relies more heavily on trade books to involve students and improve their social studies learning.

FUND-RAISERS. Avoid commercial programs that prey on schools. Most people feel held hostage by children who ask them to buy overpriced jewelry or very small bars of expensive chocolate. A good fund-raiser should enable the children to learn something. For example, one principal taught photography and darkroom procedures to sixth-grade students. Those children then organized a portrait program for families, set up appointments, shot the pictures, developed, printed, and sold them. Another teacher taught students how to make salt-and-pepper centerpieces for picnic tables, which they then constructed and sold.

HAVE CHILDREN EARN MONEY FOR BOOKS. Instead of asking children to bring money for books, contact parents and ask for support in having their child work at home doing extra chores for a standard price. All parents pay, perhaps a dollar an hour, for good, honest labor.

STUDENT STORE. During lunch, your class sells treats to the student body, keeping profits for books. Students help plan and conduct the daily business. Sometimes this gets approval more easily when it is for a specified period of time, say, one month.

Ordinarily, when you request money to buy trade books for your classroom, you will have to write some kind of rationale or proposal. Ask about and follow the procedure of each particular benefactor. If a benefactor has none, present a clear, attractive, professional-looking, but brief (one page is fine) request at the time you ask for funds. Include a specific dollar amount you seek, what kinds of books and how many you will buy, and the benefit those books will bring to your students and teaching. Frankly, if you can't make it clear how these books will benefit your students, you don't deserve the money. (See Chapters 21 and 22 for ideas, but the words in the written request must reflect your own conviction.)

WHERE TO BUY BOOKS

Books are available from a variety of places. Following are some recommended sources, including the pluses (+) and minuses (–) of each.

Book Clubs

Two of the best are The Trumpet Club, P.O. Box 604, Holmes, Pa. 19043. Phone: (800) 826-0110; and Scholastic Book Club, 730 Broadway, New York, N.Y. 10003. Phone: (800) 724-2424. Each has separate clubs according to grade levels.

+ Inexpensive. Relatively quick turnaround time—no more than two weeks, if you call in the order.
– Limited titles, like any book club. Some books are a slightly smaller size than regular bookstore editions.

Bookstores

Ask about educational discounts (if you can't get at least 20 percent, look elsewhere). Inquire about minimum orders (some stores give no discounts on small purchases). Take the school's tax-exempt number to avoid paying sales tax.

+ Immediate availability.
– Discount is small. Availability limited to stock on hand.

Local Paperback Wholesalers

Cities with populations over 100,000 are likely to have a paperback distributor. Look in the Yellow Pages under "Magazines—Distributors." Those listed generally carry a line of paperbacks, including children's books, and sell at a substantial discount to teachers who pay with a school check or purchase order. Call first for details.

+ Books available today. Can do your own book club or book fair.
– Paperback wholesalers are found only in larger metropolitan areas.

Mail-Order Discounted New Paperbacks

For any order totaling a minimum of either 25 books or $100, a 30 percent discount is available through The Booksource, 1230 Macklind Avenue, St. Louis, Mo. 63110. Phone: (800) 444-0435. FAX: (800) 647-1923. A new catalog available every August lists 7,500 titles; 20,000 more are in stock at their warehouse. (Send them a list, and they will type it up and return it at no charge with current prices for your final selections.) Shipping charges are between 5 and 8 percent. You can buy most titles pre-bound (made into hardcover) for about twice the cost of the regular paperback.

+ No one offers a better discount on single titles. Titles are organized in the catalog by subject and also alphabetically by author and title. Library processing is available. Books for all ages are available.
- No advantage for small orders under 25 titles or $100 (for those, use a local bookstore and get a 20 percent discount).

Paperback Publishers

Many paperback publishers sell books to teachers for a greatly reduced price but ship only to schools—no private addresses. Often the procedures for requesting copies are announced in publishers' catalogs. If not, ask each for its specific guidelines. Two examples follow:

BANTAM DOUBLEDAY DELL.   Bantam Doubleday Dell offers a special price of $3 per paperback (hardcovers are half price) with its examination copy offer. This is available to teaching professionals to help in evaluating Bantam Doubleday Dell books for classroom adoption.

Only one copy per title per teacher. For catalogs, which contain titles and specific ordering information, send a self-addressed label (typed or printed clearly) with your request (specify grades K–3, 4–5, or 6–8) to Bantam Doubleday Dell, 2451 Wolf Road, Des Plaines, Ill. 60018-2676.

Send your request (including your name, address, and each book's title and ISBN number on school letterhead) and a check made payable to Bantam Doubleday Dell to Examination Copy Department at the BDD address above.

AVON BOOKS.   Avon Books has slightly different procedures. Teachers still send requests on school letterhead and prepay with each order, but they are limited to six titles at a time. Paperbacks up to $4.99 are $1.50; $5.00 and over are half price. Include a $2 shipping and handling fee with each order. To receive a catalog, call (800) 223-0690. Send requests for books to Avon Books, Customer Service Department, Box 767, Dresden, Tenn. 38225.

+ Inexpensive
- Limited to titles of each particular publisher

Sources of Remaindered Books

When books go out of print, publishers frequently sell the remaining copies in bulk to a remainder house. These books are then available at tremendous savings, often discounted 80 percent from the original price. One of the easiest to use is University Book Service. Different catalogs list books for elementary, junior high, high school, and general audiences. Specify which catalog or catalogs you want. Catalogs quote reviews and offer detailed information about each book. University Book Service, P.O. Box 728, Dublin, Ohio 43017. Telephone number: (800) 634-4272.

+ Enormous savings on new books. Helpful evaluations. Not limited to institutional sales; individuals can buy for private use.
– Limited selection.

Sources of Used Books

Some bookstores specialize in used books and have decent ones for greatly reduced prices. Thrift stores have better prices, but the pickings tend to be slimmer. Garage sales? Spotty.

+ Very inexpensive.
– Very limited selection.

BOOKS FOR STUDENTS

Reading is Fundamental (RIF) will not help build a classroom library, but it does provide books to give to students. RIF is a federally funded nonprofit organization with the goal of increasing book ownership among students, particularly those with special needs (defined as meeting one criterion from a list of ten, including below-average reading skills, eligibility for free or reduced-price lunch, emotionally disturbed, without access to a library, or having disabilities). When 60 percent of the children in a school or special school program qualify, RIF will give 75 percent of necessary funds to buy paperback books for all students in the qualifying group (25 percent of the money must be provided locally). RIF provides 100 percent of the necessary funds for children of migrant or seasonal farm workers. Deadlines for submitting applications are January 14 and October 1. Contact: Reading is Fundamental (RIF), 600 Maryland Avenue, Suite 600, Washington, D.C. 20024. Phone: (202) 287-3220.

USING THE CLASSROOM LIBRARY

Once a classroom has a library, the teacher has to make some decisions about its use. Should those books be limited to reading in the classroom, or can students take them home? Are they on their honor to return the books, or should there be some kind of checkout system? How many is each child allowed to check out? How long may children keep the books? Does every book need a card pocket? Does the teacher serve as class librarian, or can children handle the job?

No universal answers exist for these questions. Each teacher has to devise a system that is personally comfortable. One fact every teacher can count on: If children borrow books from a classroom library, some titles will be lost. Period. The only way not to lose books is to keep students from touching them. For peace of mind, accepting this inevitability is essential. Yet few titles are lost to calculated theft. Most missing books are due to students misplacing them or simply forgetting to return them. So some kind of system is recommended to help students remember they have a book from the classroom library. The easiest system is to have the students themselves write their names, dates, and book titles on a form attached to a clipboard or filed in a folder. As students return books, they draw a line through their names and the other information. Appointing one or more students as librarians also works well.

PROTECTING AND PRESERVING PAPERBACKS

Many teachers do nothing to prolong the life of paperbacks, believing the books will wear out anyway. Some simple procedures can keep books looking better for a longer time, however. Using parent volunteers to cover the books with contact paper yields good results. Even easier is to use the taping machine many libraries have to repair the spines of hardbacks. Paperbacks wear most quickly along the edges. A paperback can be reinforced by running a strip of four-inch clear tape along the center of the spine, folding it over onto the front and back covers. Trim tape flush with the top and bottom of the book. Do the same to the front edges of both covers, folding the tape half to the inside and half to the outside. Now the spine and front edges of the covers are protected, prolonging significantly the looks and increasing substantially the life of the book.

When pages fall out of paperbacks, the best method for restoring them is to buy a tube of clear silicon bathtub caulk (shaped like a toothpaste tube, not one of the large cylindrical variety used in caulking guns unless you are repairing hundreds of books). By barely cutting the tip, you can run a very small bead of caulk along the back of a page if it has fallen completely out or along the spine if the back is broken. Reattach the siliconed pages, apply pressure with a rubber band or the weight of other books, and leave for a day. Those pages never will come loose again. Other glues tend to crack, but the silicon caulk, with both strength and a little flexibility, will do its job beyond your retirement.

No matter how bad the economic times, it is possible for a teacher to find free books and money for books. With perseverance and patience, any teacher can build an enviable library that will help turn kids into readers. And with little effort and expense, the books can be reinforced and repaired to offer dozens and dozens of readings.

CHAPTER 20

Teaching Reading with Children's Literature

We first published most of the information in this chapter in "Using 'Real' Books: Research Findings on Literature-based Reading Instruction," The Reading Teacher 42, *March 1989, pp. 470–477. Copyright by the International Reading Association.*

How should reading be taught and with what sorts of materials? Phonics or sight words or context clues? Basals or trade books? Do "real" books come later, after a child has mastered decoding skills? Or might the child start with real books from the library or book club and learn skills as needed in a so-called natural context? What are the best ways of leading a child to literacy?

The traditional method of teaching reading in America's classrooms has been to use the reading textbook, the basal reader. Shirley Koeller (1981, p. 553) reveals that 95 to 99 percent of teachers relied on the basal to teach reading in 1958. Although the percentage is not quite as high today, basal readers still are used in more than 90 percent of schools (Reutzel and Cooter 1996, p. 339).

Those who use literature-based reading instruction instead of basal programs boast stunning levels of success with all types of students and particularly with disabled and uninterested readers. Recently, a focus on a balanced, holistic reading program with a strong emphasis on children's books has given renewed attention to individualized reading—redefining and refining the process that uses real books to teach and foster literacy. Can reading be taught successfully with less emphasis on the basal? What does the literature in reading instruction indicate about both the success rate and the components of literature-based approaches to building literacy?

We have used the expression *real books* more than once, a term that now seems to be generally accepted in the literature about reading instruction. So-called artificial materials—such as workbooks, skill cards, textbooks, and basal readers—are the sort that children can get only through teachers. Children would seldom read a textbook by choice, much less a workbook or skill card, and neither would an adult. Real reading materials, on the other hand, are the sorts of things people read because they want to. Comic books, *Sports Illustrated for Kids*, and a McDonald's sign all count as real reading materials, although children's trade books such as *Charlotte's Web* (White 1952) and *Where the Wild Things Are* (Sendak 1963) are most commonly identified for use in literature-based or individualized reading instruction.

THE STUDIES

A number of controlled studies have compared literature-based reading with basal and mastery-learning reading instruction, and others have simply looked at literacy growth within classrooms that use literature-based reading programs.

A landmark study by Cohen (1968) used a control group of 130 second-grade students who were taught using traditional basal reader instruction and compared those students with 155 children in an experimental group using a literature component along with regular instruction. The schools in New York City were selected because of academic retardation likely due to the students' low socioeconomic backgrounds. The experimental treatment consisted mainly of reading aloud to children from 50 carefully selected children's trade picture books—books without the controlled vocabulary or fixed sentence length that existed in abundance in the 1960s but are rarely published today—and then following up with meaning-related activities. The children were encouraged to read the books anytime. Metropolitan Achievement

Tests and Free Association Vocabulary Tests were administered in October and June, and the experimental group showed significant increases over the control group in word knowledge ($P \leq .005$), reading comprehension ($P < .01$), vocabulary ($P < .05$), and quality of vocabulary ($P \leq .05$). When the six lowest classes were compared, the experimental group showed an even more significant increase over the control group. Cohen's study was replicated a few years later by Cullinan, Jaggar, and Strickland (1974), yielding basically the same results.

Another controlled study that warrants a closer look was conducted by Eldredge and Butterfield (1986), whose initial study involved 1,149 second-grade children in 50 Utah classrooms. They compared a traditional basal approach to five other experimental methods, including two that used variations of a literature-based program. Using a variety of techniques that included an instrument for evaluating phonics skills developed and validated by Eldredge, the Gates-MacGinitie Reading Test, and A Pictorial Self-Concept Scale, the researchers discovered that 14 of 20 significant differences among the different instructional methods favored the literature approach teamed with a series of special decoding lessons also developed by Eldredge—lessons taking no more than 15 minutes daily. The other literature-based group also placed highly. Eldredge and Butterfield (1986, p. 35) concluded that "the use of children's literature to teach children to read had a positive effect upon students' achievement and attitudes toward reading—much greater than the traditional methods used." (Also see Bader, Veatch, and Eldredge 1987, p. 65.)

A literature-based, developmental program for first graders called the Shared Book Experience was examined closely under the auspices of the New Zealand Department of Education. Holdaway (1982) explains that

> no grade or structured materials were used and all word-solving skills were taught in context during real reading. This experimental group proved equal or superior to other experimental and control groups on a variety of measures including Marie Clay's *Diagnostic Survey*. (p. 299)

So impressed was the Department of Education that it embarked on a countrywide program of inservice in New Zealand, and subsequently, developmental programs, such as Shared Book Experience, have taken over on a national scale.

The influence of this New Zealand program did not stay down under. The Ohio Reading Recovery program, reported by Boehnlein (1987) to be an American version of New Zealand's Reading Recovery program, is specifically targeted at beginning readers who have a profile that will make failure likely. Results of a controlled study match that of the New Zealand findings, which are best encapsulated in this remarkable statement:

> After an average of 15 to 20 weeks, or 30 to 40 hours of instruction, 90% of the children whose pretest scores were in the lowest 20 percent of their class catch up to the average of their class or above and *never need remediation again*. (Boehnlein 1987, p. 33)

The Ohio Reading Recovery program confirmed that gains are maintained, and when compared to control groups, the Reading Recovery children "not only made greater gains than the other high risk children who received no help, but they also made greater gains than the children who needed no help" (Boehnlein 1987). (Also see Pinnell 1986.)

Another experiment dealing with literature-based reading and children at high risk of failure, the Open Sesame program, was conducted at P.S. 192 on New York City's west side (Larrick 1987). Ninety-two percent of the children in P.S. 192 came from non-English speaking homes, 96 percent were below the poverty level, and 80 percent spoke no English when entering school. The Open Sesame program began with 225 kindergarten students and gave them an opportunity to read in an unpressured, pleasurable way—no basals, no workbooks. Immersion in children's literature and language experience approaches to reading and writing were the major instructional thrusts, and skills were taught primarily in meaningful context as children asked for help in writing. As the year concluded, all 225 students could read their dictated stories and many of the picture books shown in class. Some were even reading on a second-grade level. School officials were so impressed that they made a written commitment to extend the program gradually through sixth grade. The following year, all 350 first graders were happily reading English—60 percent on or above grade level. In fact, only three of the 350 failed to pass district comprehension tests, and those three had been in the United States less than six months.

White, Vaughan, and Rorie (1986) reported that first-grade children from a small, economically depressed rural community responded well to reading and writing programs not using a basal. In speaking of the methods employed, White, Vaughan, and Rorie (1986, p. 86) said that "print was something that permeated their day. . . . Books became theirs, 'in a natural way, in a real way.' " Although quick to say that the children understood far more about the reading process than could ever be measured by a pencil-and-paper test, White, Vaughan, and Rorie were also pleased that 20 of the 25 children scored a grade equivalent of 2.0 or better on the spring standardized tests. The other five children had scores of 1.6, 1.7, or 1.9, and the lowest percentile ranking was the 54th.

Purcell-Gates, McIntyre, and Freppon (1995, p. 659) discovered that children who start school with limited linguistic knowledge of books do catch up to their "well-read-to" peers when exposed to solid skills-based or literature-based reading instruction. However, in classrooms that emphasized a holistic, literature-based curriculum, the students exhibited "significantly greater growth in their knowledge of written language and more extensive breadth of knowledge of written linguistic features."

But what about children who have already failed? Chomsky (1978), in a research report aptly titled "When You Still Can't Read in Third Grade: After Decoding, What?" addressed the plight of the young "stalled" reader, who for better than one year had made absolutely no progress in reading. In a middle-class suburban community near Boston, she worked with five third-grade children who had average IQs and no apparent language or speech problems but who always had been remedial reading students, hated reading, and had made no progress in reading since first grade. Abandoning the intensive decoding program, the researcher instead asked the children to listen to tape-recorded stories from real books, and return often to each title until the story was memorized. The neurological impress method (child simultaneously sees and hears print) using natural, enjoyable text proved to be the key to eventual success.

Standardized achievement test scores (Metropolitan Achievement Test) after a year of treatment showed that these no-progress children were off and running. Average increase in the overall reading scores was 7.5 months (grade equivalent) and in word knowledge was 6.25 months (grade equivalent), a significant increase for children whose former test scores showed no progress.

Even older children who have had years of failure with reading and writing have been exposed to literature-based programs with notable success. Fader et al. (1976) flooded secondary classrooms in inner-city Detroit with paperbacks, finding great success in raising reading achievement and developing the reading interests of high school students who traditionally did not read often or well. But their literature-based program was best put to the test with hard-core subjects—students at the W. J. Maxey Boys' Training School in Whitmore Lake, Michigan. Fader et al. provided hundreds of paperbacks for the W. J. Maxey students, along with the time to read them and without requiring the usual book reports or summaries. Another midwestern boys' training school was used as a control group. Although no significant differences were found in control and experimental groups at the onset, by the end of the school year, the boys at W. J. Maxey showed significant gains over the control group on measures of self-esteem, literacy attitudes, anxiety, verbal proficiency, and reading comprehension. In some instances, the control group's scores actually decreased from the year before while the experimental group's surged ahead, even doubling control group scores.

Stalled children also showed marked improvement in a classroom study with fifth-grade children. With the entire class, Tunnell (1986) employed a literature-based reading/writing program adapted from the program suggested by Eldredge and Butterfield (1986). Eight of the 28 students in his classroom were reading disabled, receiving Chapter I or resource instruction in a pull-out program. After seven months of treatment, the standardized tests (SRA) were administered, and the average gain in the overall reading score was a grade equivalent of 1.1. The eight reading-disabled children, who also were virtually stalled in their reading achievement progress, posted an average gain of 1.3 with a comprehension gain of 2.0. Even more noteworthy was the swing in reading attitudes in all children. A thirteen-question reading attitude survey was administered to the class in August and again in April. Negative attitudes toward books and reading almost disappeared as their self-concept in relationship to literacy rose. (See also Morrison and Moser, 1998; Tunnell, Calder, Justen, and Waldrop 1988.)

It is important to note that gains in reading skills using a literature-based approach are not limited to students at risk. In the studies by Eldredge and Butterfield (1986), Holdaway (1982) and Tunnell et al. (1988), the average and above-average reader made progress equal to and most often better than students in traditional programs as measured by the typical achievement tests.

Some of the strongest evidence for the broad use of a reading program using literature comes from Ray Reutzel, an education professor who took a one-year leave to teach reading to 63 first-grade children. With a classroom library of 2,000 books, Reutzel taught the elements and skills of reading within the meaningful context of trade books. He didn't use a basal or the state program of worksheets and drill activities, called the Utah Benchmark Skills. The state goal was to have the students pass the Utah Benchmark Skills Test at an 80 percent level in May. Without teaching the program, Reutzel's students scored 93 percent in January—13 points higher than state expectations and four months earlier than the normal testing time. In March, the students took the Stanford Achievement Test (SAT). Group percentiles in reading across all categories—word study skills, reading comprehension, and total reading—for the 63 children were uniformly in the 99th percentile. Individual scores were all above grade level except for four children who scored below 1.6. The lowest score was 1.2, and that from a boy who knew only a few letters of the alphabet when entering first grade. Even a girl whose IQ tested at 68 came out at grade level. There was not one nonreading first-grade child in the school (Reutzel and Cooter 1990).

Rasinski and Deford (1985) indicate why literature-based reading approaches may have a profound positive effect on learners. They compared three first-grade classrooms, each with competent teachers using different approaches to teaching reading: content-centered mastery learning, traditional basal, and child-centered literature-based. The researchers looked less at achievement than at student conceptions about reading assessed through interviews. The responses to the basic questions "What is reading?" or "What happens when you read?" were rated by a team of raters in relation to whether they were meaning related (high score of 7) or letter–sound related (low score of 1). Mean scores showed that children from the literature-based program conceived reading to be more of a meaning-related activity than did the other children. The mean scores for the mastery group were 3.45, for the basal group 4.32, and for the literature group 4.91.

Conclusions indicate that good readers in all three groups tended to define reading as being concerned with meaning, and poor readers saw it as a process of converting symbol to sound. Natural text—the writing found in real rather than artificial reading materials—supports reading as a meaning-related activity.

That children in classroom situations can be taught to read from real books is not a new idea. Thompson (1971) examined 40 studies from 1937 through 1971 that compared the basal approach to teach reading with instruction using the individualized literature-based approach. He discovered that 24 of the studies favored individualized reading, and only one declared the basal as the better method. (The remaining studies were ties.) Thompson (1971) concluded that "individualized reading programs can facilitate reading achievement to the extent of basal programs, and . . . more often than not . . . have facilitated higher reader achievement than basal programs in controlled studies." (See also Davis and Lucas 1971.)

BASIC ELEMENTS OF LITERATURE-BASED READING PROGRAMS

Although each of the studies reviewed employed its own brand of literature-based reading instruction, several basic premises—certain guiding principles—are found often in the different approaches. Elements of instruction vary depending on the age of the students, but the following threads of commonality were overtly employed or subtly implied in all of the literature-based reading programs reported in the studies in this chapter:

Based on Premises Learned about "Natural Readers"

Advocates of balanced, holistic reading instruction tend to believe reading skills can be acquired in much the same manner as speaking skills (Forester 1977; Holdaway 1982). For example, from a pool of 5,103 new first-grade students who had received no formal reading instruction, Durkin (1961) identified 49 students who had entered school reading between a grade equivalent level of 1.5 and 4.6. She discovered this group of 49 natural readers were heterogeneous—vastly different racial and socioeconomic backgrounds and IQ levels. The factors that were common among all these children related to the reading models they had in the home: families had a high regard for reading, children were read to regularly from age two forward, and parents answered the often-asked questions about words and reading. Durkin concluded that natural readers seem to acquire abilities through experiences with whole texts provided by strong reading models.

Both Clark (1976) and Thorndike (1973) support Durkin's conclusions. Clark's study of young readers in Scotland yielded two common factors in natural readers: All were read to from an early age and all had access to books at home or through libraries. Thorndike studied reading comprehension in 15 countries and discovered two conditions that prevailed in strong readers: All had been read to from an early age and had come from homes that respected education. Immersion in natural text at an early age has the same effects on reading as immersion in aural and spoken language has on speech.

Nagy, Anderson, and Herman (1985) agree, reporting that vocabulary growth occurs 10 times faster from reading than from intensive vocabulary instruction. In fact, they suggest there is no need for direct vocabulary instruction—the time is better spent reading.

Hoskisson (1979) concurs that immersion in natural text develops skills, suggesting that natural readers "solve the problem of learning to read as they construct their knowledge of written language" (p. 490). Therefore, no formal hierarchy of reading skills should be imposed on children, because only the child can determine what can be assimilated and accommodated within that highly personal cognitive structure. Hearing the printed page read aloud is essential in formulating and testing each child's personal hypotheses about written language. Learning to read naturally begins when parents read to young children and let them handle books, and that process is continued with the teacher reading aloud and including books naturally in the classroom.

Teacher Modeling

An important element usually only hinted at by the researchers cited in this chapter is teacher modeling. Holdaway (1982) suggests this as he lists the three basic requirements of the Shared Book Experience, one of which is that teachers need to present new material (books) with whole-hearted enjoyment. According to the same principle, teachers themselves should also read during sustained silent reading (McCracken and McCracken 1978) (see also Chapter 18). A prerequisite for this sort of modeling is a teacher who values reading in his or her personal life and also knows and loves the children's books that will be read by the students.

Natural Text

In every study examined, researchers were emphatic about using trade books in the classroom—children's literature written in natural, less controlled language. Goodman (1988) supports this move away from basal reading materials, especially after evaluating the ways in which such programs select, write, or alter the stories they include. "Basals have tended to isolate sounds, letters, and words from the [language] systems. And they have given little attention to the systems and how they relate in natural texts" (Goodman 1988, p. 37). He maintains that basal materials often produce distorted abstractions, loss of contextual meanings, and loss of grammatical function—all due to letter–sound relationships taught in isolation or words used out of context. The process of controlling vocabulary and syntax also causes a loss of style and makes language less natural and less predictable. Since Goodman's examination of basal readers, companies have made efforts to do less rewriting and simplifying of the stories they include in their basals. Nevertheless, many teachers still use both trade books and reading textbooks that overly control vocabulary and syntax. (See Chapter 3.)

It is also interesting to note that the 104 books used with the second-grade children in the Eldredge and Butterfield (1986) study were not controlled for vocabulary. In fact, the researchers report that 91 percent of the books had readability scores in excess of the third-grade level, and 62 percent were at a fourth-grade level. Despite the lack of vocabulary control, the students made superior progress.

Neurological Impress

Sometimes called "shadow reading" or "buddy reading," neurological impress is simultaneously seeing and hearing print. In the studies that involved beginning readers, a variation of the neurological impress method was generally employed.

In Chomsky's (1978) study, children "read" in the trade book while following along with the recorded version on audiocassette. Eldredge and Butterfield (1986) used reading dyads (pairs) or triads (groups of three), teaming poor readers with average readers. The readers sat together and read aloud from the same book while the faster reader touched words as they were read and the slower reader repeated them. Groups changed every few days, and as proficiency was gained, the slower reader began to read silently, using the better reader as a word resource.

Even the use of Big Books, as suggested by Holdaway (1982) and White et al. (1986), allows for a form of neurological impress. Big Books usually are trade picture books that have been reproduced in a format large enough to be seen from 20 feet away. With Big Books, teachers can have their students follow their fluent reading.

Reading Aloud

Another characteristic of literature-based programs is that teachers regularly spend time reading aloud to their students. In all of the studies reviewed, reading aloud seemed to be a must. Daily reading aloud from enjoyable trade books has been the key that unlocks literacy growth for many disabled readers. Opportunities for modeling and neurological impress abound during read aloud time. And, of course, being read to is the essential element in the backgrounds of natural readers.

Sustained Silent Reading

Sustained silent reading (SSR) is the time provided for students and teacher to read materials of their own choosing without interruption. Every study examined for this chapter included as a part of its plan the time for children to be alone with books.

> The relationship between reported free voluntary reading [SSR] and literacy development is not always large, but it is remarkably consistent. Nearly every study that has examined this relationship has found a correlation, and it is present even when different tests, different methods of probing reading habits, and different definitions of free reading are used. (Krashen 1993, p. 7)

Allington (1977) suggests that the more words that pass in front of the eyes, the better the reader becomes. The time children spend in independent reading "is associated with gains in reading achievement" (Anderson et al. 1985, p. 119). A study in England tracked the reading habits of boys who participated in an SSR program for just over eight months in the sixth grade. Six years later they were still reading more than boys who did not engage in an SSR program (Greaney and Clarke 1973). The opportunity to reread favorites, reread books recorded on audiotape, or read something new is the best way to give children the practice they need to apply their newly learned skills.

Emphasis on Changing Attitudes

An affective approach to reading instruction is also a recurring element of literature-based programs. Tunnell's (1986) study showed a marked improvement of student attitudes toward the reading process. Researchers mentioned in this article tended to make comments such as that of Larrick (1987, p. 189): "Best of all, they loved to read." As mentioned in Chapter 1, Fader et al. (1976, p. 236) illustrates a shift in attitude and its benefits with his story of Bill, a 13-year-old second-grade-level reader whom he watched busily reading *Jaws*, the adult novel by Peter Benchley. When Fader asked him if the book was hard, Bill answered, "Sure it's hard, but it's worth it."

Self-Selection

Children's attitudes toward reading seem to be affected positively by allowing them to select their own reading materials. Every study examined included a time when students at every age level were encouraged to find and read books of their own choosing. Though sometimes books were read together (as with Big Books), each classroom had a large library from which children could select their own books—like Bill's *Jaws*. Sustained silent reading is unsuccessful unless children are allowed to read books of their own choosing.

Self-selection of reading materials allows students to choose books that match their interests, and interest is not a factor to be ignored in education. Several studies undertaken by one group of researchers pinpointed what helps children recall information from their reading. Two of the factors were readability—making the language simple and easy to understand—and reader interest. The experiments concluded that "interest accounted for an average of thirty times as much variance in sentence recall as readability" (Anderson et al. 1987, p. 289). In other words, what the researchers called the "interestingness" of text is 30 times more powerful than the readability of text when it comes to comprehending and remembering information from print. Because children have different interests, teachers may miss the advantages of a powerful instructional tool if they ignore "interestingness" by not allowing ample opportunity for children to learn from self-selected books. Also, one of the continuing problems of basal readers, when used as the major resource for reading instruction, is that opportunities for self-selection are limited.

Emphasis on Meaning

Most studies reviewed suggested teaching reading skills as they relate directly to the books and writings of the children (Boehnlein, 1987; Chomsky, 1978; Cohen, 1968; Holdaway, 1982; Larrick, 1987). Eldredge and Butterfield (1986) employed a brief decoding lesson, but they suggested moving quickly into "real" reading so that the lesson can be put into realistic and immediate practice.

Process Writing and Other Output Activities

In every study, a follow-up output activity periodically accompanied reading experiences, and often the output activities involved writing (Chomsky, 1978; Fader et al., 1976; Forester, 1977; Holdaway, 1982; Larrick, 1987; Tunnell, 1986; White, Vaughan, and Rorie, 1986). In fact, Chomsky (1978) states that the children who progressed the most achieved in both reading and writing.

The studies examined in this chapter often suggest process writing in particular. Process writing instruction is a mainstay of a balanced literacy philosophy wherein the process of writing is emphasized initially over the product. Children are given license to write without fear of making mistakes, and they learn to find their "voice" by beginning to write about the thing they know best—their own lives. For more about process writing, see the definitive work, *Writing: Teachers and Children at Work*, by Donald Graves (1983).

OTHER CONSIDERATIONS

Success of literature-based programs is well documented. Disabled readers are brought into the world of literacy (and not just decoding) using real books. When children learn that reading and books are worthwhile, they will spend more self-initiated time in books, as Fielding, Wilson, and Anderson (1984) point out. Children who participate in this self-initiated practice (some children read from 10 to 20 times more than others) make more progress because frequent personal reading improves the automaticity of basic reading skills. Unfortunately, in a study of after-school activities of fifth-grade children, Fielding and her colleagues (1984) discovered that only 2 percent of free time is spent reading (a daily average of 9.2 minutes). Fifty percent of the children read only four minutes or less each day, and 30 percent read two minutes or less (10 percent did not read at all). It is no surprise that television watching consumed most of their after-school time (an average of 136.4 minutes daily). Yet, these researchers concluded that

> among all the ways children can spend their leisure time, average minutes per day reading books was the best and most consistent predictor of standardized comprehension test performance, size of vocabulary, and gains in reading achievement between second and fifth grade. (Fielding, Wilson, and Anderson 1984, p. 151)

Greaney (1980, p. 339) reviewed studies concerning leisure reading and discovered that "a number of studies have reported significant relationships between amount of leisure reading and level of pupil attainment." One of the studies Greaney points to was conducted decades ago by LaBrant (1936). His longitudinal study reported that students who completed a six-year free reading program were, twenty-five years later, reading significantly more than most other groups to which they had been compared. (Also see Connor 1953/1954; Maxwell 1977.) In fact, *Becoming a Nation of Readers* (Anderson et al. 1985, p. 82) suggests that "priority should be given to independent reading."

Fielding, Wilson, and Anderson (1984) note that reading trade books deepens knowledge of the forms of written language. Early experiences with the richness and variety found in children's books seem to give children reason to read, teaching them, as Trelease (1985, p. 6) explains, not only "how to read, but to want to read."

The affectivity of literature-based programs gives purpose and pleasure to the process of learning to read, thus making skills instruction more meaningful. At the very least, it is safe to say the basal reader is not the only successful way to teach children to read.

REFERENCES

Allington, Richard. 1977. If they don't read much, how they ever gonna get good? *Journal of Reading* 21 (October): 57–61.

Anderson, Richard C., Elfrieda H. Hiebert, Judith A. Scott, and Ian A. G. Wilkinson. 1985. *Becoming a Nation of Readers: The Report of the Commission on Reading.* Washington, D.C.: The National Institute of Education, U.S. Department of Education.

Anderson, Richard C., Larry T. Shirley, Paul T. Wilson, and Linda G. Fielding. 1987. Interestingness of children's reading material. In *Aptitude, Learning and Instruction, Volume 3: Conative and Affective Process Analysis,* edited by R. E. Snow and M. J. Farr. Hillsdale, N.J.: Earlbaum.

Bader, Lois A., Jeannette Veatch, and J. Lloyd Eldredge. 1987. Trade books or basal readers? *Reading Improvement* 24 (Spring): 62–67.

Boehnlein, Mary. 1987. Reading intervention for high risk first-graders. *Educational Leadership* 44 (March): 32–37.

Chomsky, Carol. 1978. When you still can't read in third grade: After decoding, what? In *What Research Has to Say about Reading Instruction*, edited by Jay Samuels. Newark, Del.: IRA.

Clark, Margaret. 1976. *Young Fluent Readers*. London: Heinemann.

Cohen, Dorothy. 1968. The effect of literature on vocabulary and reading achievement. *Elementary English* 45 (February): 209–213, 217.

Connor, D. V. 1953/1954. The relationship between reading achievement and voluntary reading of children. *Educational Review* 6: 221–227.

Cullinan, Bernice, Angela Jaggar, and Dorothy Strickland. 1974. Language expansion for black children in the primary grades: A research report. *Young Children* 29 (January): 98–112.

Davis, Floyd W., and James S. Lucas. 1971. An experiment in individualized reading. *The Reading Teacher* 24 (May): 737–743, 747.

Durkin, Dolores. 1961. Children who read before grade one. *The Reading Teacher* 14 (January): 163–166.

Eldredge, J. Lloyd, and Dennie Butterfield. 1986. Alternatives to traditional reading instruction. *The Reading Teacher* 40 (October): 32–37.

Fader, Daniel, James Duggins, Tom Finn, and Elton McNeil. 1976. *The New Hooked On Books*. New York: Berkley.

Fielding, Linda G., Paul T. Wilson, and Richard Anderson. 1984. A new focus on free reading: The role of trade books in reading instruction. In *The Contexts of School Based Literacy*, edited by Taffy E. Raphael. New York: Random House.

Forester, Anne D. 1977. What teachers can learn from "natural readers." *The Reading Teacher* 31 (November): 160–166.

Goodman, Ken. 1988. Look what they've done to Judy Blume!: The "basalization" of children's literature. *The New Advocate* 1 (Winter): 29–41.

Graves, Donald H. 1983. *Writing: Teachers and Children at Work*. Portsmouth, N.H.: Heinemann.

Greaney, Vincent, and M. Clarke. 1973. A longitudinal study of the effects of two reading methods on leisure-time reading habits. In *Reading: What of the Future?* edited by Donald Moyle. London: United Kingdom Reading Association.

Greaney, Vincent. 1980. Factors related to amount and type of leisure reading. *Reading Research Quarterly* 15, no. 3 (1980): 337–357.

Holdaway, Don. 1982. Shared book experience: Teaching reading using favorite books. *Theory into Practice* 21 (Fall): 293–300.

Hoskisson, Kenneth. 1979. Learning to read naturally. *Language Arts* 56 (May): 489–496.

Koeller, Shirley. 1981. 25 years advocating children's literature in the reading program. *The Reading Teacher* 34 (February): 552–556.

Krashen, Stephen. 1993. *The Power of Reading*. Englewood, Colo.: Libraries Unlimited.

LaBrant, Lou L. 1936. *An Evaluation of Free Reading in Grades Ten, Eleven and Twelve*. Columbus, Ohio: Ohio State University Press.

Larrick, Nancy. 1987. Illiteracy starts too soon. *Phi Delta Kappan* 69 (November): 184–189.

Maxwell, James. 1977. *Reading Progress from 8 to 15*. Windsor, England: National Foundation for Educational Research.

McCracken, Robert, and Marlene McCracken. 1978. Modeling is the key to sustained silent reading. *The Reading Teacher* 31 (January): 406–408.

Morrison, Timothy, G., and Gary P. Moser. 1998. Increasing students' achievement and interest in reading. *Reading Horizons* 38, no. 4 (March/April): 233–245.

Nagy, William E., Richard Anderson, and Patricia A. Herman. 1985. Learning words from context. *Reading Research Quarterly* 20, no. 2 (Winter): 233–253.

Pinnell, Gay Su. 1986. *Reading Recovery in Ohio 1985–86: Final Report*. Technical Report, The Ohio State University, Columbus, Ohio.

Purcell-Gates, Victoria, Ellen McIntyre, and Penny A. Freppon. 1995. Learning written storybook language in school: A comparison of low-SES children in skills-based and whole language classrooms. *American Educational Research Journal* 32, no. 3 (Fall): 659–685.

Rasinski, Timothy V., and Diane E. Deford. 1985. *Learning within a Classroom Context: First Graders' Conceptions of Literacy*. ED 262 393. Arlington, Va.: ERIC Document Reproduction Service.

Reutzel, D. Ray, and Robert B. Cooter, Jr. 1996. *Teaching Children to Read: From Basals to Books*. Upper Saddle River, N.J.: Merrill/Prentice Hall.

Reutzel, D. Ray, and Robert B. Cooter, Jr. 1990. Whole language: Comparative effects on first-grade reading achievement. *The Journal of Educational Research* 5, no. 5 (May/June): 252–257.

Sendak, Maurice. 1963. *Where the Wild Things Are*. New York: Harper.

Thompson, Richard A. 1971. *Summarizing Research Pertaining to Individualized Reading*. ED 065 836. Arlington, Va.: ERIC Document Reproduction Service.

Thorndike, Robert L. 1973. Reading comprehension, education in 15 countries: An empirical study, Vol. 3. *International Studies in Education*. New York: Holsted-Wiley.

Trelease, Jim. 1985. *The Read Aloud Handbook*. New York: Viking/Penguin.

Tunnell, Michael O. 1986. The natural act of reading: An affective approach. *The Advocate* 5 (Winter/Spring): 156–164.

Tunnell, Michael O., James E. Calder, Joseph E. Justen, III, and Phillip B. Waldrop. 1988. An affective approach to reading: Effectively teaching reading to mainstreamed handicapped children. *The Pointer* 32 (Spring): 38–40.

White, E. B. 1952. *Charlotte's Web*. New York: Harper.

White, Jane H., Joseph L. Vaughan, and I. Laverne Rorie. 1986. Picture of a classroom where reading is for real. *The Reading Teacher* 40 (October): 84–86.

CHAPTER 21

Evaluating
Children's Reading

Reading gets more attention than any part of the curriculum in the elementary school. And for good reason. Reading is the basic skill needed for survival and continued learning in a literate society. As such, the evaluation of a child's reading has always been an important part of the public school. Parents and educators alike are concerned with how well our children are doing in this consequential area.

Although a host of definitions identify what reading is, the explanation in *Becoming a Nation of Readers* (Anderson, Hiebert, Scott, and Wilkinson 1985) is as clear and comprehensive as any.

- Skilled reading is constructive. Becoming a skilled reader requires learning to reason about written material using knowledge from everyday life and from disciplined fields of study.
- Skilled reading is fluent. Becoming a skilled reader depends on mastering basic processes to the point where they are automatic, so that attention is freed for the analysis of meaning.
- Skilled reading is strategic. Becoming a skilled reader requires learning to control one's reading in relation to one's purpose, the nature of the material, and whether one is comprehending.
- Skilled reading is motivated. Becoming a skilled reader requires learning to sustain attention and learning that written material can be interesting and informative.
- Skilled reading is a lifelong pursuit. Becoming a skilled reader is a matter of continuous practice, development, and refinement. (pp. 17–18)

To determine how well a child is reading, an accurate evaluation should at least touch on each point in this list. Until recent years, however, the standard procedure for evaluating reading was limited to administering a national test. These tests report a child's reading level in specific and tidy numbers. If a boy is reading at 4.2, for instance, that translates into his reading at the same mean level as the average American child in fourth grade, second month of instruction. Such a score would please the parents and teacher of a boy in second grade but not be such good news for the parents and teacher of a child just finishing sixth.

Although standardized tests still are used widely, we now know that reading is not so easily evaluated. Standardized reading tests measure only a narrow spectrum of total reading (Johnston 1984). They are restricted to easily measurable elements of the reading process, particularly recall of information, some literal thinking, and some vocabulary matching. Because standardized tests reflect only this limited view, they are no longer trusted as the definitive measure of a child's current reading abilities (Cambourne and Turbill 1990; Johnston 1987; Neill and Medina 1989; Valencia and Pearson 1987; Wiggins 1989). National tests are

(1) inconsistent with our knowledge of reading processes; (2) not capturing the complexities of reading acquisition and learning; (3) requiring students to engage in decontextualized tasks with ecologically invalid materials; and (4) offering teachers little help in guiding and directing students' reading instructional programs in classrooms. (Baumann and Murray 1994)

Worksheets also carry a caution. Although widely used, worksheets do not help students learn to read or help them read better. Their use is not related to year-to-year gains in reading proficiency (Leinhardt, Sigmond, and Cooley 1981; Rosenshine and Stevens 1984). Too often they are used to keep students quiet and busy, are poorly designed, and demand only the most perfunctory level of attention from students (Anderson et al. 1985, p. 76). Workbook and skill-sheet use should be cut back to the minimum.

OBSERVING AND RECORD KEEPING

How, then, can a teacher know how well a child is reading? The five points described in *Becoming a Nation of Readers* can be checked by (1) listening to the child read aloud, (2) talking with the child about the content, and (3) observing the child reading. Observations in each area should be included in an anecdotal reading record for each child. This personalized record keeps track of and compares the child's progress from one grading period to the next. Anecdotal records are idiosyncratic for each child, identifying precisely the strengths and weaknesses of each child's reading abilities. They also contain teacher observations about the child's broader orientation to reading, including difficulty or ease in finding interesting titles, attention span, involvement in books, and any other telling observations. As such, anecdotal reading records tell much more about the particular child's reading abilities and growth or regression than statistically normed tests (Wood and Algozzine 1994, Chapter 7).

LISTEN TO THE CHILD READ ALOUD

The quickest way to evaluate reading skills is to listen to the child read aloud a passage of text for the first time. Most of the individual skills of reading are evident in oral reading, and a teacher can identify areas of strength and weakness by observing how the child decodes and the child's fluency, which includes rate, expression, and smoothness. How well the child can decode is evident in which words cause the child difficulty and how the child unlocks the pronunciation. The rate should approximate normal speech. Expression, which should be as varied as the content demands, reveals how well the child understands and interacts with the text. And smoothness shows the child's confidence and competence in reading for meaning.

If the teacher follows along on a separate copy of the text as the student reads, marking specific errors and shortcomings and jotting down other observations, this sheet of notes becomes a part of the student's anecdotal reading record.

When parents wonder how their child is doing, the most helpful response a teacher can give is to ask them to listen to the child read aloud. Even the untrained adult can get a fairly accurate impression of the child's skill in recognizing familiar words, figuring out new words, and interacting with the text when hearing the child read.

TALK WITH THE CHILD ABOUT THE CONTENT

Comprehension can be checked by asking the child to tell you about the passage or story just read. The teacher should be looking for evidence of understanding of the text in literal elements (detail, sequence, vocabulary) and nonliteral elements (main idea, cause and effect, and inference). If the child hesitates, the teacher then can ask leading questions that deal with the content or element in question.

The child's understanding of content is often evident during discussions in small groups or even with the entire class. By directing questions to a specific student, the teacher can infer how well that student understood the story or information from the reading. It is impossible to keep records for all children in all discussions, but when something noteworthy occurs, it is wise to record it in the child's anecdotal record.

Whether in one-on-one interviews or in discussions, anecdotal records of comprehension should be kept periodically for each child. Note the ease (or hesitation) of response, the degree of completeness, the literal and nonliteral elements that the student voluntarily included in a response as well as responses indicating a lack of understanding.

OBSERVE THE CHILD READING

Watching the child read provides information about skills as well as motivation. Children whose lips move or fingers follow each line of print are not reading as fluently as they will be with more practice and confidence. Teachers can assess student motivation by observing how focused children are when they search the classroom library for a book, how quickly they get ready to read when it is time for sustained silent reading (SSR), how well they stay on task, how long they stay on task, and how often and eager they are to discuss what they read with their teacher or peers.

MEASURING THE AMOUNT OF READING

If teachers want to evaluate students' growth in overall reading abilities, they will want to measure the time their students spend reading in books of their own choosing. Of all outside school activities, the best predictor of reading growth in children between the second and fifth grades is the average number of minutes per day they spend reading books (Anderson et al. 1985, p. 77). Stephen Krashen (1991) confirmed that students who spend time actually reading strengthen considerably their reading skills. He examined a number of studies that compared growth in reading as a result of direct reading instruction with progress made when students simply read books.

In face-to-face comparisons, reading is consistently shown to be more efficient than direct instruction. Other studies confirm that direct instruction has little or no effect. The only conclusions we can draw from these findings can be stated easily: Reading is a powerful means of developing literacy, of developing reading comprehension ability, writing style, vocabulary, grammar, and spelling. Direct instruction is not. (p. 22)

While reading meaningful text, children practice all the subskills of the reading act. Naturally, the more children read, the better readers they become. Bernice Cullinan (1981) illustrates this principle with Figure 21–1. The diagram indicates that reading skills improve with practice, as does the ability to perform any task we repeat over and over. The more we read, the better we get at reading. The better we get at reading, the more pleasure we find in it. And the more pleasure it gives us, the more we practice—with the result that we get better.

Sometimes teachers who emphasize individual reading are challenged by those who think school is not the place for such soft approaches. A teacher walking down the hall looks in on a class where a teacher is reading aloud and says, "I wish we had time for entertainment, but we are too busy learning." A PTA president wants to emphasize "back to basics" and finds fault with providing time in the classroom for SSR and reading aloud, labeling them "entertaining" and "baby-sitting," which belong in the home but not in the rigorous atmosphere of school.

You might respond to such charges by saying, "You want children to read better and master reading skills? Those are my greatest concerns, too. I want my students to have both the ability to read and also the desire. When they want to read, they get constant practice that increases their fluency, comprehension, and overall reading skills. It is regular reading that takes them to those high levels of proficiency."

Next, quote two or three of the studies in Chapter 20 that show how improved or maintained test scores result from an emphasis on increased personal reading. Then continue, "What we are doing is not only making them better readers but also teaching them the lifelong reading habit that will prepare them for their continuing education better than anything else we can do in this classroom."

While some see a conflict between emphasizing skills instruction or focusing on engaged personal reading, there really is no conflict between the two. The aim of both approaches is to have students become more proficient, skilled, experienced readers, so avoid buying into the argument that the two ideas are at odds with each other. The

FIGURE 21–1
The more we read, the better we get.

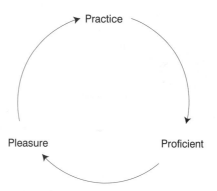

teacher who wants students to become involved in books of their own choosing has the same goal as the teacher who emphasizes skills: to help students read better.

RECORD KEEPING

If reading more helps children read better, one way to evaluate progress is to keep track of how much each child reads. This information then becomes evidence that the reader is practicing measurable reading skills as well as interacting with print. Students should know that teachers are tabulating their performance and precisely what they are counting. The three measurable parts of the individual reading activity are books, pages, and time. When children know that their reading is being recorded (and often teachers suggest a minimum or guideline), then keeping track only of the number of books presents a problem because books vary so much in length. In an effort to make things fairer, some teachers count total pages. Yet pages are hardly uniform. Because of their size and number of words, a page in one children's novel may have 60 words, while a page in another might have 450. The most democratic method of setting a goal and keeping a record is to look at the time spent reading. If a slow reader and a fast reader spend the same 20 minutes reading, the fast reader naturally will cover more ground, but each pays an identical price.

In an effort to get students reading on their own, two teachers unknown to each other and half a nation apart created similar reading programs. Kemie Nix of Atlanta, Georgia, and Katie Blake of Provo, Utah, both knew that students who read successfully only at school run the risk of losing the reading habit once June rolls around. Each reasoned that teaching children to find reading time in their own world, unaffected by the schedules and bells of the classroom, would increase their chances of becoming self-motivated readers. Samples of the record-keeping forms each developed are reproduced here. (See Figures 21–2 and 21–3.)

The plans' similarities are remarkable. Both focus on students' finding their own meaning in books outside of class and provide a nudge in that direction by reminding them to read regularly. Both give readers complete control over their reading materials. Perfection is reading five days per week. Students do not have to report on the books they read. They read for short periods of time, and the results of their reading are reported only to the teacher, not displayed on a wall for all to see.

Each differs slightly from the other. Blake assigned a specific number of minutes by grade level; Nix left the required time spent reading to each teacher's discretion. For Blake, daily reading time could be either a child's private reading, or a parent's reading to the child, or the child's reading to the parent. Blake's record-keeping system is visible in the home (she recommends putting the form on the refrigerator) and can be used easily by all students, including those in kindergarten through second grade; Nix's reading record stays in the school and is more difficult for younger children (K–2) to handle. Once individual teachers understand the principles in these two plans, they can use them to structure a program of their own.

In addition to the daily reading record, each child should also maintain a list of titles and authors read that year. These data, along with a compilation of how many

I read: ——————————————   Extra time: ————————————   Monday,
I did not read: ——————————
Author: ——————————————————— Title: ————————————————————

I read: ——————————————   Extra time: ————————————   Tuesday,
I did not read: ——————————
Author: ——————————————————— Title: ————————————————————

I read: ——————————————   Extra time: ————————————   Wednesday,
I did not read: ——————————
Author: ——————————————————— Title: ————————————————————

I read: ——————————————   Extra time: ————————————   Thursday,
I did not read: ——————————
Author: ——————————————————— Title: ————————————————————

I read: ——————————————   Extra time: ————————————   Weekend,
I did not read: ——————————
Author: ——————————————————— Title: ————————————————————

I read: ——————————————   Extra time: ————————————   Monday,
I did not read: ——————————
Author: ——————————————————— Title: ————————————————————

I read: ——————————————   Extra time: ————————————   Tuesday,
I did not read: ——————————
Author: ——————————————————— Title: ————————————————————

I read: ——————————————   Extra time: ————————————   Wednesday,
I did not read: ——————————
Author: ——————————————————— Title: ————————————————————

I read: ——————————————   Extra time: ————————————   Thursday,
I did not read: ——————————
Author: ——————————————————— Title: ————————————————————

I read: ——————————————   Extra time: ————————————   Weekend,
I did not read: ——————————
Author: ——————————————————— Title: ————————————————————

FIGURE 21–2
Kemie Nix's Out-of-School Reading Program

Kemie Nix's Out-of-School Reading Program
Atlanta, Georgia

1. Students read books of their own choosing, but daily reading at home is a part of classroom requirements.

2. Teacher makes booklet of forms for entire period of record keeping. For a school year, do the following:
   a. Make one form without dates.
   b. Duplicate number needed for one complete booklet. Because one form records 2 weeks of reading, 18 are needed for a 36-week year.
   c. Type in dates for entire year. One copy is now finished.
   d. Now duplicate—one for each student.
   e. Put in inexpensive folder secured by brads.

3. Booklets are kept in one spot in classroom and filled out daily by each student.

4. Student checks "I read" if required time was spent reading the previous day.

5. If student misses a day, the reason for not reading is to be written in the space for that day.

6. Reading does not have to be made up. Goal is to make reading delightful and easy, and no one performs without missing occasionally.

7. Grading is according to teacher prerogative. Nix uses "Excellent" for not missing, "Very Good" for missing one day, and "Good" for missing two days. Missing three or more days simply cancels the week–counts neither for nor against student.

8. Progress is checked each week by teacher, preferably with student in a one-minute visit. Whole class can open booklets on desks with teacher circulating.

9. Students write title and name of author each day, even if book takes a number of days to finish. No ditto marks. Writing the titles and authors results in students developing more confidence and competence in knowing and talking about books.

10. Include a lined page at the front of the booklet to record each title and author as books are finished. Teachers can assess progress at a glance, and students often are surprised to see how many books they have read.

FIGURE 21–2, *continued*

FIGURE 21-3

One of Nine Record-Keeping Calendars for Katie Blake's Shared Warmth Reading Program

PROVOST'S "SHARED WARMTH" RULES

Parent or guardian should initial and write the appropriate number on the calendar each day one of the following is accomplished:

1. Parent reads to child.
2. Child reads to parent.
3. Child reads silently.

Combinations are acceptable.

Required reading time per grade:

K, 1, 2--fifteen minutes per night
3, 4--twenty to thirty minutes per night
5, 6--thirty or more minutes per night

Sample:

27 KB_1	28 KB_3	29 MB_2

Katie Blake, Library/Media Coordinator

HAPPY READING!

FIGURE 21–3, *continued*

minutes the children have read in SSR and how many titles the teacher has read aloud, are formidable. In a world that sometimes seems driven by scientific research and statistical data, the number of books read, the number of pages, and amount of time spent reading can sometimes be overlooked. Yet these numbers are hard data that show genuine growth.

CHILDREN WITH READING PROBLEMS

Increasing the amount of reading will not increase automatically the reading abilities of all children. About 85 percent of the children in a given classroom will improve their reading skills markedly from spending additional time with good books. The remaining 15 percent will need more specific help (McCormick 1987, p. 12). Those 15 percent have problems in at least one of three areas: context clues, sight reading, or phonics. Roughly two-thirds of that 15 percent have difficulty with context clues and sight reading and can be helped by more contact with meaningful language, partly solved by increased involvement with trade books. The remaining third of that 15 percent need additional phonics help. When encouraged and allowed to spend more time with books of their own choosing, 85 percent of all students will respond favorably and grow in their reading abilities. The teacher then has more time to focus on those three to five children—the remaining 15 percent—who need special attention.

WAYS TO GENERATE READER RESPONSE

While increased skills come as a by-product of increased reading, many teachers are interested in what can be done to involve the hearts and minds of children in the books that they read. How can we help them become more interested in their reading? What can we do to get them to respond favorably to books?

Before we get to the specific approaches and activities, it is important to understand the principles that lead to successful involvement with books. Madeleine L'Engle outlined perhaps the main characteristic we teachers want to capitalize upon.

> Readers usually underestimate their own importance. If a reader cannot create a book along with the writer, the book will never come to life. Creative involvement: That's the difference between reading a book and watching TV.
>
> In watching TV, we are passive—sponges; we do nothing. In reading we must become creators, imagining the setting of the story, seeing the facial expressions, hearing the inflection of the voices. The author and reader "know" each other; they meet on the bridge of words. (L'Engle 1980, p. 37–38)

We want readers to "create a book along with the writer." We want them to live in the book; to be active in their experience and response. To keep them from being sponges, we must provide them the kinds of assignments and activities that allow the kind of reading to take place where reader and author "meet on the bridge of words."

If an activity allows and encourages readers to respond in a way that L'Engle calls "creative involvement," the assignment is generally a plus. When used with self-selected books, such an activity is helpful when it adheres to three principles: (1) students choose the books they wish to respond to, (2) students choose the activities, and (3) students read most books without any obligation to respond (see Figure 21-4, later in this chapter).

Even when students are enthusiastic about a certain way of responding to books, teachers need to remember that variety is the key to keeping them involved. No response or activity designed to involve readers with their books works for long. Students may love recording their personal thoughts in a reading journal, but if it is required for every book, the idea wears thin. As one teacher said, "What I want when they finish reading *Tuck Everlasting* is a gleam in their eyes." If assigned responses dim that gleam—like the traditional book report—they need to be rethought.

The traditional book report (focusing on elements of fiction, including plot, characters, setting, style, and theme) has done more to kill the love of reading in Americans ages 9 to 18 than any other idea to come from the schools (Root 1975). Traditional book reports are almost universally detested. Ask any American group how many had to write traditional book reports in school (many hands go up), and then ask how many remember the task with fondness (hardly a hand rises). They continue to be used because some teachers demand tangible evidence that the child has read the book. Of course, it is possible for students to write reports on books they have not read. Any sixth grader can offer a variety of ways. Rent the movie. Read the front flap. Talk to someone about the book. Use someone else's old book report. Read about the book in *Junior Plots*. Or, for the daring, invent the book—title, author, plot, characters—the entire thing. The only defense for traditional book reports is that they foster imagination by teaching kids to cheat creatively.

The response options that follow offer alternatives to the traditional book report.

Group Responses

Grand conversations.   For those books or poems everyone has read or has had read to them, discussions can provide the opportunities for meaningful responses. Peterson and Eeds (1990) call this approach "grand conversations," which are characterized by teachers participating fully in the discussion where they model and share their thought processes and personal interpretations about the story. The teacher is not, however, the central focus and needs to be careful that adult comments do not become pronouncements. The spotlight is on the book and the readers' responses. The teacher simply participates by being a voice with the students (Eeds and Peterson 1997; Wells 1995). Teachers allow and encourage students to share their personal responses, providing open-ended prompts when necessary for group discussion: "What did you notice in the story?" "What do you remember from the story?" "Does anything in the story remind you of your own life?" "Did you find anything in the story that was funny?"

Grand conversations can also include the discussion of literary merit and technique. As long as the questions do not have a right and wrong answer so the talk is truly a discussion, children can become involved. "What hints did the author drop to prepare us for the ending?" "Are there any facts or details in the book that let us know Josh was not to be trusted?" "Can you find an image—a picture in your mind—put there by the author that helps you to see the castle clearly?"

Teachers must be prepared for discussion that goes beyond their own preparation and understanding. In grand conversations, even a six-year-old can notice something an experienced teacher has missed.

When discussing *Sylvester and the Magic Pebble* (Steig 1969), six-year-old Tracy responded to an illustration showing Sylvester using the magic pebble to abruptly stop a rainstorm as ducks in the background peer skyward in confusion. Tracy shared with her teacher examples of things she thought were funny:

Tracy:	When Sylvester finds the red pebble—and the ducks are cute. . . .
Teacher:	The what?
Tracy:	The ducks are cute. . . .
Teacher:	The ducks *are* cute. They've got their bills up in the air like they're just enjoying the sunshine, having a grand time, uh-huh. . . .
Tracy:	Or else they're thinking, "How'd that happen?"
Teacher:	How'd what happen?
Tracy:	The rain started, then stopped.
Teacher:	Yes! Of course they're thinking that!
Tracy:	They go—"It started a little while ago—what happened?"

The teacher was looking at the picture but had not noticed the ducks. She was dumbfounded that a six-year-old had picked up on a subtle point of interpretation that an adult had overlooked (Peterson and Eeds 1990, pp. 17–18).

LITERATURE CIRCLES. After observing a number of small groups of elementary school children discussing books, Harvey Daniels identified specific kinds of responses that kept reappearing. He then named these responses, for example: Discussion Director—assumed the role of keeping things moving along; Connector—centered on connections to parts of the child's life or other books beyond the one being discussed; Vocabulary Enricher—noticed the author's specific word choices. Using a small group of students, Daniels explained the clearly defined roles, allowed the children to practice them, and then assigned each member of the group to play a particular role in a discussion. They change roles over a two-week period, allowing them both to participate and observe as each child centers on just one aspect of a discussion. The idea of a literature circle is to make students aware of the kinds of responses that are possible, give them practice with each, and move as quickly as possible to the desired end: All participants play all the roles in genuine discussions of books (Daniels 1994).

READER'S WORKSHOP. Nancie Atwell sought a way to have her students interact with books beyond the discussion. She wanted to know how each of them was responding to reading and knew that was impossible in discussion groups—time is limited; some students are shy; group dynamics can keep some students from being heard;

it is difficult for the teacher to get around to every small group. So Atwell initiated a written response program, which included personal writing about the book each student was reading. To guide their writing, she focused on reading as a process, building on the same principles used in writer's workshops: (1) Writers and readers *rehearse*, planning and predicting; (2) writers and readers *draft*, discovering meaning; and (3) writers and readers *revise*, reseeing and reseeking meaning. And to further develop awareness and skill, she used minilessons to teach the whole class about books—five to ten minutes to talk about an author, a genre, or an element of literature. Students then chose their books, read at a time provided during the school day, and wrote personal responses to her in what she called "dialogue journals" (Atwell 1987).

READING GROUPS.   The teacher forms small groups of readers by having multiple copies of a number of books and then telling the entire class about five or six of the titles. Each student is then allowed to choose one that sounds interesting. Those reading the same book naturally belong to one group.

Because children read at different rates and with different intensities, one problem in choreographing small group responses is having everyone read the same book without making it seem like work. One member of a group may finish the book overnight, while another might take a couple of weeks to get to the last page. One way to allow for this natural difference is to plan for small group responses to take about three weeks. Let students read at their natural rates, and those who finish first can move on to other titles during SSR or at home. Those who are moving more slowly have two weeks to complete the book, and then the group responds sometime during the third week.

To provide necessary variety, the teacher can offer the groups four or five response options for the first three-week period. Then the next time, each group may be allowed to choose from one section of the possibilities listed in Figure 21–4. The time after that, the students might come up with their own plan. The idea is that the responses are always honest and varied. And for that reason, small reading groups should not be in constant session but should have liberal vacations between the three-week periods.

Individual Reader Responses

No matter how interesting and varied reader responses might be, readers do not want to make even an informal response to every book they read any more than viewers want to respond to every movie they see. Insisting that students do something with every title is sure to backfire. In fact, most of the books a person reads should be left alone—the reading is sufficient.

But every so often, perhaps twice a grading period—once if small groups are being used—teachers can ask students to respond to a book they have read. Allowing the students to select the title and have some choice in the method of response are both essential if the response is to have any real meaning to the reader. Again, the list in Figure 21–4 provides some alternatives, but students may come up with their own ways to respond to the books they read.

Writing Activities

1. Rewrite part of the story, telling it from the viewpoint of a different character.
2. Write an advertisement for the book. Identify where the advertisement will be displayed.
3. Write a poem based on the book.
4. Make up riddles about the book or any parts of it.
5. Write a rebus of the book's title, a short summary, or a certain scene in the book.
6. Develop a word game based upon the book (word scramble, crossword puzzle, acrostic).
7. Write a letter to the author, particularly if you enjoyed the book or have a question. (Send the letter to the publisher of the book and it will be forwarded.)
8. Write an imaginary interview with the main character—or any character or object.
9. Make a newspaper which summarizes or presents elements from the book. Include as many regular departments of a newspaper (sports, comics, lovelorn, classified ads, business, and so on) as you desire.
10. Write your own book on the same theme, perhaps writing some and outlining the rest.
11. Rewrite a section of the book in either radio or stage script.
12. Select a passage or quotation which has special significance for you. Write it down and then tell why it is meaningful.
13. Rewrite the story or part of the story as a news article.
14. Rewrite part of the book in a different time period—space age future, cavemen, wild West, etc.
15. Write some trivia questions to exchange with someone else.
16. Write a chapter which tells what happened before or after the book.
17. If the book were made into a movie, choose who would play the characters. (See if you can select real people familiar to your classmates.)
18. Write a letter from some character to a real or fictitious person not in the story.
19. Write the same scene from three or four different points of view.
20. Write a simplified version of the story in picture book form.
21. Write a review of the book.

Art and Craft Activities

1. Make a diorama of an important scene in the book.
2. Construct a mobile representative of the book or some part of it.
3. Draw portraits of the main character(s).
4. Draw a mural which highlights events from the book or retells the story.
5. Draw a picture in the same style as the illustrator, or using the same medium (pen and ink, collage, watercolor, etc.).
6. Cut out words from newspapers and magazines for a word collage which gives a feeling for the book.
7. Use stitching or liquid embroidery to make a wall hanging or decorate a T-shirt with art related to the story.
8. Draw a coat of arms for a character(s) and explain the significance of each symbol.
9. Draw a silhouette of a person, scene, or object from the book.
10. Design a new dust jacket for the book.

FIGURE 21–4
Reader Response Activities to Enhance Reading

11. Illustrate what you believe is the most important idea or scene from the book.
12. Make a poster advertising the book.
13. Make a time line of the important events in the book.
14. Make a roll movie of the book which can be shown on a t.v. set made from a box using your own illustrations, photographs, or pictures cut from magazines.
15. Retell the story using a flannel board and bits of string, yarn and felt—or create recognizable characters to use in the retelling.
16. Identify the important places in the book on a map of your own making.
17. Make paper dolls and clothes of the main character(s).
18. Make a travel poster inviting tourists to visit the setting of the book.
19. Construct a scene or character out of clay.
20. Design a costume for a character to wear.
21. Prepare and serve a food that the characters ate or which is representative of the book.

Drama, Music, and Assorted Activities

1. Make puppets—sack masks, socks, or finger—of the characters and produce a puppet show of the book.
2. Dress as a character and present some of the character's feelings, or tell about a part of the book, or summarize very briefly the story.
3. Videotape a dramatized scene from the book.
4. Write a song which tells about the book.
5. Conduct an interview between an informed moderator and character(s) ... maybe t.v. news?
6. Research music from the time of the book, and find some songs the characters may have sung.
7. Pantomime a scene from the book.
8. Perform a scene from the book with one person taking all the parts.
9. Choosing a familiar tune, write lyrics which tell about the book.
10. For each character in the book, choose a musical selection which typifies that person.
11. Give a sales pitch to get listeners excited about the book.
12. Give a party for characters and their friends, or for characters from many books. Invite parents and have characters present themselves.
13. Research some real aspect of the book and present your newly found facts.
14. Bring something from home which reminds you of the book. Explain.
15. Choose a real life person who reminds you of a character in the book. Explain.
16. Select one passage which is the focal point of the book. Explain.
17. Collect and display a collage of quotes that you like from the book.
18. Make a board game using characters and elements from the book. Have pitfalls (lose a turn, etc.) and rewards (shake again, etc.) reflecting parts of the book.
19. Find other books on the same subject and set up a display with them.
20. Perform a choral reading from the book, or write something about the book to perform in a choral reading.
21. Emphasize the setting of the book using any or all of the following: a) objects, b) food, c) costumes, d) culture, e) music, f) art.

FIGURE 21–4, *continued*

Reading gets more attention than any part of the curriculum because it is the foundation of learning. To evaluate reading accurately, we need to do more than measure a few narrow elements. We must see the child according to the broad view of reading—mastering basic processes, learning to reason, discovering meaning, and finding personal reward that will lead to a lifetime friendship with print. Instead of relying solely on paper-and-pencil tests, teachers can more accurately identify a child's progress using a wider range of evaluative methods. When we listen to children read, talk with them about what they read, observe them with books, and watch them respond to books, we learn much of significance about their reading skills and attitudes.

REFERENCES

Anderson, Richard C., Elfrieda Hiebert, J. A. Scott, and I. A. G. Wilkinson. 1985. *Becoming a Nation of Readers: The Report of the Commission on Reading.* Washington, D.C.: National Institute of Education.

Atwell, Nancie. 1987. *In the Middle: Writing, Reading, and Learning with Adolescents*: Portsmouth, N.H.; Boynton/Cook.

Baumann, James F., and Bruce A. Murray. 1994. Current practices in reading assessment. In *Teaching Reading to High-Risk Learners,* edited by Karen D. Wood and Bob Algozzine. Boston: Allyn and Bacon.

Cambourne, B., and J. Turbill. 1990. Assessment in whole language classrooms: Theory into practice. *Elementary School Journal* 90: 337–349.

Cullinan, Bernice. 1981. The Power of Reading. Address at the annual convention of the Utah Council of the International Reading Association, Salt Lake City, Utah, 5 March.

Daniels, Harvey. 1994. *Literature Circles*: *Voice and Choice in the Student-Centered Classroom* York, Maine: Stenhouse.

Eeds, Maryann, and Ralph Peterson. 1997. Literature studies revisited: Some thoughts on talking with children about books. *The New Advocate* 10 (Winter): 49–59.

Johnston, Peter H. 1984. Prior knowledge and reading comprehension test bias. *Reading Research Quarterly* 19 (Winter): 219–239.

Johnston, Peter H. 1987. Teachers as evaluation experts. *The Reading Teacher* 40 (April): 744–748.

Krashen, Stephen. 1991. *The Power of Reading.* Englewood, Colo.: Libraries Unlimited.

L'Engle, Madeleine. 1980. *Walking on Water: Reflections on Faith and Art.* Wheaton, Ill.: H. Shaw.

Leinhardt, G., N. Sigmond, and W. W. Cooley. 1981. Reading instruction and its effects. *American Educational Research Journal* 18 (1981): 343–361.

McCormick, Sandra. 1987. *Remedial and Clinical Reading Instruction.* New York: Merrill/Macmillan.

Neill, D. M., and N. J. Medina. 1989. Standardized testing: Harmful to educational health. *Phi Delta Kappan* 70: 688–697.

Peterson, Ralph, and Maryann Eeds. 1990. *Grand Conversations: Literature Groups in Action.* Richmond Hill, Ont.: Scholastic.

Root, Shelton L., Jr. 1975. Lecture, University of Georgia, Athens, Georgia, 21 March.

Rosenshine, B., and R. Stevens. 1984. Classroom instruction in reading. In *Handbook of Reading Research*, edited by P. David Pearson. New York: Longman.

Steig, William. 1969. *Sylvester and the Magic Pebble.* New York: Windmill.

Valencia, Sheila W., and P. David Pearson. 1987. Reading assessment: Time for a change. *The Reading Teacher* 40 (April): 726–732.

Wells, D. 1995. Leading grand conversations. In *Book Talk and Beyond: Children and Teachers Respond to Literature,* edited by N. Roser and M. Martinez. Newark, Del.: International Reading Association.

Wiggins, G. 1989. Teaching to the (authentic) test. *Educational Leadership* 46 (1989): 41–47.

Winograd, Peter, Scott Paris, and Connie Bridge. 1991. Improving the assessment of literacy. *The Reading Teacher* 45 (October): 108–111.

Wood, Karen D., and Bob Algozzine. 1994. *Teaching Reading to High-Risk Students.* Boston: Allyn and Bacon.

CHAPTER 22

Teaching the Curriculum with Children's Literature

If your goal is to help children become lifelong learners, then children's literature is perhaps the most important class you will take. No discovery is more valuable to a lifelong learner than finding out there is something personally worthwhile between the covers of a book. Students who are self-motivated continue their education as long as they breathe. And an education is not always the same as having a diploma. Just as it is possible to gain a diploma without much education having taken place, it is also possible to become educated without formal instruction. Getting an education is a personal decision.

What distinguishes truly educated people, what identifies them and sets them apart, is that they are readers. This is true even for a school dropout who has spent 70 percent of his life in prison. When Wilbert Rideau was eighteen years old, he robbed a bank, killed a teller, and was sent to the Louisiana State Prison for life. After a few angry years doing nothing but sitting and rebelling, Rideau picked up a book and spent a number of weeks reading it. Then he picked up another. Although he left school in eighth grade and English was his least favorite subject, soon he was reading two books a day on a variety of subjects. But he liked history best.

> "I read about Napoleon, Muhammed, Lincoln, Washington, Bolivar, Sukarno," says Rideau. "I came to realize that a lot of people had terrible beginnings, but they lifted themselves up and gave something back to the world. I read *Profiles in Courage*. I'll never forget what it said—that a man does what he must, regardless of the cost." One day a guard passed him a copy of Ayn Rand's *Atlas Shrugged*. Its message of self-reliance became Rideau's credo. "I started seeing that no matter how bad things looked, it was all on me whether I made something of myself or I died in some nameless grave."(quoted in Colt 1993, p. 71)

What Rideau did was initiate and become editor of *The Angolite*, the convict magazine that is required reading in training classes for new correctional officers and also the first prison publication ever nominated for a National Magazine Award (an honor it has since earned six times). In addition, it is the first to win the Robert F. Kennedy Journalism Award, a George Polk Award, and the American Bar Association Silver Gavel Award (Colt 1993, p. 72).

TYPES OF BOOKS

Schools use books as tools of education, and those books fall into three distinct categories: reference, text, and trade. Each type of book is philosophically different from the others and serves a different purpose. Reference books are those volumes a person consults for an immediate answer to a specific question, such as a dictionary, encyclopedia, atlas, and thesaurus. Textbooks are designed for use in formal instruction, presenting a dispassionate view of a subject in an organized, methodical manner. *Trade books* is the term given to books published for the retail market (books written for and sold in the trade) that are typically available in bookstores and libraries. Trade books are written by people who have something personal to say and hope their words appeal to readers who seek knowledge, insight, and pleasure.

Students who read books because of a school assignment usually read textbooks. Anyone who has finished high school has only to consider how often teachers require reading from each of the three categories to determine that textbooks are used far more than the other two types. Estimates from our classes of college students about the percentage of textbook time offer no surprises. The range has been surprisingly consistent throughout the years, from a low of 60 percent to a high of 95 percent, with most responses hovering around 80 to 85 percent. Trade books are estimated to occupy between 10 and 30 percent of school reading time, and reference books 5 to 15 percent.

Although textbooks are used in the classroom much more than the other two types of books, they are not the most liked. Textbooks have been targeted as one reason social studies is the most universally disliked of all school subjects at all levels (Sewall 1988). When students from grades 3 to 12 were asked how education could be improved, 40 percent said textbooks should be improved—a higher percentage than those who think they need better teachers (Roper Organization 1987).

Jim Trelease suggests one reason why textbooks do not have student appeal:

> Textbooks are written by either committees or an author who has to please a committee of editors, who in turn must please a curriculum committee, which must please a school board (another committee).
>
> So textbook writing and publishing decisions are made on the basis of the lowest common denominator—the fewest number of committee members or special interest groups who will be offended by a pabulum text. The end result is a book without a personality and voice, a textbook without texture. And for this reason, no one grows up having a favorite textbook. (You never hear someone say, "I'll always remember my sixth-grade science book, *Meadows and Streams*.") (1988, p. xiv)

That textbooks do not excite students is not a new trend. Over 400 years ago, in the play *Romeo and Juliet*, Shakespeare referred to the feelings students have for their textbooks. The first time the two lovers meet and pledge their devotion to one another—which is so deep and consuming they are willing to forsake everything for it, including family, worldly goods, and life itself—Romeo speaks figuratively to show the intensity of their love. "Love goes toward love, as schoolboys from their books" (Shakespeare, 2.2.157–158). How powerful is their love? As powerful as the revulsion schoolboys feel for their textbooks.

A quick look at both textbooks and trade books can help us capitalize on the strengths of each in the educational process. To prepare for the points to follow, consider these two passages about dinosaurs, one from a textbook and the other from an informational picture book.

> Millions of years ago, most land animals were reptiles. Dinosaurs of all sizes roamed the land. Flying reptiles had beaks with teeth. Their wings were covered with leathery skin, not feathers. Other reptiles swam in the seas. They had fish-shaped bodies with tails and fins. Their scientific name means "fish lizard." But they were not fish. They had lungs and breathed air. (*Holt Science* [fifth grade]. Holt, Rinehart and Winston, 1989, p. 326)

Scientists long thought that dinosaurs, like today's reptiles, were cold-blooded animals. THE NEWS IS: Some dinosaurs may have been warm-blooded. *Deinonychus*—"terrible claw"—is one of those dinosaurs.

Deinonychus was fairly small. It had the sharp teeth of a meat-eater, hands shaped for grasping prey, and powerful hind legs. It also had a huge, curved claw on one toe of each hind foot. This was a claw shaped for ripping and slashing.

To attack, *Deinonychus* must have stood on one hind foot and slashed with the other. Or it must have leaped and attacked with both hind feet. Today's reptiles are not nimble enough to do anything like that. And as cold-blooded animals, they do not have the energy to attack that way. Warm-blooded animals do. . . .

Warm-blooded animals grow much faster than cold-blooded ones. A young ostrich, for example, shoots up 5 feet in a year. A young crocodile grows only about one foot.

Bones in the nesting grounds of Montana show that duckbills were 13 inches long when they hatched. Scientists think young duckbills were 10 feet long at the end of their first year. If that is right, it is a sign of an animal that grew fast—perhaps of a warm-blooded one. (*The News about Dinosaurs*. Patricia Lauber, Bradbury Press, 1989, p. 32)

Strengths of Trade Books

Trade books offer the following advantages in teaching the curriculum:

DEPTH OF CONTENT. Trade books focus on a subject and bring it to life with interesting observations and details. The reader comes away with a richer understanding of the topic. Textbooks offer a broad and consequently shallow view of subjects that do not allow for the kind of compelling presentation available in trade books. For example, the Holt science text quoted earlier devotes only that one complete paragraph to dinosaurs. It is difficult if not impossible to give readers any real insight in such a small space.

MANY PERSPECTIVES. Hundreds of books about dinosaurs are available, rounding out reader knowledge as much as one chooses. Textbooks offer one perspective. "No one book, whatever its type, can truly answer every question about a particular subject. Trade books offer the opportunity to explore a broad range of topics as well as to examine in-depth a single topic . . . " (Holmes and Ammon 1985, p. 366).

CURRENT. Trade books are produced more quickly than textbooks, offering the latest findings even on old subjects (dinosaurs and the new warm-blooded theory). Also, most school districts can afford a new textbook in each subject only every 5 to 10 years, which is a distinct disadvantage in this information-rich age.

WRITING STYLE. Trade books often are written in a conversational style; textbooks are formal. Trade books have the space to make meaningful comparisons (crocodile to ostrich) and use more detail to enlarge understanding (duckbill babies in Montana). Textbooks depend on short sentences and a "basket of facts" style (Fielding, Wilson, and Anderson 1986, p. 152).

To make a narrative "readable," publishers break up complex sentences, shorten paragraphs, and excise stylistic flourishes. The conjunctions, modifiers, and clauses that help create subtle connections and advance student understanding are routinely cut. The result is, at its best, straightforward—and, at its worst, choppy, monotonic, metallic prose. (Sewall 1988, p. 555)

VOICE. Trade books allow a human being to emerge in the writing. Information has more power to influence others when it is presented through the individual voice of a trade book author. Textbooks are detached and impersonal.

REFLECT INDIVIDUAL READING LEVELS. In a regular classroom, the reading levels of students vary widely. Because of the number and variety of trade books, even students with reading problems can locate books that they can read, enjoy, and learn from, and that allow them to contribute to class discussions.

RICH LANGUAGE. The words in trade books create images ("hands shaped for grasping prey," "leaped and attacked with both feet") and use more precise, colorful vocabulary (nimble, slashing). The sentences are varied and read more interestingly, both silently and aloud. (Read aloud the two dinosaur excerpts on pp. 283 and 284 and compare.)

VARIED FORMATS AND STRUCTURES. Trade books come in all sizes and lengths. The illustrations and diagrams tend to be larger and more appealing than those in textbooks. They tend to structure information so it is natural and clearly understood. Textbooks have a predictable industrial look, are dense and compact, and generally have smaller illustrations and diagrams. The structure of content is not always clear.

Too many social studies and science texts are simply "baskets of facts," little more than loosely connected lists of propositions about a topic. The structure of textbook chapters is likely to be murky. There are simple structures that are accepted among the cannons of exposition, such as cause–effect, temporal sequence, or comparison contrast. Yet it is seldom that one finds a content-area textbook selection that is clearly organized according to one of these structures. Students are more likely to encounter these structures and to learn to understand and appreciate them when they read good nonfiction trade books. (Fielding, Wilson, and Anderson 1986, p. 152)

TOOLS OF LIFELONG LEARNING. Trade books are available in all libraries and bookstores. They are the books people go to most often to learn about the world after they leave school. Trade books are the stuff of "real life" reading. Textbooks are limited to formal education and can be found only in classrooms and academic bookstores. Regular bookstores have none, and libraries very few, which causes some people to ask, "If schools are to prepare children for lifelong learning, why do they rely so heavily on a tool that is not available in their actual future?"

Strengths of Textbooks

Textbooks serve three useful purposes in the classroom, two for the teacher and one for the students:

IDENTIFY SUBJECT MATTER STUDENTS ARE EXPECTED TO LEARN. Textbooks provide the content boundaries for which the school district makes the teacher responsible, and teachers of all levels of experience and ability need to know what is required of them in each subject area. Even though the classroom teacher also can find this information in a state or district curriculum guide, the textbook is usually more accessible.

PROVIDE A RESOURCE FOR SUBJECT AREAS WHERE THE EDUCATOR IS UNSKILLED OR UNSURE.   New teachers, in particular, simply haven't had the time or experience to become knowledgeable and proficient in all subjects, and the text provides them with a crutch while they are gaining the knowledge, experience, and insight they need before they can call a subject area their own. The best resource in a classroom is a skilled and experienced teacher, one who knows the material and how to present it so students will be involved. The teacher should work continually to become that resource, replacing the textbook with personalized, interesting materials and approaches as soon as possible. Some teachers will be able to do this relatively quickly; others will need longer. But the situation to avoid is becoming textbook dependent. If the goal is to have excited and interested students, the text needs to become a secondary source, or sometimes even abandoned, as soon as possible.

SERVE STUDENTS WHO ALREADY HAVE AN INTEREST IN THE SUBJECT. The strength of the textbook approach is the generalized overview of a topic. When a reader comes to a textbook with an interest and curiosity about the subject, the text-book can serve as a worthwhile resource. As a successful way of exciting the uninitiated about a topic, however, textbooks largely fail. Yet they are used most frequently in the educational process as an introduction to a subject, the very way in which they do not perform well.

EDUCATION AND TRADE BOOKS

The purpose of both fiction and nonfiction trade books is not so much to inform, which they do very well, as it is to excite, to introduce, to let the reader in on the irresistible secrets of life on planet Earth. No uninteresting subjects exist on this sphere—nor are there any interesting ones. All subjects are neutral. What makes them appealing, or boring, is how we are introduced to them. What makes the difference between a reader being enthusiastic or bored is the viewpoint, the perspective, the care, and the skill of the one doing the introducing. Interesting perspectives simply are easier to find in trade books than in texts. And today's informational trade books often are tantalizing (see Chapter 12). They help create interest in young readers. Although subjects by their nature are neither interesting nor uninteresting, the books are.

In addition to using appealing informational books to generate interest in a subject, a teacher who knows fiction has another advantage in bringing students to the curriculum. Historical fiction, for instance, sheds light on history in a way that nonfiction has difficulty duplicating. By introducing historically accurate fiction, complete with its compelling plot and well-developed characters, Cynthia Stokes Brown says that history can come alive by allowing children more readily to "identify . . . with heroes and heroism and . . . explore their own lives and identity, character and convictions through heroic stories" (1994, p. 5).

When children are interested in what they read, and read broadly—whether fiction, nonfiction, or both—they can learn much of value from trade books. People are able to grow and develop intellectually without the carefully monitored presentation of information typical of textbooks, as these three examples show:

1. *Robert Howard Allen has never seen his father.*   Divorced before he was born, Robert's mother left him at age six to be raised by his grandfather, three great-aunts, and a great-uncle, all of whom lived in the same house in rural Tennessee. After his grandfather taught him to read, Robert regularly read the Bible to a blind great-aunt. "From age seven he read thousands of books—from Donald Duck comics to Homer, James Joyce and Shakespeare. . . . He began picking up books at yard sales, and by his early 20s he had some 2000 volumes" (Whittemore 1991, p. 4).

Robert Howard Allen stayed home and helped and read. He never went to school, not even for a day. At age 30 he easily passed a high school equivalency test, and at age 32 he showed up at Bethel College in McKenzie, Tennessee. Three years later he graduated summa cum laude (3.92 GPA), and continued his education by enrolling in graduate school at Vanderbilt University. Having earned his Ph.D. in English, he is currently a visiting lecturer at Murray State College in Kentucky (Whittemore 1991).

2. *During her childhood, Lauralee Summer and her mother moved frequently from one homeless shelter to another.*   She remembers sitting on her mother's lap and listening to stories. "'She was about 20 months old when I began reading to her every single night,' says [Lauralee's mother], who recalls a well-thumbed book of nursery rhymes. 'I read the same book every night. That was the only book we had' " (Gloster 1994, p. 1).

With money for her fourth birthday, Lauralee bought a See & Say book and taught herself to read. She soon was visiting libraries as mother and daughter moved among shelters and welfare hotels in three states. At age 10, Lauralee tried fourth-grade classes in two Santa Barbara schools, then quit in favor of reading to herself at the shelter. Eventually, she did attend school, an alternative program for nontraditional students during her senior year, where she took the Scholastic Aptitude Test (SAT) and scored 1460, putting her in the 99.7 percentile of America's high school seniors. Lauralee applied to Harvard University and was admitted to the 1994 freshman class with a full scholarship (Gloster 1994).

3. *Cushla Yeoman was born with multiple handicaps.*   Chromosome damage caused her spleen, kidneys, and mouth cavity to be deformed and prevented her from

holding anything in her hand until she was three years old. She could not see clearly more than a foot away. Muscle spasms kept her from sleeping more than two hours a night. She was diagnosed as mentally and physically retarded, and doctors recommended that she be institutionalized.

Cushla's parents had seen her respond to the picture books they read aloud, so they kept her home and increased their reading to fourteen picture books a day, week after week and month after month. By age five, Cushla was pronounced by doctors to be socially well adjusted and intellectually well above average (Butler 1980).

We are not suggesting that the best way to learn is outside of school. Yet people can and do learn beyond the walls of formal education. All of us need to recognize that books can create interest in readers, that people learn better when they are interested, and that people can learn a great deal by reading widely on their own.

TEACHING THE CURRICULUM WITH TRADE BOOKS

Trade books, textbooks, and reference books are different from one another and should be used differently. If we ignore those differences and, say, use trade books exactly as we use texts, the trade books lose much of their power. We need to avoid using *The Very Hungry Caterpillar* (Carle 1969) as the core of 32 separate language arts activities, or devising 19 mathematical procedures from *Frog and Toad Are Friends* (Lobel 1970). The strength of trade books is their ability to create interest. Recognizing that they also can be used for instruction, we need to choose ways to preserve their ability to stimulate readers and not turn the books into reading assignments with lists of questions to be answered.

One way to show students the appeal of trade books in the instructional program is for teachers to read and use them. Children won't see how books from the library fit into daily instruction unless the teachers include them as a natural part of classroom learning. An easy way to bring the books into lessons is to ask the librarian for titles on a subject to be taught—for instance, magnetism. Look through the books until you find enough interesting ideas, experiments, or information for a lesson or unit, and then present it to the class, showing the books that gave you the information. Teachers' use of these books is particularly important in the lower grades, where children have more limited reading abilities. Middle- and upper-grade children will be able to make more of their own discoveries, as outlined in three approaches that follow.

The Individual Reading Approach

Holmes and Ammon (1985) devised a strategy to use with an entire class, grades three and above, but it can be adapted for use with groups, individuals, or children in the lower grades. It is designed to be used as a series of lessons instead of one presentation, and has four steps: readiness, reading, response, and record keeping.

READINESS.   First, the teacher plans something to activate prior knowledge of a subject, such as a discussion in which students share facts they already know about the topic. Another way to activate prior knowledge is to generate word associations as a class. The topic "dinosaurs," for instance, may elicit words like *huge*, *fighters*, and *extinct*. After this introduction, each student generates a personally interesting question about dinosaurs, writes it on a small piece of poster board, and puts it randomly on the wall or a bulletin board. Finally, the teacher asks students if any of the questions are related. Similar questions are grouped and become a subtopic. Student groups then select a subtopic, such as "birth and death of dinosaurs," and proceed to step two.

READING.   The teacher collects dinosaur books of varied lengths and difficulty levels. Students choose their own books and read silently, focusing on the subtopic, one of the questions within it, or reading for a general overview. After the reading, the teacher directs the class in collecting data by taking each subtopic in turn, asking for information the students found, and writing it on an overhead projector or chart. During the activity, children might present conflicting facts. This provides a chance to do what seldom happens at school—return to their sources to corroborate information. In one session, for instance, a child identified the largest dinosaur as a Brachiosaurus while another said it was a Tyrannosaurus rex. A rereading showed the Tyrannosaurus rex to be the largest *meat-eating* dinosaur. If rereading offers no solution, other possibilities for clarification should be explored, such as looking at the recency of publication or consulting still other sources.

RESPONSE.   Now the class is ready to summarize together the information under each subtopic, perhaps enrich their learning (more reading, a field trip, or guest lecturer), and then make their own personal responses: art projects, constructing models, writing projects.

RECORD KEEPING.   During this series of lessons, students keep their own records of the books they consulted and their proposed responses in a folder where they also place a variety of pieces of evidence: snippets of work, drafts, note cards, and the like (Holmes and Ammon 1985). The teacher has access to their folders for evaluation.

The Large Group Reading Approach

Brozo and Tomlinson (1986) incorporate fiction as well as nonfiction into the content curriculum. They suggest using trade books, especially reading them aloud to the class, to introduce and extend the textbook in a four-step approach:

STEP 1. IDENTIFY SALIENT CONCEPTS.   Textbooks only hint at many important concepts that need a closer look if students are to identify and understand them. Consider the following description of Nazis and Jews in a fifth-grade textbook:

German soldiers rounded up and transported Jews and other minorities from all over Europe to death camps called concentration camps. The Nazis killed 11 million men, women, and children at the camps. Six million of those killed were Jews. The remaining victims included Gypsies, Russians, Poles, and others. This mass murder is known as the *Holocaust*, which means total destruction. (*Build Our Nation*, Houghton Mifflin, 1997, p. 552.)

The preceding paragraph is the entire entry for the Holocaust in that text. It hints at the drama and tragedy of the Holocaust but provides no details or insight into this terrible event. To personalize students' understanding, the teacher needs to identify the unmentioned but important concepts that underlie the Holocaust. Asking questions like the following can identify these salient concepts: What are the driving forces behind the events? What phenomena described in the textbook have affected ordinary people or may do so in the future? What universal patterns of behavior related to this event should be explained? Such questions lead us to pursue core elements of Nazi persecution of the Jews, like prejudice, inhumanity, and the abuse of power.

STEP 2. IDENTIFY APPROPRIATE TRADE BOOKS TO HELP TEACH CONCEPTS.   Subject guides, like Sharon Dreyer's *The Bookfinder* (1977–1995, vols. 1–5) and the annual publication *Subject Guide to Children's Books in Print* (1999) help teachers find books to strengthen their collections (see Appendix A plus the compact disc accompanying this text). The library can assist with immediate needs. Teachers naturally should read the books before using them in class, looking for captivating nonfiction and powerful fiction that breathe life into the important concepts to be learned. Take, for example, the following excerpt from *Friedrich* (Richter 1970). The concepts of bigotry and injustice only hinted at in the textbook entry are brought to life when an attendant at a German swimming pool in 1938 discovers that a boy retrieving his clothes is a Jew.

> "Just take a look at this!" the attendant said. . . . "This is one of the Jewish identification cards. The scoundrel lied to me . . . —a Jew that's what he is. A Jew in our swimming pool!" He looked disgusted. . . .
>   As if he could no longer bear to touch it, the attendant threw Friedrich's identification card and its case across the counter. "Think of it! Jewish things among the clothes of respectable human beings!" he screamed, flinging the coat hanger holding Friedrich's clothes on the ground so they scattered in all directions. (pp. 76–77)

STEP 3. TEACH.   The teacher then reads the trade book or books to the class as a schema and interest builder before getting to the overview presented in the textbook. After providing to the whole class a foundation for understanding, then the teacher presents the main points from the text. The teacher also introduces additional trade books that are valuable to the students for elaboration and extension of content.

STEP 4. FOLLOW-UP.   After the content is presented and students explore it, follow-up activities personalize and extend learning. They can be as varied as the people who create them: imagined on-the-scene descriptions of places or events, letters to historical figures, dramatizations, interviews, and debates are a few suggestions.

The Small Group Reading Approach

Ad Spofford teaches sixth grade and successfully uses small groups in the teaching of subject matter. He divides the students into groups of between four and six members. He then gives each group children's trade books on a common topic, making sure that there is one book less than there are members of the group. By providing fewer books than people, they have to share and work together more. He then gives the group an assignment that depends on the group's reading and compiling information from the books, such as the following: "Prepare a report for the board of directors on active volcanoes within the boundaries of the United States. They have little understanding of the number and potential threat of American volcanoes, so be sure to give background and experts' opinions on how dangerous our volcanoes are. Use visuals to help present your information."

At other times, Spofford provides the books—still one fewer than group members—and asks the group to generate a response (write a report, make a video, create charts, and so on) using information in the titles on their table. They can decide what to present and how to present it, but each person has to make a contribution.

THREE PRINCIPLES OF USING TRADE BOOKS TO TEACH SUBJECT MATTER

The individual, large group, and small group reading approaches are not the only methods teachers can use when teaching with trade books. Elements of the three techniques can be combined to form other strategies. A class can, for example, read a book together as a springboard to small group work or individual study, bypassing the textbook completely.

As long as three principles are followed, trade books may be used to spark learning in a variety of ways that will be successful:

1. *Students read trade books as they are meant to be read*—as windows to the world that do not cover a subject but, like peeling layers off the onion, uncover it.
2. *Teachers allow students to discover, or uncover, the information.* When the teacher knows *exactly* what the student should find in a given book, that book is being misused. Teachers who allow students to select their own evidence often will be pleasantly surprised at what students will bring back as proof of learning even when the assignment is fairly specific (for example, "Find evidence of how animals adapt to their environment").
3. *Students share their discoveries and insights.* Teachers reinforce genuine learning by providing some means for the excited student to present new knowledge to an audience, or make a personal response to new discoveries—through an oral or written summary, poster, display, explanation to a small group, or a diary or story from the perspective of a historical figure.

Trade books even can be used to learn beyond the curriculum. They explore so much more of the world than is covered in traditional school subjects: child labor laws, the development of dynamite, the making of baseball bats, printing paper money, living with a terminal disease, illustrating comic books, and on and on. It is difficult to find a topic in the world that is *not* the focus of a children's book. After a brief discussion of how much interesting information exists outside school subjects, children may be assigned to find a book about something they will not learn about in school yet is appealing to them. After reading it, they should have a chance to share their new knowledge. Using trade books to learn subject matter provides children freedom to discover while still keeping them accountable.

If we want children to develop intellectually, we make the greatest strides when we concentrate on helping them become curious. A curious person is observant, is aware, asks questions, and tries to find the answers. Being curious is a mind set and is a common denominator of those who discover and who solve problems. It is the curious who continue to learn under their own power. As Rabelais reportedly advised us, "Children are not vessels to be filled but fires to be lit." Because trade books reflect the curiosity and humanity of authors who have learned to see, and wish to share that vision, they have the spark that can light that flame.

REFERENCES

Brown, Cynthia Stokes. 1994. *Connecting with the Past: History Workshop in the Middle and High Schools*. Portsmouth, N.H.: Heinemann.

Brozo, William G., and Carl M. Tomlinson. 1986. Literature: The key to lively content courses. *The Reading Teacher* 40 (December): 288–293.

Build Our Nation. 1997. Boston: Houghton Mifflin.

Butler, Dorothy. 1980. *Cushla and Her Books*. Boston: The Horn Book.

Carle, Eric. 1969. *The Very Hungry Caterpillar*. New York: Philomel.

Colt, George Howe. 1993. The most rehabilitated prisoner in America. *Life Magazine* (March), pp. 69–76.

Dreyer, Sharon. 1977–1995. *The Bookfinder* (vols. 1–5). Circle Pines, Minn.: American Guidance Service.

Fielding, Linda, Paul T. Wilson, and Richard C. Anderson. 1986. A new focus on free reading. In *The Context of School-Based Literacy*, edited by Taffy Raphael. New York: Random House.

Gloster, Rob. 1994. After a childhood of disarray, girl heads to Harvard. In *The Daily Herald*, Provo, Utah, 4 June.

Holmes, Betty C., and Richard I. Ammon. 1985. Teaching content with trade books: A strategy. *Childhood Education* 61 (May/June): 366–370.

Holt Science. 1989. New York: Holt, Rinehart and Winston.

Lauber, Patricia. 1989. *The News About Dinosaurs*. New York: Bradbury Press.

Lobel, Arnold. 1970. *Frog and Toad Are Friends*. New York: Harper.

Richter, Hans Peter. 1970. *Friedrich*. New York: Holt, Rinehart and Winston.

Roper Organization. 1987. *The American Chicle Youth Poll*. New York: Roper Organization.

Sewall, Gilbert T. 1988. American history textbooks: Where do we go from here? *Phi Delta Kappan* (April): 553–558.

Subject Guide to Children's Books in Print. 1999. New York: R. R. Bowker. (Published annually.)

Trelease, Jim. 1988. Introduction. In *Eyeopeners!* by Beverly Kobrin. New York: Viking.

Whittemore, Hank. 1991. The most precious gift. *Parade Magazine,* 22 December, pp. 4–6.

APPENDIX A

Book Selection Aids

PROFESSIONAL ORGANIZATIONS

American Library Association (ALA)

50 Huron St.
Chicago, IL 60611
Phone: (312) 944-6780; (800) 545-2433
Website: http://www.ala.org

Founded in 1876, ALA is the oldest and largest national library association in the world. It works to maintain the highest quality of library and informational services in institutions available to the public. Included in its membership are libraries, librarians, library trustees, and others who are concerned with literacy and informational services. The ALA publishes *Booklist,* one of the most respected book review journals.

- *Association for Library Service to Children (ALSC).* A branch of ALA, ALSC focuses on library services for children. Through many committees, it evaluates and selects print and nonprint materials to use in libraries for children, beginning in preschool and extending through the junior high years. Other duties include serving as advocates for the child, assisting the professional development of librarians, and recognizing quality literature by giving out appropriate awards. Awards granted by ALSC include the John Newbery and Randolph Caldecott Medals, the Mildred L. Batchelder Award, and the Laura Ingalls Wilder Award. ALSC publishes, in cooperation with YALSA (see below), the *Journal of Youth Services*.

- *Young Adult Library Services Association (YALSA)*. Also a branch of ALA, YALSA is similar in purpose and responsibilities to ALSC, but its special focus is on library services for older youth beyond the elementary level. Like ALSC, YALSA is concerned with selecting and evaluating books, being advocates for young people, assisting the professional development of librarians, and making library services accessible. In cooperation with ALSC, YALSA publishes the *Journal of Youth Services*.

Children's Book Council (CBC)

568 Broadway, Suite 404
New York, NY 10012
Phone: (212) 966-1990; (800)-999-2160 (orders only)
Website: http://www.cbcbooks.org

CBC sponsors National Children's Book Week in November and develops children's book programs related to various disciplines through joint committees with library, bookselling, and education associations. Each year the council cosponsors the designation of outstanding trade books through its participation in the following: Children's Choices (with the International Reading Association), Outstanding Science Trade Books for Children (with the National Science Teachers Association), and Notable Children's Trade Books in the Field of Social Studies (with the National Council for the Social Studies). CBC also sponsors the Children's Books Mean Business Project and the Not Just for Children Anymore Program.

The Children's Literature Association (ChLA)

P.O. Box 138
Battle Creek, MI 49016-0138
Phone: (616) 965-8180
Website: http://ebbs.english.vt.edu/chla

The Children's Literature Association is an organization under the umbrella of the Modern Language Association (MLA). It encourages serious scholarship and research in the area of children's literature and provides an outlet for scholarship through conferences and publications. ChLA sponsors the Phoenix Award for books that are at least 20 years old that have not won any major awards. This organization also grants scholarships to persons doing innovative research in the field.

International Reading Association (IRA)

800 Barksdale Rd.
P.O. Box 8139
Newark, DE 19714-8139
Phone: (302) 731-1600
Website: http://www.reading.org

IRA seeks to improve the quality of reading instruction at all educational levels, to stimulate and promote the lifetime reading habit and an awareness of the impact of reading, and to encourage the development of every reader's proficiency to the highest possible level. The organization disseminates information pertaining to research on reading, including information on adult literacy, computer technology and reading, early childhood and literacy development, international education, literature for children and adolescents, and teacher education and effectiveness. IRA publishes *The Reading Teacher*, a journal for elementary-level teachers interested in reading education. IRA also promotes children's literature through its annual book awards (IRA Children's Book Awards) and through its cooperation with the Children's Book Council in administering Children's Choices, an annual booklist chosen by young readers.

National Council of Teachers of English (NCTE)

1111 Kenyon Rd.
Urbana, IL 61801
Phone: (217) 328-3870; (800) 369-6283
Website: http://www.ncte.org

NCTE works to increase the effectiveness of instruction in English language and literature. Conferences, workshops, and other presentations provide information and aids for teachers involved in formulating objectives, writing and evaluating guides, and planning in-service programs for teacher education. Children's literature is promoted through award programs for nonfiction writing (Orbis Pictus Award) and poetry (Excellence in Poetry for Children Award). NCTE publishes *Language Arts*, a journal for elementary-level teachers interested in language education.

- *Children's Literature Assembly (CLA)*. A branch of NCTE, CLA publishes *The Journal of Children's Literature*, previously known as *The Bulletin*, which includes book reviews and articles about children's literature and reading, thematic groupings of books, research updates, proceedings of NCTE workshops, and ideas for incorporating children's literature in the classroom. CLA also sponsors the NCTE Notable Books in the Language Arts, an annual list of the outstanding children's books with a language arts emphasis, and several yearly workshops and other programs that focus on children's literature.

PUBLICATIONS ABOUT CHILDREN'S LITERATURE

Review Sources

Appraisal
Children's Science Book Review Committee
Northeastern University
403 Richards Hall
Boston, MA 02215
Phone: (617) 373-7539

This quarterly periodical publishes detailed evaluative book reviews by both practicing children's librarians and subject specialists of all new children's and young adult science trade books.

Booklist
American Library Association
50 E. Huron St.
Chicago, IL 60611
Phone: (800) 545-2433
Website: http://www.ala.org

This review journal describes its purpose as "to provide a guide to current print and nonprint materials worthy of consideration for purchase by small and medium-sized public libraries and school library media centers." The journal includes subject and title, cumulative, and advertisers indexes and is published biweekly (except July and August). *Booklist* publishes annually a list of best books titled "Editor's Choice" as well as ALA Notable Children's Books and Best Books for Young Adults.

Bulletin of the Center for Children's Books
University of Illinois Press
1325 S. Oak Street
Champaign, IL 61820
Phone: (217) 244-0626
Website: http://edfu.lis.uiuc.edu/puboff/bccb

This periodical reviews and rates current children's books, classifying each by grade/age level, and includes information about adapting each for classroom use. The bulletin appears monthly from September to July, and the July issue includes the annual index.

Children's Book Review Index
Gale Research Inc.
835 Penobscot Bldg.
Detroit, MI 48226-4094
Phone: (800) 877-4253

The index includes more than 21,000 review citations that give access to reviewers' comments and opinions on more than 9,000 books written and/or recommended for children through age 10. The publication makes it easy to find a review by an author's name, book title, or illustrator, and it fully indexes over 500 periodicals.

Horn Book Magazine
Horn Book, Inc.
11 Beacon St., Suite 1000
Boston, MA 02108
Phone: (800) 325-1170
Website: http://www.hbook.com

Published six times per year, the magazine contains reviews of books that the editorial staff considers to be the best as well as articles about literature, interviews with authors, and other news about children's literature. *Horn Book* cosponsors the Boston Globe/Horn Book Awards for children's fiction, nonfiction, and picture books and publishes yearly a list of the reviewers' choices of best books called "Fanfare." The July/August issue includes the acceptance speeches for Newbery and Caldecott awards. The November/December issue includes the annual index.

Kirkus Reviews
200 Park Avenue South
New York, NY 10003-1543
Phone: (212) 777-4554

Kirkus is published on the 1st and the 15th of each month. It makes an effort to review a book two months before the book's official publication date, or as early as possible. The reviewers note outstanding books in each issue with a diamond symbol called a "pointer."

School Library Journal
P.O. Box 57559
Boulder, CO 80322
Phone: (800) 456-9409
Website: http://www.slj.com

This monthly journal is one of the most complete providers of news, information, and reviews for librarians and media specialists who serve children and young adults in school and public libraries. A special issue in December includes an index and a "Best Books" section. Subscribers can also request a free supplement, titled *Star Track: For Teachers and Other Adults Who Support Good Reading*. Sent twice each year, *Star Track* compiles reviews of outstanding books, organizing them according to genre and subject matter.

Bibliographies

A to Zoo: Subject Access to Children's Picture Books. 1998. By Carolyn W. and John A. Lima. 5th ed. New York: R. R. Bowker.

Most useful for teachers of preschool and the early grades, this source lists 12,000 picture books for children. A chapter at the beginning briefly chronicles the history of children's picture books. Indexed by author, illustrator, title, and subject.

Adventuring with Books: A Booklist for Pre-K–Grade 6. 1997. Edited by Wendy K. Sutton. 11th ed. Urbana, Ill: NCTE.

Published every five years by the NCTE, this bibliography includes annotated listings of fiction and nonfiction books recommended for children before and during the elementary school years. Books are grouped according to subject matter.

Best Books for Children: Preschool through Grade 6. 1998. 6th ed. Edited by John T. Gillespie and Corinne J. Naden. New Providence, N.J.: R. R. Bowker.

Contains over 17,000 annotated titles listed by topic, ranging from literature to history to science to recreation. Author, illustrator, title, and subject/grade level indexes are also included.

The Bookfinder: A Guide to Children's Literature About the Needs and Problems of Youth Aged 2–15. 1977, 1981, 1985, 1989. 1995. By Sharon Spredemann Dreyer. Circle Pines, Minn.: American Guidance Service.

Critical annotations of recommended books are found in subject indexes according to which needs and problems of children the books address. The third edition includes a cumulative index of the first three volumes.

Children's Books in Print. New York: R. R. Bowker (published annually).

All books in print are indexed by title, author, and illustrator. Publishers and their addresses are listed as well as detailed information relevant to purchase of books. Also available in compact disc format; monthly updates.

The Children's Catalog. 1996. Edited by Juliette Yaakov and Anne Price. 17th ed. New York: H. W. Wilson.

Published every five years, with annual supplements, this extensive retrospective source is arranged in two sections. The first lists and describes professional resources, trade books, and magazines recommended for young people, from preschool to sixth grade. The second section is a comprehensive index of entries arranged by author, title, and subject. Other editions for junior high and high school readers are also available.

The Elementary School Library Collection: A Guide to Books and other Media. 1998. Edited by Linda L. Homa. 21st ed. Williamsport, Pa.: Brodart.

Books, magazines, and nonprint media for teachers and parents of children are described according to their quality, reading level, and interest level. Entries are indexed by subject, title, author, and illustrator. A new edition is published every two years.

Eyeopeners II!: Children's Books to Answer Children's Questions About the World Around Them. 1995. By Beverly Kobrin. New York: Scholastic.

Eyeopeners II, like Kobrin's first volume *Eyeopeners*, is a terrific resource for "all adults involved with children." With over 800 nonfiction books included, this resource provides titles for topics from airplanes to words.

Horn Book Guide to Children's and Young Adult Books. Edited by Roger Sutton. Boston: Horn Book.

Published in March and September of each year since 1990, this guide lists the children's books published within each six-month period. Fiction is organized by age; nonfiction by the Dewey Decimal System. Author, subject, and title indexes, as well as ratings, further classify books.

Your Reading: An Annotated Booklist for Middle School Junior High. 1996. Edited by Barbara Samuels and G. Kylene Beers. 10th ed. Urbana, IL: NCTE.

Like *Adventuring with Books*, this source is published and frequently updated by the NCTE and includes topically arranged annotated listings of fiction and nonfiction books. Unlike *Adventuring with Books*, however, *Your Reading* is geared for young adults and is designed for use by the young readers themselves.

Other Journals

Book Links: Connecting Books, Libraries, and Classrooms
American Library Association
50 E. Huron St.
Chicago, IL 60611
Phone: (800) 545-2433
Website: http://www.ala.org

Published every two months since 1991 by ALA, this journal is designed for teachers, librarians, library media specialists, booksellers, parents, and other adults interested in exploring themes with children through literature.

Bookbird: World of Children's Books
International Board of Books for Young People (IBBY)
P.O. Box 807
Highland Park, IL 60035-0807
http://www.ibby.org

Bookbird's articles examine the children's book authors, illustrators, titles, and publishing trends from around the world.

CBC Features
CBC Order Center
350 Scotland Rd.
Orange, NJ 07050
Phone: (800) 999-2160; (212) 966-1990
Website: http://www.cbcbooks.org

Formerly titled *The Calendar*, this is a semiannual newsletter, published by the Children's Book Council. Often themed, it includes profiles of authors written by experts in the field of children's literature and listings of free or inexpensive materials.

Children's Literature in Education: An International Quarterly
Human Sciences Press, Inc.
233 Spring St.
New York, NY 10013-1578
Phone: (800) 221-9369; (212) 620-8000
Website: http://www.plenum.com/index/html

This journal is published four times each year with features that include interviews with and articles by or about authors and illustrators of children's literature, best practice ideas for the classroom, critical evaluations of books, and commentaries on social issues.

Journal of Children's Literature
Children's Literature Assembly
National Council of Teachers of English
1111 W. Kenyon Rd.
Urbana, IL 61801-1096
Phone: (800) 369-6283; (217) 328-3870
Website: http://www.ncte.org

This periodical contains articles and features on all aspects of children's literature, including news and items of interest to members.

Journal of Youth Services
American Library Association
50 Huron St.
Chicago, IL 60611
Phone: (800) 545-2433; (312) 944-6780
Website: http://www.ala.org

Published four times a year by ALSC and YALSA, *JOYS* provides news and information about ALSC and YALSA, information for librarians about current techniques and trends, and thorough reviews of professional resources.

Language Arts
National Council of Teachers of English
1111 W. Kenyon Rd.
Urbana, IL 61801-1096
Phone: (800) 369-6283; (217) 328-3870
Website: http://www.ncte.org

The periodical includes themed issues on topics relating to the teaching of English and the language arts as well as practical teaching ideas, annotations of children's books, and reviews of professional resources. It is published monthly from September through April.

The New Advocate
Christopher-Gordon Publishers Inc.
480 Washington St.
Norwood, MA 02062
Phone: (508) 543-8729

This periodical contains articles on creating, teaching, and appreciating children's literature; profiles of authors and illustrators; and reviews of children's books and literature resources for teachers. *The New Advocate* is published quarterly, with an additional issue each October devoted to one theme.

The Reading Teacher
International Reading Association
800 Barksdale Rd.
P.O. Box 8139
Newark, DE 19714-8139
Phone: (302) 731-1600
Website: http://www.reading.org

This periodical focuses on the theory and practice of teaching reading skills to elementary school children. Features include children's and professional book reviews, research reports, and practical teaching ideas. Published eight times a year.

TALL (Teaching and Learning Literature with Children and Young Adults)
Essmont Publishing
P.O. Box 186
Brandon, Vermont 05733-0186
Phone: (802) 247-3488

TALL "is published in an effort to promote the reading of literature and engagement in the genuine literary experience." It is published five times during the school year and includes articles about teaching with and evaluating trade books and the creative process of writing and illustrating. The journal also reviews both children's and young adult books.

APPENDIX B

Magazines for Children

Approximately 280 magazines for children and young adults currently are available in North America. Never have we had such a variety: magazines for young pianists (*Clavier's Piano Explorer*), racing enthusiasts (*Racing for Kids*), chess fans (*School Mates*), Barbie collectors (*Barbie, the Magazine for Girls*), or lovers of math (*Quantum*). Successful magazines can, and do, have circulations from 100 (*Acorn*) to 3 million (*Highlights*). Some successful magazines target national readership, and others aim at a small audience. For instance, *The Goldfinch* is limited to the history of Iowa, and *Signatures from the Big Sky* presents writing and art only from students living in Montana.

A selection of children's magazines belongs in every elementary school because magazines

- Offer the latest, freshest information about many subjects
- Present a variety of viewpoints on a specific topic
- Draw the attention and interest of young readers with appealing layouts and photography
- Are not imposing, thus attracting readers who hesitate to open a book
- Support and strengthen the elementary school curriculum

Following is a variety of titles selected for their quality, energy, and general appeal.

Babybug (6 months–2 years). "A board-book magazine designed for small hands" (cardboard pages, 6¼ × 7 inches with rounded edges and no staples). *Babybug* contains simple stories, rhymes, and colorful pictures. Subscription: $32.97 per year (12 issues). *Babybug*, P.O. Box 7436, Red Oak, IA 51591-4436. Phone: (800) 827-0227.

Boy's Life (ages 7–17). Published by Boy Scouts of America, the magazine covers electronics, cartoon features, sports, hobbies and crafts, careers, history and science, and scouting projects and programs. Fiction is also included. Subscription: $18.00 per year (12 issues). *Boy's Life,* Boy Scouts of America, 1325 Walnut Hill Lane, P.O. Box 152350, Irving, TX 75015-2350. Phone: (972) 580-2512.

Boys' Quest (ages 6–12). Besides fiction and nonfiction pieces, *Boys' Quest* has many exploratory, investigative, and problem-solving pages. This publication "emphasizes wholesome, innocent, childhood interests" and is designed "to inspire boys to develop interest in reading at an early age." Subscription: $15.00 per year (six issues). *Boys' Quest*, P.O. Box 227, Bluffton, OH 45817-0227. Phone: (419) 358-4610.

Calliope (ages 8–15). World history and archeology are presented to young readers through fiction and nonfiction, time lines, maps, activities, and historical photographs, demonstrating that history is a continuation of events, not a series of isolated, unrelated occurrences. Subscription: $26.95 per year (9 issues). *Calliope*, Cobblestone Publishing, 30 Grove St., Suite C, Peterborough, NH 03458. Phone: (603) 924-7209; (800) 821-0115. Website: http://www.cobblestonepub.com

Chickadee (ages 6–9). *Chickadee* is a science and nature magazine from Canada for younger children. Illustrated with drawings and color photographs, each issue contains a short story or poem, an easy-to-read animal story, puzzles, a science experiment, and a pull-out poster. Subscription: $22.95 per year (Canada), $15.95 (U.S.) (9 issues). *Chickadee*, P.O. Box 726, STN Main Markham, Ontario, Canada L3P 7V9. For U.S. orders: 25 Boxwood Lane, Buffalo, NY 14227. Phone: (416) 340-2700; (800) 387-4379. Website: http://www.owl.on.ca

ChildArt (6–14). Published by the International Child Art Foundation, a nonprofit organization dedicated to promoting child art and visual learning, *ChildArt* presents a broad view of the world of art. Often written from a child's perspective, the magazine looks at art history, contemporary art and artists, and the variety of forms art may assume. Children's artwork also appears in this publication. Subscription: $15.00 (student rate); $25.00 (school/library rate) (4 issues). *ChildArt* P.O. Box 33099, Washington, DC 20033-0099. Phone: (202) 436-3941. Website: http://www.icaf.org

Cobblestone (ages 8–15). American history comes alive through articles, maps, illustrations, songs, poems, puzzles, crafts, and activities. Subscription: $26.95 per year (9 issues). Cobblestone Publishing, 30 Grove St., Suite C, Peterborough, NH 03458. Phone: (603) 924-7209; (800) 821-0115. Website: http://www.cobblestonepub.com

Creative Kids (ages 8–14). *Creative Kids* is a forum for children's writing. Young writers' work about almost any subject may be accepted for publication. Subscription: $19.95 per year (6 issues). Prufrock Press, P.O. Box 8813, Waco, TX 76714-8813. Phone: (800) 998-2208. Website: http://www.prufrock.com

Cricket (ages 7–14). The magazine publishes quality stories, poems, and nonfiction pieces often written by well-known names in the field of children's literature. It is nicely illustrated in full color. Subscription: $32.97 per year (12 issues). *Cricket*, P.O. Box 7433, Red Oak, IA 51591-4433. Phone: (800) 827-0227.

Dolphin Log (ages 7–15). Published by The Cousteau Society, *Dolphin Log* focuses on science, the environment, and marine biology in relation to our global water system. Each issue includes an illustrated "Cousteau Adventure." Subscription: $15.00 per year (6 issues). *Dolphin Log,* The Cousteau Society, 870 Greenbriar Circle, Suite 402, Chesapeake, VA 23320. Phone: (757) 523-9335; (800) 441-4395. Website: http://www.dolphinlog.org

Faces (ages 8–14). The magazine explores and celebrates human diversity. The editorial staff is aided by the Anthropology Department of the American Museum of Natural History in creating a magazine that examines the lifestyles, beliefs, and customs of world cultures. Subscription: $26.95 per year (9 issues). *Faces,* Cobblestone Publishing, 30 Grove St., Suite C, Peterborough, NH 03458. Phone: (603) 924-7209; (800) 821-0115. Website: http://www.cobblestonepub.com

Highlights for Children (ages 2–12). *Highlights* contains fiction, nonfiction, science projects and experiments, craft projects, games, puzzles, and hidden pictures. It emphasizes "values instead of violence" and "fun with a purpose." Subscription: $29.64 per year (12 issues). *Highlights for Children*, P.O. Box 269, Columbus, OH 43216-0269. Phone: (800) 848-8922.

Hopscotch (ages 6–12). *Hopscotch* is a magazine for young girls that includes articles and features, short stories, poetry, nonfiction, games, crafts, and activities. It is one of the few magazines targeted at younger girls. Subscription: $15.00 per year (6 issues). *Hopscotch*, P.O. Box 164, Bluffton, OH 45817-0164. Phone: (419) 358-4610; (800) 358-4732.

Kids Discover (ages 6–12). Each issue is themed, focusing on a fascinating subject that is sure to stimulate young curiosities. Illustrations, diagrams, and photographs illuminate each topic, such as the construction and use of skyscrapers. Subscription: $19.95 per year (12 issues), $16.95 (10 issues). *Kids Discover*, 170 Fifth Ave., 6th Floor, New York, NY 10010. Phone: (212) 242-5133; (800) 284-8276.

Ladybug (ages 2–7). Each issue includes songs, finger plays, poems, nursery rhymes, longer read-aloud stories illustrated by award-winning illustrators, and activities for preschool and primary grade children. *Ladybug* is designed to encourage a lifetime of reading and learning in youngsters. Subscription: $32.97 per year (12 issues). *Ladybug*, P.O. Box 7433, Red Oak, IA 51591-4433. Phone: (800) 827-0227.

Muse (ages 6–14). The *Smithsonian* magazine for children, *Muse* is produced by the editors and publishers of *Cricket Magazine*. It features articles covering the breadth and wonder of the Smithsonian's collections and research, including topics such as the latest technology, architecture, paleontology, music, physics, theater, math, visual arts, earth sciences, space travel, ancient and modern world history, and almost everything else in the universe. Subscription: $24.00 per year (6 issues). *Muse*, P.O. Box 7433, Red Oak, IA 51591. Phone: (800) 827-0227.

National Geographic World (ages 8–14). Designed to encourage geographic awareness in young readers, *National Geographic World* includes full-color pictures, short articles, far-out facts, and activities. Children who subscribe become members of the National Geographic Society. Subscription: $17.95 per year (12 issues). *National Geographic World*, P.O. Box 63001, Tampa, FL 33660-0001. Phone: (800) 638 4077; (800) 548-9797. Website: http://www.nationalgeographic.com

Nickelodeon Magazine (ages 6–14). *Nickelodeon Magazine* is a humorous publication with the same irreverent tone of the Nickelodeon cable channel. It focuses on popular culture and is formatted in a busy, energetic style. Subscription: $19.97 per year (10 issues). Subscription: *Nickelodeon Magazine*, P.O. Box 37216, Boone, IA 50037. Phone: (515) 280-8750; (800) 947-7052. Website: http://www.nick.com

Odyssey (ages 10–16). With a focus on physical and natural science, the magazine contains full-length articles, star charts, spectacular photographs, activities, contests, puzzles, and interviews. Subscription: $26.95 (9 issues). *Odyssey*, Cobblestone Publishing, 30 Grove Street., Suite C, Peterborough, NH 03458. Phone: (603) 924-7209; (800) 821-0115. Website: http://www.cobblestonepub.com

Owl (ages 9–14). *Owl* is a beautifully illustrated nature magazine from Canada. Full-color photographs and paintings illustrate an interesting assortment of articles, stories, and experiments concerning the environment. Subscription: $22.95 per year (Canada), $15.95 (U.S.) (10 issues). *Owl*, P.O. Box 726, STN Main Markham, Ontario, Canada L3P 7V9. For U.S. orders: 25 Boxwood Lane, Buffalo, NY 14227. Phone: (416) 971-5275; (800) 387-4379. Website: http://www.owl.on.ca

Ranger Rick (ages 6–12). The magazine contains nonfiction, fiction, jokes and riddles, crafts and activities, plays, and poetry—all focused on nature and natural history. This well-illustrated magazine comes with membership in the Ranger Rick Nature Club. Subscription: $17.00 per year (12 issues). *Ranger Rick*, P.O. Box 777, Mt. Morris, IL 61054. Phone: (703) 790-4000; (800) 588-1650. Website: http://www.nwf.org/rrick

Scienceland (ages 5–10). Each issue focuses on a single topic, such as plants, animals, friction, motion, or lenses. Illustrated in brilliant, full-page color, each issue also may serve as a unit of study and is adaptable for use with preschool children or upper-grade elementary students. Subscription: $18.00 per year (4 issues). Scienceland, Inc., 501 Fifth Avenue, Suite 2108, New York, NY 10017-6102. Phone: (212) 490-2180.

Skipping Stones (ages 7–16). *Skipping Stones* is a multicultural, multilingual magazine accepting art and original writings from people of all ages and from all corners of the globe. Issues have included photos, stories, and art by children from Russia; traditional arts and crafts of East Africa; environmental games in Spanish and English; and songs from India. Subscription: $25.00 per year for individuals, $35.00 for institutions (5 issues). *Skipping Stones*, P.O. Box 3939, Eugene, OR 97403. Phone: (541) 342-4956. Website: http://www.nonviolence.org/skipping

Spider (ages 5–9). *Spider* includes quality stories, poems, and nonfiction pieces. It is nicely illustrated in full color. Subscription: $32.97 per year (12 issues). *Spider*, P.O. Box 7433, Red Oak, IA 51591. Phone: (800) 827-0227.

Sports Illustrated for Kids (ages 8–13). The magazine focuses on sports-related subjects and introduces young readers to professional and amateur sports figures, including athletes who began their careers at young ages. Departments include sports cards, legends, puzzles, activities, and "Tips from the Pros." Subscription: $27.96 per year (12 issues). *Sports Illustrated for Kids,* Time Inc. Magazine Co., P.O. Box 830609, Birmingham, AL 35283-0609. Phone: (800) 334-2229. Website: http://www.sikids.com

Stone Soup (ages 6–13). *Stone Soup* is a bimonthly literary magazine that publishes fiction, poetry, book reviews, and art produced by children. Subscription: $32.00 per year (6 issues). *Stone Soup*, Children's Art Foundation, P.O. Box 83, Santa Cruz, CA 95063. Phone: (800) 447-4569. Website: http://www.stonesoup.com

3-2-1 Contact (ages 8–14). With appealing photography and artwork, the magazine covers various physical, natural, and social science topics, such as mathematics and technology, through articles, fiction, puzzles, projects, and experiments. Subscription: $19.90 per year (10 issues). *3-2-1 Contact*, 7690 Red Oak, IA 51591-0691. Phone: (800) 840-9392.

Your Big Backyard (ages 3–5). The magazine presents a conservation message by focusing on animals and nature. Each issue contains a "read-to-me" story and encourages language and number skills in very young children. Subscription: $15.00 per year (12 issues). *Your Big Backyard*, P.O. Box 777, Mt. Morris, IL 61054. Phone: (800) 588-1650. Website: http://www.nwf.org/ybby

Zillions (ages 8–14). This publication is a children's version of *Consumer Reports* that tests and rates selected consumer items. *Zillions* helps make young readers aware of advertising ploys, as well as ways to earn, save, and manage money. Subscription:

$16.00 per year (6 issues). *Zillions* Subscription Dept., P.O. Box 54832, Boulder, CO 80322. Phone: (800) 234-2078.

Zoobooks (ages 5–14). The magazine contains photographs, artwork, and scientific facts about wildlife and often focuses on a particular animal. Subscription: $20.95 per year (12 issues). *ZooBooks*, P.O. Box 85384, San Diego, CA 92186. Phone: (619) 578-2440; (800) 992-5034. Website: http://www.zoobooks.com

For other magazine titles see *Magazines for Kids and Teens,* 1997, edited by Donald R. Stoll and copublished by Educational Press Association of America and the International Reading Association.

APPENDIX C

Publishing Children's Books

Children generally do not come to school knowing that books are written and illustrated by people. In their minds books simply *are*, appearing magically on library and bookstore shelves. Teachers familiar with the publishing process can round out children's perceptions by helping them see how books come to be.

Reflecting a general business trend, large corporations have been buying independent publishers, so that today most national publishing houses are owned by someone other than the company whose name appears on the book. But the business of getting a book published remains the same.

STEPS IN GETTING A FIRST BOOK PUBLISHED

Because submission procedures can vary from publisher to publisher, an aspiring author benefits from checking one of the many publishing guides like *Children's Writer's and Illustrator's Market*, published by Writer's Digest. Some publishers announce they currently are not accepting picture book manuscripts, for instance. Or the hopeful author will learn that a query letter is needed before submitting anything. (A query letter is a letter sent to the publisher describing the manuscript to see if the publisher is interested in seeing the actual work.) Then the submission process is generally as follows:

1. **Author sends query letter or the manuscript to a publisher.** Depending on information gleaned from a publisher's guide, the would-be author sends off a query letter or the manuscript. After the final rewriting, the author of a picture book prints out a double-spaced manuscript of the complete text, and the author of a chapter book either prints out a few chapters and prepares a detailed outline of the rest or submits the entire manuscript. A short cover letter of no more than one page should accompany the manuscript. It is becoming an accepted practice for authors to submit to more than one publisher at a time. Once frowned on by publishers, their acquiescence to this practice recognizes that publishers may hold onto unsolicited manuscripts for a few months to more than a year. The manuscript will be looked at by a staff member or freelance reader. If not acceptable, it is returned to the author with a rejection notice. If the first reader finds some promise in the manuscript, it is passed to another staff member and eventually to the editor, usually the fourth or fifth reader. An editor who likes the manuscript will present it to the rest of the editorial staff for approval.

2. **Author signs contract.** When the publisher decides to accept the manuscript, a multipage contract is sent to the author. The contract states the financial conditions as well as scores of other income-producing possibilities, such as translation into other languages; adaptation into film, stage play, or audiocassette; paperback rights; and the right to consider for publication the author's next manuscript. Half of the advance goes to the author when the contract is signed. The editor will ask the author to make some changes, usually when the contract is signed, but sometimes as a condition of signing. The changes can be small or extensive, but almost always the author has revisions to make. The author now works on the corrections suggested by the publisher, and eventually the publisher declares the manuscript ready for publication. When the final copy is sent in, the remaining half of the advance is sent to the author.

3. **Book is printed**. The publisher sees that the manuscript is edited, proofread, and polished, laying out all the plans for printing: typeface style and size, where page numbers go, placement of text with art, weight of paper, finish of paper, color of paper, style of endpapers, and so on. Because publishers do not own printing presses (too expensive), a printer is selected to produce the book according to the publisher's specifications. Unless the printer has binding facilities, the printed sheets then go to a binder to be made into books. Finished books are delivered to the warehouse.

4. **Book is sold.** Marketing people at the publishing house decide how to feature the book in a catalog and whether to promote the book with a poster, display, or advertisements in book review journals. Except for sending sample copies to book reviewers, the publisher has no say if or how the book is reviewed, but author and publisher alike hope for favorable reviews to appear.

OFTEN-ASKED QUESTIONS

WHERE DO AUTHORS GET THEIR IDEAS? This is the question asked most often of authors. Like all people, they get their ideas from living and thinking. Russell Freedman visits an exhibition of old photographs and comes away with the idea for a book about immigrant children (*Immigrant Kids,* 1980). Lloyd Alexander sees in his mind an adolescent boy running up wide steps leading to an official government building in what seems to be Europe about 200 years ago. He then has to determine who this boy is, why he is hurrying, and what is going on in the world around him. After months of asking and answering his own questions, Alexander eventually fashions the idea for *The Marvelous Misadventures of Sebastian* (1970). Eric Kimmel scours collections of folktales to locate one that strikes his fancy and can be turned into the text for a picture book. Richard Peck hears a librarian say that any book with "secret" in the title won't stay on the shelf. His next book is *The Secrets of the Shopping Mall* (1979). Where authors get their ideas is as varied as human personalities and the books that line library shelves, but the common denominator is that each seems interesting or important to the writer.

WHAT IS THE CHANCE A PUBLISHER WILL BUY AN AUTHOR'S FIRST BOOK?   About one manuscript of every 5,000 received will be published. But, as one publisher pointed out, "some people win the lottery." Every author was once a new author, and new authors must persevere. Madeleine L'Engle's *A Wrinkle in Time* (1962) was rejected by every publisher in New York, so she started at the top of the list again. This time Farrar, Straus and Giroux took it, and the book promptly won the Newbery Medal.

WHY ARE MOST PICTURE BOOKS 32 PAGES LONG?   Books are not printed on small pieces of paper that are then collated but on one large sheet that is folded four times by a machine and then made into pages by trimming the folds on three sides. The most economical way to produce a short book, like a picture book, is to print only one sheet—32 book pages when folded and trimmed. (Sometimes the first and last four pages—eight total—are used as endpapers, making the book itself 24 pages.)

IF THE AUTHOR OF A PICTURE BOOK CAN'T DRAW, HOW IS AN ARTIST CHOSEN TO DO THE ILLUSTRATIONS?   The publisher chooses the artist. Traditionally, the author has no say in who is chosen to illustrate the manuscript and gets no chance to approve the artwork. If the two had to agree, people could grow old waiting for a successful compromise. So the author is in charge of the words, the artist is given authority to interpret the story, and the book gets printed on time.

WHEN AN AUTHOR FINISHES A BOOK, HOW LONG BEFORE IT IS ON BOOKSTORE SHELVES?   Time varies, but one year is customary.

HOW MANY COPIES OF AN AUTHOR'S FIRST BOOK ARE PRINTED?   The usual number printed is around 8,500 for picture books and 5,000 for novels. Considering that the population of the United States is about 270 million, that translates into one copy of a new book for approximately every 35,000 Americans. Enough copies of R. L. Stine's Goosebumps books, on the other hand, have been printed (over 200 million) so that all the children and most adults in the United States could have one for themselves.

When authors are well known, the press run is much larger than for an author's first book. Based on the sales and popularity of author John Scieszka and artist Lane Smith, the publisher ordered 200,000 copies of their new picture book, *Squids Will Be Squids* (1998).

WHAT DO *IN PRINT,* *OUT OF STOCK,* **AND** *OUT OF PRINT* **MEAN?**   *In print* means the book is currently available; the publisher has copies stacked in a warehouse ready to ship to bookstores and libraries when ordered. *Out of stock* means the books aren't in the warehouse but probably will be reprinted and available in the near future. *Out of print* means the book is no longer available and the publisher has no plans to reprint it.

WHAT DO *FIRST PRINTING, SECOND PRINTING,* **AND** *THIRD PRINTING* **MEAN?**   The first time a book is printed is the first printing. When the first printing sells out within a reasonable time, the plates are put back on the presses and a second group of books is printed—a second printing. Printings are identified on the back of the title page with a row of numbers, usually 1 through 10. When the book is printed again, the 1 is removed leaving 2 as the lowest number, indicating the second printing. The next time the 3 will be the lowest, and so on.

WHAT IS A ROYALTY?   In trade book publishing, the royalty is a percentage paid to the author for each copy sold. The standard royalty is 10 percent of the retail price. Royalties are calculated and checks are mailed twice a year, so an author living solely from creative works usually needs to budget well.

WHAT IS AN ADVANCE?   When the publisher agrees to buy a book, the author is given an advance against royalties—good faith money that will be paid back with future earnings from the book. Only when the advance is repaid to the publisher does the author receive additional money. An advance for a first-time author of children's books might range from $3,000 to $8,000. (Established authors, of course, get a much larger advance.) If the book does not sell enough to repay the advance, the author still keeps the money.

HOW MUCH MONEY DO AUTHORS MAKE?   At a 10 percent royalty, an $18 picture book earns $1.80 for the author. If the press run is 8,500 copies and all sell, the author will make $15,300 (8,500 multiplied by $1.80). If the picture book has both an author and an illustrator, the two share the royalty with the usual split 50/50: $7,650 each. A first novel, on the other hand, will sell for about $16 and print 5,000 copies for total earnings of $8,000 if the entire print run sells out. Production time for a book is about a year, royalties are calculated every six months, and the money the book first earns repays the advance, so it is not unusual for an author to wait two or three years after publication before receiving money beyond the advance. Of course, the author hopes the book will go into additional printings. For instance, *Make Way for Ducklings*, first published in 1941, is in its 65th printing. Robert McCloskey must be satisfied when a book he created almost 60 years ago is still being bought and read, as well as continuing to produce income.

Why do books cost so much, particularly picture books?   The $18 a consumer pays for a picture book usually is split into the categories listed below, but the percentages vary from publisher to publisher and year to year. They depend on the general health of the publishing industry and the economy. The following ball-park figures show the approximate percentages of where a book buyer's dollar goes:

- **50 percent** discount to the bookseller (jobbers, chain stores, and warehouse stores receive a slightly higher discount; independent bookstores slightly lower) = $9.00, which leaves the publisher with $9.00
- **10 percent** of the retail price to the author and illustrator = $1.80, which leaves the publisher with $7.20
- **20 percent** for manufacturing costs (color separations, press plates, paper, printing, binding, shipping) = $3.60, which leaves the publisher with $3.60
- **13 percent** for overhead (salaries, rent, office equipment, utilities, advertising, marketing, and warehousing) = $2.34, which leaves the publisher with = $1.26
- **7 percent** profit = $1.26 left after paying all expenses

Chapter books cost less than picture books because of the expense related to color printing. Producing full-color books requires each press sheet to be printed four separate times, which takes longer and demands more sophisticated technology, thus costing more. Chapter books, usually printed only in black and white, simply are cheaper to produce.

Does every book make money for the publisher?   No. Much like the movie industry, some make a profit and some don't. In children's books, about 65 percent of the books never pay out, which means they don't make back enough money to reimburse the publisher for expenses—author's advance, some overhead costs, preparing the manuscript for printing, making the plates for the press, and paper and ink for printing. Approximately 35 percent of the children's books published do pay out, and they must earn enough additional money to bear the expenses of those titles that do not meet their expenses. Naturally the publisher hopes that each title will be profitable, even though two-thirds will become financial liabilities. When a book has proven it is not selling enough to meet expenses, those additional copies remaining in the warehouse often are sold in bulk to a remainder house, which pays from 20¢ to $1 for each hardcover book. Those remaindered books then are resold to chain stores and bookstores, where customers can buy titles for a fraction of their list price.

What about the future of book publishing?   Some people predict that computers will replace books. Others say books always will occupy the place in society they now have. But computers are making an impact in the publishing world. In 1998, print on demand became a reality. In that year, both Ingram Book Group and IBM displayed the technology to store books electronically and print and bind them one copy at a time on one machine. Ingram included print-on-demand titles in its catalog. The print-on-demand machines currently produce paperbacks only, but the finished copies have colored covers and are of a quality so similar to traditionally published books the average customer can't tell the difference. Ingram had nearly 2,000 titles electronically stored by the beginning of 1999. The expectation is that print on demand eventually will make its way into bookstores where a customer walks in, asks for a copy of a novel not on the shelf, and the clerk calls it up on the computerized machine that prints and binds the book during the time it takes the customer to pay.

REFERENCES

Alexander, Lloyd. 1970. *The Marvelous Misadventures of Sebastian*. New York: Dutton.

Freedman, Russell. 1980. *Immigrant Kids*. New York: Dutton.

L'Engle, Madeleine. 1962. *A Wrinkle in Time*. New York: Farrar, Straus & Giroux.

McCloskey, Robert. 1941. *Make Way for Ducklings*. New York: Viking.

Peck, Richard. 1979. *The Secrets of the Shopping Mall*. New York: Delacorte.

Scieszka, Jon. 1998. *Squids Will Be Squids*. New York: Viking.

APPENDIX D

Audiovisual Media and Children's Books

When a novel is made into a commercial movie, public response generally is a mixture of cheers and jeers. Those who cheer welcome a good story appearing on the screen. Those who jeer decry how the moviemakers mutilate the book by omitting parts, adding parts, or in some other way deviating from the original. Regardless of the type of book or composition of the audience, the consensus generally is that the book is better than the movie.

CHILDREN'S BOOKS INTO NONPRINT MEDIA

While the book generally reaches more directly and deeply into the human being, sometimes a video or filmstrip made from a children's book can serve a teacher's purpose as well or even better than the paper copy. The audiovisual version of a book can benefit the teacher and students in the following ways:

- When a picture book is too small to be seen by the whole class.
- As an introduction or a bridge to printed stories for those children whose focus primarily has been electronic.
- By providing variety. The teacher who reads aloud frequently should continue to do so, but she can spice things up by occasionally using a video or filmstrip of a book.

- By offering a professional reading of the story that models a new way to interpret and present the text.
- When used by small groups so the teacher can spend time with other students.
- In developing and strengthening reading skills as children listen to a cassette tape of the story while they follow along in the book.

Children's books appear as videos, filmstrips, and audiotapes in three separate categories:

- *Book unchanged.*   Every effort is made to be faithful to the book as it is translated into sight and sound. Although modifications inevitably occur—a soundtrack adds background noises or a book illustration may appear twice, once as a medium shot and once as a close-up—the producers change as little as possible.
- *Book changed.*   The book is used as the basis for a video or audiotape, but liberties are taken. The artist's drawn character may give way to a human being who takes the role in a live-action movie, dialogue may be altered, and scenes may be eliminated or added. Most audiovisual versions of books fall into this category, and many of them are excellent. However, many also do great damage to the integrity of the original work.
- *Book adapted from another medium.*   An original movie or television show that receives strong attention becomes the basis for a book, generally paperback.

Some companies that produce audiovisual materials from books make a strong effort to be true to the book. Weston Woods of Weston, Connecticut, for example, sees itself as producing audio and visual renderings of picture books that will stimulate children to return to each book with a greater appreciation. If a teacher plans to use an audiotape as a read-along experience for a student who needs a boost, it is important that the tape be faithful to the book. When ordering cassette tapes, catalog descriptions specify if a tape is unabridged (or complete). If no such designation is present, the buyer generally may assume the book is abridged.

For all ages, the experience of comparing the printed page to a video or audiocassette yields insight about how different media tell a story. Read a book or a segment from a book, and then present that part as it appears in a commercially prepared audiovisual medium. Then ask one question: "What differences did you notice in the two?" Discussion inevitably leads children to discover the strengths of each medium, including the difficulty moviemakers experience when turning a 250-page book into a two-hour film.

AUDIOVISUAL PRODUCTS

Beyond the books themselves, a wealth of media materials provides information and insight into the field of children's literature. Scores of cassette tapes help teachers understand the world of children's books, offering suggestions for using poetry in the classroom, finding humorous books, or reading aloud. (See, among others, the offerings from the Children's Book Council [Appendix A].) Artists Gerald McDermott, Steven Kellogg, and Gail Hailey explain in filmstrips, produced by Weston Woods, how they go about creating books. But the "meet the author" video is one of the most popular supplementary media. Authors speak from their homes and workplaces directly to viewers, sharing life experiences and talking about their work while answering many of the questions readers usually ask. Not all publishers offer author videos, but more and more are producing them. Houghton Mifflin and Trumpet Club (Scholastic) keep adding to growing lists of author videos. Harcourt and Penguin Putnam list a few.

A smattering of interactive books on CD-ROM is on the market, but to date they offer little beyond gimmickry. A typical technique, for example, transfers a double-page spread in a book to a computer screen. It shows the outside view of a house and yard with a bird perched in a tree. Click on the computer bird, and it flies from the tree. Click on the bunny, and it rushes into the house. Initially these actions draw attention, but they add nothing of significance to the story. And the actions lose their charm soon after readers discover them.

Interactive books also offer supplementary material. In a story where a boy is walking to school, for example, the reader can click on the sidewalk to learn additional facts and history about sidewalks, or the reader can click on the boy's legs to obtain information about walking and the health benefits that result from that activity. The information is fine, but it tends not to be germane to the story and does not extend the reading experience. We expect in the near future books will be translated to CD-ROM with more imagination and substance.

A few companies already have succeeded. DK Publishing's CD-ROM of *The Way Things Work* by David Macaulay (1997) extends the information in the book by adding movement and action to Macaulay's explanations of technology, like how helicopters fly, toilets flush, and lasers shoot their powerful light beams. In addition, the CD adds historical perspective, shows scientific principles, and provides information about the inventors. IBM has enhanced *Talking Walls* (Margy Burns Knight 1998), an illustrated book focusing on the significance of walls around the world, which includes the Berlin Wall, the Great Wall of China, the Wailing Wall and many others. The CD-ROM based on the book includes a wealth of related information like historical facts, movie snippets and news clips, and actual speeches and background sounds. In addition, it provides activities for young readers and Internet connections that the user can pursue. IBM has two series, *Stories and More I* and *Stories and More II,* that help children read and respond to picture books without trivializing or altering the original works. Scholastic does the same for picture books in its *Wiggle Works* series and for novels and nonfiction in the *Smart Books* series.

Audiovisual materials for children have their own award. The American Library Association initiated the Carnegie Medal for Excellence in Children's Video in 1991 to honor the most distinguished American video for children. The winners have been

1991   *Ralph S. Mouse* by George McQuilkin and John Matthews (Churchill Films)

1992   *Harry Comes Home* by Peter Matulavich (Barr Films)

1993   *The Pool Party* by John Kelly and Gary Soto (Distributed by Gary Soto)

1994   *Eric Carle: Picture Writer* by Rawn Fulton (Searchlight Films)

1995   *Whitewash* by Michael Sporn (Churchill Media)

1996   *Owen* by Paul R. Gagne (Weston Woods)

1997   *Notes Alive! On the Day You Were Born* by Tacy Mangan (What a Gal Productions)

1998   *Willa: An American Snow White* by Tom Davenport (Davenport Films)

1999   *The First Christmas* by Frank Moynihan (Billy Budd Films)

More information on audiovisual materials for children is available in *Booklist*, a review journal published by the American Library Association. In each issue, reviews of films, audiotapes, video productions, and other media forms, including media relating to children's books, appear in the section titled "Audiovisual Media." Also, for literature-related audiovisual materials geared to elementary students, see the latest edition of *The Elementary School Library Collection: A Guide to Books and Other Media*, published by Brodart.

CHILDREN'S LITERATURE AND THE INTERNET

Internet possibilities continue to stagger the mind. Ask a search engine to scan "children's literature," and as of this writing, six categories plus almost 200 specific sites pop up. Click on the first category, and find authors (356 sites), book awards (13), companies @ (simply type in a name), electronic literature (8), events (5), fairy tales and folktales (27), illustrators (28), magazines (6), organizations (4), poetry (16), recommended reading lists (10), reviews (18), series (54), titles (9), web-published fiction (71), writing (8), and indices (7).

Scan the almost 200 sites, and find reading courses; bestseller lists (both current and lifetime); specialized bibliographies; guidelines for children to read, write, illustrate, and review books; specialized cultures and groups who promote reading; collections of various libraries; festivals and conferences; catalogs of antique, rare, and used books; electronic journals dealing with almost every imaginable aspect of children's literature; author studies; scholarly reviews and criticisms; individual reviews and criticisms; articles, links, and resources for editors; foreign books; books in English other than from America; magazines for children; and much, much more.

We selected four sites in early 1999 as practical and representative, two dealing exclusively with children's literature and two focusing on literature in general.

The Children's Literature Web Guide

http://www.acs.ucalgary.ca/~dkbrown/index.html

Compiled by David K. Brown of the University of Calgary, this site is "an attempt to gather together and categorize the growing number of internet resources related to books for children and young adults." Brown's audience is "teachers, librarians, parents, book professionals (writers, editors, booksellers, and storytellers) and kids." The Children's Literature Web Guide contains the most comprehensive lists on the Internet of awards given to children's books written in English. The home page lists four main categories.

- Features: What's new?; Newbery and Caldecott winners; best books of the year—a roundup of lists from all over; What We're Reading—commentary on children's books; Web-Traveler's Toolkit—essential kid lit websites
- Discussion Boards: Readers Helping Readers, Conference Bulletin Board
- Quick Reference: Children's Book Awards, Children's Bestsellers, the Doucette Index—teaching ideas for children's books
- More Links: Authors on the Web; Stories on the Web; Readers' Theater; Lots of Lists—recommended books; Journals and Book Reviews; Resources for Teachers; Resources for Parents; Resources for Storytellers; Resources for Writers and Illustrators; Digging Deeper—research guides and indexes; Internet Book Discussion Groups; children's literature organizations on the Internet; children's publishers and booksellers on the Internet.

Electronic Resources for Youth Services

http://chebucto.ns.ca/~aa331/childlit.html

Dedicated to "reviewing WWW resources related to children's literature and youth services," this site is geared toward school librarians, children's writers, illustrators, book reviewers, storytellers, parents, and anyone interested in children's books. The home page lists these categories, each of which offers links to additional sites: award-winning books; book reviews; reading and storytelling; writing resources; on-line children's literature; educational entertainment; authors; publishers and booksellers; associations; miscellaneous resources; listserve; news groups; submit a site.

The Library of Congress Experimental Search System

http://lcweb2.loc.gov/catalog

This site allows users to search the entire holdings of the Library of Congress in a number of ways: by author, title, subject, notes, publisher, category, date, collection, ISBN, and Dewey Decimal or Library of Congress call number. Specialized searches are also possible. Among other possibilities, users can locate the complete output of one author (all titles appear here, even out-of-print), check the exact wording of the title, determine the correct date of publication, find out which books are on the library shelf next to a certain title, or see how many different editions of a title have been published. For other library of congress electronic catalogs, use the following address: http://lcweb.loc.gov/catalog

Bibliofind

http://www.bibliofind.com

Locating out-of-print books has been a frustrating pursuit—until now. Bibliofind brings together a worldwide inventory of nine million volumes from more than 4,000 individual book dealers who specialize in used, hard-to-find, and rare books. Simply type in the title or author, and a list of available books appears on the screen. After looking at price and a detailed description of the condition, the user selects the desired copy and then is given all the necessary ordering information. (To locate both new and used books, try Bookfinder [http://www.bookfinder.com].)

REFERENCES

Knight, Margy Burns. 1998. *Talking Walls*. Atlanta: IBM.

Macaulay, David. 1997. *The Way Things Work*. New York: DK Publishing.

APPENDIX E

Author and Illustrator Visits

For both children and adults, the benefits of visiting with an author or illustrator by phone or in person often last a lifetime. Once people see and hear someone who has created a title they know, their view of books enters a different sphere and is never quite the same again. They always remember the day they talked on the phone with Lloyd Alexander or saw Steven Kellogg draw pictures as he talked about his stories.

A visit to a class or a school requires preparation that may take as long as a year. All publishers have someone who helps schedule visits with their authors and illustrators, usually called an author-appearance coordinator, who is very helpful in answering any questions or making suggestions.

To carry off a successful visit by an author or illustrator, you need to ask yourself the following questions and make the following arrangements at each preparatory stage.

PLANNING STAGE

Six Months to One Year before Visit

HOW MUCH WILL A VISIT COST?   The general range for an honorarium is between $750 and $1,500 per day but can vary from $300 to $2,000. The price generally depends on how established the author is—beginning people charge at the $300–$500 end of the scale. If you have limited funds, you can ask the author-appearance coordinator, "Who can I get for 'X' dollars?" Remember that all expenses connected with the visit also need to be paid—travel, lodging, and food. Many times two or more schools or organizations plan together so expenses can be shared.

HOW MUCH FOR A TELEPHONE INTERVIEW?   Again, rates vary. But offering $100 for a half-hour conversation is reasonable. A speaker phone works best so the whole class can hear and individual students can ask questions.

WHAT DO I NEED TO KNOW BEFORE CONTACTING THE PUBLISHER? So you can present the details to the publisher in an organized fashion, prepare an outline of the general itinerary for the visit—what types of presentations, how many presentations, length of each, type of audience (children? adults? professionals?), and times for autographing.

WHO CAN I GET TO COME?   Most authors and illustrators make school visits, but not all. If you have one or more specific authors or illustrators in mind, contact the author-appearance coordinator at the publisher responsible for the author's or illustrator's latest book. (Often an author or illustrator has books with more than one publisher.) If you have no person in mind but wish to invite a specific kind of author or illustrator (one who specializes in nonfiction or creates books for a certain age level) or are open to any author or illustrator, get in touch with an author-appearance coordinator at a larger publisher. The coordinator can make suggestions. Once the coordinator and you have agreed on a person, the type of visit (personal or phone), and a price, you can begin making specific arrangements.

PREPARATION STAGE

Two to Three Months before Visit

COORDINATE WITH THE PUBLISHER.   Now that your author or illustrator is confirmed and the date is final, keep in touch with your contact person at the publisher (usually the author-appearance coordinator). Prepare a checklist to ensure that you or the publisher make the following arrangements:

- *Order books.*   Choose the titles and quantity of each of the author's or illustrator's books that you want to have on hand for participants to buy and have autographed. Select a place for them to be sold and someone to be in charge of sales. Often, a local bookstore will take over these responsibilities. Determine if you are going to sell books at a discount, and if some of the money made from books will be returned to the school or district to cover expenses for future visits.
- *Make transportation and lodging reservations.*   Sometimes the publisher makes these arrangements, sometimes the local host, and sometimes the author chooses to oversee these details personally. Be sure you are clear about who is responsible for reservations.

- *Make local assignments.* Secure the necessary help in organizing the program, overseeing publicity, making arrangements for the room, chauffeuring the visitor, and planning the social functions.
- *Send the publisher an itinerary.* Include everything the author or illustrator needs to know: the composition and size of the groups, time for meeting with children, time for socializing with faculty and administrators, time between presentations for rest room breaks or simply recharging, and mealtimes. Include names and phone numbers of the hotel and the people responsible for meeting and hosting the visitor.
- *Ask about the visitor's personal preferences.* Determine what special needs the author or illustrator has—audiovisual requests (easel and pad? whiteboard and marker?), specific physical arrangements for the presentation (lavalier microphone?), dietary restrictions or preferences, or anything you should know that will make the visit more agreeable or comfortable.
- *Request publicity materials from the publisher.* The contact person will tell you what promotional materials are available, but generally you may request a short biography (sometimes enough to provide one for each participant) and a black-and-white glossy photograph for the local newspaper. Other materials may be available: book lists, posters, bookmarks, and book jackets.
- *Arrange for an honorarium check to be available.* Contact the payroll department to determine what must be done so the check will be ready to give the author/illustrator after the presentation.

PREPARE THE AUDIENCE. The most satisfying visit is one where the audience is familiar with the author's or illustrator's books before the visit. Teachers should read some books aloud and allow students (or audience members) to read selected titles individually. Children who have spent time with the visitor's works—discussing, writing responses, creating artwork relating to the books—anticipate the visit more eagerly and reward the guest by being enthusiastic.

FINAL CHECK

Ten Days before Visit

CHECK ALL ITEMS MENTIONED PREVIOUSLY. Go over the list to see what needs your attention.

CALL THE CONTACT PERSON AT THE PUBLISHER. This call is to let the publisher know that all is arranged and to determine if any last-minute concerns have arisen.

The Following Day

WRITE NECESSARY THANK-YOU NOTES.   Write to the visitor, and be sure to drop a note to the contact person at the publishing house. You may also consider having selected audience members write to the visitor.

WRITE AN EVALUATION OF THE AUTHOR'S OR ILLUSTRATOR'S PERFORMANCE FOR THE PUBLISHER.   Feedback is helpful to the publisher for future visits.

Bask in the warmth of a successful visit, and begin thinking about the next one.

APPENDIX F

Children's Book Awards

Children's book awards have proliferated in recent years; today there are well over 100 different awards and prizes presented by a variety of organizations in the United States alone. The awards may be given for books of a specific genre or simply for the best of all children's books published within a given period. An award may honor a particular book or an author/illustrator for a lifetime contribution to the world of children's literature. Most children's book awards are chosen by adults, but now a growing number of children's choice book awards exist. The larger national awards given in most countries are the most influential and have helped considerably to raise public awareness about the fine books being published for young readers. Of course, readers are wise not to put too much faith in award-winning books. An award doesn't necessarily mean a good reading experience, but it does provide a starting place when choosing books.

NATIONAL AWARDS

United States of America

RANDOLPH CALDECOTT MEDAL.   Sponsored and administered by the Association for Library Service to Children, an arm of the American Library Association, the Caldecott Medal is presented to the illustrator of the most distinguished picture book for children published in the United States during the preceding year. A variable number of honor books also may be named by the Caldecott Selection Committee. Eligibility for this award is limited to U.S. citizens and residents. Named for the nineteenth-century British illustrator, the Caldecott Medal is America's major picture book award.

1938   *Animals of the Bible, a Picture Book.* Text selected from the *King James Bible* by Helen Dean Fish. Illustrated by Dorothy P. Lathrop. Lippincott.

Honor Books:

Seven Simeons: A Russian Tale by Boris Artzybasheff. Viking.

Four and Twenty Blackbirds compiled by Helen Dean Fish. Illustrated by Robert Lawson. Stokes/Lippincott.

1939   *Mei Li* by Thomas Handforth. Doubleday.

Honor Books:

The Forest Pool by Laura Adams Armer. McKay/Longmans.

Wee Gillis by Munro Leaf. Illustrated by Robert Lawson. Viking.

Snow White and the Seven Dwarfs. Translated and illustrated by Wanda Gág. Coward-McCann.

Barkis by Clare Turlay Newberry. Harper.

Andy and the Lion by James Daugherty. Viking.

1940   *Abraham Lincoln* by Ingri d'Aulaire and Edgar Parin d'Aulaire. Doubleday.

Honor Books:

Cock-a-Doodle-Doo by Berta and Elmer Hader. Macmillan.

Madeline by Ludwig Bemelmans. Viking.

The Ageless Story by Lauren Ford. Dodd.

1941   *They Were Strong and Good* by Robert Lawson. Viking.

Honor Book:

April's Kittens by Clare Turlay Newberry. Harper.

1942   *Make Way for Ducklings* by Robert McCloskey. Viking.

Honor Books:

An American ABC by Maud and Miska Petersham. Macmillan.

In My Mother's House by Ann Nolan Clark. Illustrated by Velino Herrera. Viking.

Paddle-to-the-Sea by Holling Clancy Holling. Houghton Mifflin.

Nothing at All by Wanda Gág. Coward-McCann.

1943   *The Little House* by Virginia Lee Burton. Houghton Mifflin.

Honor Books:

Dash and Dart by Mary and Conrad Buff. Viking.

Marshmallow by Clare Turlay Newberry. Harper.

1944 *Many Moons* by James Thurber. Illustrated by Louis Slobodkin. Harcourt.

Honor Books:

Small Rain: Verses from the Bible. Text arranged from the Bible by Jessie Orton Jones. Illustrated by Elizabeth Orton Jones. Viking.

Pierre Pigeon by Lee Kingman. Illustrated by Arnold Edwin Bare. Houghton Mifflin.

The Mighty Hunter by Berta and Elmer Hader. Macmillan.

A Child's Good Night Book by Margaret Wise Brown. Illustrated by Jean Charlot. Scott.

Good Luck Horse by Chih-Yi Chan. Illustrated by Plato Chan. Whittlesey.

1945 *Prayer for a Child* by Rachel Field. Illustrated by Elizabeth Orton Jones. Macmillan.

Honor Books:

Mother Goose: Seventy-Seven Verses With Pictures. Illustrated by Tasha Tudor. Walck.

In the Forest by Marie Hall Ets. Viking.

Yonie Wondernose by Marguerite de Angeli. Doubleday.

The Christmas Anna Angel by Ruth Sawyer. Illustrated by Kate Seredy. Viking.

1946 *The Rooster Crows* selected and illustrated by Maud and Miska Petersham. Macmillan.

Honor Books:

Little Lost Lamb by Golden MacDonald. Illustrated by Leonard Weisgard. Doubleday.

Sing Mother Goose by Opal Wheeler. Illustrated by Marjorie Torrey. Dutton.

My Mother Is the Most Beautiful Woman in the World retold by Becky Reyher. Illustrated by Ruth Gannett. Lothrop.

You Can Write Chinese by Kurt Wiese. Viking.

1947 *The Little Island* by Golden MacDonald. Illustrated by Leonard Weisgard. Doubleday.

Honor Books:

Rain Drop Splash by Alvin Tresselt. Illustrated by Leonard Weisgard. Lothrop.

Boats on the River by Marjorie Flack. Illustrated by Jay Hyde Barnum. Viking.

Timothy Turtle by Al Graham. Illustrated by Tony Palazzo. Viking.

Pedro, the Angel of Olvera Street by Leo Politi. Scribner's.

Sing in Praise: A Collection of the Best Loved Hymns by Opal Wheeler. Illustrated by Marjorie Torrey. Dutton.

1948   *White Snow, Bright Snow* by Alvin Tresselt. Illustrated by Roger Duvoisin. Lothrop.

Honor Books:

Stone Soup: An Old Tale by Marcia Brown. Scribner's.

McElligot's Pool by Dr. Seuss (pseud. for Theodor Geisel). Random.

Bambino the Clown by George Schreiber. Viking.

Roger and the Fox by Lavinia Davis. Illustrated by Hildegard Woodward. Doubleday.

Song of Robin Hood edited by Anne Malcolmson. Illustrated by Virginia Lee Burton. Houghton Mifflin.

1949   *The Big Snow* by Berta and Elmer Hader. Macmillan.

Honor Books:

Blueberries for Sal by Robert McCloskey. Viking.

All Around Town by Phyllis McGinley. Illustrated by Helen Stone. Lippincott.

Juanita by Leo Politi. Scribner's.

Fish in the Air by Kurt Wiese. Viking.

1950   *Song of the Swallows* by Leo Politi. Scribner's.

Honor Books:

America's Ethan Allen by Stewart Holbrook. Illustrated by Lynd Ward. Houghton Mifflin.

The Wild Birthday Cake by Lavinia R. Davis. Illustrated by Hildegard Woodward. Doubleday.

The Happy Day by Ruth Krauss. Illustrated by Marc Simont. Harper.

Henry, Fisherman: A Story of the Virgin Islands by Marcia Brown. Scribner's.

Bartholomew and the Oobleck by Dr. Seuss (pseud. for Theodor Geisel). Random.

1951   *The Egg Tree* by Katherine Milhous. Scribner's.

Honor Books:

Dick Whittington and His Cat translated and illustrated by Marcia Brown. Scribner's.

The Two Reds by Will (pseud. for William Lipkind). Illustrated by Nicolas (pseud. for Nicolas Mordvinoff). Harcourt.

If I Ran the Zoo by Dr. Seuss (pseud. for Theodor Geisel). Random.

T-Bone, the Baby-Sitter by Clare Turlay Newberry. Harper.

The Most Wonderful Doll in the World by Phyllis McGinley. Illustrated by Helen Stone. Lippincott.

1952 *Finders Keepers* by Will (pseud. for William Lipkind). Illustrated by Nicolas (pseud. for Nicolas Mordvinoff). Harcourt.

Honor Books:

Mr. T. W. Anthony Woo by Marie Hall Ets. Viking.

Skipper John's Cook by Marcia Brown. Scribner's.

All Falling Down by Gene Zion. Illustrated by Margaret Bloy Graham. Harper.

Bear Party by William Pène du Bois. Viking.

Feather Mountain by Elizabeth Olds. Houghton Mifflin.

1953 *The Biggest Bear* by Lynd Ward. Houghton Mifflin.

Honor Books:

Puss in Boots translated and illustrated by Marcia Brown. Scribner's.

One Morning in Maine by Robert McCloskey. Viking.

Ape in a Cape: An Alphabet of Odd Animals by Fritz Eichenberg. Harcourt.

The Storm Book by Charlotte Zolotow. Illustrated by Margaret Bloy Graham. Harper.

Five Little Monkeys by Juliet Kepes. Houghton Mifflin.

1954 *Madeline's Rescue* by Ludwig Bemelmans. Viking.

Honor Books:

Journey Cake, Ho! by Ruth Sawyer. Illustrated by Robert McCloskey. Viking.

When Will the World Be Mine? by Miriam Schlein. Illustrated by Jean Charlot. Scott.

The Steadfast Tin Soldier by Hans Christian Andersen. Translated by M. R. James. Illustrated by Marcia Brown. Scribner's.

A Very Special House by Ruth Krauss. Illustrated by Maurice Sendak. Harper.

Green Eyes by Abe Birnbaum. Capitol.

1955 *Cinderella, or the Little Glass Slipper* by Charles Perrault. Translated and illustrated by Marcia Brown. Scribner's.

Honor Books:

Book of Nursery and Mother Goose Rhymes compiled and illustrated by Marguerite de Angeli. Doubleday.

Wheel on the Chimney by Margaret Wise Brown. Illustrated by Tibor Gergely. Lippincott.

The Thanksgiving Story by Alice Dalgliesh. Illustrated by Helen Sewell. Scribner's.

1956   *Frog Went A-Courtin'* retold by John Langstaff. Illustrated by Feodor Rojankovsky. Harcourt.

Honor Books:

Play With Me by Marie Hall Ets. Viking.

Crow Boy by Taro Yashima. Viking.

1957   *A Tree Is Nice* by Janice May Udry. Illustrated by Marc Simont. Harper.

Honor Books:

Mr. Penny's Race Horse by Marie Hall Ets. Viking.

1 Is One by Tasha Tudor. Walck.

Anatole by Eve Titus. Illustrated by Paul Galdone. McGraw.

Gillespie and the Guards by Benjamin Elkin. Illustrated by James Daugherty. Viking.

Lion by William Pène du Bois. Viking.

1958   *Time of Wonder* by Robert McCloskey. Viking.

Honor Books:

Fly High, Fly Low by Don Freeman. Viking.

Anatole and the Cat by Eve Titus. Illustrated by Paul Galdone. McGraw.

1959   *Chanticleer and the Fox* by Chaucer. Adapted and illustrated by Barbara Cooney. Crowell.

Honor Books:

The House That Jack Built ("La Maison Que Jacques a Bâtie"): A Picture Book in Two Languages by Antonio Frasconi. Harcourt.

What Do You Say, Dear? A Book of Manners for All Occasions by Sesyle Joslin. Illustrated by Maurice Sendak. Scott.

Umbrella by Taro Yashima. Viking.

1960   *Nine Days to Christmas* by Marie Hall Ets and Aurora Labastida. Illustrated by Marie Hall Ets. Viking.

Honor Books:

Houses from the Sea by Alice E. Goudey. Illustrated by Adrienne Adams. Scribner's.

The Moon Jumpers by Janice May Udry. Illustrated by Maurice Sendak. Harper.

1961   *Baboushka and the Three Kings* by Ruth Robbins. Illustrated by Nicolas Sidjakov. Parnassus.

Honor Book:

Inch by Inch by Leo Lionni. Obolensky.

1962 *Once a Mouse. . . A Fable Cut in Wood* retold by Marcia Brown. Scribner's.

Honor Books:

The Fox Went Out on a Chilly Night: An Old Song by Peter Spier. Doubleday.

Little Bear's Visit by Else Minarik. Illustrated by Maurice Sendak. Harper.

The Day We Saw the Sun Come Up by Alice Goudey. Illustrated by Adrienne Adams. Scribner's.

1963 *The Snowy Day* by Ezra Jack Keats. Viking.

Honor Books:

The Sun Is a Golden Earring by Natalia Belting. Illustrated by Bernarda Bryson. Holt.

Mr. Rabbit and the Lovely Present by Charlotte Zolotow. Illustrated by Maurice Sendak. Harper.

1964 *Where the Wild Things Are* by Maurice Sendak. Harper.

Honor Books:

Swimmy by Leo Lionni. Pantheon.

All in the Morning Early by Sorche Nic Leodhas (pseud. for Leclaire Alger). Illustrated by Evaline Ness. Holt.

Mother Goose and Nursery Rhymes by Philip Reed. Atheneum.

1965 *May I Bring a Friend?* by Beatrice Schenk de Regniers. Illustrated by Beni Montresor. Atheneum.

Honor Books:

Rain Makes Applesauce by Julian Scheer. Illustrated by Marvin Bileck. Holiday House.

The Wave by Margaret Hodges. Illustrated by Blair Lent. Houghton Mifflin.

A Pocketful of Cricket by Rebecca Caudill. Illustrated by Evaline Ness. Holt.

1966 *Always Room for One More* by Sorche Nic Leodhas (pseud. for Leclaire Alger). Illustrated by Nonny Hogrogian. Holt.

Honor Books:

Hide and Seek Fog by Alvin Tresselt. Illustrated by Roger Duvoisin. Lothrop.

Just Me by Marie Hall Ets. Viking.

Tom Tit Tot adapted by Joseph Jacobs. Illustrated by Evaline Ness. Scribner's.

1967   *Sam, Bangs and Moonshine* by Evaline Ness. Holt.

Honor Book:

One Wide River to Cross adapted by Barbara Emberley. Illustrated by Ed Emberley. Prentice Hall.

1968   *Drummer Hoff* adapted by Barbara Emberley. Illustrated by Ed Emberley. Prentice Hall.

Honor Books:

Frederick by Leo Lionni. Pantheon.

Seashore Story by Taro Yashima. Viking.

The Emperor and the Kite by Jane Yolen. Illustrated by Ed Young. World.

1969   *The Fool of the World and the Flying Ship: A Russian Tale* by Arthur Ransome. Illustrated by Uri Shulevitz. Farrar.

Honor Book:

Why the Sun and the Moon Live in the Sky: An African Folktale by Elphinstone Dayrell. Illustrated by Blair Lent. Houghton Mifflin.

1970   *Sylvester and the Magic Pebble* by William Steig. Windmill.

Honor Books:

Goggles! by Ezra Jack Keats. Macmillan.

Alexander and the Wind-Up Mouse by Leo Lionni. Pantheon.

Pop Corn and Ma Goodness by Edna Mitchell Preston. Illustrated by Robert Andrew Parker. Viking.

Thy Friend, Obadiah by Brinton Turkle. Viking.

The Judge: An Untrue Tale by Harve Zemach. Illustrated by Margot Zemach. Farrar.

1971   *A Story, a Story: An African Tale* by Gail E. Haley. Atheneum.

Honor Books:

The Angry Moon retold by William Sleator. Illustrated by Blair Lent. Atlantic/Little, Brown.

Frog and Toad Are Friends by Arnold Lobel. Harper.

In the Night Kitchen by Maurice Sendak. Harper.

1972   *One Fine Day* by Nonny Hogrogian. Macmillan.

Honor Books:

If All the Seas Were One Sea by Janina Domanska. Macmillan.

Moja Means One: Swahili Counting Book by Muriel Feelings. Illustrated by Tom Feelings. Dial.

Hildilid's Night by Cheli Duran Ryan. Illustrated by Arnold Lobel. Macmillan.

1973   *The Funny Little Woman* retold by Arlene Mosel. Illustrated by Blair Lent. Dutton.

Honor Books:

Hosie's Alphabet by Hosea Baskin, Tobias Baskin, and Lisa Baskin. Illustrated by Leonard Baskin. Viking.

When Clay Sings by Byrd Baylor. Illustrated by Tom Bahti. Scribner's.

Snow-White and the Seven Dwarfs by the Brothers Grimm. Translated by Randall Jarrell. Illustrated by Nancy Ekholm Burkert. Farrar.

Anansi the Spider: A Tale from the Ashanti adapted and illustrated by Gerald McDermott. Holt.

1974   *Duffy and the Devil* retold by Harve Zemach. Illustrated by Margot Zemach. Farrar.

Honor Books:

Three Jovial Huntsmen adapted and illustrated by Susan Jeffers. Bradbury.

Cathedral: The Story of Its Construction by David Macaulay. Houghton Mifflin.

1975   *Arrow to the Sun* adapted and illustrated by Gerald McDermott. Viking.

Honor Book:

Jambo Means Hello: Swahili Alphabet Book by Muriel Feelings. Illustrated by Tom Feelings. Dial.

1976   *Why Mosquitoes Buzz in People's Ears* retold by Verna Aardema. Illustrated by Leo and Diane Dillon. Dial.

Honor Books:

The Desert Is Theirs by Byrd Baylor. Illustrated by Peter Parnall. Scribner's.

Strega Nona retold and illustrated by Tomie de Paola. Prentice Hall.

1977   *Ashanti to Zulu: African Traditions* by Margaret Musgrove. Illustrated by Leo and Diane Dillon. Dial.

Honor Books:

The Amazing Bone by William Steig. Farrar.

The Contest by Nonny Hogrogian. Greenwillow.

Fish for Supper by M. B. Goffstein. Dial.

The Golem: A Jewish Legend retold and illustrated by Beverly Brodsky McDermott. Lippincott.

Hawk, I'm Your Brother by Byrd Baylor. Illustrated by Peter Parnall. Scribner's.

1978   *Noah's Ark* by Peter Spier. Doubleday.

Honor Books:

Castle by David Macaulay. Houghton Mifflin.

It Could Always Be Worse retold and illustrated by Margot Zemach. Farrar.

1979   *The Girl Who Loved Wild Horses* by Paul Goble. Bradbury.

Honor Books:

Freight Train by Donald Crews. Greenwillow.

The Way to Start a Day by Byrd Baylor. Illustrated by Peter Parnall. Scribner's.

1980   *Ox-Cart Man* by Donald Hall. Illustrated by Barbara Cooney. Viking.

Honor Books:

Ben's Trumpet by Rachel Isadora. Greenwillow.

The Treasure by Uri Schulevitz. Farrar.

The Garden of Abdul Gasazi by Chris Van Allsburg. Houghton Mifflin.

1981   *Fables* by Arnold Lobel. Harper.

Honor Books:

The Bremen-Town Musicians retold and illustrated by Ilse Plume. Doubleday.

The Grey Lady and the Strawberry Snatcher by Molly Bang. Four Winds.

Mice Twice by Joseph Low. Atheneum.

Truck by Donald Crews. Greenwillow.

1982   *Jumanji* by Chris Van Allsburg. Houghton Mifflin.

Honor Books:

A Visit to William Blake's Inn: Poems for Innocent and Experienced Travelers by Nancy Willard. Illustrated by Alice and Martin Provensen. Harcourt.

Where the Buffaloes Begin by Olaf Baker. Illustrated by Stephen Gammell. Warne.

On Market Street by Arnold Lobel. Illustrated by Anita Lobel. Greenwillow.

Outside Over There by Maurice Sendak. Harper.

1983   *Shadow* by Blaise Cendrars. Translated and illustrated by Marcia Brown. Scribner's.

Honor Books:

When I Was Young in the Mountains by Cynthia Rylant. Illustrated by Diane Goode. Dutton.

A Chair for My Mother by Vera B. Williams. Greenwillow.

1984   *The Glorious Flight: Across the Channel with Louis Blériot* by Alice and Martin Provensen. Viking.

Honor Books:

Ten, Nine, Eight by Molly Bang. Greenwillow.

Little Red Riding Hood by the Brothers Grimm. Retold and illustrated by Trina Schart Hyman. Holiday House.

1985　*Saint George and the Dragon* adapted by Margaret Hodges. Illustrated by Trina Schart Hyman. Little, Brown.

Honor Books:

Hansel and Gretel adapted by Rika Lesser. Illustrated by Paul O. Zelinksy. Dodd.

The Story of Jumping Mouse retold and illustrated by John Steptoe. Lothrop.

Have You Seen My Duckling? by Nancy Tafuri. Greenwillow.

1986　*The Polar Express* by Chris Van Allsburg. Houghton Mifflin.

Honor Books:

The Relatives Came by Cynthia Rylant. Illustrated by Stephen Gammell. Bradbury.

King Bidgood's in the Bathtub by Audrey Wood. Illustrated by Don Wood. Harcourt.

1987　*Hey, Al* by Arthur Yorinks. Illustrated by Richard Egielski. Farrar.

Honor Books:

The Village of Round and Square Houses by Ann Grifalconi. Little, Brown.

Alphabatics by Suse MacDonald. Bradbury.

Rumpelstiltskin by the Brothers Grimm. Retold and illustrated by Paul O. Zelinsky. Dutton.

1988　*Owl Moon* by Jane Yolen. Illustrated by John Schoenherr. Philomel.

Honor Book:

Mufaro's Beautiful Daughters: An African Tale retold and illustrated by John Steptoe. Lothrop.

1989　*Song and Dance Man* by Karen Ackerman. Illustrated by Stephen Gammell. Knopf.

Honor Books:

Free Fall by David Wiesner. Lothrop.

Goldilocks and the Three Bears retold and illustrated by James Marshall. Dial.

Mirandy and Brother Wind by Patricia McKissack. Illustrated by Jerry Pinkney. Knopf.

The Boy of the Three-Year Nap by Diane Snyder. Illustrated by Allen Say. Houghton Mifflin.

1990　*Lon Po Po: A Red-Riding Hood Story from China* translated and illustrated by Ed Young. Philomel.

Honor Books:

Hershel and the Hanukkah Goblins by Eric Kimmel. Illustrated by Trina Schart Hyman. Holiday House.

The Talking Eggs adapted by Robert D. San Souci. Illustrated by Jerry Pinkney. Dial.

Bill Peet: An Autobiography by Bill Peet. Houghton Mifflin.

Color Zoo by Lois Ehlert. Lippincott.

1991   *Black and White* by David Macaulay. Houghton Mifflin.

Honor Books:

Puss in Boots by Charles Perrault. Illustrated by Fred Marcellino. Farrar.

"More, More, More," Said the Baby: 3 Love Stories by Vera B. Williams. Greenwillow.

1992   *Tuesday* by David Wiesner. Clarion.

Honor Book:

Tar Beach by Faith Ringgold. Crown.

1993   *Mirette on the High Wire* by Emily Arnold McCully. Putnam.

Honor Books:

Seven Blind Mice by Ed Young. Philomel.

The Stinky Cheese Man and Other Fairly Stupid Tales by Jon Scieszka. Illustrated by Lane Smith. Viking.

Working Cotton by Sherley Anne Williams. Illustrated by Carole Byard. Harcourt.

1994   *Grandfather's Journey* by Allen Say. Houghton Mifflin.

Honor Books:

Peppe the Lamplighter by Elisa Bartone. Illustrated by Ted Lewin. Lothrop.

In the Small, Small Pond by Denise Fleming. Holt.

Owen by Kevin Henkes. Greenwillow.

Raven: A Trickster Tale from the Pacific Northwest by Gerald McDermott. Harcourt.

Yo! Yes? by Chris Raschka. Orchard.

1995   *Smoky Night* by Eve Bunting. Illustrated by David Diaz. Harcourt.

Honor Books:

Swamp Angel by Anne Isaacs. Illustrated by Paul O. Zelinsky. Dutton.

John Henry by Julius Lester. Illustrated by Jerry Pinkney. Dial.

Time Flies by Eric Rohmann. Crown.

1996   *Officer Buckle and Gloria* by Peggy Rathmann. Putnam.

Honor Books:

Alphabet City by Stephen T. Johnson. Viking.

Tops and Bottoms by Janet Stevens. Harcourt.

The Faithful Friend by Robert D. San Souci. Illustrated by Brian Pinkney. Simon & Schuster.

Zin! Zin! Zin! a Violin by Lloyd Moss. Illustrated by Marjorie Priceman. Simon & Schuster.

1997   *The Golem* by David Wisniewski. Clarion.

Honor Books:

Hush! A Thai Lullaby by Minfong Ho. Illustrated by Holly Meade. Orchard.

The Graphic Alphabet edited by Neal Porter. Illustrated by David Pelletier. Orchard.

The Paperboy by Dav Pilkey. Orchard.

Starry Messenger by Peter Sís. Farrar, Straus & Giroux.

1998   *Rapunzel* retold and illustrated by Paul O. Zelinsky. Dutton.

Honor Books:

The Gardner by Sarah Stewart. Illustrated by David Small. Farrar.

Harlem by Walter Dean Myers. Illustrated by Christopher Myers. Scholastic.

There Was an Old Lady Who Swallowed a Fly by Simms Taback. Viking.

1999   *Snowflake Bentley* by Jacqueline Briggs Martin. Illustrated by Mary Azarian. Houghton.

Honor Books:

Duke Ellington: The Piano Prince and His Orchestra by Andrea Davis Pinkney. Illustrated by Brian Pinkney. Hyperion.

No, David! by David Shannon. Blue Sky/Scholastic.

Snow by Uri Shulevitz. Farrar, Straus & Giroux.

Tibet Through the Red Box by Peter Sís. Farrar, Straus & Giroux.

JOHN NEWBERY MEDAL.   Sponsored and administered by the Association for Library Service to Children, an arm of the American Library Association, the Newbery Medal is presented to the author of the most distinguished contribution to children's literature published in the United States during the preceding year. A variable number of honor books also may be named by the Newbery Selection Committee. Eligibility for this award is limited to U.S. citizens and residents. Named for the eighteenth-century British publisher, the Newbery Medal is one of the world's oldest and most prestigious children's book prizes.

1922   *The Story of Mankind* by Hendrik Willem Van Loon. Liveright.

Honor Books

The Great Quest by Charles Boardman Hawes. Little, Brown.

Cedric the Forester by Bernard G. Marshall. Appleton.

The Old Tobacco Shop by William Bowen. Macmillan.

The Golden Fleece and the Heroes Who Lived Before Achilles by Padraic Colum. Macmillan.

Windy Hill by Cornelia Meigs. Macmillan.

1923   *The Voyages of Doctor Dolittle* by Hugh Lofting. Lippincott.

(No record of the honor books.)

1924   *The Dark Frigate* by Charles Boardman Hawes. Little, Brown.

(No record of the honor books.)

1925   *Tales from Silver Lands* by Charles J. Finger. Illustrated by Paul Honoré. Doubleday.

Honor Books:

Nicholas by Anne Carroll Moore. Putnam.

Dream Coach by Anne and Dillwyn Parrish. Macmillan.

1926   *Shen of the Sea* by Arthur Bowie Chrisman. Illustrated by Else Hasselriis. Dutton.

Honor Book:

The Voyagers by Padraic Colum. Macmillan.

1927   *Smoky, the Cowhorse* by Will James. Scribner's.

(No record of the honor books.)

1928   *Gay-Neck, The Story of a Pigeon* by Dhan Gopal Mukerji. Illustrated by Boris Artzybasheff. Dutton.

Honor Books:

The Wonder Smith and His Son by Ella Young. McKay/Longmans.

Downright Dencey by Caroline Dale Snedeker. Doubleday.

1929   *The Trumpeter of Krakow* by Eric P. Kelly. Illustrated by Angela Pruszynska. Macmillan.

Honor Books:

The Pigtail of Ah Lee Ben Loo by John Bennett. McKay/Longmans.

Millions of Cats by Wanda Gág. Coward-McCann.

The Boy Who Was by Grace T. Hallock. Dutton.

Clearing Weather by Cornelia Meigs. Little, Brown.

The Runaway Papoose by Grace P. Moon. Doubleday.

Tod of the Fens by Eleanor Whitney. Macmillan.

1930   *Hitty: Her First Hundred Years* by Rachel Field. Illustrated by Dorothy P. Lathrop. Macmillan.

Honor Books:

The Tangle-Coated Horse and Other Tales: Episodes from the Fionn Saga by Ella Young. Illustrated by Vera Brock. Longmans.

Vaino: A Boy of New Finland by Julia Davis Adams. Illustrated by Lempi Ostman. Dutton.

Pran of Albania by Elizabeth C. Miller. Doubleday.

The Jumping-Off Place by Marian Hurd McNeely. McKay/Longmans.

A Daughter of the Seine by Jeanette Eaton. Harper.

Little Blacknose by Hildegarde Hoyt Swift. Illustrated by Lynd Ward. Harcourt.

1931   *The Cat Who Went to Heaven* by Elizabeth Coatsworth. Illustrated by Lynd Ward. Macmillan.

Honor Books:

Floating Island by Anne Parrish. Harper.

The Dark Star of Itza by Alida Malkus. Harcourt.

Queer Person by Ralph Hubbard. Doubleday.

Mountains Are Free by Julia Davis Adams. Dutton.

Spice and the Devil's Cave by Agnes D. Hewes. Knopf.

Meggy McIntosh by Elizabeth Janet Gray. Doubleday.

Garram the Hunter: A Boy of the Hill Tribes by Herbert Best. Illustrated by Allena Best (Erick Berry). Doubleday.

Ood-Le-Uk, the Wanderer by Alice Lide and Margaret Johansen. Illustrated by Raymond Lufkin. Little, Brown.

1932   *Waterless Mountain* by Laura Adams Armer. Illustrated by Sidney Armer and Laura Adams Armer. McKay/Longmans.

Honor Books:

The Fairy Circus by Dorothy Lathrop. Macmillan.

Calico Bush by Rachel Field. Macmillan.

Boy of the South Seas by Eunice Tietjens. Coward-McCann.

Out of the Flame by Eloise Lownsbery. McKay/Longmans.

Jane's Island by Marjorie Hill Alee. Houghton Mifflin.

The Truce of the Wolf and Other Tales of Old Italy by Mary Gould Davis. Harcourt.

1933   *Young Fu of the Upper Yangtze* by Elizabeth Foreman Lewis. Illustrated by Kurt Wiese. Holt.

Honor Books:

Swift Rivers by Cornelia Meigs. Little, Brown.

The Railroad to Freedom by Hildegarde Swift. Harcourt.

Children of the Soil by Nora Burglon. Doubleday.

1934   *Invincible Louisa: The Story of the Author of "Little Women"* by Cornelia Meigs. Little, Brown.

Honor Books:

The Forgotten Daughter by Caroline Dale Snedeker. Doubleday.

Swords of Steel by Elsie Singmaster. Houghton Mifflin.

ABC Bunny by Wanda Gág. Coward-McCann.

Winged Girl of Knossos by Erick Berry. Appleton.

New Land by Sarah L. Schmidt. McBride.

The Apprentice of Florence by Anne Kyle. Houghton Mifflin.

The Big Tree of Bunlahy: Stories of My Own Countryside by Padraic Colum. Illustrated by Jack Yeats. Macmillan.

Glory of the Seas by Agnes D. Hewes. Illustrated by N. C. Wyeth. Knopf.

1935   *Dobry* by Monica Shannon. Illustrated by Atanas Katchamakoff. Viking.

Honor Books:

The Pageant of Chinese History by Elizabeth Seeger. McKay/Longmans.

Davy Crockett by Constance Rourke. Harcourt.

A Day on Skates: The Story of a Dutch Picnic by Hilda Van Stockum. Harper.

1936   *Caddie Woodlawn* by Carol Ryrie Brink. Illustrated by Kate Seredy. Macmillan.

Honor Books:

Honk: The Moose by Philip Stong. Illustrated by Kurt Wiese. Dodd.

The Good Master by Kate Seredy. Viking.

Young Walter Scott by Elizabeth Janet Gray. Viking.

All Sail Set: A Romance of the "Flying Cloud" by Armstrong Sperry. Winston.

1937   *Roller Skates* by Ruth Sawyer. Illustrated by Valenti Angelo. Viking.

Honor Books:

Phoebe Fairchild: Her Book by Lois Lenski. Lippincott.

Whistler's Van by Idwal Jones. Viking.

The Golden Basket by Ludwig Bemelmans. Viking.

Winterbound by Margery Bianco. Viking.

Audubon by Constance Rourke. Harcourt.

The Codfish Musket by Agnes D. Hewes. Doubleday.

1938 *The White Stag* by Kate Seredy. Viking.

Honor Books:

Bright Island by Mabel L. Robinson. Random.

Pecos Bill by James Cloyd Bowman. Little, Brown.

On the Banks of Plum Creek by Laura Ingalls Wilder. Harper.

1939 *Thimble Summer* by Elizabeth Enright. Holt.

Honor Books:

Leader by Destiny: George Washington, Man and Patriot by Jeanette Eaton. Harcourt.

Penn by Elizabeth Janet Gray. Viking.

Nino by Valenti Angelo. Viking.

"Hello, the Boat!" by Phyllis Crawford. Holt.

Mr. Popper's Penguins by Richard and Florence Atwater. Little, Brown.

1940 *Daniel Boone* by James H. Daugherty. Viking.

Honor Books:

The Singing Tree by Kate Seredy. Viking.

Runner of the Mountain Tops: The Life of Louis Agassiz by Mabel L. Robinson. Random.

By the Shores of Silver Lake by Laura Ingalls Wilder. Harper.

Boy with a Pack by Stephen W. Meader. Harcourt.

1941 *Call It Courage* by Armstrong Sperry. Macmillan.

Honor Books:

Blue Willow by Doris Gates. Viking.

Young Mac of Fort Vancouver by Mary Jane Carr. Crowell.

The Long Winter by Laura Ingalls Wilder. Harper.

Nansen by Anna Gertrude Hall. Viking.

1942 *The Matchlock Gun* by Walter D. Edmonds. Illustrated by Paul Lantz. Dodd.

Honor Books:

Little Town on the Prairie by Laura Ingalls Wilder. Harper.

George Washington's World by Genevieve Foster. Scribner's.

Indian Captive: The Story of Mary Jemison by Lois Lenski. Lippincott.

Down Ryton Water by Eva Roe Gaggin. Illustrated by Elmer Hader. Viking.

1943 *Adam of the Road* by Elizabeth Janet Gray. Illustrated by Robert Lawson. Viking.

Honor Books:

The Middle Moffat by Eleanor Estes. Harcourt.

"Have You Seen Tom Thumb?" by Mabel Leigh Hunt. Lippincott.

1944   *Johnny Tremain* by Esther Forbes. Illustrated by Lynd Ward. Houghton Mifflin.

Honor Books:

These Happy Golden Years by Laura Ingalls Wilder. Harper.

Fog Magic by Julia L. Sauer. Viking.

Rufus M. by Eleanor Estes. Harcourt.

Mountain Born by Elizabeth Yates. Coward-McCann.

1945   *Rabbit Hill* by Robert Lawson. Viking.

Honor Books:

The Hundred Dresses by Eleanor Estes. Harcourt.

The Silver Pencil by Alice Dalgliesh. Scribner's.

Abraham Lincoln's World by Genevieve Foster. Scribner's.

Lone Journey: The Life of Roger Williams by Jeanette Eaton. Illustrated by Woodi Ishmael. Harcourt.

1946   *Strawberry Girl* by Lois Lenski. Lippincott.

Honor Books:

Justin Morgan Had a Horse by Marguerite Henry. Follett.

The Moved-Outers by Florence Crannell Means. Houghton Mifflin.

Bhimsa, the Dancing Bear by Christine Weston. Scribner's.

New Found World by Katherine B. Shippen. Viking.

1947   *Miss Hickory* by Carolyn Sherwin Bailey. Illustrated by Ruth Gannett. Viking.

Honor Books:

The Wonderful Year by Nancy Barnes. Messner.

The Big Tree by Mary and Conrad Buff. Viking.

The Heavenly Tenants by William Maxwell. Harper.

The Avion My Uncle Flew by Cyrus Fisher. Appleton.

The Hidden Treasure of Glaston by Eleanore M. Jewett. Viking.

1948   *The Twenty-One Balloons* by William Pène du Bois. Lothrop.

Honor Books:

Pancakes-Paris by Claire Huchet Bishop. Viking.

Li Lun, Lad of Courage by Carolyn Treffinger. Abingdon.

The Quaint and Curious Quest of Johnny Longfoot, The Shoe-King's Son by Catherine Besterman. Bobbs-Merrill.

The Cow-Tail Switch, And Other West African Stories by Harold Courlander and George Herzog. Holt.

Misty of Chincoteague by Marguerite Henry. Illustrated by Wesley Dennis. Rand.

1949   *King of the Wind* by Marguerite Henry. Illustrated by Wesley Dennis. Rand.

Honor Books:

Seabird by Holling Clancy Holling. Houghton Mifflin.

Daughter of the Mountains by Louise Rankin. Viking.

My Father's Dragon by Ruth S. Gannett. Random.

Story of the Negro by Arna Bontemps. Knopf.

1950   *The Door in the Wall* by Marguerite de Angeli. Doubleday.

Honor Books:

Tree of Freedom by Rebecca Caudill. Viking.

The Blue Cat of Castle Town by Catherine Coblentz. McKay/Longmans.

Kildee House by Rutherford Montgomery. Doubleday.

George Washington by Genevieve Foster. Scribner's.

Song of the Pines: A Story of Norwegian Lumbering in Wisconsin by Walter and Marion Havighurst. Holt.

1951   *Amos Fortune, Free Man* by Elizabeth Yates. Illustrated by Nora Unwin. Dutton.

Honor Books:

Better Known as Johnny Appleseed by Mabel Leigh Hunt. Lippincott.

Gandhi, Fighter Without a Sword by Jeanette Eaton. Morrow.

Abraham Lincoln, Friend of the People by Clara I. Judson. Follett.

The Story of Appleby Capple by Anne Parrish. Harper.

1952   *Ginger Pye* by Eleanor Estes. Harcourt.

Honor Books:

Americans Before Columbus by Elizabeth Chesley Baity. Viking.

Minn of the Mississippi by Holling Clancy Holling. Houghton Mifflin.

The Defender by Nicholas Kalashnikoff. Scribner's.

The Light at Tern Rock by Julia L. Sauer. Viking.

The Apple and the Arrow by Mary and Conrad Buff. Houghton Mifflin.

1953   *Secret of the Andes* by Ann Nolan Clark. Illustrated by Jean Charlot. Viking.

Honor Books:

Charlotte's Web by E. B. White. Harper.

Moccasin Trail by Eloise J. McGraw. Coward-McCann.

Red Sails to Capri by Ann Weil. Viking.

The Bears on Hemlock Mountain by Alice Dalgliesh. Scribner's.

Birthdays of Freedom, Vol. 1 by Genevieve Foster. Scribner's.

1954   *. . . And Now Miguel* by Joseph Krumgold. Illustrated by Jean Charlot. Crowell.

Honor Books:

All Alone by Claire Huchet Bishop. Viking.

Shadrach by Meindert DeJong. Harper.

Hurry Home, Candy by Meindert DeJong. Harper.

Theodore Roosevelt, Fighting Patriot by Clara I. Judson. Follett.

Magic Maize by Mary and Conrad Buff. Houghton Mifflin.

1955   *The Wheel on the School* by Meindert DeJong. Illustrated by Maurice Sendak. Harper.

Honor Books:

The Courage of Sarah Noble by Alice Dalgliesh. Scribner's.

Banner in the Sky by James Ramsey Ullman. Lippincott.

1956   *Carry on, Mr. Bowditch* by Jean Lee Latham. Houghton Mifflin.

Honor Books:

The Golden Name Day by Jennie D. Lindquist. Harper.

The Secret River by Marjorie Kinnan Rawlings. Scribner's.

Men, Microscopes and Living Things by Katherine B. Shippen. Viking.

1957   *Miracles on Maple Hill* by Virginia Sorensen. Illustrated by Beth and Joe Krush. Harcourt.

Honor Books:

Old Yeller by Fred Gipson. Harper.

The House of Sixty Fathers by Meindert DeJong. Harper.

Mr. Justice Holmes by Clara I. Judson. Follett.

The Corn Grows Ripe by Dorothy Rhoads. Viking.

The Black Fox of Lorne by Marguerite de Angeli. Doubleday.

1958   *Rifles for Watie* by Harold Keith. Illustrated by Peter Burchard. Crowell.

Honor Books:

The Horsecatcher by Mari Sandoz. Westminster.

Gone-Away Lake by Elizabeth Enright. Harcourt.

The Great Wheel by Robert Lawson. Viking.

Tom Paine, Freedom's Apostle by Leo Gurko. Crowell.

1959   *The Witch of Blackbird Pond* by Elizabeth George Speare. Houghton Mifflin.

Honor Books:

The Family Under the Bridge by Natalie S. Carlson. Harper.

Along Came a Dog by Meindert DeJong. Harper.

Chúcaro: Wild Pony of the Pampa by Francis Kalnay. Harcourt.

The Perilous Road by William O. Steele. Harcourt.

1960   *Onion John* by Joseph Krumgold. Illustrated by Symeon Shimin. Crowell.

Honor Books:

My Side of the Mountain by Jean George. Dutton.

America Is Born by Gerald Johnson. Morrow.

The Gammage Cup by Carol Kendall. Harcourt.

1961   *Island of the Blue Dolphins* by Scott O'Dell. Houghton Mifflin.

Honor Books:

America Moves Forward by Gerald Johnson. Morrow.

Old Ramon by Jack Schaefer. Houghton Mifflin.

The Cricket in Times Square by George Selden. Farrar.

1962   *The Bronze Bow* by Elizabeth George Speare. Houghton Mifflin.

Honor Books:

Frontier Living by Edwin Tunis. World.

The Golden Goblet by Eloise J. McGraw. Coward.

Belling the Tiger by Mary Stolz. Harper.

1963   *A Wrinkle in Time* by Madeleine L'Engle. Farrar.

Honor Books:

Thistle and Thyme: Tales and Legends from Scotland by Sorche Nic Leodhas (pseud. for Leclaire Alger). Holt.

Men of Athens by Olivia Coolidge. Houghton Mifflin.

1964   *It's Like This, Cat* by Emily Cheney Neville. Harper.

Honor Books:

Rascal: A Memoir of a Better Era by Sterling North. Dutton.

The Loner by Esther Wier. McKay/Longmans.

1965   *Shadow of a Bull* by Maia Wojciechowska. Atheneum.

Honor Book:

Across Five Aprils by Irene Hunt. Follett.

1966   *I, Juan de Pareja* by Elizabeth Borten de Treviño. Farrar.

Honor Books:

The Black Cauldron by Lloyd Alexander. Holt.

The Animal Family by Randall Jarrell. Pantheon.

The Noonday Friends by Mary Stolz. Harper.

1967   *Up a Road Slowly* by Irene Hunt. Follett.

Honor Books:

The King's Fifth by Scott O'Dell. Houghton Mifflin.

Zlateh the Goat and Other Stories by Isaac Bashevis Singer. Harper.

The Jazz Man by Mary H. Weik. Atheneum.

1968   *From the Mixed-Up Files of Mrs. Basil E. Frankweiler* by E. L. Konigsburg. Atheneum.

Honor Books:

Jennifer, Hecate, Macbeth, William McKinley, and Me, Elizabeth by E. L. Konigsburg. Atheneum.

The Black Pearl by Scott O'Dell. Houghton Mifflin.

The Fearsome Inn by Isaac Bashevis Singer. Scribner's.

The Egypt Game by Zilpha Keatley Snyder. Atheneum.

1969   *The High King* by Lloyd Alexander. Holt.

Honor Books:

To Be a Slave by Julius Lester. Dial.

When Shlemiel Went to Warsaw and Other Stories by Isaac Bashevis Singer. Farrar.

1970   *Sounder* by William H. Armstrong. Harper.

Honor Books:

Our Eddie by Sulamith Ish-Kishor. Pantheon.

The Many Ways of Seeing: An Introduction to the Pleasure of Art by Janet Gaylord Moore. World.

Journey Outside by Mary Q. Steele. Viking.

1971   *Summer of the Swans* by Betsy Byars. Viking.

Honor Books:

Kneeknock Rise by Natalie Babbitt. Farrar.

Enchantress from the Stars by Sylvia Louise Engdahl. Atheneum.

Sing Down the Moon by Scott O'Dell. Houghton Mifflin.

1972   *Mrs. Frisby and the Rats of NIMH* by Robert C. O'Brien. Atheneum.

Honor Books:

Incident at Hawk's Hill by Allan W. Eckert. Little, Brown.

The Planet of Junior Brown by Virginia Hamilton. Macmillan.

The Tombs of Atuan by Ursula K. LeGuin. Atheneum.

Annie and the Old One by Miska Miles. Little, Brown.

The Headless Cupid by Zilpha Keatley Snyder. Atheneum.

1973   *Julie of the Wolves* by Jean Craighead George. Harper.

Honor Books:

Frog and Toad Together by Arnold Lobel. Harper.

The Upstairs Room by Johanna Reiss. Crowell.

The Witches of Worm by Zilpha Keatley Snyder. Atheneum.

1974   *The Slave Dancer* by Paula Fox. Bradbury.

Honor Book:

The Dark Is Rising by Susan Cooper. Atheneum/McElderry.

1975   *M. C. Higgins, the Great* by Virginia Hamilton. Macmillan.

Honor Books:

Figgs & Phantoms by Ellen Raskin. Dutton.

My Brother Sam Is Dead by James Lincoln Collier and Christopher Collier. Four Winds.

The Perilous Gard by Elizabeth Marie Pope. Houghton Mifflin.

Philip Hall Likes Me, I Reckon Maybe by Bette Greene. Dial.

1976   *The Grey King* by Susan Cooper. Atheneum/McElderry.

Honor Books:

The Hundred Penny Box by Sharon Bell Mathis. Viking.

Dragonwings by Lawrence Yep. Harper.

1977   *Roll of Thunder, Hear My Cry* by Mildred D. Taylor. Dial.

Honor Books:

Abel's Island by William Steig. Farrar.

A String in the Harp by Nancy Bond. Atheneum/McElderry.

1978   *Bridge to Terabithia* by Katherine Paterson. Crowell.

Honor Books:

Anpao: An American Indian Odyssey by Jamake Highwater. Lippincott.

Ramona and Her Father by Beverly Cleary. Morrow.

1979   *The Westing Game* by Ellen Raskin. Dutton.

Honor Book:

The Great Gilly Hopkins by Katherine Paterson. Crowell.

1980   *A Gathering of Days: A New England Girl's Journal, 1830–32* by Joan Blos. Scribner's.

Honor Book:

The Road from Home: The Story of an Armenian Girl by David Kherdian. Greenwillow.

1981   *Jacob Have I Loved* by Katherine Paterson. Crowell.

Honor Books:

The Fledgling by Jane Langton. Harper.

A Ring of Endless Light by Madeleine L'Engle. Farrar.

1982   *A Visit to William Blake's Inn: Poems for Innocent and Experienced Travelers* by Nancy Willard. Illustrated by Alice and Martin Provensen. Harcourt.

Honor Books:

Ramona Quimby, Age 8 by Beverly Cleary. Morrow.

Upon the Head of the Goat: A Childhood in Hungary, 1939–1944 by Aranka Siegal. Farrar.

1983   *Dicey's Song* by Cynthia Voigt. Atheneum.

Honor Books:

The Blue Sword by Robin McKinley. Greenwillow.

Doctor DeSoto by William Steig. Farrar.

Graven Images by Paul Fleischman. Harper.

Homesick: My Own Story by Jean Fritz. Putnam.

Sweet Whispers, Brother Rush by Virginia Hamilton. Philomel.

1984   *Dear Mr. Henshaw* by Beverly Cleary. Morrow.

Honor Books:

The Sign of the Beaver by Elizabeth George Speare. Houghton Mifflin.

A Solitary Blue by Cynthia Voigt. Atheneum.

Sugaring Time by Kathryn Lasky. Photographs by Christopher Knight. Macmillan.

The Wish Giver: Three Tales Coven Tree by Bill Brittain. Harper.

1985   *The Hero and the Crown* by Robin McKinley. Greenwillow.

Honor Books:

Like Jake and Me by Mavis Jukes. Illustrated by Lloyd Bloom. Knopf.

The Moves Make the Man by Bruce Brooks. Harper.

One-Eyed Cat by Paula Fox. Bradbury.

1986   *Sarah, Plain and Tall* by Patricia MacLachlan. Harper.

Honor Books:

Commodore Perry in the Land of the Shogun by Rhoda Blumberg. Lothrop.

Dogsong by Gary Paulsen. Bradbury.

1987   *The Whipping Boy* by Sid Fleischman. Greenwillow.

Honor Books:

On My Honor by Marion Dane Bauer. Clarion.

Volcano: The Eruption and Healing of Mount St. Helens by Patricia Lauber. Bradbury.

A Fine White Dust by Cynthia Rylant. Bradbury.

1988   *Lincoln: A Photobiography* by Russell Freedman. Clarion.

Honor Books:

After the Rain by Norma Fox Mazer. Morrow.

Hatchet by Gary Paulsen. Bradbury.

1989   *Joyful Noise: Poems for Two Voices* by Paul Fleischman. Harper.

Honor Books:

In the Beginning: Creation Stories from Around the World by Virginia Hamilton. Harcourt.

Scorpions by Walter Dean Myers. Harper.

1990   *Number the Stars* by Lois Lowry. Houghton Mifflin.

Honor Books:

Afternoon of the Elves by Janet Taylor Lisle. Orchard.

Shabanu, Daughter of the Wind by Suzanne Fisher Staples. Knopf.

The Winter Room by Gary Paulsen. Orchard.

1991   *Maniac Magee* by Jerry Spinelli. Little, Brown.

Honor Book:

The True Confessions of Charlotte Doyle by Avi. Orchard.

1992   *Shiloh* by Phyllis Reynolds Naylor. Atheneum.

Honor Books:

Nothing But the Truth: A Documentary Novel by Avi. Orchard.

The Wright Brothers: How They Invented the Airplane by Russell Freedman. Holiday House.

1993   *Missing May* by Cynthia Rylant. Orchard.

Honor Books:

The Dark-Thirty: Southern Tales of the Supernatural by Patricia McKissack. Illustrated by Brian Pinkney. Knopf.

Somewhere in Darkness by Walter Dean Myers. Scholastic.

What Hearts by Bruce Brooks. Laura Geringer Books (Harper).

1994   *The Giver* by Lois Lowry. Houghton Mifflin.

Honor Books:

Crazy Lady! by Jane Leslie Conly. Harper.

Dragon's Gate by Laurence Yep. Harper.

Eleanor Roosevelt: A Life of Discovery by Russell Freedman. Clarion.

1995   *Walk Two Moons* by Sharon Creech. Harper.

Honor Books:

Catherine, Called Birdy by Karen Cushman. Clarion.

The Ear, the Eye and the Arm by Nancy Farmer. Orchard.

1996   *The Midwife's Apprentice* by Karen Cushman. Clarion

Honor Books:

The Watsons Go to Birmingham—1963 by Christopher Paul Curtis. Delacorte.

The Great Fire by Jim Murphy. Scholastic.

What Jamie Saw by Carolyn Coman. Front Street.

Yolanda's Genius by Carol Fenner. McElderry.

1997   *The View from Saturday* by E. L Konigsburg. Atheneum.

Honor Books:

A Girl Named Disaster by Nancy Farmer. Orchard.

Moorchild by Eloise McGraw. McElderry.

The Thief by Megan Whalen Turner. Greenwillow.

Belle Prater's Boy by Ruth White. Farrar, Straus & Giroux.

1998   *Out of the Dust* by Karen Hesse. Scholastic.

Honor Books:

Ella Enchanted by Gail Carson Levine. HarperCollins.

Lily's Crossing by Patricia Reilly Giff. Delacorte.

Wringer by Jerry Spinelli. HarperCollins.

1999   *Holes* by Louis Sachar. Farrar, Straus & Giroux.

Honor Book:

A Long Way from Chicago by Richard Peck. Dial.

Canada

AMELIA FRANCES HOWARD-GIBBON MEDAL.   Sponsored and administered by the Canadian Library Association since 1971, the Amelia Frances Howard-Gibbon Medal is presented to the illustrator of the most outstanding artwork in a children's book published in Canada during the preceding year. Eligibility for this award is limited to citizens and residents of Canada.

CANADIAN LIBRARY ASSOCIATION BOOK OF THE YEAR FOR CHILDREN AWARD.   Sponsored and administered by the Canadian Library Association since 1947, the Canadian Library Association Book of the Year for Children Award is presented to the authors of the outstanding children's books published during the preceding year. Only Canadian citizens are eligible for this award.

Great Britain

CARNEGIE MEDAL.   Sponsored and administered since 1937 by the British Library Association, the Carnegie Medal is presented to the author of a children's book of outstanding merit, written in English and first published in the United Kingdom in the preceding year.

KATE GREENAWAY MEDAL.   Sponsored and administered since 1956 by the British Library Association, the Kate Greenaway Medal is presented to the illustrator of the most distinguished picture book first published in the United Kingdom in the preceding year.

Australia

CHILDREN'S BOOKS OF THE YEAR AWARDS.   The Children's Books of the Year Awards program began in 1946 under the direction of various agencies in Australia. In 1959, the administration of the award program was taken over by the Children's Book Council of Australia. Currently, four awards are given annually: The Picture Book of the Year Award, The Children's Book for Younger Readers Award, The Children's Book of the Year for Older Readers Award, and The Eve Pownall Award for Information Books. Eligibility for the awards is limited to authors and illustrators who are Australian residents or citizens.

New Zealand

RUSSELL CLARK AWARD.   Sponsored and administered by the New Zealand Library and Information Association since 1978, the Russell Clark Award is given "for the most distinguished illustrations for a children's book; the illustrator must be a citizen or resident of New Zealand." The award is given annually to a book published in the previous year.

ESTHER GLEN AWARD.   Sponsored and administered by the New Zealand Library and Information Association since 1945, the Esther Glen Award is presented to the author of the most distinguished contribution to New Zealand's literature for children published in the previous year. Eligibility for the Esther Glen Award is limited to New Zealand residents and citizens.

AWARDS FOR A BODY OF WORK

Hans Christian Andersen Award

Sponsored and administered by the International Board on Books for Young People, the Hans Christian Andersen Awards honor biennially one author (since 1956) and one illustrator (since 1966) for his or her entire body of work. This truly international award is chosen by a panel of judges representing several foreign countries. The award must be given to a living author or illustrator who has made important and time-proven contributions to international children's literature. The Americans who have won the Hans Christian Andersen Medal are Meindert DeJong (1962), Maurice Sendak (1970), Scott O'Dell (1972), Paula Fox (1978), and Virginia Hamilton (1992), and Katherine Paterson (1998).

NCTE Award for Excellence in Poetry for Children

Sponsored and administered by the National Council of Teachers of English, the Excellence in Poetry for Children Award was given annually from 1977 to 1982, but beginning with the 1985 award, it is now presented every three years. The award is presented to a living American poet whose body of work is considered an outstanding contribution to poetry for children ages 3 through 13. (See Chapter 14 for a listing of the winners.)

Laura Ingalls Wilder Award

Sponsored and administered by the Association for Library Service to Children, an arm of the American Library Association, the Laura Ingalls Wilder Award is presented to a U.S. author or illustrator whose body of work is deemed to have made a substantial and lasting contribution to literature for children. The Wilder Award was first given in 1954. Between 1960 and 1980, it was presented every five years, but as of 1983 it has been awarded every three years. Winners include Laura Ingalls Wilder (1954), Clara Ingram Judson (1960), Ruth Sawyer (1965), E. B. White (1970), Beverly Cleary (1975), Theodor S. Geisel (Dr. Seuss) (1980), Maurice Sendak (1983), Jean Fritz (1986), Elizabeth George Speare (1989), Marcia Brown (1992), Virginia Hamilton (1995), and Russell Freedman (1998).

OTHER SELECTED AWARDS

Boston Globe/Horn Book Award

Since 1967, *The Boston Globe* and *The Horn Book Magazine*, one of America's oldest and most prestigious children's book review sources, have sponsored awards for children's book writing and illustration. As of 1976, three Boston Globe/Horn Book Awards have been presented annually: Outstanding Fiction or Poetry, Outstanding Nonfiction, and Outstanding Illustration.

Carter G. Woodsen Award

Since 1974, the National Council for the Social Studies has sponsored awards for the most distinguished social science books for young readers that treat topics related to ethnic minorities and race relations within the United States with sensitivity and accuracy. The annual awards are given to books published in the United States in the preceding year, and since 1980, winners for both elementary and secondary school readers have been named.

Coretta Scott King Award

Since 1970, the Social Responsibilities Round Table, with the support of the American Library Association, has sponsored and administered the Coretta Scott King Award. This award commemorates the life and dreams of Dr. Martin Luther King as well as the continued work of his wife, Coretta Scott King, for peace and world brotherhood. It also recognizes the creative work of black authors. Beginning in 1974, two awards have been presented, one to a black author and one to a black illustrator whose books for young readers published in the preceding year are deemed outstanding, educational, and inspirational.

Edgar Allan Poe Award

Since 1962, The Mystery Writers of America have presented an award for the Best Juvenile Novel in the fields of mystery, suspense, crime, and intrigue. In 1989, a second category was added: Best Young Adult Novel. A ceramic bust of Edgar Allan Poe is presented to the winners in all categories, which include adult fiction and filmmaking. The Edgars are the mystery writers' equivalent of Hollywood's Oscars.

International Reading Association Children's Book Award

Since 1975, the International Reading Association has sponsored and administered an award presented to new authors of children's books. Publishers worldwide nominate books whose authors show special promise for a successful career in writing for children. As of 1987, two awards were given annually, one for novels and another for picture books. In 1995, a third award was added for informational books.

Mildred L. Batchelder Award

Since 1968, the Association for Library Service to Children, an arm of the American Library Association, has presented an award to an American publisher for the most outstanding children's book originally published in another country in a language other than English and subsequently translated and published in the United States during the previous year.

National Book Awards

A consortium of book publishing groups has presented the National Book Awards since 1950. The sponsors' goal was to enhance the public's awareness of exceptional books written by fellow Americans and to increase the popularity of reading in general. The awards are given in these categories: Fiction, Nonfiction, Poetry, and Young People's Literature.

Orbis Pictus Award for Outstanding Nonfiction for Children

The Orbis Pictus Award has been given annually since 1990 by the National Council of Teachers of English. Only nonfiction or informational children's books published in the United States during the preceding year are considered. The selection committee chooses the most outstanding contribution by examining each candidate's "accuracy, organization, design, writing style, and usefulness for classroom teaching in grades K–8." One winner and up to five honor books are selected each year. The award is named for the book *Orbis Pictus* (*The World in Pictures*), which is considered to be the first book created exclusively for children. This nonfiction work was written and illustrated by Johann Amos Comenius in 1659.

Phoenix Award

Since 1985, the Children's Literature Association has sponsored an award for "a book for children published twenty years earlier which did not win a major award at the time of its publication but which, from the perspective of time, is deemed worthy of special recognition for its literary quality." Consideration is limited to titles published originally in English.

Pura Belpré Award

The Pura Belpré Award is cosponsored by the Association for Library Services to Children and the National Association to Promote Library Services to the Spanish

Speaking, both part of the American Library Association. First presented in 1996, this award is given biennially to a writer and an illustrator who are Latino/Latina and who have produced works that best portray, affirm, and celebrate the Latino cultural experience. The Pura Belpré Award is named after the first Latina librarian from the New York Public Library.

Scott O'Dell Award for Historical Fiction

The Scott O'Dell Award, first presented in 1984, is given to the author of a distinguished work of historical fiction written for children or adolescent readers. The winning books must be written in English, published by a U.S. publisher, and set in the New World (North, Central, or South America). The award was originated and donated by the celebrated children's author Scott O'Dell and is administered and selected by an Advisory Board chaired by Zena Sutherland, formerly of the *Bulletin of the Center for Children's Books.*

STATE CHILDREN'S CHOICE AWARDS

Most U.S. states now have an organization, such as a state library or children's literature association, that sponsors a children's choice book award. Typically, schoolchildren nominate books, and an adult committee narrows the list to about 20 titles. Then during the year, schools participating in the award process will make the books available to children. To vote, the children must have read or had read to them a specified number of the titles. Only children may vote. Following is a list of the state children's choice award programs for specific states and regions:

Alabama	Emphasis on Reading: Children's Choice Book Award Program, since 1980 (three categories: grades K–2, 3–5, 6–8)
Arizona	Arizona Young Readers Award, since 1977 (grades K–4)
Arkansas	Charlie May Simon Children's Book Award, since 1971 (grades 4–6)
California	California Young Reader Medals, since 1975 (four categories: primary, intermediate, junior high, and senior high)
Colorado	Colorado Children's Book Award, since 1976 (elementary grades)
	Blue Spruce Award, since 1985 (young adult).
Connecticut	Nutmeg Children's Book Award, since 1993 (grades 4–6)
Florida	Florida Reading Association Children's Book Award, since 1987 (grades K–2)
	Sunshine State Young Reader's Award, since 1984 (grades 3–8)

Georgia	Georgia Children's Book Award, since 1969 (grades 4–8)
	Georgia Children's Picture Storybook Award, since 1977 (grades K–3)
Hawaii	Nene Award, since 1964 (grades 4–6)
Illinois	Rebecca Caudill Young Readers' Book Award, since 1988 (grades 4–8)
Indiana	Young Hoosier Award, since 1975 (two awards: grades 4–6, grades 6–8)
	Young Hoosier Picture Book Award, since 1992 (grades K–3)
Iowa	Iowa Children's Choice Award, since 1980 (grades 3–6)
	Iowa Teen Award, since 1985 (grades 6–9)
Kansas	William Allen White Children's Book Award, since 1953 (grades 4–8)
Kentucky	Kentucky Bluegrass Award, since 1983 (two divisions: grades K–3 and grades 4–8)
Maine	Maine Student Book Award, since 1989 (grades 4–8)
Maryland	Maryland Children's Book Award, since 1988 (three categories: primary, intermediate, middle school)
Massachusetts	Massachusetts Children's Book Award, since 1976 (grades 4–6). An award for grades 7–9 was presented during the years 1978–1983.
Michigan	Michigan Young Readers' Awards, since 1980
Minnesota	Maud Hart Lovelace Award, since 1980 (grades 3–8)
Missouri	Mark Twain Award, since 1972 (grades 4–8)
Montana	Treasure State Award, since 1991 (grades K–3)
Nebraska	Golden Sower Award for Fiction, since 1981 (grades 4–6)
	Golden Sower Award for Picture Book, since 1983 (grades K–3)
	Golden Sower Award for Young Adults, since 1993 (grades 6–9)
Nevada	Nevada Young Readers' Award, since 1988 (four categories: primary, grades K–3; young reader, grades 4–6; intermediate, grades 6–8; young adult, grades 9–12)
New Hampshire	Great Stone Face Award, since 1980 (grades 4–6)
New Jersey	Garden State Children's Book Awards, since 1977 (three categories: easy to read, younger fiction, younger nonfiction)
	The New Jersey Reading Association M. Jerry Weiss Award, since 1994 (three divisions: primary, intermediate, secondary; award for each division presented every third year on a revolving basis)

	Garden State Teen Book Award, since 1995 (three categories: fiction, grades 6–8; fiction, grades 9–12; nonfiction)
New Mexico	Land of Enchantment Book Award, since 1981 (grades 4–8)
North Dakota	Flicker Tale Children's Book Award, since 1978 (two categories: picture book and juvenile)
Ohio	Buckeye Children's Book Awards, since 1982 (three divisions: grades K–2, grades 3–5, grades 6–8)
Oklahoma	Sequoyah Children's Book Award, since 1959 (grades 3–6)
	Sequoyah Young Adult Book Award, since 1988 (grades 7–9)
Pacific Northwest	Young Reader's Choice Awards (Alaska, U.S.A.; Alberta, Canada; British Columbia, Canada; Idaho, U.S.A.; Montana, U.S.A.; Oregon, U.S.A.; Washington, U.S.A.), since 1940 (grades 4–8). Since 1991, an award for grades 9–12 has also been given.
Pennsylvania	Keystone to Reading Book Award, since 1984
	Pennsylvania Young Reader's Choice Award, since 1992 (grades K–8 with some variation in grade categories from year to year)
Rhode Island	Rhode Island Children's Book Award, since 1991 (grades 3–6)
South Carolina	South Carolina Children's Book Award, since 1976 (grades 3–6)
	South Carolina Junior Book Award, since 1993 (grades 6–9)
	South Carolina Young Adult Book Award, since 1980 (grades 9–12)
South Dakota	Prairie Pasque Children's Book Award, since 1987 (grades 4–6)
Tennessee	Volunteer State Book Award, since 1979 (three divisions: grades K–3, grades 4–6, young adult)
Texas	The Texas Bluebonnet Award, since 1981 (grades 3–6)
Utah	Utah Children's Book Award, since 1980 (grades 3–6)
	Utah Informational Book Award, since 1986 (grades 3–6)
	Utah Young Adults' Book Award, since 1991 (grades 7–12)
	Utah Picture Book Award, since 1996
Vermont	Dorothy Canfield Fisher Children's Book Award, since 1957 (grades 4–8)
Virginia	Virginia Young Readers Program, since 1982 (four divisions: primary, elementary, middle school, high school)
Washington	Washington Children's Choice Picture Book Award, since 1982 (grades K–3)
West Virginia	West Virginia Children's Book Award, since 1985 (grades 3–6)

Wisconsin	Golden Archer Award, since 1974 (three categories: primary, intermediate, middle/junior high)
Wyoming	Indian Paintbrush Book Award, since 1986 (grades 4–6)
	Soaring Eagle Young Adult Book Award, since 1989 (two divisions: grades 7–9, grades 10–12); since 1992, a single award (grades 7–12)

LISTS OF THE BEST BOOKS

The American Library Association

Notable Children's Books, an annual list of outstanding children's books chosen by a committee of the Association for Library Service to Children. Available on the Web (www.ala.org), in pamphlet form (American Library Association, 50 Huron Street, Chicago, IL 60611), or in *Booklist* (March).

Best Books for Young Adults, an annual list of outstanding young adult books chosen by a committee of the Young Adult Library Services Association. Available on the Web (www.ala.org), in pamphlet form (American Library Association, 50 Huron Street, Chicago, IL 60611), or in *Booklist* (March). YALSA also offers two other lists, Quick Picks for reluctant teenage readers and Popular Paperbacks for Young Adult Readers.

School Library Journal

School Library Journal Best Books, an annual list of the best books reviewed in *School Library Journal*. Appears in the December issue and on the Web (www.slj.com).

The Horn Book Magazine

Hornbook Fanfare, an extremely selective annual list of highly recommended books chosen from among the books reviewed in *The Horn Book Magazine*. Appears in the March/April issue and on the Web (www.hbook.com).

The Children's Book Council

Children's Choices. In cooperation with the International Reading Association, the Children's Book Council sponsors a project that produces an annual list of about 100 titles that 10,000 young readers from five project locations across the country have selected as their "best reads." Appears in the October issue of IRA's journal *The Reading Teacher* and on the Web (www.cbcbooks.org).

Outstanding Science Trade Books for Children. In cooperation with The National Science Teachers Association (NSTA), the CBC sponsors an annual listing of the best science books for young readers. Appears in the March issue of NSTA's journal *Science and Children* and on the Web (www.cbcbooks.org).

Notable Children's Trade Books in the Field of Social Studies. In cooperation with The National Council for the Social Studies (NCSS), the CBC sponsors an annual listing of the best social studies trade books (fiction and nonfiction) for young readers. Appears in the April/May issue of NCSS's journal *Social Studies* and on the Web (www.cbcbooks.org).

Others

There are many other "best books" lists prepared by a variety of organizations and individuals. Some others of note include

- Blue Ribbons (*The Bulletin of the Center for Children's Books*)
- Books for the Teenage Reader; 100 Titles for Reading and Sharing (New York Public Library)
- Children's Books of the Year (Children's Literature Center, Library of Congress)
- Editor's Choice (*Booklist*, American Library Association)
- *New York Times* Best Illustrated Children's Books of the Year (*New York Times Book Review Supplement*)
- Notable Books for a Global Society (International Reading Association, Children's Literature Special Interest Group)
- Notable Books in the Language Arts (National Council of Teachers of English, Children's Literature Assembly)
- Parents' Choice Awards (Parents' Choice Foundation)
- Teachers' Choices (International Reading Association)
- VOYA Nonfiction Honor List (*Voice of Youth Advocates*, Young Adult Library Services Association, American Library Association)

For complete lists of all the awards and the award-winning books, see the latest edition of ***Children's Books: Awards and Prizes*** published by the Children's Book Council.

APPENDIX G

Publishers' Addresses

Following is a list of selected publishers. Publishers' addresses and names may have changed since this list was compiled. Many of the changes reflect publishing houses' mergers and acquisitions. For example, Bradbury Press was subsumed by Simon & Schuster Books for Young Readers. Despite the change in the publisher's name and ownership, a student in your class who wants to write a letter to Judy Blume could write the author at the address for Bradbury Press, one of the publishing names long associated with Blume's books. That address would get the student's letter to Simon & Schuster. For up-to-date information and for a more complete listing, however, consult the most current edition of *Books in Print* or *Children's Books in Print*.

Abrams
100 Fifth Ave.
New York, NY 10010

Addison-Wesley Publishing Co.,
Inc.
One Jacob Way
Reading, MA 01867

Aladdin Books
1230 Avenue of the Americas
New York, NY 10020

Atheneum Publishers
1230 Avenue of the Americas
New York, NY 10020

Avon Books
1350 Avenue of the Americas
New York, NY 10019

Bantam Books, Inc.
1540 Broadway
New York, NY 10036

Peter Bedrick Books, Inc.
2112 Broadway, Suite 318
New York, NY 10023

Beech Tree Books
1350 Avenue of the Americas
New York, NY 10019

Berkley Publishing Group
200 Madison Ave.
New York, NY 10010

Blue Sky Press
555 Broadway
New York, NY 10012

Boyds Mills Press
815 Church St.
Honesdale, PA 18431

Bradbury Press
1230 Avenue of the Americas
New York, NY 10020

Browndeer Press
525 B St., Suite 1900
San Diego, CA 92101

Camelot
1350 Avenue of the Americas
New York, NY 10019

Candlewick Press
2067 Massachusetts Ave.
Cambridge, MA 02140

Carolrhoda Books, Inc.
241 First Ave. N.
Minneapolis, MN 55401

Chelsea House Publishers
1974 Sproul Road, Suite 400
Broomall, PA 19008-0914

Children's Book Press
6400 Hollis St., Suite 4
Emeryville, CA 94608

Children's Press
Sherman Turnpike
Danbury, CT 06816

Chronicle Books
85 2nd St., Sixth Floor
San Francisco, CA 94105

Clarion Books
215 Park Ave. S.
New York, NY 10003

Cobblehill Books
375 Hudson St.
New York, NY 10014

Creative Education, Inc.
123 S. Broad St.
P.O. Box 227
Mankato, MN 56001

Crowell
10 East 53rd St.
New York, NY 10022

Crown Publishing Group
201 E. 50th St.
New York, NY 10022

Delacorte
1540 Broadway
New York, NY 10036

Dell Publishing Co., Inc.
1540 Broadway
New York, NY 10036

Dial Books for Young Readers
345 Hudson St.
New York, NY 10014

Dillon Press
1230 Avenue of the Americas
New York, NY 10020

DK Publishing, Inc. (Dorling
Kindersley)
95 Madison Avenue
New York, NY 10016

Dover
180 Varick Street
New York, NY 10014

Doubleday
1540 Broadway
New York, NY 10036

Dutton
345 Hudson St.
New York, NY 10014

Farrar, Straus & Giroux, Inc.
19 Union Square W.
New York, NY 10003

Four Winds Press
1230 Avenue of the Americas
New York, NY 10020

Front Street Books
P.O. Box 280
Arden, NC 28704

David R. Godine, Publisher, Inc.
9 Lewis St.
P.O. Box 9103
Lincoln, MA 01773

Golden Books/Western
850 Third Ave.
New York, NY 10022

Green Tiger Press
1230 Avenue of the Americas
New York, NY 10020

Greenwillow Books
1350 Avenue of the Americas
New York, NY 10019

Grosset & Dunlap
345 Hudson St.
New York, NY 10014

Gulliver Books
525 B St., Suite 1900
San Diego, CA 92101

Harcourt Brace and Co.
525 B St., Suite 1900
San Diego, CA 92101

HarperCollins Children's Books
10 E. 53rd St.
New York, NY 10022

Harper Trophy
10 East 53rd St.
New York, NY 10022

Holiday House, Inc.
425 Madison Ave.
New York, NY 10017

Henry Holt & Co.
115 W. 18th St.
New York, NY 10011

Houghton Mifflin Co.
222 Berkeley St.
Boston, MA 02116

Hyperion Books for Children
114 Fifth Ave.
New York, NY 10011

Jewish Publication Society
1930 Chestnut St.
Philadelphia, PA 19103

Joy Street Books
3 Center Plaza
Boston, MA 02108

Kane/Miller Book Publishers
P.O. Box 315229
Brooklyn, NY 11231-0529

Alfred A. Knopf, Inc.
201 E. 50th St.
New York, NY 10022

Lee and Low Books
95 Madison Ave.
New York, NY 10016

Lerner Publications Co.
241 First Ave. N.
Minneapolis, MN 55401

Lippincott
10 East 53rd St.
New York, NY 10022

Little, Brown & Co., Inc.
3 Center Plaza
Boston, MA 02108

Lodestar Publishing
345 Hudson St.
New York, NY 10014

Lothrop, Lee & Shepard Books
1350 Avenue of the Americas
New York, NY 10019

Macmillan Publishing Co.
1230 Avenue of the Americas
New York, NY 10020

Margaret K. McElderry Books
1230 Avenue of the Americas
New York, NY 10020

McGraw-Hill Book Co.
1221 Avenue of the Americas
New York, NY 10020

William Morrow & Co., Inc.
1350 Avenue of the Americas
New York, NY 10019

Morrow Junior Books
1350 Avenue of the Americas
New York, NY 10019

John Muir Publications
P.O. Box 613
Santa Fe, NM 87504

Mulberry Books
1350 Avenue of the Americas
New York, NY 10019

National Geographic Press
1145 17th Street NW
Washington, DC 20036

North-South Books
1123 Broadway, Suite 800
New York, NY 10010

Orchard Books
95 Madison Ave.
New York, NY 10016

Oxford University Press, Inc.
198 Madison Ave.
New York, NY 10016

Parents Magazine Press
685 Third Avenue
New York, NY 10017

Pantheon Books, Inc.
201 E. 50th St.
New York, NY 10022

Penguin Putnam Books for Young
Readers
345 Hudson St.
New York, NY 10014

Philomel Books
345 Hudson St.
New York, NY 10014

Picture Book Studio
1230 Avenue of the Americas
New York, NY 10020

Price Stern Sloan, Inc.
11835 W. Olympic Blvd., 5th
Floor
Los Angeles, CA 90064

Puffin Books
345 Hudson St.
New York, NY 10014

G. P. Putnam Sons
345 Hudson St.
New York, NY 10014

Random House, Inc.
201 E. 50th St.
New York, NY 10022

Rizzoli International Publications, Inc.
300 Park Ave. S.
New York, NY 10010

Scholastic, Inc.
555 Broadway
New York, NY 10012

Charles Scribner's Sons
1230 Avenue of the Americas
New York, NY 10020

Sierra Club Books for Children
3 Center Plaza
Boston, MA 02108

Simon & Schuster Books for
Young Readers
1230 Avenue of the Americas
New York, NY 10020

Steward, Tabori & Chang, Inc.
575 Broadway
New York, NY 10012

St. Martin's Press
175 Fifth Avenue
New York, NY 10010

Tambourine Books
1350 Avenue of the Americas
New York, NY 10019

Troll Communications
100 Corporate Dr.
Mahwah, NJ 07430

Tundra Books
P.O. Box 1030
Plattsburgh, NY 12901

Tupelo
1350 Avenue of the Americas
New York, NY 10019

Viking
345 Hudson St.
New York, NY 10014

Walker & Co.
435 Hudson St.
New York, NY 10014

Frederick Warne & Co., Inc.
345 Hudson St.
New York, NY 10014

Franklin Watts, Inc.
Sherman Turnpike
Danbury, CT 06816

Albert Whitman & Co.
6340 Oakton St.
Morton Grove, IL 60053

Wordsong
815 Church St.
Honesdale, PA 18431

NAME INDEX

SUBJECT INDEX

The *Children's Literature, Briefly* children's literature database allows you to:

- Find books quickly in a database of over 10,000 titles
- List books by title, author, grade level, and/or other information
- Trim a list to browse as much or as little of this information as you want
- View a complete record of information for any book on the database
- Search for specific key words (such as names, titles, topics, etc.)
- Access several HELP screens to aid in using the program, such as instructions for more sophisticated searching techniques
- Print a summary or complete record of all of the books in a selected list
- Annotate books of interest with your own User Comments
- Add your own books to the database

Menus and buttons allow you to proceed with just a few mouse clicks or keystrokes. All of the frequently used commands have shortcut keys that are displayed in the menus for easy reference. On-line Help guides you through the more complex commands. And an Undo command allows you to undo your most recent action.

To access instructions for use of your database, insert the diskette into your computer and display the document entitled "Read me."